The Adams Women

Abigail Smith Adams in 1800, by Gilbert
Stuart, copy by his daughter Jane Stuart.
The beautiful apparel does not hide the
mark left upon the first lady by worry and
illness. *Courtesy of the National Park Service.*

Louisa Johnson Adams in a portrait Gilbert Stuart completed in 1826. The woes
in the executive mansion are obvious on
the face of the first lady. *Courtesy of the
White House.*

The Adams Women

ABIGAIL AND LOUISA ADAMS, THEIR SISTERS AND DAUGHTERS

Paul C. Nagel

HARVARD UNIVERSITY PRESS
Cambridge, Massachusetts
London, England

First Harvard University Press paperback edition, 1999

Published by arrangement with Oxford University Press, Inc.

Library of Congress Cataloging-in-Publication Data

Nagel, Paul C.
The Adams Women

Bibliography: p.   Includes index.

1. Adams, Abigail, 1744–1818.   2. Adams, Louisa Catherine, 1775–1852.
3. Adams, John, 1735–1826—Family.   4. Adams, John Quincy, 1767–1848—Family.
5. Adams family.   6. Presidents—United States—Wives—Biography.   I. Title.
E322.1.A38N34   1987   973.4´092´2 [B]   86-31262

ISBN 0-674-00410-8 (pbk.)

This book is dedicated to dear ones, past and present,
who have taught me about women:

my grandmothers,
Ida Groenemann Nagel and Emma Blank Sabrowsky;

my mother,
Freda Sabrowsky Nagel;

my daughters-in-law,
Monica O'Brien Nagel and Maggie Dowd Nagel;

but, most of all, my wife,
Joan Peterson Nagel,
who, throughout our forty years together,
has brought me to treasure
what meant so much to Abigail and Louisa.

Foreword

This book has been a delight to write. Its principal characters form an amazing and attractive group which collectively offers the biographer an intimate view of how women lived and thought between 1750 and 1850. Reading the letters and journals of Abigail and Louisa Adams—two of America's first ladies—and of the women close to them, I found myself dealing one moment with their perceptive observations about human nature and democracy, and the next with their recipes for making rouge, for plum pudding, or for treating piles. At some points, I had before me their keen judgments about the strengths and weaknesses of males, and then their formula for enduring menopause. Present at every turn was their indignation at how a society ruled by men treated women, an indignation soothed by their humility before a very personal God. The manuscripts left by Abigail, Louisa, and the other Adams women are so revealing and detailed that even a man ought to be capable of giving a fair and thoughtful account of their lives.

Fifteen years ago, I began to think about the Adams family. It took a while before I recognized that more might be learned from their personal stories than from their public lives. It was even later when I realized the women in the Adams annals deserve at least as much attention from a biographer as their male counterparts have received. By then, it was 1981 and I had nearly finished writing *Descent from Glory: Four Generations of the John Adams Family*, its pages dominated by famous statesmen and historians. Fortunately, even the comparatively minor role played in the book by the Adams females led many readers to ask for more about "those wonderful women."

Encouraged by Sheldon Meyer and Oxford University Press, I went back to the Adams family papers. From that awesome treasury I have woven into one story the lives and thoughts of several highly talented and perceptive women, each of whom has an appeal and significance of her own. The association of the characters in this book with the Adams family provides only a background. In the foreground are women who triumphed in an era when it was more difficult to soften or disguise such fundamentals of existence as the endless childbirths, the preparation of daily bread, the need for mutual assistance, the acknowledgment before God of sinning, the enfeeblements of age, and the omnipresence of death. Seeing how these were confronted by the Adams women makes it difficult to give the latter enough credit.

Personally, I am thankful that friends kept after me to write this biography. A deepened acquaintance with the Adams women has humbled me as a male and helped dispel the fog from my perspective on American life and thought. Had I not returned to the Adams manuscripts, I would have missed knowing Mary Cranch, Elizabeth Shaw Peabody, Betsy Norton, Lucy Greenleaf, Nancy Harrod, Mary Hellen, Abby Brooks, and other companions to those American first ladies, Abigail and Louisa Adams. Now it is the reader's turn to enjoy their company.

Richmond, Virginia   P.C.N
November 1986

Contents

Illustrations

The Adams Women

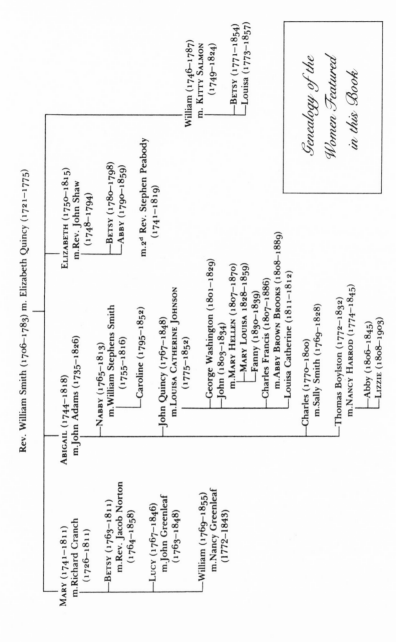

Rev. William Smith (1706–1783) m. Elizabeth Quincy (1721–1775)

MARY (1741–1811)
m.Richard Cranch (1726–1811)

ABIGAIL (1744–1818)
m.John Adams (1735–1826)

ELIZABETH (1750–1815)
m.Rev. John Shaw (1748–1794)
m.2d Rev. Stephen Peabody (1741–1819)

William (1746–1787)
m. KITTY SALMON (1749–1824)

—BETSY (1763–1811)
m.Rev. Jacob Norton (1764–1858)

—LUCY (1767–1846)
m.John Greenleaf (1763–1848)

—William (1769–1855)
m.Nancy Greenleaf (1772–1843)

—NABBY (1765–1813)
m.William Stephens Smith (1755–1816)
└Caroline (1795–1852)

—John Quincy (1767–1848)
m.LOUISA CATHERINE JOHNSON (1775–1852)
├George Washington (1801–1829)
├John (1803–1834)
│m.MARY HELLEN (1807–1870)
│└MARY LOUISA 1828–1859
│ └Fanny (1830–1839)
├Charles Francis (1807–1886)
│m.ABBY BROWN BROOKS (1808–1889)
└Louisa Catherine (1811–1812)

—Charles (1770–1800)
m.Sally Smith (1769–1828)

—Thomas Boylston (1772–1832)
m.NANCY HARROD (1774–1845)
├Abby (1806–1845)
└LIZZIE (1808–1903)

—BETSY (1780–1798)
—ABBY (1790–1859)

—BETSY (1771–1854)
—Louisa (1773–1857)

*Genealogy of the
Women Featured
in this Book*

PROLOGUE

The White House

Tucked away in a pile of Adams family manuscripts is a copy of the November 1888 issue of *Wide Awake*. This popular magazine was published in Boston for readers of all ages, and its pages reflected the conventional American outlook, particularly on women and history. The November number was no exception; it featured an illustrated piece by Harriett Upton depicting the life of Mrs. John Quincy Adams during her husband's presidency. Perhaps the closest Mrs. Upton came to reality was when she called Louisa Adams "the most scholarly woman who has presided at the White House."

While this tribute might have pleased Louisa, she would have been astounded at *Wide Awake*'s contention that "the family life at the White House during the John Quincy Adams administration was nearly ideally complete." Harriett Upton described Louisa as enjoying an existence of "wooings and weddings, baby life and christenings and many frolics, long old-fashioned visits from relatives, quiet hours when the President read aloud." The article pictured a first lady who, like all right-minded women, happily served in a man's world. Whether it was the White House or a laborer's cottage, the purpose of the home was to comfort a husband as he strove to meet the demands of the masculine life.

It is unlikely that the editors of *Wide Awake* realized how misleading was their version of the Adams White House. Mrs. Upton's portrayal of a contented Louisa acknowledged no dark side. The author probably did not know, for example, that Louisa despaired over two orphaned nephews who put the White House in an uproar because of their amorous romps with a chambermaid whom Louisa called "a bold and cunning minx." The first lady observed it would be impossible to say whether the nephews or the maid were the most "wheedled and dastardized."

Nor did Mrs. Upton mention that the sister of these nephews used the White House for scandalous behavior with one of Louisa's sons, although she was engaged to be married. These antics were not what *Wide Awake* had in mind when it said Louisa's White House was ruled by "family pride and family love." Mrs. Upton insisted that President and Mrs. Adams must have spent many quiet hours together. In fact, Louisa was left mostly alone, and called the White House her "prison," a place "which depresses my spirits beyond expression."

The fancifulness of *Wide Awake* may seem extreme, but it is a fair representation of how far the nineteenth century had gone in its senti-mental view of women. Only now are historians and biographers seeking to understand the lives and thoughts of American women who lived a century and more ago. For this quest we can have no better guides than the Adams women.

Nor is there a more convincing place to introduce the story of these Adams women than the very location exalted by *Wide Awake*, the White House. For in that residence two female Adamses demonstrated a tough-minded realism which readers of Mrs. Upton's essay would most likely have considered unfeminine. Abigail Adams was mistress of the new executive mansion only during the winter of 1800–1801. Louisa Adams had a full four-year lease, from 1825 until 1829. Having had far from rapturous experiences in the president's house, both first ladies were impatient to leave the place. Both were also deeply pessimistic about the nation's political future; both suffered much personal tragedy while their husbands were in office; and both were indignant that America's women were beginning to be the victims of degradation. In short, Abigail and Louisa were independent, strong persons, and bore no resemblance to the gentle, retiring females portrayed in journals like *Wide Awake*.

There was no starry-eyed nonsense when Louisa described the presi-dent's residence in 1825 as a "half-finished barn," with windows so loose the wind rattled them in a din that made a person's head burst. The East Room, so grand today, was then an undecorated space. No running water entered the house, except for rain accumulated by attic cisterns on which two toilets depended. Otherwise, water was drawn from wells located where the presidential horses and cows were kept, not far from the west wing. Bathing for the first family was difficult, there being no space for this amenity. *Wide Awake* readers were spared these discouraging facts about what Louisa laughingly dubbed "this great palace."

Even so, a distant observer might be forgiven for calling Louisa Adams the most fortunate woman in America. Indeed, she had much for which to be grateful. She had grown up in England and France, and had lived abroad with her diplomat husband in several great cities. She was a gifted writer of prose and poetry, a translator of the classics, and a discerning critic of society and politics. She also sang beautifully and performed on the harp and piano. She possessed a special talent for healing the sick and comforting the sorrowful and had proved herself the most accomplished hostess in Washington society. Her letters were rivaled only by those of another first lady, her mother-in-law Abigail Adams.

Yet with all of this attainment and advantage, Louisa was angry. She was angry about what she believed men were doing to humiliate women. Like Abigail, Louisa insisted that the relationship between men and women should be that of partners. The two contended that, while individuals in a marriage had different makeups, they deserved to be seen as equals. In eighteenth-century America life was concentrated in the home. There men and women labored together to sustain themselves and their children. In this setting, as Louisa and Abigail agreed, males and females needed each other, as both filled roles which nature and civilization had assigned them. John and Abigail Adams were speaking literally when they referred to each other as partners.

But with national independence had come centralization—in economy, politics, and society. To the alarm of perceptive women, the collaboration once characteristic of relations between the sexes began to disappear. The Adams first ladies never advocated that females should demand admission to roles for which males appeared obviously designed. There were already enough duties and specialties for women. The diverse talents that divided men and women were, in Abigail and Louisa's outlook, intended by the Creator to be combined in marriage. Marital partners were to live on an equal footing, in spite of differences.

When she was the president's wife, Abigail wrote to her sister Elizabeth, "I shall never consent to have our sex considered in an inferior point of light." Thick-skinned and aggressive, Abigail was very different from her daughter-in-law Louisa. After her childhood in a rural Massachusetts parsonage, Abigail had spent many years as a domestic and community leader while John Adams was off to Philadelphia or Europe on government business. Yet Abigail was no less disgusted with the White House and Washington than Louisa would be twenty-five years later. The elder woman called the new federal capital "the very dirtyest hole I ever saw for a place of any trade or respectability of inhabitants." She found every room in the president's house unfinished, and thirteen fires were required if the occupants were not to sleep in the damp. The autumn rains turned the city streets into bottomless tracks of mud. And though the town had merely three thousand citizens, this was humanity enough for Abigail to witness an abundance of greed, sensuality, and corruption, the elements she and Louisa feared were soon to rule and ruin American politics.

"My residence in this city has not served to endear the world to me," was Abigail's understatement just before she returned to Massachusetts. "I am sick, sick, sick of publick life." In this mood Abigail announced she would rather watch her promising son John Quincy "thrown as a log on the fire than see him President of the United States." Louisa knew what her mother-in-law meant by this statement. "Experience had taught her," said Louisa approvingly, "how valueless are such honours." This heresy, typical of Abigail Adams, was ignored by sentimentalists like Harriett Upton, who rendered Abigail as unreal for later generations as they did Louisa.

In mid-February 1801, Abigail Adams left Washington, starting out for her home in Quincy, Massachusetts. She was convinced that the election of 1800 would prove to be the nation's last, and that Thomas Jefferson's recent victory over John Adams was intended by God to punish America "for our sins and transgressions." Abigail predicted that a great darkness must cross the land, and that the day was coming when the United States would be "kindled into flames." Sixty years later, the horrors of the Civil War made a prophet of Abigail Adams.

It took until 10 March for Abigail to reach home, "bent and bang'd enough" despite frequent stops. She traveled with the aid of no man but the driver, having only her tiny granddaughter Susan Adams and a niece, Louisa Smith, as companions. As they lurched along, Louisa was bold enough to ask her aunt about the absence of males on the trip. Abigail replied that she was "too independent to want a gentleman always at my apronstring." She amused herself by contemplating what suitable punishment the terrible roads would be for the Jeffersonians if they could be compelled to make the same journey.

Abigail's mood rapidly improved as she drove into Quincy. But then, in her haste to alight, she thrust a leg through a snow-covered hole in the bottom of her carriage. Now bruised in body as well as soul, the retiring first lady turned for comfort to her sisters, her daughter, and her nieces, the women who dominate the following chapters. This circle of remarkable females had sustained one another during fifty years of sorrows and joys in scenes extending from New England farms and parsonages to the White House and they eagerly welcomed Abigail home.

The lives of these Adams women began in Weymouth, the oldest hamlet in Massachusetts, and the opening scene is the local parsonage, the center of life at that time in all New England villages. The setting of this book is thus as different from our late-twentieth-century existence as it would be if this were a biography of women in the age of the Pharaohs. However, the three daughters who grew up in that parsonage had the talent and charm to enliven any age.

1

Three Daughters

The village of Weymouth, where Abigail and her sisters grew up, was founded in 1622, the first community established in Massachusetts Bay Colony. It was also the last settlement through which early travelers passed in proceeding south from Massachusetts Bay into Plymouth Plantation. Such a trip remained rough going even in Abigail's time, for the road between Boston and Weymouth was little more than a path with dangerous crossings at the brooks and rivers. Journeys were taken by foot, horseback, or chaise, a sort of chair on wheels. The ten miles from Weymouth to Boston followed an ancient Indian trail that led north through Braintree, the next town, thence to the village of Milton, on the Neponset River. After ferrying the stream, travelers picked up the road again; it touched three hamlets—Dorchester, Roxbury, and Jamaica Plain—before it reached Boston. Another destination might be the nearby town of Cambridge, the site of Harvard College. These communities played important roles in the lives of the Adams women.

In 1750 this stretch of Atlantic coast between Weymouth and Boston was still a small world where residents knew virtually every neighbor along the route. The area retained much of its original beauty, although New England's cold winters had compelled settlers to harvest many trees for firewood. Even so, the region resembled what Thomas Morton, one of the earliest settlers, saw when he arrived in 1622. Morton later recalled how he doubted "that in all the known world" a place could be found which would match the "fair endowments" of this Massachusetts shore. Unforgettable to him were the "many goodly groves of trees, dainty, fine, round, rising hillocks, delicate, fair, large plains, sweet, crystal fountains, and clear, running streams," the latter twining through the land and "making so sweet a murmuring noise . . . as would even lull the senses with delight asleep."

For Thomas Morton, the area around Weymouth was "Nature's masterpiece." Indeed, said he, "If this land be not rich, then is the whole world poor." Today's visitor must accept on faith what Thomas Morton saw. The Atlantic may still lie to the east and the Blue Hills to the west of Weymouth, but the rural beauty cherished by Abigail and, after her, by Louisa Adams and their dear ones has been obliterated by urban sprawl.

The story of the Adams women began in 1734 when the Weymouth congregation chose a new minister, a twenty-seven-year-old bachelor named William Smith. He was ordained on 4 December 1734 and accepted £160 as his annual salary. He also was given a settlement amount of £300. In those days a clergyman was appointed for life, so he and his family needed money for a residence befitting their place in the community. It took four years for the Reverend Smith to acquire the parsonage he preferred; his negotiations attested to his astuteness about money. In fact, business was in his blood.

Although William Smith's forebears had not been present at the beginning of Massachusetts Bay, they contributed to the colony's prosperity soon after its inception. No one knows when the family's founder, Thomas Smith, arrived in Boston, but by 1663 he had a butcher's business in Charlestown, just across the river from Boston, and had married Sarah, from the prominent Boylston family. Of their several children, two sons are remembered. One, the second Thomas Smith, established himself in South Carolina after prospering as a seafarer. His descendants would be important in politics, one serving as governor of South Carolina.

The other son who grew up in the Charlestown butcher shop was Abigail Adams's grandfather, the first William Smith, who, like his brother, succeeded as a mariner and earned the title of captain. Born in March 1667, Captain Smith lived mostly in the town of Medford, above Cambridge, northwest of Boston, where he had a farm on the Mystic River. After marrying Abigail Fowle, Smith gave his name to a son born in February 1707. The second William Smith graduated from Harvard College in 1725 with a reputation for piety and a fondness for recording rather tasteless jests in his journal.

After serving in Weymouth, the Reverend William Smith evidently improved his sense of humor; his parishioners admired how the biblical texts he selected for his sermons had a clever appropriateness to local or colonial events. He also became known as a crafty conciliator. By all accounts, Smith's most astute move was to marry Elizabeth Quincy on 16 October 1740. The bride was from Braintree, the town next to Weymouth, and was a daughter of that locale's leading citizen, Colonel John Quincy.

The bride was eighteen, and the groom thirty-three, an age difference typical among couples in a society where males were expected to be well established before marrying.

William and Elizabeth Smith spent the rest of their lives in the parsonage in Weymouth. As pastor for forty-five years, Smith was respected for his conservative theological views and for his ability to keep the parish united during the worrisome 1740s and 50s, when the so-called Great Awakening in American religion brought proposals even in staid Weymouth for a more spirited approach to faith and worship. The assistance Parson Smith received from his wife Elizabeth was, in the opinion of some Weymouth residents, the main reason for his successful ministry. His daughter Abigail and her sisters shared this view.

The bride who joined William in Weymouth was soon known for her open and affable manner. She brilliantly displayed the virtues and performed the deeds expected of a minister's wife. This came as no surprise since Elizabeth Quincy Smith had distinguished forebears on both sides. Her father Colonel John Quincy and her mother Elizabeth Norton Quincy lived, as befitted their prominence, on a large, oceanside Braintree estate called Mount Wollaston. The land had been in the family since the colony granted it in 1637 to the first Edmund Quincy, who brought to America a family line of which his descendants would be proud. It delighted Abigail that in 1066 an ancestor had traveled from Normandy with William the Conqueror to rescue Britain from misrule, and that a Quincy was present when King John was compelled to sign Magna Carta. When an ancient parchment of genealogical information about the Quincys was mislaid, it was Abigail who set up a search, saying of her Quincy lineage, "Money should not purchase it from me." Other families whose bloodline Abigail claimed with pleasure were the Nortons and the Shepards, who both filled New England pulpits with distinction. When he wrote the story of his grandmother Abigail, Charles Francis Adams asserted that her stock went back "to the most noted of the most respected class of their day."

Elizabeth Quincy had grown up with two sisters and a brother. Anna Quincy married Colonel John Thaxter of Hingham, and Lucy Quincy's husband was Dr. Cotton Tufts of Weymouth. Elizabeth's brother Norton became a recluse on the Mount Wollaston estate, which he had inherited. Colonel and Mrs. John Quincy's three successful daughters were thus left to worry over a disappointing brother. Curiously, this was precisely the outcome for Elizabeth and William Smith. Their children had the best possible beginnings at a time when a minister's family was treated with great deference. Yet it did their son as little good as it spurred their daughters.

The Smiths' first child was Mary, born 9 December 1741. Next came

Abigail, on 11 November 1744, a son, William, in 1746, and on 7 April 1750, a last daughter, Elizabeth, named after her mother. No portrait survives of Mary, but what likenesses we have of Abigail and Elizabeth show a remarkable resemblance among the sisters. All three seem to have been petite, even frail, but with strength to survive into old age despite two crippling disorders which relatives before and after them would also suffer—rheumatism and tuberculosis. Mary, Abigail, and Elizabeth often spoke of "the infirmity of our family" and the "natural tendency in our family" for these diseases.

They were less frank about alcoholism, their most devastating inheritance. It carried off their brother and would destroy several of their sons. As Charles Francis Adams later observed, "The Smith blood seems to have had the scourge of intemperance dreadfully applied to it. Yet the first example of the race whom I know of, was an exemplary clergyman. A son, grandchildren in two branches and great grandchildren have defied all the efforts of the most careful education. Here have been the causes of the bitterest sorrows of our family."

Parson and Mrs. Smith's eldest daughter, Mary, was the quiet child, often tending her siblings while her mother cared for the community. Abigail, the second daughter, was high-spirited, but still mindful of lessons from home life. What she recalled as "my own volatile, giddy disposition" caused her parents to comfort each other with such words of hope as "wild colts make the best horses." Family lore stressed the difference between Abigail and Mary. Abigail herself remembered how "a thread would govern one, a cable would be necessary for the other." She was once told, "You will either make a very bad or a very good woman."

While each of the three Smith daughters was known for an "uncommon force of intellect," it was the third sister, Betsy, as little Elizabeth was known until her mother died, who possessed the strongest mind and the most ardent appreciation of learning. Unfortunately, none of the girls, not even Betsy, attended school. In eighteenth-century Weymouth, the church and the home were considered edification enough for young women. Much later the Smith sisters would remind each other how "it was not the fashion for females to know more than writing and a little arithmetic. No books on female education were then in vogue, no academies for female instruction were then established." As late as 1813, two years before she died, Betsy still spoke of how ardently she had wished to master languages, philosophy, and literature, and how little she felt she had succeeded.

Fortunately, unusual resources for learning existed within the parsonage. The Smith girls had the advantage of a lively and literate group of relatives and friends who were often found at the fireside talking with Parson and

Mrs. Smith. While the girls' parents seemed less concerned about female education, Betsy did recall that her mother—a "dear, excellent woman"— explained reading to her by using Isaac Watts' hymnal as the primer. In these songs Betsy found a heartwarming introduction to divine truths.

Abigail usually described Grandmother Quincy in nearby Braintree as her teacher, saying she never forgot the older woman's "wise and just observations upon nature." Perhaps Elizabeth Norton Quincy knew how to apply patience and diplomacy to her headstrong granddaughter, who invariably was stirred by the memory of sitting beside the elderly woman, whose "lively, cheerful disposition animated all around her whilst she edified all by her unaffected piety." The secret of successful teaching, Abigail concluded from this experience, was "never to give in to laxity, while leading through a tender firmness." Thus, to Abigail, Grandmother Quincy remained an "oracle of wisdom" thanks to her "happy method of mixing instruction and amusement." She addressed "certain principles the utility of which I could not but see and approve, when a child." In her old age, Abigail claimed, however, that her introduction to reading came from her grandfather, Colonel John Quincy.

As the youngest Smith sister, Betsy had the benefit of older siblings and their suitors to encourage her education, and "treasured up in my little store house" much of value, she later recalled. Betsy always praised the inspiration she received from three men who often visited the Weymouth parsonage. These were Richard Cranch, who eventually married Mary; John Adams, who became Abigail's husband; and Dr. Cotton Tufts, who was both uncle and cousin to the three young women.

The three sisters all profited from informal instruction gathered at their domestic setting. In later life, they enjoyed debating why it was, as Mary put it in 1800, "that so totally secluded as we were in childhood from the world, we came to be so interested in the politics of it at so early a period of life." Mary answered herself by remembering how she and her sisters would huddle at the edge of the parsonage sitting room, out of the fire's light, listening to their parents and guests explore the public questions of the 1750s and 60s. Especially memorable were the stimulating opinions of "our venerable Grandfather, Major Humphery, Doctor Tufts, and a few more of our dear Parents' particular friends." Indeed, Mary said, these encounters "furnished us with valuable ideas" and "led us to read the foreign news in the public prints, to read the debates of the British Parliament, and to turn over the Historick page of Nations."

Mary acknowledged that "method was wanting in our studies and we had no one to point us to it," for their relatives seemed to overlook "with what avidity we attended to and treasured up the observations which fell from their lips." In fact, Mary asserted, Parson and Mrs. Smith based their idea about educating women upon "the necessity of keeping us from scenes of dissipation and frivolity, and left the rest to nature and I will say genius." In one subject, however, the sisters were carefully trained. This was to prepare them for the woman's role decreed by tradition. Their instructor was an expert, their mother.

As the partner of a clergyman, Elizabeth Smith had to embody all those feminine qualities which her daughters were taught to consider admirable. Thus did Elizabeth impart the importance of family affection and, especially, compassion. "We should never wait to be requested to do a kind office, an act of love," was one of Mary's favorites among her mother's admonitions. Elizabeth Smith also prized the habit of early rising, respect for domestic duties, caring for the ill and the dying, and thrift—to the extent of making use of apple peelings. The girls also learned an unforgettable lesson from Parson Smith. He urged them to speak harshly of no one, to stress the "handsome" aspects of an individual, and then to switch the conversation to "things rather than persons."

Since the parents in Weymouth's parsonage seem to have concentrated on "all the charities of social life," as Betsy summed it up later, it was actually the three young men—Richard Cranch, John Adams, and Cotton Tufts—who brought the sisters into the world of literature—"Bell Letters," Mary spelled it—and encouraged them to delight in learning. The young women owed their biggest debt to Richard Cranch, a self-taught theologian and student of literature, and also a watch repairman. Tall and thin, with a gentle manner and fond of talk, Richard was an appealing figure said to bear a remarkable resemblance to John Locke. Like another great thinker, Isaac Newton, Richard's favorite hobby was drawing prophecy from the Christian Scripture.

This erudite man was born in 1726 in Devonshire. There the Cranches pursued the woolen trade and were religious dissenters. They claimed Lucas Cranach, the German painter, as an ancestor. Richard, the youngest of seven children, let his elders do the wool working while he turned to books and watch-making. When his sister Mary and her husband Joseph Palmer sailed to Masschusetts in 1746, the twenty-year-old Richard accompanied them. As a man of business and worldly affairs he was mostly a failure in America. As one who could teach, talk, inspire, and think, he was successful. Cranch's piety and vigor of mind made him many friends in New England, among them the renowned Reverend Jonathan Mayhew, into whose West Church he was admitted in 1749, and Robert Treat Paine, son of Thomas Paine, a clergyman who had traded the pulpit for business.

Finding little prosperity in Boston, Richard tried Weymouth after 1755, hoping that the hamlet would have enough work to keep him busy. He was disappointed, but he received a warm welcome from William and

Elizabeth Smith, at whose table he first read John Locke. Richard returned the favor in overflowing measure; Abigail was endlessly grateful that "brother Cranch" had made her "a lover of literature," teaching her that "the true female character consisted not in the tincture of the skin or a fine set of features." "Female excellence," Richard admonished, rested "beyond the exterior form."

Abigail contended that this early association with Richard Cranch made her always enjoy the company "of the gentlemen more than [that of] the ladies." What a pity most women had no Richard Cranch in their background, Abigail lamented. Females were usually offered little to learn that was worth remembering, dooming them, said Abigail, to a life of talking about insipid and trifling topics, while males had the advantage of training and experience from which to make worthwhile comments. Believing that all women should be well-read, Richard Cranch had his three pupils begin with Shakespeare, Milton, Pope, and Richardson. The last of these became the young women's favorite. Abigail recalled that she learned to appreciate delicacy of sentiment and refined tastes from Richardson. She remembered how Richardson had created in the character of Charles Grandison such an ideal male that some observers feared the English-speaking world would be "over run with old maids" who spent their lives vainly seeking the Grandison type to wed.

Richard Cranch had arrived in Weymouth for another reason—to put a sad romance behind him. This fact doubled his attractiveness in the eyes of the Smith daughters, particularly Mary, who was seventeen when Cranch became a fixture at the parsonage dining table and fireside. While living in Boston, Richard had fallen in love with Eunice Paine, sister of his friend Robert Treat Paine and daughter of Thomas Paine. Eunice's surviving letters and the comments of her many friends attest to her zest and wit. She was born in 1733, making her seven years younger than Richard, and twenty years old when he applied for her hand in 1753.

Alas, Eunice's father had just suffered business reversals which, he said, prevented him from providing a proper dowry. As Thomas Paine described his daughter's situation, "The necessary supplys to settle her in the world are at present perplexed." While emphasizing that Eunice was free to select her husband, Mr. Paine chose to add, "I can't think it prudent for her to engage herself in marriage while I am in these circumstances." Although young Cranch was assured that the Paine family fortune "will doubtless be altered and better in a short time," nothing apparently changed, and Eunice never married. She did, however, remain close to Richard and his family until her death in 1803.

About the time he lost Eunice, Richard became friends with a younger man who also had bookish leanings. This was the Braintree attorney, John

Adams, who was nine years Richard's junior. Taciturn, abrupt, worldly-wise, and ambitious, Adams' qualities generally contrasted with Cranch's, except for a shared love of literature. It was John who urged his friend to spend less time being "swallowed up in raptures" by biblical study, and to try instead a more aggressive and stern approach to life. With this advice, Richard redoubled his business efforts in Weymouth, but the books and the eager sisters in the parsonage soon called him back to his gentle ways, his quiet wit, and his open, confiding manner.

Richard's intellectual nature was encouraged by Dr. Cotton Tufts, another new friend he made in Weymouth. In 1752, at age twenty, Tufts had begun practicing medicine in Weymouth. He was Parson Smith's nephew and the three sisters' cousin. Like other talented persons, Tufts borrowed books from the Weymouth parsonage library and stayed around to talk, especially after he met the sister-in-law of Parson Smith, Lucy Quincy. Although she was older than he by three years, Cotton married Lucy on 2 December 1755, his Uncle William officiating. This union made Dr. Tufts uncle as well as cousin to the daughters of the parsonage. He was but nine years senior to Mary Smith.

Although nearly every venture to which Cotton Tufts gave his attention succeeded, unlike those of the luckless Richard Cranch, the two men were very similar—compassionate, witty, devout, and hungry for knowledge. And when the pair was joined at the fireside by John Adams, who began enjoying the Weymouth parsonage fellowship in 1759, it is easy to imagine why the Smith daughters never forgot the talk they heard. The bonds formed between the young women and these gentlemen lasted until death, and represented unity of mind, effort, and matrimony. The pity is that the conversations around the circle, which must have been among the best in the colonies, went unreported, left to linger only in affectionate recollection.

Nor is there any record of how Richard Cranch wooed Mary Smith, fifteen years his junior. When Parson Smith married them on 25 November 1762, family legend claims that he chose as a text for his sermon "And Mary hath chosen that good part, which shall not be taken away from her" (Luke 10:42). However, not even a parsonage setting could waive the customary male fellowship after the ceremony, when, as Dr. Tufts put it, the men stood around and told "good matrimonial stories to raise our spirits." On this occasion, Dr. Tufts himself related one anecdote which apparently was a hit with everyone. It concerned a bride who "was very anxious, she feared, she trembled, she could not go to bed." But there being no turning back, as the story went, "she mustered up her spirits, committed her soul to God and into bed she leaped—and in the morning she was amazed, she could not think for her life what it was that scared her so." The story may have been more appropriate than the assembly appreciated since Mary conceded to Abigail many years later that she had been terrified on her wedding day.

Mr. and Mrs. Cranch remained for a time in Weymouth, where the bride soon recognized how books had done little to help Richard master the world at hand. One day, the new husband went forth to purchase a chaise against the advice of shrewd Parson Smith. He brought home a broken-down buggy, loosened spokes, torn leather, and all, for which he paid an outrageous price. Richard excused his folly by explaining that the seller was poor, and it would have shown a "narrowness of purse" to bargain. But this was not all. The man who sold the chaise saw his advantage and quickly offered Richard his horse, a miserable specimen, for five times its worth. Mary's husband bought it, even though he and his bride did not need the animal. According to John Adams, his good friend Cranch had been "miserably bubbled by his own vanity and credulity."

Two years after Mary took Richard to the altar, Abigail married John Adams, concluding a romance about which something can be known, because in this case letters between the lovers have survived. During the smallpox scare in 1764, John went off to Boston for the lengthy ordeal of inoculation. The messages he and Abigail exchanged during April and May 1764 show how completely John's heart had been won by Parson Smith's second daughter.

Before Abigail entered his life, John Adams had been an uncertain, often melancholy person, alternately ambitious and subdued. He thus had to marvel at the effect wrought by the nineteen-year-old Abigail Smith. She had "always softened and warmed my heart," John told her during his inoculation quarantine. From her he knew would come the strength he badly needed for his benevolence, his health, and his tranquility. "You will polish and refine my sentiments of life and manners, banish all the unsocial and ill-natured particles in my composition, and form me to that happy temper, that can reconcile a quick discernment with a perfect candour." Such attention and adoration pleased Abigail, who confessed she wanted to be courted by no village Lothario. "I always despised the appelation woman's man," she later asserted to a nephew. "To be a gallant, a man must have a little of the fop. Nothing pleases me and gratifies me so much as to know myself the sole monopolizer."

Perhaps Abigail never knew how nearly she missed having John Adams as a suitor. While Abigail was still in her early teens, John, nine years her senior, had pursued one of her distant cousins, Hannah Quincy. He became so ardent that his father, Deacon John Adams, had to caution him that the Quincy family considered the romance serious. The parent advised the son that if he did not marry Miss Quincy, John rather than Hannah would suffer. "A story will be spread that she repelled me," John reported, as he considered his father's contention that in such episodes it was the male who usually lost. Undeterred for a time, John pressed his cause, and the result was a close call. One evening John was so swept away by Hannah Quincy that he began to propose in the moonlight, only to be interrupted by friends. John quickly took to safer ground. Since this episode occurred in 1759, when he was as yet unable to support a wife, John talked himself into being thankful that a premature marriage was so narrowly averted.

Actually, Hannah had enjoyed collecting suitors, and her flirtatious ways had often dismayed John, who knew she had toyed with the affections of persons he claimed as good friends, including Anthony Wibird, the eccentric minister of the Braintree church. On the night John nearly proposed to Hannah, she was evidently engaged already to Bela Lincoln, a physician who lived in Hingham. When John's ardor cooled, Hannah promptly married Dr. Lincoln, leaving a disgruntled John to try to forget her, not an easy task. It soon was clear that Hannah had made a poor choice. Dr. Lincoln abused his wife, once even in the presence of a shocked John Adams, who was moved to forgive the unhappy Hannah. Her plight made him review the merits of divorce, and he tried to think of ways to rescue her, a step which proved unnecessary, for Bela Lincoln soon died and Hannah entered marriage a second time, in this case to the prosperous and amiable Ebenezer Storer, treasurer of Harvard College.

Thereafter, Hannah and John saw nothing of each other until they were both nearly ninety. The elderly woman was brought to visit ex-President Adams some years after Abigail's death. When Hannah confronted John, the old man delightedly exclaimed, "What! Madam, shall we not go walk in Cupid's Grove together?" Hannah was taken aback for only a moment, and then, with sixty years vanishing between them, she replied, "Ah, sir, it would not be the first time that we have walked there!" This exchange left such an impression upon its witness, a young member of the Quincy family, that he kept it as his favorite memory of John Adams, claiming it showed the natural, genuine side of a person whom history long misunderstood.

Back in 1759, however, frustration over Hannah made John an even sterner judge of himself and mankind. Then he met Abigail Smith and his outlook brightened, for the parson's daughter reproached him for being so severe. She confessed that in his presence she sometimes felt frightened, particularly when she heard John's condemnations of optimistic talk about human nature. Humanity, said Abigail's suitor, was devoted primarily to "hunger and thirst and desire for copulation." Abigail confessed to John that "as a critic I fear you more than any other person on earth." After saying as much, Abigail was proud of her frankness and asked John, "What say you? Do you approve of that speech? Don't you think me a courageous being? Courage is a laudable, a glorious virtue in your sex, why not in mine?"

Abigail Smith's letters to John displayed her talent as a writer, and her spirit as a person. Certainly not lawyer Adams, nor probably any male, could resist Abigail's winsome pledge made just before their wedding: "Gold and silver have I none, but such as I have, give I unto you." Her writing was unrestrained and lilting. As the editors of the Adams Papers have observed, Abigail did not know how to pen a dull paragraph, so that her letters still have charm today. They surely entranced John Adams, above all when Abigail spoke of the mutual dependence and concern which love should entail. Such comments and his agreeable responses formed the spirit of partnership which imbued their marriage for over half a century. It was a union the pair was desperately eager to enter in 1764, now that John's law practice was established.

While she was being courted, Abigail seems to have yearned for John and regretted the necessity for chaste behavior. She chose to discuss her feelings with, of all persons, her cousin and John's former love, Hannah Quincy, to whom Abigail wrote in November 1763 after she and John had traveled together on one of his circuits as an attorney. During this trip the couple evidently had found it very difficult to preserve their virtue. While Abigail's letter is missing, she received a sympathetic reply from her cousin, who told her that, tantalizing though the trip with John had been, it could not have given a true glimpse of the joy of matrimony. Not even "the gaiety of your fancy," Hannah assured Abigail, could imagine wedded pleasure.

Hannah was encouraging, urging Abigail to marry immediately. "I know of nothing more irksome than being just at the door of bliss, and not being in a capacity to enter." She knew, too, how the prenuptial interlude held another annoyance, the many "ill-natured" acquaintances who made "rude, unpolished" jokes about the eager couple's frustrations. "They may call it wit, if they please," Hannah growled, "but I think it bears the name of shocking indecency." Remembering how she listened to such taunting, Hannah said, "it galls me everytime I think of it." However, for Abigail's cheer, she added, "I am now happily rewarded for what I then suffered." Hannah hoped these inhuman jokesters would spare Abigail their outrageous indelicacies. Meanwhile Hannah urged Abigail to prepare for her share of "all those transports my fond heart experiences."

Even less is known about the wedding of Abigail and John than of Mary and Richard's. Somehow the pair survived the torment of delay, although two weeks before the ceremony Abigail took refuge with relatives in

Boston. There she became ill, weak, and "low-spirited," as she reported to
John, while she tried to believe Dr. Tuft's good-humored assurance that
"I shall be better in a few days." When that short time had passed, Abigail
returned to Weymouth, where on 25 October 1764 she was married to
John Adams in a ceremony overseen by her father.

All that survives from the occasion is a family story which claimed that
Parson Smith took note of how eyebrows were raised in Braintree and
Weymouth because a young woman with Abigail's lineage had accepted a
lawyer as mate. In the province of Massachusetts Bay, as was generally
true in the American colonies, it was still said that no right-thinking male
would aspire to an attorney's career. Full-time lawyers were pictured as
troublesome leeches on the social body. It was argued that legal services
could be provided as a sideline by farmers, ministers, and businessmen.
To these insinuations about his daughter's choice the Reverend Smith is
reported to have preached a wedding sermon drawn from a gently rebuking
text, "For John came neither eating nor drinking, and they say he hath a
devil." (Matthew 11:18)

Abigail accompanied John to Braintree, the village next door, where
they set up housekeeping in a cottage John had inherited from his father,
Deacon John Adams, who had died in 1761. Deacon John was descended
from Henry Adams, an early settler in Braintree. The deacon was typical
of his forebears: hard-working, independent, well-regarded, and—at least
in Deacon John's case—modestly ambitious. A deacon's position in town
ranked next to that of the minister, thus awarding John's father considerable influence among those who filled the Braintree church pews. He
was a farmer, shoemaker, militia officer, constable, and probably did other
tasks, for Deacon Adams, like most men of the day, dabbled in many
occupations to support a family.

The deacon was fortunate in marriage, his wife and John's mother being
Susanna Boylston, a member of a prominent Brookline clan whose men
were celebrated for their contributions to medical science. Susanna probably became an Adams because Deacon John's brother Ebenezer had
married Susanna's older sister Ann several years earlier. Deacon John was
eighteen years Susanna's senior. The pair had three sons, of whom John
was the eldest, and apparently the only one who inherited his mother's
love of books.

When Abigail arrived in Braintree, she found her mother-in-law living
a few feet away in the house where John had been born. The widowed
Susanna soon took another husband, John Hall, in October 1766. He died
in 1780, but the redoubtable Susanna lived until April 1797, long enough
to see her oldest son become President of the United States. Abigail and
Susanna were good friends, perhaps because the older woman had an

admirable mind and read every paper and book that came to hand. She was never a dull companion, said Abigail, and John could not forget how she taught him to prize reading.

If ever companionship blossomed out of marriage, it did so for Abigail and John. This bond grew stronger despite the fact that soon after they were married the two often found themselves apart. For thirty years or more, John's professional and public life compelled him to be away from home, a circumstance forever regretted by the couple, though it produced one of the most interesting and touching correspondences in American history. When separated, Abigail and John seemed to write to each other constantly, and many of these letters have survived.

Looking back, Abigail considered the first ten years of her marriage to have been the best part. From that time she liked to recall the "humble cottage" she and John shared at the foot of Penn's Hill, from which Abigail gave her children a view of the sea and Boston. There were to be five youngsters, four of whom survived childhood. Abigail recognized early that managing these offspring as well as her home and farm would largely be her lot as she watched John, "my good gentleman," strive as a "practitioner at the Bar."

Some memories were less delightful, of course, as when Abigail, married barely a year, caught "hooping cough" from her first infant, and had to remain home sick in May 1766 when all of Boston was celebrating the repeal of the Stamp Act. She bitterly resented missing the excitement, especially when John could not stay to comfort her. Typically, he had to be away in Plymouth attending the superior court. Thus Abigail coughed alone, grumbling that Braintree was "insensible to the common joy."

Her need to be involved persuaded Abigail that she and her little ones should move into Boston whenever John's practice kept him there. In this way, the first decade of marriage passed, with Abigail and John as close as his work permitted. It meant that Abigail sometimes was in Weymouth, occasionally in Boston, but usually in Braintree. Then, in 1774, when Continental Congress duty took John to Philadelphia, Abigail gave up trying to stay with her husband, except through the letters they exchanged. Between 1774 and 1778, John was mostly occupied with congressional duties. Thereafter, he was sent to Europe as a diplomat, and for six years the couple's letters had to cross the Atlantic, until Abigail was able to join her husband in 1784.

As much as Abigail deplored their separation, John's toil as a delegate to the Continental Congress brought her much satisfaction. His letters opened her eyes to new scenes of which she became a shrewd observer from afar as John played an ever more significant part in the movement toward American independence. It was he who in late spring 1775 proposed George Washington as commander-in-chief of the infant nation's military forces. By autumn, John had become the leader in establishing the American navy, an accomplishment which the Adams family would cherish in the nineteenth century.

In 1776, John's role on the national stage was enlarged even further. He wrote *Thoughts on Government*, a treatise which influenced those who were drafting constitutions for the newly independent states. Abigail was soon hearing how John had taken on the frustrating, all-consuming assignment of managing the country's military operation, for Congress had appointed him president of the Continental Board of War and Ordnance. In spite of these burdens, during congressional debate John was present, often the strongest voice for separation of the colonies from England and for their transformation into independent states. It was fitting, then, that he should join Thomas Jefferson in drafting the Declaration of Independence and that he should give the speech which Jefferson believed rallied Congress to adopt the Declaration.

The strain imposed on John by Revolutionary politics alone was enough to make Abigail's epistles indispensable to his good humor, and he paid no heed to her plea that he "burn all these letters lest they should fall from your pocket and thus expose your most affectionate friend." Beyond their sentimental value, John cherished their cogent descriptions of home life during the struggle for Independence. This correspondence showed that after ten years of marriage Abigail and John shared a complete partnership. A good example of this is their debate about how best to educate their oldest son, John Quincy. Abigail was determined that he be trained at home by his absent father's law clerks. The alternative was "going to the town school," which Abigail dreaded as being filled with impure language and corrupt behavior. After emphasizing her concern to her husband, Abigail tactfully conceded that, after John returned from Philadelphia, "we can then consult what will be best."

At such times, Abigail expressed her yearning to have her husband with her, and pictured for him how they should settle down to farming and reading. Allowing sentiment momentarily to stifle her ambitious spirit, Abigail told John of her willingness to be a "dairy woman" while "our boys shall go into the field and work with you, and my girl shall stay in the house and assist me."

This kind of talk was intended to comfort John, who, no matter how lofty his station, always pined for the agricultural life. Abigail's encouragements were wasted, however, for she and John were unable to farm quietly together until he retired from the presidency in 1801. Abigail was mostly alone in Braintree after 1774, thankful that Mary Cranch was nearby. Mary had settled in Braintree with Richard when he and his watch-repairing business failed again, this time in Salem. Mary and Abigail took pleasure not only in being neighbors but also in taking trips to Weymouth to the parsonage where they grew up. Abigail's son John Quincy Adams claimed that his Smith grandparents "seemed to me as a second father and mother," adding that his grandmother Elizabeth "can never be to me any other than a guardian angel of my childhood."

Mary and Abigail made frequent visits to Weymouth not only to see their parents, but also to keep an eye on their younger sister, Betsy. She remained behind in the parsonage after Mary and Abigail went with their husbands to new homes, being fourteen when Abigail was married in 1764. Soon afterward, Betsy's strong will began to alarm some family members. As the youngest child, she had greatly profited from the opportunities for learning and for conversation with older persons, so that at age eighteen her letters disclosed a keen mind, a delight in literature, an appealing personality, and a character that was both romantic and devout.

Betsy's most notable trait was an independence which gave her sturdiness and self-possession, attributes that shaped her views of love and marriage. Even when she reached her sixties, Betsy disagreed with the conventional notion that courting was the most desirable part of a person's life. "I do not believe it," she told Abigail, reflecting on her own painful love affairs. These had taught her to deplore the stilted and artificial behavior forced on young persons in their search for romance. Betsy was twenty-seven when she eventually married in 1777 after being courted by three young ministers, each of whom lived in the Weymouth parsonage at some point, having come under the tutelage of Parson Smith, who prepared many young men for careers in the pulpit.

The first minister in Betsy's love life was her cousin Isaac Smith, Jr., son of the Boston merchant Isaac Smith, who himself was brother to Parson William Smith. In those days attachments between first cousins were common. Isaac was a year older than Betsy, a Harvard graduate, and shared Betsy's enthusiasm for literature and wide-ranging talk. The earliest surviving letter of Betsy's—written in 1768 when she was eighteen—is one of many she exchanged with Isaac Smith; in it she expressed her lively views on books.

Betsy had a way, however, of using such edifying chat to introduce more personal considerations. Once, when she was discussing Mary, Queen of Scots, Betsy switched topics charmingly to deny Isaac's contention that she herself had claimed to prefer being unmarried. Conceding that she might once have asked Isaac if he did not agree that there were some advantages to remaining single, Betsy assured him that she abhorred the thought. She then refused to clarify her attitude, for to do so would "necessarily lead to topics that I do not like very well to be concerned in." Instead she took up the subject of letters written by prominent French women, these, in turn, prompting her to observe that it often was easier to wage war than to fall in love.

Isaac's visits to Weymouth were a delight for Betsy. The couple walked along the Atlantic shore, a perfect setting for their literary conversation. If their talks moved down more personal avenues, Betsy had to conduct them; Isaac Smith displayed a sluggishness about matters of the heart which eventually kept him a bachelor forever. It was Betsy who showed an interest in addressing such matters as whether desire was an acceptable companion to virtuous love. She tried to coax Isaac into conversing about how it was the "natural propensity in the human species to love."

But Isaac, a short, rotund, lethargic fellow, preferred to ruminate about the way authors treated subjects, which of course also appealed to Betsy— up to a point. She did not share Isaac's main enthusiasm, English scenery, a preference that, in fact, took him away from Betsy in 1770, when he visited England. So stirred was he by the British Isles that he returned to Massachusetts a Tory. He opposed the call for disobedience to British rule which other men like John Adams and Richard Cranch eagerly answered. Isaac's outlook seems not to have troubled Betsy at first. Her interest in him lasted long enough to make her ignore the attentions of another ministerial candidate, Stephen Peabody, who came to the parsonage in Weymouth during the autumn of 1769.

Peabody was somewhat older than most divinity aspirants. He was twenty-two when he matriculated at Harvard, arriving from his home in Andover with enough changes of underwear to last a college term; at any rate such was the goal of his sisters, who were seamstresses. He was almost nine years Betsy's senior when he studied with Parson Smith during the time Isaac Smith was abroad. Whenever possible, Peabody escorted "Miss Betsy," but these outings apparently were limited to practical occasions, such as trips into Boston. There were no long walks beside the ocean. Nevertheless, the slender diary which Stephen Peabody kept during his stay in Weymouth assumed a sprightlier tone when he recorded the moments he spent with Betsy, uneventful though they were.

In complete contrast to Isaac Smith, Stephen Peabody was a giant whose physical strength perhaps exceeded his intellectual powers. He was almost intimidating in his gusto, singing loudly and well at any opportunity— Handel arias were his favorite—and he could build a stone wall by himself. His views on most matters were conventional and thus, for Betsy, unstimulating. She wrote to Isaac of a conversation—a "small debate," she called it—with Peabody who had insisted to her that "it was impossible to acquire a knowledge of the world without being deeply infected with its vices." Betsy countered this by stressing how knowledge brought awareness and with it vigilance. Peabody evidently contended that travel, which he could not afford, exposed a person to profanity and lewdness. Maybe so, Betsy replied, but one need not succumb.

Late in 1771, Stephen Peabody accepted a call from the newly formed parish in Atkinson, New Hampshire. He took with him the gratitude of Weymouth, for he had preached twice on many Sabbaths during a long illness suffered by Parson Smith. Peabody filled the Atkinson pulpit for nearly fifty years, and during the last twenty-five Betsy joined him as his second wife. When Peabody left Weymouth, however, Betsy's thoughts were fixed on Isaac Smith's impending return from England. She lost sleep because of her excitement, and when he arrived, she communicated her wish to see him "soon," and told him of her unabated affection. To Betsy's dismay, Isaac's stay abroad had left him an even less inspired swain. His thoughts were more than ever about England.

For a time, the faithful Betsy kept Isaac as her favorite, watching him become ordained and then serve as a minister in Cambridge. By 1774, however, she seemed to have abandoned hope, particularly after a new ministerial candidate arrived in the Weymouth parsonage. These developments alarmed Mary and Abigail, for they had encouraged Betsy's interest in cousin Isaac; but they were also disgusted with Isaac for becoming embarrassingly vocal in opposing colonial rights. This latter folly led Mary Cranch to scold him, perhaps in the hope that a new regard for America might lead Isaac to more aggressive behavior toward Betsy.

Mary wrote with ill-disguised irritation in the autumn of 1774 to remind Isaac that "Orthodoxy in politics is full as necessary a qualification for settling a minister at the present day as orthodoxy in divinity was formerly." If he supported injustice from London his usefulness would soon be over. After informing Isaac of the "trouble" he had caused, Mary asked him if he realized how, if one Smith seemed a loyalist, the public would suspect the entire family. Isaac assured Mary she had been misinformed and suggested they talk about her alarm, although he warned her he must be faithful to his views.

This exchange between Mary and Isaac further discouraged family hopes that Betsy would marry him. As for Betsy, however, the issue was already closed, a fact which Abigail discovered to her dismay when she urged the younger sister to be patient with their cousin. Betsy was embarked on a new romance, with John Shaw, the third clergyman in her life, and asked Abigail to stop interfering. Considerably miffed, Abigail reported to Mary, "I really think she must take her own way and nobody say her Nay." Betsy was now a woman of twenty-four, with views strongly reasoned and tenaciously held, particularly on the topic of marriage. She informed Abigail that, although it took a long time to know another individual's nature, many persons hurried into marriage dreaming of perpetual bliss, only to find themselves, as Betsy put it, "dragging out a miserable load of life, in domestic quarrels and perpetual uneasiness."

When Abigail insisted on knowing more about what happened to the relationship with Isaac, Betsy was less than forthcoming. She told her older sister that she cheerfully broke the bond, and that Abigail should drop the subject. The redoubtable Abigail persisted, fearing Betsy's relationship with John Shaw might flourish and end Isaac's chances. She urged Betsy to take a vacation in Boston where she could stay at Uncle Smith's residence and thus hardly avoid Isaac. Betsy might have received this advice in silence had Abigail left off at this point. Unfortunately, she went on to accuse Betsy by letter of flirtatiousness, a charge that brought Betsy's disgust to a boil.

The letter containing Abigail's scolding is missing, but its contents can be reconstructed from Betsy's indignant reply written in Weymouth on 7 March 1774. Obviously straining to remain courteous, Betsy conceded that she was still angry, particularly over Abigail's charge that she trifled with men. She had found this indictment so bewildering, Betsy said, that she asked her mother to explain Abigail's words. Once she understood that Abigail considered her a flirt, Betsy was outraged, perhaps too much so. *"Let me beg you my Sister to remember,"* Betsy wrote, that she was free to enjoy the companionship of all worthy persons. And if her liveliness in such company led some men to think she took a romantic interest in them, then that revealed their own designs. Men and women ought to be able to talk together without anyone, including themselves, considering the exchange a façade for amorousness.

Then Betsy examined Abigail's motives for rebuking her. She had waited to reply, the younger sister said, until "reason convinced me" that what at first had seemed jealousy on Abigail's part actually manifested "an over anxious concern for my welfare and happiness." This led Betsy to face Abigail's "insinuations" concerning her new friend, John Shaw. Although Betsy strongly defended Shaw, her letter leaves unclear what Abigail disliked about the young theologian. Certainly some folly or indiscretion must have been known or rumored to lurk in Shaw's background. Whatever it may have been, Betsy dismissed the stories, claiming that John deserved more generous treatment. She recommended Abigail check with other families with whom he had boarded while teaching school. For Betsy, John Shaw fully deserved kindness and friendship, besides which, Betsy acknowledged she enjoyed talking with him.

Betsy saved for last her retort to Abigail's suggestion that something improper hovered over the relationship with Shaw. "You cannot think how much I was astonished to be told that I had excited fears in some of the family," Betsy responded, emphasizing how Abigail's doubts filled her with "the *gall of bitterness.*" She was doubly indignant, Betsy said, because she had resisted adopting the coquettish manner the world seemed to expect of young women. How ironical it was, Betsy suggested, that she should be distrusted because she approached men with candor, friendliness, and compassion.

How could society and Abigail, Betsy wondered, discourage such openness or forbid men from acting in a frank, natural way with women? Must the male be either haughty and reserved, or else be judged to have romantic designs? Betsy proudly told Abigail that John Shaw was not imprisoned in this role. Nothing he had said or done could alarm "the most jealous prude," Betsy informed Abigail, adding that John's blameless behavior could lead no one to claim that romance was on either party's mind.

In a biting postscript Betsy implied that Abigail was so trapped by suspicion that a simple assurance was not enough. Therefore Betsy enclosed a mock deposition attesting "that we, John Shaw and Elizabeth Smith, have no such purpose in our hearts, as has been unjustly surmised. This we do solemnly declare as witness our hand." Betsy signed the statement herself, affixed Shaw's signature, clipped from one of his letters, and added the names of the Reverend and Mrs. Smith as witnesses. After sending this letter, Betsy continued to behave as she had before. She "talked down the summer sun" and held "converse with the stars" in the company of John Shaw, who, she exclaimed, was "such a friend."

It is impossible to know whether Betsy's sharp reply to Abigail came only from the indignation of innocence, or if she felt defensive or even guilty about her association with John Shaw. At any rate, either then or later, Betsy was indeed in love with him, and took him as a mate on the basis of her oft-declared belief that the marital bond should be formed from affection and compatibility and nothing else. Their marriage occurred well after Betsy's exchange with Abigail, but it seems unlikely that any delay was caused by the furor in 1774. The lovers were interrupted instead by a period of distress, when Elizabeth Smith, mother to Betsy, Abigail, and Mary, died in 1775. The event left Betsy to care for her infirm father, the two of them bound by deep grief. It is not known if John Shaw was then living in the Weymouth parsonage, although he was still seeking ordination. Only after the accustomed year of mourning had ended, early in 1777, did the romance between John and Betsy resume.

Betsy's renewed association with Shaw dismayed Abigail more than ever, leading her to hint ill-naturedly that Betsy was seeking marriage out of fear her time was running out. The older sister even exaggerated Betsy's age, claiming she was nearly thirty when, in fact, she was twenty-seven, still alarmingly late in those days for a woman to linger in maidenhood. As for Shaw, Abigail's dislike was at least as strong and certainly as mysterious as ever. If John Shaw had weaknesses, however, lineage was not one of them. He was the great grandson of Harvard's president Urian Oakes. His father and grandfather had been ministers; the former occupied the pulpit in Bridgewater's First Church for sixty years.

John Shaw was born on 14 September 1748, the tenth child in his family, and graduated from Harvard College in 1772. No one knows what caused the delay in his ordination. Personal difficulties, the excitement of the Revolution, perhaps uncertainty about Christian doctrine. He may have intended to remain a schoolmaster, for John shared his father's—and Betsy's—love of books. The elder John Shaw had run an academy as part of his ministry; the son was a teacher almost from birth. It was natural that he, with Betsy's help, opened a small school with a classical curriculum after his ordination and marriage. Such scholarly inclinations possibly endeared Shaw to Mary and Richard Cranch, for they evidently did not share the dislike that seemed to consume Abigail Adams.

Shaw's credentials also satisfied John Adams, who at this time was in Philadelphia attending the Continental Congress. When Betsy Smith and John Shaw announced their engagement in 1777, John Adams asked Abigail to send the pair his good wishes, suggesting as a message, "Tell him he may be a Calvinist if he will, provided always that he preserves his candour, charity, and moderation." But Abigail was unimpressed. "I cannot do your message to Betsy since the mortification I endure at the mention of it is so great that I have never changed a word with her upon the subject," she said. Again, Abigail's wrath remains a mystery, although one cause might have been the sting left by Betsy's scathing letter of 1774.

Whatever Abigail's views, Betsy went on serenely preparing for her wedding. John Shaw's ordination took place on 12 March 1777 in Haverhill, Massachusetts, where he had been called to settle. Shaw's selection by Haverhill did nothing to calm Abigail. "I would not make an exchange with her [Betsy] for all the mountains [gold] of Mexico and Peru." Abigail went on: "She has forfeited all her character with me and the world for taste, etc. All her acquaintances stand amazed." Abigail claimed that reaching age thirty without marriage drove some women to "do very unaccountable things." But not even Abigail was startled when Betsy dropped her nickname. It was no longer Betsy but Elizabeth Smith who married John Shaw on 16 October 1777.

In selecting a text for the occasion, Parson Smith may have intended to chasten those, including daughter Abigail, who might discredit his new son-in-law. Elizabeth's father chose a striking passage from the Gospel of John, the sixth verse of the first chapter: "There was a man sent from God, whose name was John." After the ceremony, Elizabeth Smith Shaw accompanied her husband to their new home, a handsome two-story parsonage which stood on the main street. Haverhill was a community of more wealth and sophistication than either Weymouth or Braintree, although as recently as 1709 a minister had been slain during an Indian raid. The town was almost on the New Hampshire border. A mile or so into New Hampshire was the village of Atkinson, where Stephen Peabody served as minister.

Two interested parties received terse reports of Elizabeth's marriage. Isaac Smith was notified by his father simply that "cousin Betsy Smith" had married John Shaw and moved to Haverhill. Isaac was now a Tory refugee in England where, ironically, he preached to the dissenting citizens of Exeter. In Philadelphia John Adams received a similar bulletin from Abigail, who pointedly stressed the more worthwhile news about cousin Hannah Quincy taking a second husband.

For the next six months no word was exchanged between Elizabeth and Abigail until the latter, hearing the bride had become pregnant, extended a peace offering, writing that reports concerning Betsy's health and happiness were pleasing, both of these subjects being "very dear to me." The older sister then asked to be remembered "in affectionate terms" to John Shaw, acknowledging that he had a "sympathetic soul." Promising to visit Haverhill soon, Abigail made a point of reiterating that "the knowledge of your happiness will always give joy to Your Sister."

Elizabeth accepted reconcilation at once, telling Abigail that her letter was fresh proof of "your goodness, piety of heart, sweetness of disposition, and greatness of mind." The younger woman assured the older of her love and that a visit "would afford the greatest pleasure to your truly affectionate sister." Elizabeth added a word about her once reviled husband, who indeed did have a sympathetic heart, which made him grateful for Abigail's gracious words. In fact, Elizabeth said, her mate's capacity for affection might make him more tenderly concerned about others than was wise "for his own comfort and advantage." Elizabeth had already noticed how members of the Haverhill congregation, like many others, were slow to pay their pastor, and also how the Reverend Shaw was too kindhearted to go out and press for his due.

Soon there was even stronger evidence that Abigail decided to accept Elizabeth's marriage to John Shaw. When she went abroad to join John Adams in 1784, she entrusted her sons Charles and Thomas to them. There was equally impressive proof of conciliation when John Shaw was asked by Abigail to prepare John Quincy Adams for Harvard. By this time, however, the three daughters from Weymouth's parsonage had been drawn into a unity which helped sustain them in their very different careers. All three—Mary, Abigail, and Elizabeth—demonstrated their prized rule, that in marriage the female deserved full and equal partnership.

2

Belonging to Everyone

The life of Mary Cranch wearies the observer even after two centuries. She toiled for the benefit of her impractical husband, her children, her sister Abigail, and for the entire Braintree community. She had little time for herself, but rarely complained except to lament those lost moments which might have been used for reading. Once, however, Mary felt so put upon by home and town that she broke down long enough to tell Abigail in disgust: "I am not my own. I belong to everybody." It was no exaggeration, for this eldest daughter from the Weymouth parsonage had become a guardian angel to her neighbors and relatives.

Mary and Richard Cranch settled with their three children in Braintree in 1771, after Richard found neither Salem nor Boston could support his efforts at selling and repairing watches. They rented a large house in the center of Braintree where Mary could enlarge the family income by taking in boarders since the town had no inn. Richard decided to make farming a supplement to his business in timepieces, while Mary undertook to manage a dairy. The farm project was a meager attempt to till thirty-two rocky acres located on a hill above the town. The land, purchased with aid from Mary's father and Uncle Norton Quincy, was an easy walk from home, as was the residence of Abigail and John Adams, located only half a mile south of the Cranch house.

In this setting, a little agriculture, dairying, watch-repairing, tutoring, and taking boarders kept the Cranches in provisions. Mary, of course, made clothes, prepared or preserved food, nursed her frequently ill husband, and oversaw all chores, including milking the cows and doing laundry. From the outset of all this activity, Mary realized that she would have to be the strong figure, looking after her mate and three children—two daughters and a son. Her husband, unlike Abigail's John, had no

family inheritance, no college degree, and no profession. Richard Cranch
had abundant wit, but he devoted it to literature and divinity, no less after
marriage than before. He was content to have Mary administer their
domestic life. Richard admired her ability as a partner. In his will he said
of her, "She has always conducted in the management of my family with
the greatest prudence and wisdom."

The Cranch union was extremely close. Richard was devoted to Mary,
his letters often beginning "My Dearest Love!" and closing "I am yours
with all that affection dictates and reason approves." To his relatives in
England, Richard wrote that marriage was "the happiest state in life." Well
might he have said so, for no man was better cared-for than Richard
Cranch. An example of this occurred when Richard developed a severely
infected leg. Mary was the only available person who could endure changing
his bandages. The limb was so putrid that she was perpetually nauseated,
and the odor seemed never to leave the house. The ordeal, Mary said to
Abigail, displayed how crucial women's strengths were to men, who were,
as a rule, helpless in affliction.

Braintree esteemed Richard Cranch, sending him to Boston as a representative in the legislature. He became a justice of the peace, a local
jurist, and parish treasurer, duties which served mostly to keep him even
less involved in household chores. Innocently, Richard caused so many
additional cares for Mary that she sometimes marveled how other tasks
got done. It was not easy to be patient with males, Mary observed to
Abigail, illustrating this remark with the story of how an ill Richard insisted
on leaving his bed to supervise some plastering, even though Mary was
quite capable of doing so herself. The result was what any good wife would
foresee—a husband's overexertion, sweating, and then a terrible cold.
None of this surprised Abigail, Mary knew, so in her own defense she
added a good-humored postscript: "And where was you, I hear you say"
when Richard was misbehaving? I was, said Mary, "reasoning, entreating,
and at last almost holding before I could get him into his chamber."

Never at a loss for suggestions, Abigail urged that flannel underwear be
put on Richard, and while she was seeing to this, Mary as well should
"wear it next to your skin." Abigail said that she too would don such a
garment if she had as much "spare room in my stays as you have." Mary
replied that she cherished "the kind soothings of my sister," and as Cranch
affairs worsened, she unburdened herself more often. "My prospects are
gloomy," she wrote, adding that she was left with only the strength that
came from "patience and resignation." Not that Richard ignored this.
Mary's partner emerged occasionally from the solitude of his thoughts
and was sympathetic—in his own style. He liked to remind his hardworking
wife that "the ways of Heaven are unsearchable." The blessed assurance,

in Richard's view, was that they could "hope that great moral good will arise from much natural evil."

Mary's career as a wife exemplified just how vigorous female partners needed to be. The cost was often high, both to her health and her morale. Confiding to Abigail during some especially trying circumstances in 1790, Mary was moved to make a remark that ought to humble husbands and males in any age: "Nobody but I know half the difficulties I have had to encounter. I have thought sometimes it would be too hard, for you and I have been better wives than the world will ever know or give us credit for."

Mary's labors usually necessitated taking in a girl or two from destitute or broken households to help with the tasks required in running a residence full of family and guests. "I am stiff from head to foot," she announced soon after dawn one summer morning, telling Abigail that she would like nothing better than to continue the agreeable task of writing a letter, but "my irons are hot and I must work before the heat of the day." Much of the laundry and ironing was the result of both children and adult boarders whose payment of rent was often the house's only income, particularly when the cows were ill or dying, a frequent occurrence in Mary's dairy. As she worked, Mary clung valiantly to the comfort of knowing that her lot was "from the hand of a good providence and I must not complain."

Yet there were moments when Mary felt she could not continue. Her house was a public gathering place, her children presented worries, her husband always needed supervision, and the community looked to her for numerous services and guidance. There was even difficulty finding a quiet place to read, for if she had a spare moment to herself, there was scarcely a corner not occupied by the paying guests who filled the Cranch home. It seemed to Mary that it took forever for her to finish reading a biography of King Philip II of Spain. When Mary's nephew John Quincy Adams visited the Cranch household, he complained that the hubbub was more than even his powers of concentration could withstand.

Much as John Quincy cherished his Aunt Mary, he was not the sort to appreciate the extent to which chores in the Cranch residence were increased when Abigail was often absent from Braintree between 1784 and 1801. It proved difficult for Abigail to resist John's lonely words, whether written from the great distance of Europe or from Philadelphia. The letters often ended with a poignant plea: "I hope I shall not be obliged to lie alone next Winter." When these sentiments carried Abigail away to be with John abroad or in the federal capital, it was up to Mary Cranch to supervise the real estate and the personal relationships which constituted Abigail's empire in Braintree.

After helping forge the peace treaty ending the American Revolution, John had been named the United States' first minister to Great Britain. As soon as peace was confirmed in 1784, Abigail went to Europe and remained there with John until they returned in 1788, when it was clear John would become vice president. Although Abigail lamented how public affairs frequently separated her from her husband and took them both from the beloved scenes around Braintree, at heart she did not regret her husband's success as a statesman. In fact, it was John Adams who more often deplored his entanglements in politics. Ambitious though her husband often was, Abigail's aspiring nature was more steadfast.

When John shrank from carrying on, it was his wife who prodded him forward. For this he was usually grateful, acknowledging how much his career owed to Abigail, "that excellent Lady who has always encouraged me." One of Abigail's proudest moments came in November 1789 when President George Washington visited Boston and, alongside John and Samuel Adams, was presented to a vast audience. With Abigail thrilled to listen, this sight prompted some in the crowd to shout: "Behold three men . . . who can make a revolution when they please."

Not even Abigail, however, could play her role beside John and also discharge the responsibilities at home which had been hers since she was married. When his law practice and political career took John from home, necessity made Abigail a skilled and aggressive manager. When away from Braintree, the instructions Abigail sent to Mary breathed a spirit of command and a mastery of detail which make it possible even today to appreciate how formidable Abigail Adams must have been in person. When it was time to paint rooms in her house, for example, the absent Abigail directed that Mary locate a competent painter. She warned, "I once suffered and was obliged to have a room three times painted when once would have answered."

On those occasions when John intervened in her domestic management, Abigail often quietly countermanded him by sending Mary or Uncle Cotton Tufts private messages. Usually John was interested in buying another parcel of land, but Abigail would tell her relatives at home, "between you and I, don't be in a hurry about that." Mrs. Adams was convinced her husband was gullible, especially about realty, and that she was the means of preventing his perpetually being swindled. Someone had to be tough, Abigail acknowledged, and no one viewed the world through shrewder eyes than hers.

No domestic detail was beneath Abigail's attention and she expected Mary to follow her example, whether in seeing to spreading manure or in caring for a horse stricken with laminitus, a hoof disorder. In a case of the latter, Abigail's tactics were instructive for Mary. The first lady sent careful directions to the Adams stable hand, Michael, concerning an ill horse. The oats fed to "Favorite" must be reduced, Abigail ordered. When that availed nothing, Abigail herself took the animal to two blacksmiths, each of whom announced that her horse's feet were the most afflicted encountered in their experience, and that she should give up "Favorite" as hopeless. Undaunted, Abigail informed her relatives that she herself had finally solved the crisis by having the horse's old shoes put back on and afterward personally seeing that "Favorite" ate "only two quarts oats a day."

Mary's love and admiration for Abigail was great, and her efforts to please her were earnest. So awesome did Abigail often appear that Mary never fully appreciated that her services to the Adamses—superintending their home, garden, farm, John's mother, and, at critical junctures, their children—were crucial. Abigail was profuse with her gratitude. Otherwise, as she pointed out, to whom could she entrust her precious offspring and farm? As Abigail put the problem to Mary, "It is very hard that mankind are so little trustworthy." Anyone but Mary, Abigail said, would likely injure the Adams property and "plunder me besides." Thus, whether in Paris, London, or the federal seat, Abigail appreciatively sent commands to Mary and, in turn, gratefully looked for letters from Mary to keep her aware of what was happening at home and in the village. In turn, Mary was eager to hear about the larger world, with its fashions, politics, and all the sights her sister saw.

The two sisters wrote in complete confidence, trusting each other to read aloud to relatives and friends only the less private passages. Mary's sharing with neighbors portions of Abigail's epistles became a village event. And woe to anyone who pried beyond what was thus revealed. Not even the president of the United States felt free to peruse Mary's messages. On one occasion Abigail caught John opening and reading one of Mary's letters. The consequence can be imagined from Abigail's terse words: "He has not opened any since I scolded so hard." John humbly promised to be "satisfied with such parts as I am willing to communicate."

Frank as they were, these exchanges between Mary and Abigail were still merely letters, and thus contain only a hint of what was said in conversation when any two—or all three—of the sisters were together. Whenever she was away, Abigail yearned to be back in Mary's kitchen, a setting that allowed much more of the personal banter the sisters enjoyed. A hint of what the face-to-face teasing was like appears in a note Abigail sent Elizabeth Shaw from London in 1787. It accompanied the gift of a beautiful piece of silk. "I was deliberating some time whether it should be virgin white or sky blue," Abigail quipped. "Upon the whole, I concluded that you had more pretensions to the sky than to the appellation annexed to the white." Since it was illegal to export silk, Abigail urged Elizabeth to keep the gift secret, meanwhile picturing "how pretty you will look in it." And Elizabeth was to be mindful that in London blue was "vastly the present taste." In time it occurred to Abigail that the finery she was sending her sisters might leave a false impression. So she took pains to assure them that her style of dress in England was no different from that worn in Braintree—"calico, chintz, muslin, a double gauze handkerchief, and an apron."

This pledge, along with Abigail's longing for the corn and beans in Braintree and for simple travel by chaise, helped reassure the sisters that Abigail was impervious to the worldly temptations of Paris, London, and Philadelphia. Not everyone in Abigail's entourage was so strong, however. Mary received a disturbing report from Abigail just as the Adamses prepared to leave London and return to Massachusetts in 1788. A Braintree woman well known to Mary, Esther Field, had accompanied Abigail to Europe as a maid. At the same time, another Braintree citizen, John Briesler, joined the group as manservant. Obviously shocked, Abigail wrote that Esther had become pregnant by John Briesler during an affair which had escaped Abigail's keen eye. It did not help matters when Esther claimed she had not known how women conceived. Briesler, it seemed, had explained nothing.

Abigail told Mary that eventually Esther rushed to her "in the utmost distress," to beg forgiveness. She assured her mistress that she and Briesler intended to marry when they returned to America. Abigail was sympathetic; the pair were excellent workers—Briesler was "as good a servant as ever bore the name." Hastening the couple off to be wed, Abigail shuddered at the likely prospect of superintending a childbirth at sea. But chiefly, she was amazed at the ignorance of poor Esther, saying to Mary, "however foolish it may appear to us, I must believe that she had no idea of being with child."

Mary was cautioned to keep this report a complete secret. Elizabeth, of course, also heard the amazing story, and was more skeptical about the astounding innocence of Miss Field. Thinking out loud to Mary, Elizabeth marveled that any female who read her Bible would not know some basic facts about conception. Calling Esther a "silly girl," Elizabeth turned her thoughts to the sinning male in the melodrama. How, she wondered, had Abigail confronted Briesler with his iniquity? Shaking her head, Elizabeth could only say, "I pity sister."

While Abigail worried over Esther in London, Mary struggled to maintain the Adams residence in Braintree. There were problems. In cold weather, Mary could never thwart the annual invasion of field mice, no matter what tactics were used. The rodents were so successful that, on one occasion,

Abigail had to be told that her bed coverings held a layer of "mice dung." Mary summoned a cat, but this noble animal could do little about the mice that had broken into the stove and devoured most of the loaf sugar Abigail had hidden there. Mary found it easier to supervise Abigail's garden.

The greatest burden was imposed whenever Abigail's return was imminent. Mary then had to recruit new servants, and not always to Mrs. Adams' satisfaction. Once, in 1800, Abigail had to remind Mary that she must put only a woman in charge of the kitchen. "I will have no more men cooks." Abigail also insisted that the family's coach driver must be a "decent, civil, sober man, and a Native American."

Mary was instructed to make many purchases before Abigail reached town. The Adams household must be ready, even to the extent of having refreshments at hand should neighbors walk in to welcome Abigail. In the summer of 1798, for example, Abigail sent $100 to be used to buy nine gallons of brandy, various spices, fresh bedding, coffee, tea—both "Hyson and Sonchong"—and brown sugar. Mary had to see that the beds were reassembled, and was told exactly where to find the screws for this project: "over the top of the granary chamber window."

Perhaps Mary's greatest service to Abigail took place not in Braintree but in Cambridge, where Mary arranged commencement parties when two of the Adams sons received their Harvard degrees in the absence of their parents. Mary took a more personal interest in the ceremonies of July 1787 when her son William graduated with his cousin John Quincy Adams. She had the two young men entertain friends together, for Mary was by no means so otherworldly as not to appreciate the social advantages that came with directing the graduation party for the son of America's minister to Great Britain. Under Mary's supervision, these commencement parties proved to be great successes.

At least they seem so in a glowing account sent by Mary to London. Two rooms had been rented in Cambridge where Mary oversaw dinner served to one hundred guests, with cake and wine later offered to four hundred more. The governor and other dignitaries were present. Three years later, Mary repeated the triumph for Abigail's youngest son Thomas, an affair including one hundred for dinner and a "multitude" more thereafter for cake and drink. The diners consumed thirty-one chickens, two legs of pork, four tongues, and a rump of beef.

Despite the extent to which she helped Abigail, Mary often was embarrassed when her sister tried to reciprocate. In part, this was because of the impractical forms occasionally taken by Abigail's generous payment. When beautiful shawls once arrived from London for Mary and her daughters, Mary found them so "costly" that to wear them around the village would be out of character for the Cranch women. Abigail seemed not always to understand how serious her sister's basic needs were. Mary tearfully had to ask Abigail for money to help the Cranches care for the Adams sons in their parents' absence. Stressing that times were difficult, Mary reluctantly requested ten shillings per week for feeding the lads. On these occasions, Mary tried tactfully to explain that money would be far more helpful to her than more glamorous gifts.

Even with assistance from Abigail, the Cranches' worries grew. By 1796 Richard himself recognized the family's peril. He passed his seventieth birthday with little to show except mounting debts and declining income. Usually Mary did the fretting, but at this point Richard spent a sleepless night contemplating their needs. The next day he wrote to Abigail for help, a deed that annoyed Mary when she learned about it. Mary had previously been responsible for all financial contact with the Adamses, taking pains not to seem complaining. Now that Richard had been so bold and frank, Mary had to confess before Abigail that Mr. Cranch was correct. "We are doomed to always be the obliged," she mourned.

Richard Cranch may have acted on more than impulse. His family's pathetic situation was presented to the Adamses with what could have been shrewd timing, for when Richard wrote, he knew that his dear "brother Adams" would soon be president of the United States. A year later, Richard became village postmaster, to Abigail's satisfaction. Although the Cranch household drew back from destitution, the appointment did not boost Richard's health, and the post office and an ailing postmaster were both left to Mary's care. Money problems therefore persisted.

In 1798, in order to pay the bills, Mary supervised the sale of their small farm to John Adams, who was bent on owning all the land thereabouts. Abigail was quick to advise Mary to protect the principal received from the sale. Invest it, use the income, and above all, Abigail warned, Mary must keep an eye on Richard, whose cavalier approach to money might prompt him to give it all to their children. "I repeat, pray do not let the bank be touched," Abigail advised, reminding Mary of the many pathetic instances where parents became their children's dependents.

Mary's larger role in the community obviously was the result of who and what she was as a person, and not because of material or financial glamor. Since contrasts in earthly possessions were not yet sharp in New England, most villages were not tempted to accept governance by a powerful purse. Mary's leadership in Braintree represented the sway of her personality, for she often appeared in apparel cast off by her famous sister. Mary put the family's plight before her son William as he set out for study at Harvard. "Our station in life is above our fortune," Mary cautioned. "We find the greatest prudence and economy necessary to feed and clothe our family and to give you my dear children the education we wish."

Although Abigail helped lessen Mary's woes, she could only stand aside and watch admiringly as Mary cheerfully cared for the village of Braintree. When Abigail sent money to use in helping the "worthy poor," Mary replied, "Happy, happy woman, to have the ability and the will to do so much good." To this, Abigail's answer was swift and to the point. It was Mary's role which deserved all the praise. "You prove that it is possible to be very benevolent and charitable tho with small pecuniary means."

Abigail was referring to the manner in which Mary dispensed charity and encouragement and offered commiseration, services usually assigned to the wife of the village minister; Mary's mother had excelled in playing this part. Braintree, however, not only had a bachelor parson, Anthony Wibird, but this astonishing man was himself one of Mary's chief worries. Nearly every dinner hour he could be found at Mary's table. The story of the Reverend Wibird was entwined with that of Mary and Richard. Even the youthful John Adams, writing in his diary in the 1750s, was taken aback by Wibird, who had recently become parish minister. There could hardly have been a more colorful or exasperating figure among Massachusetts' clergy than this man.

Anthony Wibird was born in New Hampshire in 1729, left a good record at Harvard College, and made an early display of his shrewdness when, in negotiating during 1754 to be minister for Braintree's north precinct, he bargained for and received £100 annual salary. The parish had offered £80 and a settlement allowance for establishing a home and family. Wibird rejected this generous offer, foreseeing accurately that he was unlikely to marry.

The new minister's person and his physical habits were not attractive, because Wibird possibly suffered from a neurological affliction. His bodily motions were erratic—"his head and half his body have a list one way, the other half declines the other way, and his lower parts from his middle incline another way," John Adams wrote. When he walked one leg stepped twice as far as its mate. Wibird seemed unable to sit quietly, but twisted himself around a chair, and when he spoke, he rolled his eyes, his head shook, and he "jerks his body about." He was far from handsome. His teeth were described by John Adams as black "and foul," his chin was huge, and his nose even larger, "with a prodigious bunch protuberance upon the upper part of it." There was said to be little industry in Wibird, and even less delicacy and politeness. But he did enjoy the company of people, could tell stories endlessly, and was exceedingly adept at keeping out of disputes. Wibird, his friend Adams acknowledged, had "wit and humour."

These latter attributes evidently never entered Wibird's sermons, most of which he repeated often. Richard Cranch, rarely a complainer, grumbled that he had heard one of Wibird's sermons ten times. A more severe judge, John Quincy Adams, confessed, "There is none of my time that I regret more than that I spend in hearing him . . . doze over a couple of sermons." In those days and well into the nineteenth century, Sabbath services were held morning and afternoon, so boredom must have been hard to avoid with Wibird in the pulpit. After even the patient Mary complained about the preacher, Elizabeth Shaw, herself a minister's wife, tried to defend Braintree's parson: "Are you not too hard upon Father Wibird? Perhaps you do not hear aright." But it was less the parson's sermons and more his behavior which distressed Mary.

Wibird's craftiness once involved the Cranches in an annoying way. In 1792 the north precinct of Braintree became an independent town and faced the question of what to call itself. The community turned to its pastor for guidance, a role Wibird dodged because the precinct was divided between two factions, one campaigning for "Quincy" as the new town's name, the other urging "Hancock," after a family which, years before, had provided the community with a much beloved minister and, more recently, had sent forth John Hancock to attain fame at the Continental Congress and become governor of Massachusetts. The name "Quincy" would, of course, honor the area's most prominent early landholders as well as Mary Cranch's grandfather, Colonel John Quincy. The issue of choosing a name actually pointed to serious political differences, since it kindled antagonisms between Tories and Whigs.

Wibird recognized that he could devise no solution pleasing to all his flock, and avoided the issue. The town turned to Richard Cranch, its leading layman. He arose in the first town meeting and courageously nominated "Quincy." In view of Mary's lineage, any other choice probably would have made him very uncomfortable at home. But even Richard's considerable influence did not quiet the tumult, though his recommendation was adopted. Rancor persisted until the next official gathering when the "Hancock" forces sought to repeal the choice of "Quincy." They failed, in a close ballot, but the political divisions in the newly created community lingered for more than a generation, making life unpleasant at times for the Cranches, the Adamses, and their descendants, all of whom represented a conservative outlook.

As the years passed, Wibird seemed to become more irresponsible, even in matters of appearance and his residence. He lived in a "vile house," said Mary, amid disgusting filth, leaving others to assure visitors that the town's minister was actually "alright." Finally, Mary spoke to Wibird, warning him that "the house had become so scandalous that if it was in

Boston the selectmen would pull it down." Even worse, in Mary's opinion, the minister looked like a "dirty beast." The parson refused to make any improvement, even in his clothing. Abigail, hearing about this behavior, nodded knowingly. What should people expect? she asked. It was clear to her that Wibird "like most old bachelors is become nearly useless and fears his own shadow." Mary's other sister, Elizabeth, still tried to be charitable, making a point of taking tea with Wibird when she visited Quincy and marveling at his inquisitiveness and capacity for gossip.

The parish's patience with Wibird was spent by 1796. If something must be done, who else could lead the way but Mary and Richard Cranch? The congregation put Richard—which actually meant Mary—in charge of a committee to select a young clergyman who could "assist" Anthony Wibird and thus shunt the old parson aside. It was a strategy familiar in New England churches; it had been used when Mary's father had grown old. But in Quincy this scheme proved difficult, for the parish became contentious. Just what created the schism is unclear. On the surface, the dispute was over the choice of the new minister, specifically regarding his personality and salary. Beneath these questions, however, simmered many personal animosities and jealousies that had developed during Wibird's long tenure, legacies of the continuing social upheaval fostered by the Revolution.

And so the parish quarreled, no one quite certain why. "We have turbulent spirits to engage. Tis well we are not all so waspish," Mary reported to Abigail. This unhappy mood was apparent to the clergymen invited to preach trial sermons. One of them became so uneasy that he suffered a stroke and died while standing in the pulpit. Other candidates took one look and fled, accepting calls from less quarrelsome parishes. Finally, in the spring 1797, a choice seemed possible. The candidacy of Peter Whitney drew the support of a majority—until Abigail Adams intruded. Despite good intentions, the first lady created two more years of hard work for Richard and Mary and their pulpit committee.

This happened because Abigail, back from Philadelphia temporarily, asked young Mr. Whitney to tea. Characteristically, Abigail advised Whitney on his tactics, particularly that he seek a larger salary. The community, she told the young cleric, would try to be stingy, since it must keep paying Parson Wibird something until he died, in this case £50 per year. Armed with such counsel from a powerful parishioner, Peter Whitney told the congregation, in writing, what Mrs. Adams had said. The result brought to flame every resentment and jealousy smoldering in the pews. When a stalemate ensued, the Cranches found that opposition to Whitney could now count on Peter Boylston Adams, John's brother and frequent critic, and Deacon Moses Black, once Abigail's close friend. When Mary tactfully informed Abigail the trouble her chat with Whitney had caused, the first lady was furious. "The man must have lost his senses." But she also acknowledged her need to be more "close mouthed." Abigail reluctantly remained on the sidelines during the rest of the controversy, while a worried Mary wrote, "I hope that we shall get fixed soon or we shall split to pieces." She worked to pacify the opposition, whose leaders at first refused to hear a favorable word said about her injudicious candidate, saying they would sooner do their own preaching than submit to Whitney.

Not until the end of 1799 was the controversy settled. Mary's efforts to calm the parish succeeded finally in marshaling a majority behind an offer to Whitney of $500 annual salary and $500 settlement money. The amazing Mary even persuaded Peter Adams and Deacon Bass that they personally issue the invitation to Whitney, as proof of amity in the community. Whitney's cause was also aided by some citizens' alarm over those Sabbaths when no visiting pastor was available to open the meetinghouse. It appeared that boisterous drinking parties were replacing worship in some circles of Quincy.

With parish unity restored, the town had to await Whitney's recovery from the mumps to have his decision. After he finally accepted the call, the congregation selected 5 February 1800 as the day when Whitney would be ordained, a good choice, since it would be precisely forty-five years to the hour that Anthony Wibird first was welcomed to the Braintree church. Mary's residence was the logical headquarters for out-of-towners expected to attend the event, including all the relatives of the new parson. On 3 February, celebrants from afar began appearing, including a young lady who Mary discovered was the Reverend Whitney's betrothed. She brought with her Whitney's father and several of his sisters, all of them arriving during a sudden thaw and downpour. Thoroughly drenched, these persons were met by Mary and one servant with courtesy and compassion.

Mrs. Cranch had set about lighting fires to dry the travelers when more knocks announced additional sodden and hungry pilgrims, followed by still others, including Peter Whitney's three brothers. Mary soon had no more room. She dispatched one bedraggled group to a neighbor, only to have them turned away. "I think I never felt more disagreeably in my life," an indignant Mary told Abigail. "I felt for the town." Somehow Mary managed, but the toll in food, brandy, and wine was astonishing. During the week-long festivities, Mary would get to bed around 2:00 A.M., sleep fitfully, and then arise to prepare a huge breakfast for guests and others who simply walked in. "They eat like farmers," she observed.

Once the morning meal was over, Mary had to load a table with ham, cake, cider, wine, and brandy for all-day refreshment. The perpetual cooking was too much for the chimney, which caught fire. Since the house was wet inside and out, as Mary put it, flames spread slowly. A member of the former opposition to Whitney, Benjamin Beale, displayed his Christian charity, as well as courage fortified with Cranch brandy, by ascending the roof carrying pails of water to douse the fire. With order restored, Mary then placed dinner before fifty persons, the menu including plum pludding, roast turkey and geese, beef roast, chicken "pye," apple "pye," squash and rice pudding—all of it "in plenty," an exhausted Mary assured Abigail.

Despite the persistently foul weather, the ordination was a happy occasion, even if half the expected audience chose to remain dry at home. "Everything was conducted with peace, love, and harmony," a gratified Mary recorded. Whitney's father preached the main sermon (most said the son's remarks were superior), after which a fine gown was presented to the new minister. To everyone's surprise, Anthony Wibird acted properly. While he refused to attend the new parson's installation, he met a group of official well-wishers in a clean shirt, "though not a white one," Mary lamented, relieved to be at the end of her duties—or so she thought. The triumphant occasion closed with a huge snowfall which trapped all her guests for two more days.

Anthony Wibird continued to worry Mary only a short while longer. During the next six weeks he refused to remove the shirt donned for ordination day, and in April 1800, Mary announced sadly, "He certainly has not the use of his reason and ought to be treated like a person insane." With the warm weather, vermin beset the old parson, who still lived in filth, so that in late April it became an "absolute necessity" to rescue him. In Mary's words, "He was covered with sores from his shoulders to his toes." After preparing an ointment and gathering some of her husband's underwear, Mary deputized several men to help her and marched them to Wibird's wretched quarters. She bathed and anointed the aged patient, packed a few of his things, and told him he must abandon his squalid surroundings. Wibird proved stubborn and ill-tempered, "although the blood was streaming from his shoulders and stomach." Mary persisted, and even persuaded Captain Moses Brackett to give the pathetic figure a room.

There Wibird began to behave and even attempted to remain clean. He read his books, and received callers from the parish whom Mary prodded into visiting him. The reform may have been too much for the venerable theologian, however. Parson Wibird died on 4 June 1800; along with others, Abigail praised Mary for having rescued "that poor forlorn man," but she could not resist drawing a moral from Wibird's career: he never had a wife, and without such a partner to stimulate him, he naturally fell indolent, apathetic, "like waters that stagnate if they cease to flow." Wibird should serve as a warning to all men, said Abigail, "not to contract habits of sloth and inaction, to consider that no man liveth for himself."

The story of the old and new parsons, Wibird and Whitney, was but one instance in the chronicle of Mary Cranch's involvement in the village's welfare. Little escaped her eye or ear, and her letters to Abigail occasionally read like case reports from a dedicated social welfare worker. Quincy had become a community where virtue, at least in Mary's opinion, was declining, and she had no doubts about who was to blame. "All the gentry that have come to the town for these several years have rather injured than otherwise our morals," she wrote in 1784, mindful of the dislocations caused by the Revolutionary War. Mary cited a Mrs. Thomas, whose husband was away in the West Indies, leaving her afraid to sleep alone, or, as Mary put it, "without a man—in the next parlor at least." Mrs. Thomas persuaded a bachelor, Josiah Vesey, to be her *"protector"* and to move in with her. "Scandal, hold thy tongue," Mary chided herself.

Mary took on more wholesome projects, including Mr. and Mrs. Allen, who were newlyweds, but not exactly youthful. The bride was hardworking and cheerful, said Mary, one who loved her husband "and studies to make him happy." Mrs. Allen had an unimproved mind, though, which in Mary's view might smother her natural virtues. So, Mary planned for Mr. Allen to turn instructor. "It would be a pretty amusement for him in a winter evening to employ himself in teaching her the different meaning that is affixed to certain words. That *exceed* does not mean *succeed* nor *rebellious—bilious*, nor *distinguish—extinguish*." A wife who knew not these distinctions, in Mary's view, could mortify a "man of sensibility." Thus improved, Mrs. Allen would become what Mary wanted for her, to be both a good and an entertaining wife.

Most of Mary's cases were less hopeful than that of Mrs. Allen. "Do you remember Hannah Nightingale who wanted a gown that looked like a rainbow?" Mary asked Abigail. It seemed she had other desires as well, some which apparently led her astray, for Mr. Nightingale turned her "nearly naked" out of their house, leaving Mrs. Nightingale, "near lying in," as a worry for Mrs. Cranch. It was up to Mary and her team of helpers to aid such a woman, especially one in advanced pregnancy. Less sympathy went to Mrs. Howard, "who is or has been a widow bewitched," Mary reported, for when the disconsolate woman became with child, she pointed to a highly regarded citizen as the father, "but he will not marry her."

Much of Mary's time went to repairing broken family circles. She fretted over the Clarks, who seemed unable to live together in peace; the wife returned to her parents while Mr. Clark found a room and took his meals like a bachelor. Sadly, the couple's children were "put out" to other homes, the New England way of rescuing youngsters who were orphans or casualties of disrupted marriages. Mary herself often removed girls from these circumstances to train them for domestic service. In the case of Tobias Bass, however, his children were grown when he and Mrs. Bass parted in 1785.

Mary described the outcome with some amazement. Mr. Bass sold all his property, dividing the proceeds into four parts, giving one to his wife, one each to their two sons, and retaining the last. All this was edifying, except—as Mary pointed out—Bass hastily departed to the empty wastes of Maine, taking with him a young lady "to help people it." It turned out, Mary revealed, that the woman in question had been a maid in the Bass household, and had given birth to twins. The new mother swore before the court that Leonard Cleverly was the father and engaged counsel, with Mr. Bass' help. When Cleverly "most solemnly" denied paternity, he was so convincing that Mrs. Bass lost patience, and banished her husband and her former maid.

Mary reported less spectacularly on her efforts to assist families stricken with illness. There were no hospitals, making nursing a community responsibility. She saw that village women come to help as "watchers" during the night. When a neighbor died, it was mostly Mary's task to organize friends in aiding the bereaved with food and companionship. Such a practice occasionally had unexpected results, as in 1799 when James Apthorp died. Mary described how the deceased's grown offspring, after viewing their father in his coffin, decided that corpse and coffin would look improved if the casket were "lined with white flannel." Whereupon Mary asserted, "the son and daughter went to work with a hammer and nails. One held up his [the corpse's] head while the other tacked it [the flannel] on." Then the bereaved widow "got her brush and paint and painted the edge black." All the guests were then summoned "to see what an addition to the beauty of the coffin it was." The family should have applied finishing touches to the deceased, observed Mary, by "putting a little rouge on his face."

Closer to home were two widowed relatives, Uncle Norton Quincy and Uncle Cotton Tufts, gentlemen whose names figured prominently in Mary's reports to Abigail. Uncle Norton, brother to Mary's mother, remained isolated on the estate of Colonel John Quincy, his late father. Norton's wife had died within a year after their marriage in 1748. What disturbed Mary was that, to relieve his loneliness, her uncle had taken in "a vixen" who also served as housekeeper, and that occasionally one Sally Taylor came "to help his repose and to amuse him in his retirement." Mary did not approve, but she was sympathetic, telling Abigail what a pity it was that Uncle Norton had not found "a sprightly wife." Men, his niece concluded, needed feminine companionship more in advanced years than in youth.

Uncle Cotton Tufts, who still lived in Weymouth, discovered the wisdom of Mary's observation without having to be told. The results were not wholly pleasing to Mary and her sisters, who remembered lovingly his first wife, Lucy Quincy, their mother's—and Uncle Norton's—sister. Soon after the customary year's mourning for his wife, Uncle Cotton began in 1787 to search for a new mate, asking help from Mary. She did her best, regretting that Josiah Quincy's widow would lose her property if she remarried. The supply of candidates seemed scant, and Mary had no time for serious matchmaking, so she urged Abigail to send suggestions from London. Their uncle was impatient, she informed her far-off sister. This news displeased Abigail who wondered why they were acting with such haste. Second marriages at Uncle Cotton's age—fifty-five—"can be considered only an affair of convenience, the heyday of the blood is tame." Indeed, said Abigail, signs of youthful ardor in their uncle "would be ridiculous."

Whatever Uncle Tufts' reasons, he soon found a thirty-three-year-old bride, Susanna Warner, and promptly antagonized his son, who feared that children might arise from this second marriage and diminish his prospects as heir to Dr. Tufts' considerable estate. "There will be no *heart* felt harmony between the son and new mother," Mary predicted, wondering how to restore peace. There was no help when John Adams returned from Europe and hastened to greet the bride of his old friend. "I have seen the new Mrs. Tufts and admire the Dr.'s taste," he reported to Abigail. "She is in appearance a fine woman." This opinion alarmed Mary even more, leaving her to watch anxiously for a second Tufts family. It proved a groundless concern, since bride and groom lived happy and childless for many years.

Not all family dangers were so conveniently averted. Another of Mary's kindly errands required visiting the family of Dr. Thomas Welsh, whose wife, Abigail Kent, was a cousin dear to the Smith sisters. The Welsh household, in Boston, was a favorite stopping place for the country relatives. Welsh was from the Braintree area, and his widowed mother still lived there under Mary's careful attention. On 24 May 1798 Mary was driving her chaise into Boston when she was confronted with the stunning news that Thomas Welsh, who seemed so prosperous and prudent, had failed financially. The blow was especially severe since the Adamses and even the Cranches had turned over sums for Dr. Welsh to invest.

"Vanity of vanity! and the consequence of it is vexation of spirit," Mary advised Abigail, after learning that the Welsh catastrophe came from extravagant living and wild speculation. Dr. Welsh was less than fifty years old, so well regarded that he had no difficulty borrowing money from relatives, who now all repented of their generosity. Welsh's debts were discovered to be above $30,000, a fortune. Mary asserted that never had she seen some of their connections so agitated and enraged. Cousin Abigail Welsh was left speechless and nearly insensible by the news of her husband's disgrace. And Abigail Adams was compelled to inform her son John Quincy, U.S. minister in Berlin: "I fear you are a sufferer." Young Adams had left his savings under the care of Dr. Welsh before going to Europe.

Abigail could say nothing to the Welshes, and her words to Mary were hardly comforting. "The longer we live in the world, the more do troubles ·hicken upon us, yet we hug the fleeting shadow." Mary's shock lingered for days, as she wondered what could have "swallowed up" so large a sum. It grieved her, of course, that she and Richard had entrusted most of their scant savings to Dr. Welsh, some $70 now lost. Mary doubted if the Welshes, accustomed to grand living, could learn those arts of simple existence the Smith girls had acquired in the Weymouth parsonage. Nothing would save the Welshes but those economies "our dear and venerable Mother taught us, even to the importance of saving an apple paring." The man once hailed as a prospective mayor of Boston did his best, living ascetically until his death in 1831.

Imprudence among her relatives, however, was no surprise to Mary. Twelve years before the Welsh fiasco, General Joseph Palmer, Richard's brother-in-law who lived in the Germantown district of Braintree, had been a sensational failure. Palmer had emigrated from England with Richard in 1746 and become a highly successful manufacturer. Then, in 1785, Palmer's career, which for forty years had seemed such a contrast to Richard's, was in ruins. By November 1786, the Palmers' handsome home and property, which had often forced Mary to struggle against envy, was sold, and the family took refuge with the Cranches before moving on to other relatives in Charlestown.

For Mary and her sisters, this downfall was astounding and sobering. Joseph Palmer had been a model of immigrant success. For Abigail, in London, report of this disaster proved once again the folly of pride. Elizabeth Shaw was more compassionate. "Alas! how I lament the unhappy situation of General Palmer," she said, recalling "those fair possessions" now swept away. Better to look "to the realms above" even while enjoying the earth, for only above "we may place our trust." General Palmer soon suffered a stroke and died but not before displaying his old pride by opposing his daughter Betsy's marriage to Richard's nephew, Joseph Cranch. Even Mary admitted that Joseph was no match for the talented Betsy—"the superiority is in the wrong side," while young Cranch was an unambitious gunsmith. Reluctantly and after a scene witnessed by much of Boston, General Palmer finally gave in, having greatly strained the bond between the Palmers and the Cranches.

Now the widow Palmer needed Mary's help, hardly a welcome prospect for the Cranches; Mrs. Palmer had always been a difficult person, wholly unlike her brother Richard. Mary arranged for her to live in one of Abigail and John's houses, easily available for Mary's visits, which were needed until 1790 when the widow died, leaving unmarried daughters for Mary to look after. In their impoverished state, the Palmer maidens' future was bleak, prompting Abigail to observe: "If ever convents were useful, it would be for persons thus circumstanced." How much better if the Palmers had been content with a little, rather than pursuing grand visions.

The fates of the Welsh and Palmer families were sad enough, but even more painful was the sorrow befalling one of Mary and Abigail's closest friends, Mercy Otis Warren, who lived in the nearby village of Milton. Once much admired by the Smith sisters, Mercy Warren and her husband James had become increasingly consumed by ambition and jealousy. Equally distressing were Mrs. Warren's writings. A historian of the recent Revolution, she was considered by Mary and Abigail to have unfairly presented John Adams' role, an offense that weakened the link between the Warren and the Adams circles. Still, Mary was alarmed when the behavior of Mercy Warren's several sons, once judged model offspring, became scandalous.

Alcohol and lust took command of the Warren boys, convincing Mary, who could do little to help the unhappy family, that of all the years "there [were] none more critical for a gentleman than from eighteen to twenty-two." During that time, "Passion is then strongest and is too apt to prove an overmatch for reason." It now meant that the Warren lads were ruined in the world. Mary did not care to give Abigail details in writing, but Abigail's son John Quincy told the ironical story in his diary thirty years later. "Among the earliest and profoundest of my recollections are the constant and urgent admonitions of my dear mother to look to those [Warren] children as my model and to imitate their deportment and manners." Typical of their downfall was the fate of Winslow Warren, whose story especially troubled Mary Cranch.

Winslow Warren, said J. Q. Adams, "led a licentious and adventurous life"—a gamester and dissipator whose time was spent fulfilling "the longings of prurient virgins," or else gladly serving as "the plaything of practiced harlots." Fleeing debtor's prison, Warren joined the army and was killed during General Arthur St. Clair's defeat by the Ohio Indians in 1791. John Quincy recorded all this in his diary on 2 February 1820, noting that the epidemic of Warren trouble was not over, since, even as he wrote, another of Mercy Otis Warren's sons, Henry, was being forced from office for stealing public money and was imploring John Quincy, then secretary of state, for help. Drawing a lesson from this wretched history, John Quincy's reflections were identical to those of his Aunt Mary Cranch a quarter century earlier: "Among the vicissitudes of human affairs, the fate of that family of Warren is to me a source of melancholy and would it might be of useful reflection."

Mary had felt compassion toward Mrs. Warren, as she did generally toward those around her who were caught by the seemingly endless misfortunes of life. It was difficult in a rural village to disguise sin and distress, so that Mary's realism about affairs in Quincy could not exalt human nature. Yet there was no "revolt from the village" in Mary's time, as there would be when early twentieth-century writers began ridiculing small-town America. In the eighteenth century, the Mary Cranches attributed trouble to the nature of men and women, not to their environment, no matter how rude or pinched. Mary knew what to expect when the foe was greed, pride, lust, and intemperance. She tried to teach everyone that no mortal was safe from human baseness.

However, one example of virtue's triumph was at hand to cheer Mary. This was the career of a black woman, Phebe, who had been enslaved to Mary's father, Parson Smith. Mary and her sisters were almost as devoted to Phebe as to each other, for Phebe had been treated as a family member. During the dreadful time as Parson Smith suffered his final illness from a blocked urinary tract, Phebe was his nurse. When the Weymouth patriarch died in 1783, he stressed in his will that Phebe should take her freedom, and he set £100 annual income aside for her support. If she refused the arrangement, the sum would go to the daughter who kept her as a slave.

Phebe accepted her liberty and the money. After marrying a Braintree resident named Abdi on 28 January 1784, in a ceremony consecrated by the Reverend Wibird, Phebe settled with her husband into the absent Abigail's cottage, helping Mary look after the place for many years. Like Mary, Phebe made her home a refuge for any person in need, particularly blacks living in the area or passing through. Phebe's husband usually was willing to support his wife's humanitarianism, hesitating only when Phebe insisted on caring for Quincy's most disreputable woman, a certain Sally Traxter. But there were other "such creatures," and Phebe's husband once spoke to Mary about the propriety of sheltering such a "vile crew" within the property of the president of the United States. Phebe, however, sadly reproved her mate, saying, "He has no compassion."

Mary sided with Phebe, but admitted to a dismayed Abigail, "Tis as you say, while Phebe has a house, every Black thing will be living with her." Mary was emphatic about the value of Phebe's charity, however. As an example she cited the shameful case of Jonathan Rawson, who sent a sick Negro woman to Phebe with only a little rice, one hard biscuit, and a few sticks of firewood to ward off a blizzard's chill. The pitiful creature "was so ill Phebe could not send her back in the storm," Mary sympathized. For her pains, Phebe had to care all night for the refugee, who suffered from fits and was so weak she could not even undress herself.

Phebe and Mary Cranch were remarkable partners, a team composed of a black and a white woman whose Samaritan labor made them belong to everyone. Phebe did not outlive Mary by much, and in her last illness she was attended by Mary's daughter, Lucy Greenleaf, who was, of course, supervised by Abigail. Elizabeth sent her farewell to Phebe, asking Abigail to urge the venerable black woman to trust God for He "made of one blood all the nations of the earth." The dying former slave received Elizabeth's reminder that all persons who feared and served God would be accepted by Him regardless of their color.

These were comfortable words, and no one knew their solace better than Elizabeth, who uttered them out of a religious faith that had sustained her in a life spent far from the familiar scenes of her childhood. First in one parsonage with John Shaw and then in another with Stephen Peabody, Elizabeth had cared for her family and community in the same spirit of love and compassion that had characterized Mary Cranch's career, even though Elizabeth's trouble sometimes outweighed even Mary's and Abigail's burdens. Despite her sorrows, the youngest of the Smith daughters never lost for long the lively and literate charm that had enlivened her youth.

3

From One Parsonage . . .

It must have been a happy autumn wedding day in 1777 for Elizabeth and John Shaw. Unlike Mary, Elizabeth never recalled being terrified at the time, but of approaching the event with "delightful anticipation." It was a day's ride to Haverhill from Weymouth, distance enough to make Elizabeth feel far away from the two sisters and the scenes she cherished. Because she remained along the Massachusetts–New Hampshire border for the rest of her life, Elizabeth never overcame a disagreeable sense of remoteness from her sisters. Yet with this distance came an advantage which Elizabeth could not entirely recognize. In Haverhill her unusual personality flourished without having to compete against the restraints that might have been imposed on her had she lived near Mary and Abigail.

Elizabeth's marriage to John Shaw was at first a triumph, although soon after the wedding her husband fell desperately ill. Elizabeth, well-trained by her mother, nursed him expertly, and before long was praising Heaven for saving "the life of *my* kind and affectionate friend." A witness to the Reverend Shaw's professional success was his nephew, John Quincy Adams, whose standards were not easily satisfied. Young Adams had only admiration for "Uncle Shaw's" sermons and for his management of a difficult position.

Parson Shaw's duties extended beyond the pulpit. After a parishioner startled everyone by dying while astride his horse, John remained with the bereaved family until well after midnight. His consoling and inspiring presence was widely comforting, although Elizabeth was too much a realist not to see that the Haverhill congregation was no different than others. "People love their minister, at least love to have him with them when they are in trouble, if at no other time."

As part of his stewardship, John Shaw performed as a schoolmaster, as his father had done, taking on a few students, including his son and nephews, who wished to prepare for Harvard College, a tutoring project at which he became a specialist. From London Abigail sent Elizabeth a book originally given to John Adams by Benjamin Franklin: "Mr. Adams thought it might be more useful to Mr. Shaw than it would be to him." The book was a treatise on education, and thus belonged to Shaw's "department," Abigail asserted. Even the Harvard faculty admired Elizabeth's husband's skill in coaching students for admission, a fact that pleased Elizabeth. After all, it was their shared devotion to learning and literature that had drawn the two together.

Haverhill's parsonage and meetinghouse stood in the center of town on a hill overlooking the Merrimack River valley. Elizabeth's large and handsome residence was built in 1773 and lasted until 1908, when progress pulled it down. The comparative splendor of the parsonage hinted at the brief moment of wealth enjoyed by Haverhill until after the American Revolution, when it was deposed as the region's commercial center. John Shaw's salary was £100, payable in money and kind. He would find it difficult to collect. The meetinghouse, erected in 1766, was replaced in 1837—the congregation finally lost patience with the unusual design of the pews. The seats needed to be lifted and then dropped as worshipers took their positions. The result was a noise said to resemble an artillery battle. John Shaw was constantly urged by his congregation to remind worshipers to lower their seats gently.

Another kind of congregational uproar was still audible at the time Elizabeth and John moved into the parsonage. This was an ongoing quarrel caused by the Arminian views held by John's pastoral predecessor, Edward Barnard, who had died in 1774. He left the parish so agitated that no new minister could be agreed upon until Shaw was chosen in 1777. The Reverend Barnard's advocacy of universal salvation created confusion and unhappiness in Haverhill, but John Shaw's mild Calvinism and his even milder manner soon restored the town's confidence in its parson, and during the seventeen years of John's ministry the congregation grew steadily. Thirty persons were received as members, and he married 107 couples and baptized 163 infants, a creditable record for a town in decline.

In Haverhill the Shaws were seen everywhere, for Elizabeth usually accompanied John on his rounds. In her first letter to Mary, Elizabeth reported that her new circumstances left her "exceedingly pleased." She believed she had won over the townsfolk through friendliness, for she learned her parishioners were saying " 'that she talks, and is as sociable as one of us.' " The children called her " 'a dear pretty woman.' "

All this was the benefit, Elizabeth conceded, of the many hours she gave to visiting and to receiving calls. It was not the way she preferred to spend time, she admitted, but being a minister's wife meant conforming to duty and tolerating disagreeable company. Only Elizabeth knew what she put up with in order that people of Haverhill would "say my character was very good and they are no ways disappointed." Even more than Mary, Elizabeth yearned for quiet to read and write, but she was determined to help her husband succeed, which obligated her to sit center stage in the town's social life. Her independent spirit was suppressed but undefeated. In a letter Elizabeth sent to Mary in 1780, three years after arriving in Haverhill, she said that her existence required a deep faith in God, for such was needed "to calm our passions amid the disagreeable scenes of life." She confessed herself "surfeited with dress and all the gee gaw appertenances. But I forbear."

Indeed, Elizabeth had found that life in Haverhill consisted of more than piety, learning, and household duties. The town was a much livelier place than the more rural Weymouth and Braintree, and thus enjoyed numerous social occasions in addition to the two Sunday meetings. Located on an important river, the Merrimack, between Newburyport and Lawrence, Haverhill's citizens were involved in commerce and early manufacturing as well as in agriculture, creating an atmosphere more worldly and sophisticated than was common in the region where Elizabeth grew up. Haverhill carried on formal social activity, into which the Shaws immediately entered. Every fortnight, during fall, winter, and spring, citizens gathered in "Assembly" for fellowship, which included dancing, games, and conversation. Back in Braintree/Quincy, Mary Cranch succeeded in preventing such village frolics until she gave up the fight after 1800. Scripture, she believing, frowned on dancing.

For some Haverhill neighbors official entertainment every two weeks was insufficient. Certain homes therefore took turns being the setting for almost nightly socializing. When he was studying with Uncle Shaw in 1785 and 1786, John Quincy Adams faithfully attended these sessions, not because they were animated, which was not always the case, but because he could meet young ladies, a benefit for both sexes which may have caused parents to instigate the arrangement. In these evening confrontations, those present, young and old, sometimes simply stared at each other, or settled for small talk and gossip. At other times, the participants would be moved to play whist, to dance, and to sing, all the while displaying an amazing capacity to drink tea. For these gatherings Elizabeth of course took her turn as hostess.

One of Elizabeth's "evenings" had been so successful that she sent to Abigail, by then in glamorous London, words of praise for life in small-town America. The younger sister, who probably yearned to see the larger world, occasionally showed herself somewhat thin-skinned, especially when

Abigail rhapsodized lengthily about English society. It was true, Elizabeth acknowledged, that there were no lords and ladies to dignify a Haverhill gathering, but in these fellowships one could "feel that glow of generous love and friendship which those who always move in the higher walks of life are too often a stranger to." Elizabeth's defensive tone continued as long as she sensed Abigail's condescension and received her irritating lectures, so that she often reminded "my Sister" of the comparative genuineness of a simple life against the artificiality of high society.

When he arrived in Haverhill in 1785 to take up study with Uncle Shaw, John Quincy described Elizabeth's household, which, he said, "presents as perfect a scene of happiness as I ever saw, but it is entirely owing to the disposition of the persons." For his Aunt and Uncle Shaw, "a life of tranquility is to them a life of bliss." In this setting, the most exciting event for many years occurred on 4 November 1789, when President George Washington visited Haverhill during his tour of New England. It was proper that the parish minister should be one of the first to call upon the president, who was staying at Joseph Harrod's tavern, near the parsonage. There John Shaw paid the requisite call, taking along his nine-year-old daughter Betsy, who, of course, was also the niece of Vice President and Mrs. Adams. George Washington lifted Betsy to his knee, gave her his glove to mend, and when she returned it, "imprinted a kiss" upon her lips. Since many other young ladies craved the same honor, the gallant first magistrate gladly proceeded, according to contemporary accounts, to fulfill the wishes of Haverhill's maidens.

Not everyone enjoyed the usually placid existence in Haverhill. In 1785, the town was horrified when Elizabeth Duncan, wife of a leading citizen, drowned herself after battling depression for several months. This was a severe blow to the Shaws, who considered the Duncans close friends. When she was discovered to be missing, Elizabeth and others from the parsonage led an all-night search, peering down wells and up at barn rafters. Dawn revealed a corpse "floating a little way off one of the wharfs."

There was some consolation in knowing that the suicidal disposition had been inherited; Mrs. Duncan's brother had earlier taken his life. No such rationale was available when Elizabeth Shaw's good friend Captain Porter also died by his own hand. He was one of the persons with whom Elizabeth discussed literature. Several days after one such chat, Porter went to a barn where later he was found "suspended by a rope upon a beam." Much saddened, Elizabeth called Porter "the philanthropist, the good member of society, and the unfortunate lover." She recollected that although his life had been full of financial and romantic misfortune he refused to talk with her about his problems, seeing himself only as weak and inadequate. "He had long rowed against the tide," she murmured in benediction. "Let us throw the mantle of charity over his name, and pray that we enter not into temptation."

The one feature of Haverhill that made Elizabeth uncharacteristically impatient and even angry was the town's distance from Braintree, which isolated her from her sisters. In 1788, she begged Mary and Richard Cranch to make an early visit "before Sister Adams arrives [from England], for I shall not then get one of you to look this way for a twelve month, I fear." Mary conceded that often Elizabeth seemed as far away as if she resided on the moon. The parsonage in Haverhill had genuine cause to complain of being ignored, since the Shaws had frequently watched for the arrival of relatives from Braintree, only to be disappointed. Once, in honor of an anticipated visit from her sisters, Elizabeth had roasted lamb, an especially handsome thing to serve, for it had been a gift from the parish. But the Cranches and Adamses had allowed their own guests to detain them, and the Shaws waited in vain.

Finally, after another such snub, Elizabeth spoke her mind. In February 1789, Abigail had promised solemnly to appear in Haverhill, but the day came and went without her and she sent neither apology nor explanation. The old friction between the two echoed in Elizabeth's rebuke. "In the full assurance of seeing you here," Elizabeth began, "we had made all the preparations in our power. Perhaps you may say 'that would not be much.' However true the remark," she went on, she nevertheless hoped that Abigail "will never measure Love and Affection by the ability I have to express it." Out of much esteem and delighted anticipation, she had made the beds, set the table, bidden the guests—and no sister appeared. "So you may fancy to yourself what a curious figure we made to our neighbors," many of whom, Elizabeth indicated, had plans of their own to welcome the great Mrs. Adams.

Small wonder, said the younger sister, that people were murmuring that the Adamses cared little for their Shaw relatives. These were the same good folk of Haverhill, Elizabeth pointed out, who had been very kind to Abigail's sons when they lived with the Shaws while their mother was enjoying life in England. The letter became more scathing, and included a reminder to Abigail that in Weymouth their father, old Parson Smith, had been considerate of all kinsmen. "If you had one drop of his blood stirring in your veins, you would have pushed forward and not have failed coming." True, the visit had been set for February, but the weather had been beautiful and the roads open, Elizabeth caustically observed, knowing that only a few weeks before, Abigail had not hesitated to make a long winter trip to Long Island for a visit with her daughter and new grandchild.

Up until 1790, Elizabeth received little of Abigail's attention, leaving the younger sister resentful, although she generously tried to ascribe Abigail's manner to her sister's travels. "I fear she will always be moving from us," Elizabeth told Mary. "She is so connected in public life and must have so large a sphere to act in." Elizabeth feared Abigail must lose that "sweet enjoyment . . . which we used to experience in the private circle of dear friends [relatives]." Usually, however, Elizabeth forgave and forgot, and tried as often as she could to visit her sisters.

How little Elizabeth had changed since her youth was apparent in her gleeful report about returning to Haverhill by stagecoach from one such reunion. She had to board the stage at dawn with several men. To make the best of the trip, Elizabeth jested, she invited the gentleman with the most "literary and classical appearance" to sit beside her. Alas, no spirited discussion ensued, for all the men promptly went to sleep, including Elizabeth's companion. Soon, she said, "my swain's" head was on her shoulder, making so comical a scene that she shook with suppressed laughter and awakened the slumberer. Amused though Abigail was by this tale, the older sister felt compelled to comment on it. The story, Abigail chided Elizabeth, was "as fanciful, as romantic" as any told by a young girl, rather than by a parson's wife. Who was the sleepy gentleman? Abigail demanded to know. Elizabeth would not answer.

Like Abigail, Elizabeth had a strong and complex personality. She claimed her "presence of mind" never forsook her. Eventually, Abigail gained unbounded respect and admiration for her younger sister, as did many others. Long after the latter's death, a distant cousin, Josiah Quincy, who would become president of Harvard University, asserted that Mrs. Shaw "was not less distinguished than her sister [Abigail] for intellectual power and literary attainments." The only difference between them, said Quincy, was that marriage to a famous husband had put Abigail's talents before the public eye. Elizabeth's circle was much smaller, Quincy added, but "in it she gave proof of being alike gifted by nature and distinguished for attainments of mind and virtues of heart." Because she married late, Elizabeth had used her free time to cultivate her intellectual interests.

She knew what she was giving up when she joined her lot to that of a country parson, for Elizabeth often deplored how intellectually enervating a woman's domestic tasks could be, particularly after offspring arrived. The first Shaw child, a son named William, was born in August 1778, ten months after Elizabeth and John were married. Later there were two daughters. Still angry over what the next generation of Adamses would call "Aunt Elizabeth's Affair" with John Shaw, Abigail could not resist a sardonic comment about Elizabeth's baby. She wrote to cousin John Thaxter about this "new nephew." The infant was, said Abigail, "bettered I hope by the mother's side." Thaxter obviously knew what Abigail had in mind, for he replied, "I hope it is 'bettered by the mother's side' in all conscience, else I pity it. May it be an heir to its sweet Mother's perfections and an alien to its Father's." Thaxter's letter survived even though he wrote on the margin, "This is too imprudent. The flames will purify." We can only conjecture why this pair of letters was not burned when so many other highly delicate exchanges were destroyed.

By 1781, Elizabeth had two tiny children, which led her to tell Mary Cranch how she envied her for having offspring that were nearly grown. In Haverhill, the parsonage contained nothing but distraction. "For if ideas present themselves to my mind," Elizabeth lamented, "it is too much like the good seed sown among thorns. They are soon erased and swallowed up by the cares of the world, the noise and wants of my family and children." Her baby girl, another Betsy, slept little and cried much, caring not "whether her mamma works, thinks, or plays. I have no patience with the saucy girl." If there was a spare moment, Elizabeth had to use it in training an incompetent hired girl to spin. What a life, she said, for a woman who preferred books. "I hate it."

Even so, the children grew and the chores got done, leaving Elizabeth time to sustain her thoughtful side. Reading and talk with her husband were a special joy, and there was a friend, one Mrs. Spearhawk, with whom Elizabeth said she always found happiness. "Our souls were in unison," Elizabeth told Abigail. "She was a woman of reading and sentiment, and those seldom fail of pleasing. Such are the salt of the world. How soon must Society grow insipid and conversation wearisome unless it is enlivened by a taste for literature."

Late in life, Elizabeth's zeal for literature was unabated. When Richard Cranch died in 1811, she sought to buy his complete set of Alexander Pope: "I am almost sometimes mentally starved. I long to gratify my thirst, but I do not believe I could get more than one volume of his [Pope's] works within twenty miles." Another lifelong favorite was Samuel Richardson, one of the founders of the modern novel, whose *Clarissa* was Elizabeth's particular joy. All women, young and old, should read it, she contended. It was a fine vehicle for moral improvement.

"I long to make the young feel as *you* and *I* do," Elizabeth confessed to Abigail, namely, to "hate to leave a book." So loath sometimes was Elizabeth to put aside her latest volume that John Shaw was obliged to chide her, calling his wife "Pelican," for seeming to think less of her family and surroundings than of the pages in front of her. Elizabeth knew how to cherish her moments of quiet. "There is nothing more agreeable to me for a little while than what the world calls solitude," she said. It was bliss to sit and read, hearing nothing "but the hum of flies and the warbling of a wren."

These idylls were cheerfully interrupted when Elizabeth could help her husband's students. "I often ask my heart, is there any way in which I can render myself more useful to society than by rearing these human buds," even though, Elizabeth admitted, the young scholars were "not of my own vine." She described herself as a "general Mother," and her province included Abigail's sons during much of their youth. Seasons like Thanksgiving brought Elizabeth special pleasure. Once, when she had an unusually large group of family and students gathered around her table, all in high spirits, she found herself too stirred to eat.

The love for Elizabeth displayed by John Quincy Adams, his brothers Thomas and Charles, and countless other young people was kindled by her gentle and sympathetic manner. Elizabeth admitted her style was different from that of John Shaw's—"praise and approbation" were her tactics. They were "more congenial to my nature than reproof," Elizabeth said. Although it pained her to see youngsters assigned a writing task and then "waste paper and pens most wretchedly," she kept after them to do better, saying that each of them must "stretch our wings." Only thus, she reminded Abigail, could they see how high they could fly.

A chore Elizabeth performed all her life was writing to parents of students sent to her and her husband. She did not seem to resent doing this, though it often pulled her from "reading and the sweets of literary improvement." To all parents Elizabeth added the same exhortation after she had reported on their child's progress. She asserted that mothers had special assignments in their partnerships with fathers. One of these was to take particular interest in educating their children, a job which, though "arduous," was a "pleasant task." A mother must rear children "in the fear and love of God, teaching them sacredly to keep his commandments," said Elizabeth, warning women that their husbands would be less likely to do the Lord's work, given the tiring nature of a male's labor. To all matrons went Elizabeth's charge: "It devolves upon you to form their [children] minds in all that is 'lovely' and of 'good report.'" Elizabeth predicted no youngster could be truly happy without humility, patience, modesty, magnanimity, and perseverance.

Although the style and content of Elizabeth's letters brought wide praise, including the commendation of her sisters, she always remained severely critical of her own literary efforts: "I feel myself so deficient as often makes me feel ashamed." She pointed out that usually when time came for her to write, she took up her pen amid the hubbub of student boarders working around her. "If they would not apply to me, I should not care if they talked so much," she told Mary. "But I hate to be interrupted." The results of her striving, hidden today in family manuscripts, were far better than she would ever acknowledge. In 1811,

Abigail Adams willingly conceded "the palm of excellence to the pen of my sister."

More than once, in far-off Haverhill or Atkinson where she was usually surrounded by a mound of clothing to wash or mend for her boarders, Elizabeth would speculate about what she might have written had she enjoyed the leisure "of ladies of fortune." After her fiftieth birthday, she gave up her secret hope that, through "literary improvements," she might become "a more respectable figure in life." By then, Elizabeth confessed that her struggles with time had "dampened the ardor of youth, depressed my genius, and extinguished almost every latent spark." If talent was "to soar on fancy's wings," she said it needed hope and support. Where were these after a long day as partner to a parson and schoolmaster? "When I feel determined to write, coats, jackets, and stockings call so loud for my attention that my purposes are quite altered."

No matter what the distractions, Elizabeth still infused her letters with sentiment and spirit. She left no feeling disguised, particularly her own soul's deep division. Of the three sisters, Elizabeth excelled in standing aside from daily existence to ponder its ironies and contradictions. Part of her, she knew, yearned to make her marital partnership succeed, but she always believed her life was wasted in domesticity. Her letters are marvels of style and commentary from New England's frontier. Among Abigail and Mary's circle of female friends, Elizabeth's mind had the most strength, ranging easily across literature, mathematics, and history.

In addition to recording her academic interests, Elizabeth wrote confidently of social, spiritual, and political concerns, though she felt her pen often grew careless on such topics. These high standards could make Abigail impatient, and she begged Elizabeth to worry less about style and content when she wrote. Elizabeth should not feel ashamed, Abigail advised, if what she penned in haste was from the heart—like Abigail's own letters. Elizabeth should be "more careless."

No matter how little free time she had, Elizabeth kept up her interest in the world of letters and public affairs. Like Mary, she urged Abigail to send newspapers and journals from abroad or from New York and Philadelphia. In 1793, only a year after Mary Wollstonecraft published *A Vindication of the Rights of Women*, Elizabeth implored Abigail to locate a copy for her at "the first opportunity." This request was made in a letter in which Elizabeth described the ideal male character. Naturally, she contended that a man should possess zeal for religion, but "without too great a degree of enthusiasm." He should be "meek—and serious—without affectation—cheerful without levity, complacent and affable . . . gentle in his manners, excellent in his morals."

Elizabeth did not overlook other important attributes, however. Once, advising a niece about what to seek in a man, she acknowledged that "the phlegmatic lover and the cold, indifferent husband are especially the objects of my aversion." Still, one must be realistic, Elizabeth warned. The male who "adores and burns" would soon grow calmer, for "the life of rapture is not the life of a man." Females needed to be cautious amid the joys of courtship and young love, recognizing that eventually such bliss would be cooled by the daily demands of a household. Elizabeth discussed with Mary how, while daughters surely needed to be prepared to work hard "with their hands," they ought to be taught to find consolation in literature. In this fashion, strengthened in both mind and body, Elizabeth felt a young bride would more readily hasten into the sweetness of "conjugal affection."

It was talk like this which made Abigail set out early to advise Elizabeth against frequent pregnancies, once her duty to be fruitful seemed fulfilled. In 1782, with Elizabeth the mother of a healthy son and daughter, Abigail sent an admonitory message: "I hope you are not in the increasing way, as I think your health ill able to bear it." Not that Elizabeth need feel singled out, for Abigail added, "We have none of us nursing constitutions—twice my life was nearly sacrificed to it." Whether Abigail sensed that the always romantically inclined Elizabeth might be incautious is uncertain, but Abigail seemed to be warning her younger sister again in a letter written in 1787, two years before Elizabeth conceived her last child. "Tis hardly fit to begin a business at a time of life when one should be leaving off," Abigail commented pointedly. How Elizabeth reacted to this advice is unknown, but in 1789, her fortieth year, she became pregnant.

None of Elizabeth's surviving letters refers to her condition, and the exchanges on the topic between Mary and Abigail naturally were restrained, for in those days it was unseemly, even among sisters, to write openly about pregnancy. Abigail was clearly upset, however, stressing how "really surprised" she was by Sister Shaw's condition. Elizabeth was foolish "to begin after so many years, a second crop." The news from Haverhill left Abigail with what she acknowledged was one of her "Nervous Headaches." In Mary's reply to Abigail, the page where she began discussing Sister Shaw's belated pregnancy is torn out.

Elizabeth was not shy about her achievement. On 14 March 1790, she sent the news to Abigail—2 March had been the birthday of "a fine little daughter"—"She has little bones and weighed nine pounds." The infant was "plump as a partridge." With obvious satisfaction, Elizabeth stressed to Abigail what wonderful health had accompanied her pregnant state, as much a blessing as the infant's fine condition. Not only that, but the delivery had been early and easy. Her neighbor could not believe it when the parsonage summoned her to assist Elizabeth. Actually, said the new mother, her only distress at the time of delivery was a melancholy feeling, "the vapours" Elizabeth called it, at being so distant from her sisters.

The baby was to be christened Abigail Adams Shaw if her namesake would allow it. The choice was made "in respect and gratitude to a much loved Sister . . . endeared to me by a thousand kindnesses." Thus did Elizabeth cause Abigail's cup to overflow by pouring into it affection and forgiveness. Elizabeth stressed how she had yearned for a daughter, one who might some day emulate her Aunt Abigail's career of "adorning every station she may be called to act in." Little Abby was said even to resemble her famous relative; her tiny mouth was identical to Abigail's, Elizabeth claimed. It was a charming gesture, typical of the generous and clever Elizabeth. Abigail's reaction is not recorded. There is only an expression of her relief that "Sister Shaw got well to bed with a daughter added to her family."

Soon after this episode, another of the perils of midlife caught the sisters' attention. At age forty-eight, Abigail announced to Mary in 1792 that her slow recovery from a recent illness was hampered by the fact that she had begun menopause. Abigail noted that this "critical period of life augments my complaints." To treat the condition, Abigail summoned a physician to bleed her, her remedy for so many other ailments. In 1799, menopause came upon Elizabeth, then forty-nine. Puzzled by her symptoms, Elizabeth sought an explanation from Abigail. "I have contracted a very bad habit. I do not know but it will prove my ruin," Elizabeth confessed. "It is that of profusely sweating. I find it increasing upon me— for this fortnight past, it will stand in drops all over me, perhaps once an hour or two and sometimes oftener."

By return mail, Abigail hastened words of reassurance: "Your own complaint, my sister, arises from your period of life. You must take elixer vitrol, the bark, and whatever can invigorate your constitution." Bleeding must not have helped, for Abigail did not advise it as a remedy. Indeed she confessed she was still suffering from the very symptoms Elizabeth had reported. The younger sister may have had an easier passage through her change of life, since Mary (whose own menopausal experience is unrecorded) observed with some astonishment a year later that Elizabeth "was in good spirits and full of humor."

Elizabeth's capacity to continue joyful in outlook is particularly astonishing considering that the decade of the 1790s brought her much worry and grief. In this difficult era, her son became a cripple, the Reverend John Shaw died, and her oldest daughter suffered a lingering death. This succession of events interrupted Elizabeth's faithful exchange of letters with her sisters, causing frequent and lengthy gaps. Enough was written, however, to disclose how Elizabeth's strength and her unwavering religious faith sustained her.

William Shaw, the son who was born in 1778, inherited Elizabeth's love of literature but not her powerful character. From the beginning he seemed sentenced to a difficult life, despite his enormous intelligence—he could read written words before he could pronounce them. In pre-dawn darkness, Elizabeth would find the youngster looking at a book by candlelight. A dreamy lad, he often seemed oblivious to where he was or what he was doing. At age eight he ran carelessly into a clotheslines which caught his neck, injuring his windpipe and wrenching his spine. Nearly suffocated, Billy Shaw lay lifeless for twelve hours before he began a slow recovery.

Then, in 1792, the boy stepped into a posthole, damaging an ankle and leaving him permanently lame. He suffered as an invalid for a year, with Elizabeth dividing what time she could between him and his infant sister, little Abigail Adams Shaw. Her son's travail diminished Elizabeth's hopes that Billy Shaw would match the attainments promised by the sons of Abigail and Mary. Elizabeth was so distressed she could only say, "It is a disagreeable situation not to dare to trust ourselves with our own thoughts." I am "nearly crazed," she confessed to her sisters at one point.

At this time Elizabeth assumed a burden so heavy she could not describe it even to Mary and Abigail. One can only guess at her stress. It occurred in the months before September 1794 when John Shaw lost his battle with intemperance. When the disease began is unclear, but John evidently was still sober in 1786 when the keen-eyed children of Abigail and Mary were living with the Shaws. John Quincy Adams' diary at the time records nothing but praise for the life and labor of his Uncle Shaw. Even Abigail commended this man whom she earlier despised. "The success your worthy partner has met in preparing youths for their admission at the university," Abigail informed Elizabeth, "shows him to be peculiarly adapted to 'rear the tender thought and teach the young idea how to shout.'"

Elizabeth liked to recall how young people "loved and feared" her husband and how successful he was as a disciplinarian. She remembered, too, how she would lie on the bed in their room, reading aloud to John as he contentedly smoked his pipe. He was "the friend and partner of my life," Elizabeth told Mary. Yet at some point, Shaw's command over himself gave way, leaving Elizabeth to strive for him and herself. The only hint of trouble she gave in letters written before Shaw's death were reminders to Mary of how unstable the world was. She also seemed unusually emphatic when she advised Abigail that their Father in Heaven brought peace when all else was sorrow. A few days after Elizabeth wrote these devout lines, her husband, who had preached his usual two sermons on Sunday, 28 September 1794, was suddenly dead the next morning at age forty-five.

It happened without warning. On Sunday evening, Elizabeth and John entertained guests until 9:00 P.M. The parson complained of being tired and went to bed, moments later calling his wife to bring him his nightcap. My last "kind office" for him, Elizabeth remembered. She retired at 11:00 P.M., noticing that her mate was breathing with difficulty; he often did so, and she went to sleep without worry. Waking at 6:00 A.M., Elizabeth tried to rouse John. "Have you not slept enough?" she recalled asking. "Is it not time to get up?" Shaw was unconscious, beyond the reach even of the pleas of his tiny daughter Abby. "Poppa, Poppa, do wake him Momma." A physician arrived, but Shaw was pronounced dead at 9:30 A.M. The history of Haverhill records that because of the general affection and respect for this minister—"a bright example of meekness, patience, and charity"—the town meeting, scheduled for that time, was postponed, an unprecedented occurrence.

Throughout this great trial, Elizabeth's self-possession sustained her, and she shed no tears. She had only her children with her, and no solace reached her from Shaw's family. They did not contact her for many weeks, although later Elizabeth had a cordial association with them. The funeral took place on a rainy day, after which Elizabeth returned to the parsonage. She stayed close to her room for a month, mourning and reflecting. When she emerged, her spirits were restored, though she knew John had left her destitute. He had saved no money, and the parsonage belonged to the parish. She could live in it only until a new minister was called.

One source of income was available to Elizabeth, though a weaker character might have shrunk from exploiting it. Many citizens of Haverhill had habitually been remiss in paying their share of the minister's salary. Her husband had been unwilling to press them for their obligations, but Elizabeth did not hesitate; she politely demanded what was due her, expressing the hope that the next minister "will never submit to be treated as Mr. Shaw has been." Even though many of the parishioners who were in arrears were themselves impoverished, Elizabeth was unrelenting. "I pity them," she conceded to sister Mary, "but myself and children are the real sufferers. Many who never paid a copper of money must now pay back taxes, which might have been settled two or three years ago."

This income helped only in part, however, and Elizabeth was obliged to accept boarders into the roomy parsonage. Three gentlemen renters did much to keep the widow cheerful. Dinnertime was therefore often festive as the three guests talked with the attractive Mrs. Shaw and her children about the ladies in their lives. In the presence of this male enthusiasm, Elizabeth reported that she and her oldest daughter Betsy "sit perfectly mute. Sometimes it makes me swallow hard [to suppress laughter], and Betsy draw her head closer into her hankerchief." Writing a few short weeks after John Shaw's interment, Elizabeth conceded that perhaps she should be chided. "How can I indulge gaiety for one moment?" she asked, and then explained that "the natural bias" of her temper was cheerfulness. Surely that was not wrong.

It is difficult to avoid concluding that Elizabeth was, unconsciously perhaps, relieved by the sudden removal of her husband. She was emphatic in late 1794 when she said to Mary, "All is well." She loved Haverhill, she said, and the parishioners were kindness itself, piling up firewood by the parsonage as winter set in. She had lived there for seventeen years and had watched a generation grow up. In town she felt "beloved" by young and old. "Few women ever lived happier with a people than I have with this," Elizabeth said. To leave would be like Eve departing the Garden— with children but no Adam. It was to her youngsters that Elizabeth announced she would now devote her life.

This attitude greatly impressed Abigail Adams, who praised Elizabeth's "Christian deportment" and her "firmness and dignity." Still, worried over the Widow Shaw's impoverished state, Abigail arranged for her son, Billy Shaw, to be secretary to John Adams, the vice president. This would produce enough income to pay the young man's bills as he now entered Harvard. Abigail also had another idea for assisting Elizabeth. Soon after Shaw's death, Abigail made a trip to Haverhill in order to purchase Elizabeth's half of the old Smith family farm near Medford which their father had bequeathed them jointly.

Abigail was not prepared for Elizabeth's talent as a business negotiator. The younger sister was pleasant under pressure, but asserted that she was willing to sell only if she could be certain of investing the proceeds in something as productive as the Medford property. Abigail showed how eager she was to own the entire farm by continuing to prod Elizabeth into selling. But the more she did so, the more cautious Elizabeth became, asking for independent appraisals, and eventually deciding to keep her share of the land.

And so a year of mourning passed, Elizabeth kindly treated by her neighbors, all of whom, at least according to the town historian, considered her late husband's character to have been "unspotted." Elizabeth found widowhood a lonely lot late at night, and she had difficulty sleeping. "At times it feels as if my heart was too, too big for its little tenement." Usually she found repose by reciting lines from favorite poems, particularly Alexander Pope's apostrophe to a good woman, "O' blessed with temper, whose unclouded ray / Can make tomorrow as cheerful as today."

During these twelve months, neither Abigail nor Mary raised a question about John Shaw's health or spoke of any rumor about his behavior. Nonetheless Elizabeth apparently expected eventually to be asked about what actually had precipitated her husband's death. She volunteered nothing to her sisters, perhaps in the desperate hope that the unhappy story of Shaw's drinking would die with him. However, in September 1795, Mary and Abigail together sent word to Elizabeth reporting that unfortunate stories were reaching them about their deceased brother-in-law. Their letter does not remain among the family manuscripts, but Elizabeth's reply survives.

In a statement of 24 September 1795 addressed to both sisters, Elizabeth defended her late husband without quite defining the nature of his sin. Instead, she stressed that "My Friend" had many virtues, and these she hoped God would allow to balance his failings—even if his faults had led him "to disgrace a sacred office." All her tears and pleadings with him had not brought him to draw back "from the *worst of slavery* and make him stand fast." Thus, her partner's death had been a blessing, Elizabeth acknowledged, for it was better indeed that he should be "stretched a pale corpse before me" than that she should "endure the anguish, the torture that I daily experienced." Elizabeth challenged her sisters to imagine marital circumstances so wretched that a wife would prefer a mate's death. Yet this had been her plight, Elizabeth said, once it was clear that God would not "grant me the *unspeakable joy* of being the happy means of his reformation."

Elizabeth inquired how it was her sisters learned the secret since her friends and neighbors seemed not to know about it. Her children, perhaps? Quite possibly so, Elizabeth conceded, admitting they had been "too old not to perceive there was something very wrong." As for the servants, their eyes "have been blinded, and their lips sealed." She admitted that a "friend" had been visiting her, and that she had told him everything after he had noticed the "tremor of my nerves, and the anguish of my heart." But, this person was too generous and delicate to have divulged the story. Then, deciding she had said enough, Elizabeth thereafter never spoke again about the missteps of John Shaw.

She turned instead to another question raised by her sisters in their joint letter. Had Mary and Abigail heard correctly that Elizabeth would soon marry again? If so, the older sisters chided the younger for considering such a move, which they assumed she was contemplating only in order to ease her destitution. Elizabeth took the high road, replying that it was true she was engaged to be wed. She was not surprised, she said, at her sisters' astonishment: "After having so unexpectedly suffered in one tender connection, who can wonder if I feel extremely timid and reluctant in forming a new?" Elizabeth did not name the suitor, but implied it was the "friend" who had recently been such a comfort and whose discretion she could trust. Elizabeth emphasized that her financial embarrassments, serious though they were, constituted the least of her reasons for remarrying. She could have found another house and kept boarders, she insisted.

At this point in her reply, Elizabeth's naturally romantic temperament spoke, a spirit unextinguished by her recent suffering. The wedding would occur soon, she indicated, because of her regard for her suitor and because he yearned to marry her. "Our attachments I find very strong toward each other." Obviously pleased, Elizabeth reminded Mary and Abigail that "to be esteemed and loved is and has been the solace of my life, the soft soother of my woe, the chief ingredient that has sweetened my cup of life."

Nor did Mary and Abigail know how full their sister's cup was. The Widow Shaw had been wooed by three suitors, not astonishing considering that Elizabeth was very attractive at forty-five. One of the three was John Shaw's successor as minister for Haverhill, Abiel Abbot. Elizabeth dismissed him with a smile, saying that he was a fine person and that she had a good wife in mind for him. She reserved her interest for two men who had first been drawn to her many years before.

One was Isaac Smith, her cousin and first love, who had lately become preceptor at Dummer Academy in the village of Byfield, not far from Haverhill. Isaac had never married and never found a pulpit, most parishes remaining uneasy over his taking refuge as a Tory in England during the Revolution. For a time he had served as librarian for Harvard College. He was modestly wealthy, rotund, absentminded, and still devoted to Elizabeth in his temperate way. Unfortunately for Isaac, the other male whom the Widow Shaw found attractive was almost intemperate in pursuing Elizabeth. This was the familiar figure of Stephen Peabody, once Parson Smith's divinity student, who had left Weymouth long before to serve Atkinson, New Hampshire, as minister.

Stephen Peabody's differences from Isaac Smith were as apparent in 1795 as they had been twenty-five years earlier. Peabody was such a giant that his wife had to make his gloves; none could be bought that would fit him. Although he gained fame as an educator in New England, Stephen was not by nature bookish, preferring the hard work of a farmer. Agriculture was a necessity for him, since he was a poor man. A year before Elizabeth became a widow, Peabody's wife, Polly Haseltine, died after a protracted illness. Losing Polly left Stephen lonely and grieving, dampening his uproarious good humor, his singing, and his fiddle playing. Without a wife the Reverend Peabody could not be himself. He was fifty-four years old.

The contest between these two inveterate admirers of Elizabeth Smith

Shaw became a delightful episode in New England folklore. With Haverhill and Atkinson so closely situated, the Peabodys and the Shaws had been good friends. When Mrs. Peabody died, Stephen took comfort and advice from Mrs. Shaw. In fact, Elizabeth, then still married, had the awkward pleasure of hearing Peabody say he wanted to marry again soon, and that he wished for a wife just like her. His search was under way when John Shaw died. After preaching the sermon at Shaw's funeral, Stephen impatiently prepared to wait out the mourning period. Probably one reason Elizabeth stuck closely to her room for the first month was to keep the eager Parson Peabody from calling on what to others would have seemed an innocent pastoral visit.

Atkinson was only six miles from Haverhill, giving Stephen an advantage over Isaac Smith, who had fifteen miles to travel from Byfield. How strongly Elizabeth suspected Isaac's interests is unclear, but considering the distance between the towns and Smith's lethargic style, she may not have been fully aware of his hope to win her. Stephen Peabody, meanwhile, made no secret of his intentions. Had Elizabeth chosen strictly according to her preference she might have taken Isaac. At least that was the opinion of her friend and servant of many decades, Lydia Springer. It was she who described the final moments of the competition.

The year of mourning closed in the autumn of 1795, with the weather chilly and wet. Never a man of action, Isaac Smith took the climate as a sign to move slowly as he made his way one afternoon to propose marriage to Mrs. Shaw. It was after dark when he reached the parsonage in Haverhill, and he was soaking wet. Lydia greeted him with a gesture that told all. She pointed to a giant coat, already dry by the fire, for Peabody had arrived much earlier and was courting Elizabeth in the parlor. Isaac Smith took one look and departed without stating his case. Eventually he moved to Boston, where, still a bachelor, he lived with his books and his sister until he died at age eighty.

Although there is no clear evidence that Elizabeth was disappointed the winner turned out to be Stephen Peabody, her letters contain a hint that she may have wished Isaac Smith had possessed the courage to knock on the parlor door that rainy evening. Two years after she became Mrs. Peabody, Elizabeth wrote to Abigail in what she confessed was one of her melancholy moods. "It is the *mind* that gives the tincture to every surrounding object," she noted as she observed the birds that usually brought her such cheer with their songs today left her unstirred. How necessary it was, she said, for every person to learn how to find some solace in every disappointing circumstance.

Lest Abigail be mystified by such an uncharacteristic outburst, Elizabeth confessed that Isaac Smith was visiting Stephen Peabody on ministerial business that day. Watching the two men walk in the garden, Elizabeth suddenly paused in her writing to announce she wished to tell Abigail something about the past. Then, just as quickly, she drew up short, asserting that her thoughts were better kept to herself. She ought to be grateful, said Elizabeth, that it seemed the worst of life's trials were now over for her.

Many months earlier, Elizabeth had sent Abigail a lengthy description of what happened on the day of her wedding to Stephen Peabody. This was in reply to Sister Adams' scolding upon having been so little informed about Sister Shaw's marriage a month before, in December 1795. The bride replied that there had been several reasons for proceeding quietly. Mainly it was because she cherished the outlook of her favorite poet, Pope, who had wished to live and die " 'unseen, unknown.' " After the stormy close of her life with John Shaw, Elizabeth yearned for quiet. Even so, her sense of humor led her to share with Abigail just how far from quiet her wedding day had been.

"Everything took a contrary turn," said the bride when 8 December 1795 dawned. Haverhill awoke that morning to a northeast storm of rain and wind. It grew worse as the hours passed, leaving Elizabeth to contend that "had I lived in ancient days, I should have stood aghast and believed all the gods and goddesses had conspired against me." Why should they? she wondered. Perhaps, said Elizabeth somewhat enigmatically, "old Juno [the goddess of women and marriage]" was angry because "she thought I had not asserted my rights in previous times." The storm was not the only affliction. Haverhill was suffering from a widespread throat disorder that claimed many children. On the morning of the wedding, Betsy Smith, Elizabeth's niece and the child of the unfortunate brother William Smith, started to have fainting fits.

In addition, Elizabeth said she began to sense that she was being hurried into her second marriage. Stephen Peabody had not objected to Elizabeth's wish to be wed in the Haverhill parsonage, but he was emphatic about leaving immediately after the ceremony for Atkinson, where members of his congregation would have a feast of turkey awaiting the bridal couple and the entire community. It seemed a bit like pressure even to Elizabeth when a wagon arrived in the driving rain, along with men who were instructed by the impatient groom to load all the Widow Shaw's possessions for swift transfer to Atkinson.

The determination of her husband-to-be amazed Elizabeth, who had awakened on that wild and wet day assuming Stephen would use good judgment and postpone the ceremony. The groom, however, was not to be discouraged by an old-fashioned New England storm, although he arrived a bit late at the Haverhill parsonage, a delay which allowed

Elizabeth a few moments to hope she would remain a widow until nicer weather dawned. When Stephen Peabody presented himself at her door, dripping wet but full of joy, Elizabeth was so astonished that she blurted out that surely the Reverend Peabody did not intend to be married in such weather. Immediately, she told Abigail, she regretted her exclamation—"I confess it was rather too cavalier treatment"—and her heart went out at once to the giant on her stoop, "cold and wet as he was."

No matter what the elements, the ardent groom was not put off. Stephen looked at her with what Elizabeth called "much good humor," and said, " 'Is it *possible* you can be in earnest? What if it does storm, is it not often a prelude to a calm sunshine?' " There was nothing Elizabeth could say, so the ceremony began. "I would have given the world not to have been the chief actor in this gloomy, solemn scene," said the bride. Then, was it another omen? She wondered. As she and Stephen stood together for the ritual, shouts of fire were heard. The parsonage chimney was ablaze. "Good Lord (thought I), what next. This was not a vain exclamation, I assure you," Elizabeth confessed to Abigail. However, the fire was soon out, and the wedding proceeded to its close, Elizabeth acknowledging that her thoughts strayed to her children and her neighbors gathered in the parsonage she must now leave.

Then, putting all this behind her, Elizabeth said she had made the best of the situation and gratefully accepted the support and encouragement of her new husband, whom she called the "kindest of friends." At the parsonage door in Atkinson she was met by Stephen's daughter, who showed Elizabeth, "so much sweetness, benevolence, and affectionate respect, as has left an indelible impression on my heart, and has bound me to her forever." With this welcome came the obvious happiness of the Atkinson community over its good fortune to have this new "Ma'm" for their minister. Thus ended the wedding day that had begun in storm and misgiving. Elizabeth joined Stephen Peabody that night in her new parsonage home, where, she delicately informed Abigail, Elizabeth found that the groom was "supremely blest in the power of making—" at which point in the letter the bride carefully obliterated whatever word she had first written and added instead—"others happy."

4

. . . To Another

Once the storm and uncertainty passed, Elizabeth became happy as Stephen's wife and as the leading lady in Atkinson. Her husband had dominated the community for nearly a quarter century, and his parish had grown with him. When Stephen arrived in Atkinson for ordination late in 1772, the village had been incorporated but five years. As first minister, Stephen led his flock of nineteen members in worship at the parishioners' residences. And lead them he undoubtedly did, for the Reverend Peabody accepted the charge given him in the sermon preached by the Reverend John Searl at his ordination. The message had stressed that every minister was called to transmit what was in God's mind. Searl chose in his address to indict Arminianism and its trappings of rationalism and universal salvation. Stephen Peabody had agreed with this denunciation, and so did his new wife, for Elizabeth was no friend of the newfangled theology which was dividing New England's churches.

Whether in the pulpit, walking through town, being the center of music and fun at a party, or moving rocks in his fields, Stephen Peabody impressed people. With his black, bushy hair, dark eyes, imposing height, great strength, and booming voice, he was an unforgettable figure. Elizabeth saw that he went out into society wearing an old-fashioned, three-cornered beaver hat, a single-breasted coat with a lengthy vest, white knee trousers, and white stockings with what were even then old-fashioned, square-buckled shoes.

Since her new partner was always singing, Elizabeth could not have slept late if she wished. Stephen usually arose at 4:30 A.M. and promptly filled the large parsonage with melody. He was invariably busy, either lifting the stones that went into the rock fences surrounding his farm, grafting apple trees, making a very popular white-clover honey, or breeding cattle and horses. His practical nature made him the local expert on preparing wills, drawing deeds, and settling disputes. Not to be outdone by this vigorous new husband, Elizabeth soon was known in Atkinson as equally hardworking. Not long after her move, she stacked a large load of firewood by herself in Stephen's absence. Upon returning, her astonished husband said, simply, "I am sure you need not have done so," and proceeded to nurse Elizabeth through the cold she caught as a result of her exertions.

As her busy schedule permitted, Elizabeth continued to send letters to her sisters in Quincy, to whom she proudly announced that not only was the Reverend Peabody "an attentive Partner," but he was also "one of the warmest advocates of female education." Abigail was favorably impressed by these reports and spoke of her esteem for this new brother-in-law who seemed properly to value the "treasure" he had brought from Haverhill. When Billy Shaw, Elizabeth's son, had difficulty accepting his mother's decision to wed again, Abigail used her considerable influence with him. It was hard for any youngster, Abigail assured Elizabeth, who saw "another in the room of him whom he had lost." With his aunt's encouragement, young Shaw "spoke of Mr. Peabody with respect and regard," or so Abigail reported.

Young Shaw soon saw, however, that little had changed for his mother in the move from Haverhill. Youthful boarders in the Peabody parsonage recalled how the beautiful "Ma'm" would settle into a rocking chair during her few spare moments to read such staples of her library as William Paley's popular *View of the Evidences of Christianity*, published in 1794. If Elizabeth ever became impatient with life in Atkinson, it was because the forlorn village rarely attracted visitors "whose education might improve [her mind] and whose tastes and sentiments were more congenial."

Elizabeth needed that stimulation for she was busier as a teacher in Atkinson. The academy she and Stephen managed began its classes at 5:30 A.M. A pioneer for education in New Hampshire, Stephen nonetheless left most of the teaching in the Atkinson Academy to his preceptors and Elizabeth. The latter was elated by the chance to teach girls as well as boys. Peabody had opened the Atkinson Academy in 1787 and he had chosen to admit women in 1791. Only the Leister Academy had preceded him in this bold step. When Elizabeth arrived, the school already had a reputation for excellence. One of its earliest pupils was Grace Fletcher, who would marry Daniel Webster.

While such an environment of books and study pleased Elizabeth, it also brought drudgery. She found herself working much harder in Atkinson than in Haverhill, where John Shaw's pupils were few and taught informally at home. Now, with only the indefatigable Lydia Springer to aid her, Elizabeth cared for a household which often contained sixteen boarders.

Usually, there were eighty students in the Academy. Four teachers, whom Elizabeth generally admired, were in charge of instruction, and achieved such favorable results that many of Mary's and Abigail's grandchildren were dispatched to Atkinson for schooling. They were told to bring a dictionary and a Latin book. There was a nine-shilling entrance fee, tuition was nine shillings for each week, and the terms of boarding were nine shillings per week. Boarders were escorted by Elizabeth to the third floor of the parsonage, which she had converted into a dormitory.

Elizabeth's specialty as an instructor was composition. She told Abigail that, even with sixteen pupils around her, each writing three essays per week, she could not refuse their pleas for help. "They will come and beg 'What shall I do, Ma'm. I am a fool, I believe.'" It was Elizabeth's view that even the poorest scholar improved with kindness and attention. "But it would make some women crazed for sometimes they will all crowd upon me at a time." Once, she worked with twenty-one pupils, two of them girls, she reported with delight.

"For this purpose came I into the world," Elizabeth reminded herself when she was worn out. And when the female students succeeded, she needed no more reward. One especially talented young woman was sent by Elizabeth to accompany Stephen Peabody at Harvard's commencement exercises. It would do much for this bright girl "to see the Beau monde," Elizabeth explained to Abigail, for the young lady had "wit and quick discernment, but her mind must suffer from want [lack] of earlier cultivation."

The great annual event for Atkinson Academy occurred each autumn when Exhibition Week brought parents to hear their progeny declaim. The parsonage had to be readied so that parents and friends could be greeted and fed. The week brought much extra work, but it usually left Elizabeth contented. The events provided a happy change from the routine of presiding over the kitchen, the laundry, the table, and the sickroom. In the winter, she marveled at how much of her time went into preparing poultices for youthful ear infections. As with her other strengths, Elizabeth attributed her nursing talents to the training her mother offered in the Weymouth parsonage. There the theme had always been, as Elizabeth reminded herself, that "we were not born for ourselves."

Funds permitting, Elizabeth tried to hire help in the parsonage for Lydia and herself, usually with little success. "Pride reigns, and those who are rich give large wages, and *think* they want [need] a long list of servants. It was a real injury," Elizabeth continued in a letter to Abigail, "to the community for the supernumerary might be better employed in filling the earth than in riding on carriages." Yet, in spite of her load, Elizabeth rarely complained to her sisters, and then only to cite work as her reason for failing to correspond. She occasionally spoke of physical exhaustion, and just once murmured that when she had remarried she had not expected she would be caring for more boarders than ever before.

One cold January night in 1803, it seemed for a time that Elizabeth might lose her boarders. About 2:00 A.M., she and Stephen were awakened by shouts of "fire!" Their immediate thought was that students might have carelessly set the parsonage ablaze. Instead, the danger was to the academy building, which sat within sight of Elizabeth's window. From there she watched her husband and two students struggle to halt the blaze. They were hopelessly overmatched and before the village could turn out to help, the school burned to the ground. As she sat helplessly in the parsonage, Elizabeth could think only that life was precarious and that, as she told Mary, "man is born to trouble."

So ashamed was the community by its tardiness in leaving warm beds to fight a fire on a cold night that citizens spoke nobly about contributing funds at once for a fine new building, talk that led to naught. The Peabodys were obliged to raise the money themselves. Their main hope for assistance had been Nathaniel Peabody, a distant cousin and Atkinson's leading layman, but Nathaniel was taken to the debtor's prison in 1803, leaving Stephen and Elizabeth alone in their efforts to reestablish the school. Somehow, a new academy building was swiftly erected, a structure still in use two centuries later, an enduring tribute to the labors of Ma'm and Sir Peabody.

In order to raise the money needed to continue his school, Stephen borrowed $1,840 of the $2,500 required, and this was after he and Elizabeth had already contributed $100. The parson thought he would be compensated through a sale by lottery of 13,000 acres of land granted by the New Hampshire legislature. But then Stephen learned that chances for the drawing could be sold only in New Hampshire, a serious blow since he had expected his Massachusetts friends to participate. The lottery failed, leaving the Peabodys saddled with the heavy debt of rebuilding. Not until 1818, the year before he died, was Stephen repaid. Elizabeth's view of human nature darkened as she watched her husband grow old and disillusioned with the neighbors in Atkinson whom he had aided so often but who now left the Peabodys to struggle alone.

Helpfulness toward others characterized Elizabeth's life just as it did Mary Cranch's. While Mary cared for a community, Elizabeth supported countless young persons. Elizabeth took particular joy in infants, and she confessed more than once before the belated birth of her second daughter Abby that she regretted her arms had not held another tot. When Abigail became a grandmother in England, several years before Elizabeth's last child was born, Mrs. Shaw could not resist trying to reach across the

Atlantic to Abigail's grandson. "Kiss the sweet fellow once, twice, thrice for me," she instructed her sister, "and tell the little cherub his aunt sent all she could as a token of her ardent wishes that his life and health may be preserved."

As Aunt Shaw and then Aunt Peabody, in two parsonages, Elizabeth frequently wielded a more important parental influence in the lives of nephews and nieces than these youngsters found at home. By 1782, Abigail and Mary were sending children to Haverhill for study with Parson and Mrs. Shaw. Elizabeth received them—and the financial support they brought—gladly. But she established firm rules. She and her husband were the sole arbiters of the conduct of their students, Elizabeth warned her sisters, adding that their authority was not confined to scholarly matters. Guides for play, for forming friendships—the whole person would be subject to Elizabeth's direction.

Once assured of a free hand, Elizabeth was happy to accept material aid from Mary and Abigail. The charge for each child was $2 per week. She welcomed clothes, even cast-offs. So scarce was money at the Shaws that Elizabeth had been obliged to seek Abigail's discarded clothing. "Perhaps there may sometimes be things that with you are out of date, which if they are not in too high a style, may be of great service to me, and will not be valued the less by your sister."

In return, Abigail's sons received an overflowing measure of what Elizabeth quietly recognized they did not get from their stern mother, relaxed and sympathetic affection. Only once did Elizabeth betray her misgivings about Abigail's severity with her children. This was in 1788, when John Quincy returned to Haverhill after visiting his mother in Braintree. He reappeared in what Elizabeth considered a woeful state. "What did you do to him?" Elizabeth asked Abigail. The young man could not sleep and his "nervous system seems much affected." At this time, Abigail had been stressing to her son, who had just turned twenty-one, that he must put aside his dawdling and be in earnest about success. John Quincy was continually reminded by his mother that great things were expected of him.

To offset this, Elizabeth gave John Quincy, then a fledgling lawyer who lived not far from Haverhill, what she called "a little of my maternal love." He soon improved, Elizabeth pointedly reported to Abigail. Then, with remarkable bluntness, Elizabeth urged Abigail to be less "censorious" with John Quincy. Leave him to me, suggested Mrs. Shaw, for "there is more medicine in *my bed* than in all the Dr. Drugs." Reading over what she had written, Elizabeth decided her treatment needed clarifying, so she told Abigail that she was referring to the medication which came with "a little kind attention." As a result, John Quincy showed his Aunt Elizabeth a degree of warmth and affection he displayed to no one else. He confided in her about the frustrations in his love life, while he kept such matters from Abigail.

Undismayed, Elizabeth watched John Quincy rebel by showing an independence about his dress. After he was twenty-one, he adopted slovenliness as his personal style. Both Abigail and Mary were aghast at the news from Boston, where John Quincy was living in 1790 with the Thomas Welsh family, that a woman had to be hired for the sole task of making young Adams' linen respectable. "Not a pair of stockings or drawers fit to put on," Abigail was informed. Mary Cranch had been in Boston and seen for herself. The young man's underwear was so disgraceful "that it looked like Parson Wibird's." When Aunt Mary had a chance, she tried to soak her nephew's filthy shirts in buttermilk, a favorite cleanser.

At one point, however, Abigail's stern approach was appreciated by Elizabeth. This was when Billy Shaw entered Abigail's care at the time he became secretary to President Adams. It relieved her, Elizabeth acknowledged, that Abigail's "vigilent eye" was watching as her son passed through the dangerous years that began at eighteen. Elizabeth was not one to underestimate the "lures of the world" and the "destructive paths" down which they beckoned. Doubtless remembering Parson Shaw's sad end, Elizabeth took hope from Abigail's assurance that young Shaw was "free from habits of vice."

"A mother's heart, and thoughts, are ever on the wing," Elizabeth told Abigail, "spreading out in tender affections, ready to nourish the virtues of her children." When she could, Elizabeth reminded Billy of his father's better side, especially on matters of debt. "Your father used to say if he owed a man, it made him unhappy, and he could not make that progress in his studies that he wished."

There was a charming intimacy in the tone of Elizabeth's letters to her son, a cordiality never quite matched in Mary and Abigail's messages to their offspring. With Billy away amid the temptations of Harvard or Philadelphia, his mother would remind him of how, when he was younger, he would put his books away and come to sit beside her for talk. He should do that now, she suggested, by joining her in an exchange of letters. Writing to her son whenever she could, Elizabeth urged him to keep her messages and not to emulate his cousin John Quincy, who sometimes tossed Abigail's letters away.

When Elizabeth turned her son over to Abigail's care, the latter began supervision at once. Elizabeth had acknowledged that in a city's sinful surroundings Abigail would know "how to be of service to him," and when "to throw in your cautions and encouragements." Billy got much attention, so that Abigail soon confided to Mary that "we have rubbed off so many of his peculiarities that he has scarcely one left for us to laugh at." Still, Abigail conceded, young William Shaw "is a good creature."

Abigail spoke too soon. Billy Shaw became an eccentric Boston attorney and bibliophile, eventually dying at the same age his father had, and from the same disorder—intemperance. Elizabeth did not live to see this lamentable end, but she survived long enough to notice how her son visited her less and less. Shortly before she died, Elizabeth remarked to Abigail that "few children I believe are half attentive enough to the feelings and wishes of their parents." Yet even for this shortcoming Elizabeth had a gentle answer. Parents, she said, should overlook this filial failing out of the devoted love which ought to be a mother and father's nature.

By the time Elizabeth had entrusted her son to Abigail, a remarkable sisterhood had developed between Mary, Abigail, and Elizabeth, partly because Elizabeth now felt accepted by the older women, and no longer received the lecturing that once had so annoyed her. The sisters came increasingly to share their thoughts and experiences with verve and candor, making their letters a valuable example of the female perspective of their time and place. The foundation of that outlook was the sisters' acceptance of God's omnipresence and wisdom. They admitted how divine purposes were at times difficult to comprehend, particularly as they eyed the evil afoot in the world. How, they wondered, could young men and women skirt all the temptations of life in a new epoch? A concerned Elizabeth observed, "I do not wonder that Milton says when Sin was introduced into the world, that *all nature* gave a groan."

Over and over, the trio encouraged—or cautioned—each other with such favorite biblical texts as Isaiah 26:4: "Trust ye in the Lord forever, for in the Lord Jehovah is everlasting strength." As Abigail put it to Mary, "If it was not for that trust and confidence our hearts would often fail us." And Elizabeth stressed that she and her sisters were "fellow workers" in "the service of our ascended Lord!" May they be steadfast in stewardship— "and so improve those talents he has given, as to receive at the closing scenes his gracious plaudit."

As all the sisters endured sorrow and travail, their religious faith appears never to have faltered. If in times of lamentation they were tempted to repine, such thoughts were quickly stifled in praise of God's mercy and in pledges for renewed service through faith as they looked with hope toward the vindication of Judgment Day. Meanwhile they gave thanks for the earthly strength they supplied each other. Elizabeth Shaw summed up this fruitful association best: "For when three sisters love each other with such sincere affection, the one does not experience sorrow, pain, or affliction of any kind, but the others' heart wishes to relieve, and vibrates in tenderness. Like a well-organized musical instrument."

To this, Elizabeth added, "One string cannot be touched without the whole being sensibly affected." A sister's care and pity, the threesome agreed, were the most precious consolation, "so pleasing, so tender." The only comparable comfort, according to Elizabeth, was "what we experienced from our Mother's fond assiduity and affectionate tenderness." To the satisfaction of Weymouth's three daughters, they had become what Elizabeth liked to call a "Happy Triumvirate."

There were some events and topics too delicate, however, even for the remarkably candid letters exchanged between the sisters. After completing a long missive to sister Mary, Abigail remarked tantalizingly, "When we get together, we may say to each other what would not be proper to write." In their letters, the trio's favorite topic seemed to be relationships between women and men. Since Mary, Abigail, and Elizabeth never hesitated to praise the institution of marriage, they deplored that some males remained bachelors. Could not every man, they wondered, grasp why the Creator, when he "formed Adam, pronounced it not good for him to be alone"? To the sisters, bachelors were "poor, forlorn beings" left alone to "contract singular habits." Nothing, observed Abigail, made a male so "fractious" as "living without females about him." It was women, she said, who "knew how to temper the wind to the shorn lamb, and to soothe into good humor the jarring elements."

When Elizabeth feared her son William Shaw was "becoming a confirmed Old Batchelor in the most extensive sense of the word," she mournfully observed, "O, how solitary his joys—how lessened his happiness." Abigail liked to speak of the miseries suffered by men who lacked female partners to "hover" about them, to "bind up" their sorrows, and to "pour out" their coffee. Concurring with Benjamin Franklin, the Smith sisters believed that a man without a woman was only half useful. A "single lady" was different, however. She could be very helpful.

Abigail put concisely the point she and her sisters agreed on: "I know that men were made for us and we for men." On this foundation was built their belief that marriage was a partnership. This concept of matrimony was a topic Abigail was particularly prone to stress in letters. "I have ever been a warm advocate of matrimony," she wrote. The "principal felicity" of life came from "the affections between the sexes." She passed this view on to her cousin John Thaxter when he was still a bachelor, taking care to stress that these affections must arise from "purity of sentiment and politeness of behavior." Elizabeth remained more ecstatically inclined as she chose her words about marriage. Her charm can be sensed in her comment, made after thirty years of marriage, that the conjugal state required "twin-born" souls, men and women who welcomed being "yoke fellows," willing to share and "bless the dear bondage."

Here Elizabeth approached a subject on which the sisters often exchanged views: how to make marriage endure. When Elizabeth's daughter
Abby was preparing for matrimony, Abigail cheerlessly admonished Elizabeth that the younger woman must " . . . look out well. The die once
cast, there is no retreat, until death." This was spoken from a somewhat
calculating approach to wedlock which Abigail increasingly came to see as
a social more than sexual partnership. It should be a union between two
persons whose talents, endeavors, and bodies complemented one another.
"No man ever prospered in the world without the consent and cooperation
of his wife," said Abigail. "The all-wise creator made woman a help mate
for man, and she who fails in these duties does not answer to the end of
her creation." Marriage thus must be founded upon ground far more
solid than sexual attraction, which Abigail insisted withered so soon.

The sisters' most interesting difference of opinion was over cases of
second marriages or of unions involving older persons. Of the three, of
course, Elizabeth was the one who insisted that romance was no respecter
of age, and she rejoiced when older women found mates. In 1780, Elizabeth
regaled Mary with the stories of two Haverhill widowers recently remarried,
"from hence we may conclude," said Elizabeth, "no widower will ever die
with grief." Mrs. Shaw could even be poetic at times as she praised the
sexual bond between male and female as the only source of "genuine
happiness." After thirty years of marriage, Elizabeth wished that everyone
could "taste the fruit of Eden." She sturdily defended marriages between
old persons, and she always challenged her sisters when they appeared to
accept the conventional view that love welcomed only the youthful.

When news arrived that a very mature cousin of the sisters had found
a husband, it was Elizabeth who led the rejoicing. A male had casually
courted the cousin for four years. Suddenly, the suitor discovered how
much he wished to marry, and thereafter, Elizabeth observed delightedly,
he moved with the speed of a lion. Such was his haste to build a house
for his betrothed that he compelled the carpenters to work daily until
nine. He even insisted on the earliest convenient date for their wedding,
although it was Friday, considered an unlucky day by everyone.

The groom set out for nuptials in January 1786, using a sleigh because
the road was covered with snow. Soon, however, he ran out of snow. The
poor fellow arrived late and in a ludicrous state. Nonetheless, said
Elizabeth, who was a witness, the wedding was grand and the "plumb"
cake the largest ever. As for their cousin, the bride, Elizabeth described
her being "full of joy and gratitude" as she departed with her impatient
groom. She was headed, an elated Elizabeth predicted, to "the Temple of
his arms."

Abigail could not agree with Elizabeth's views about the enduring quality of passion. Years should subdue ardor, the older sister frequently observed to John, adding that "in lieu thereof a friendship and affection deep-rooted subsists which defies the ravages of time." Twenty years after her wedding, Abigail reported that for her, "the age of romance has long ago passed, leaving mature affection." This was welcome, according to Abigail's outlook, for she saw woman as more prone than man to animal desire. "Desire" was inflicted upon women "as a punishment for the transgressions of Eve." Consequently, Abigail professed to understand what the philosopher meant "who thanked the Gods he was created a Man rather than a Woman." In short, women were designed for "more exquisite sensations" than were men. It was this compulsion which Abigail believed drove many older woman ardently—and unwisely—into marriage past the season.

From this point it was often easy for the sisters to take up their concern for women of whatever age who surrendered to natural weaknesses, despite their heavy responsibilities. In letter after letter the trio cited the disaster sure to ensue when a woman allowed "violence of passion to blind her." It was agreed that women more than men faced a struggle in sustaining "judgment" and "reason." Abigail was particularly vigilant about this subject, as when she condemned plans the widowed Mrs. John Hancock made in 1794 to marry James Scott, a sailor. How often woman's name was frailty, fumed Abigail. "We cannot call it love, for at her age [forty-seven] the hey day in the blood is tame." Now was the time for a woman to show how good sense could master the impulses. "And what judgment would stoop so low?" Abigail raged.

In 1818, the year she died, Abigail was still scolding. This time her target was behavior by the Widow Barlow, whose late husband Joel was the famous American poet. Mrs. Barlow had just died at age sixty-two, from a broken heart, it was said, since she yearned to marry a much younger man. Her family had forbidden the match. To die "at *that age*" in a struggle "to subdue her own inclinations and ardent passions" was beyond understanding, said Abigail. "I can conceive of such things in the green tree, but not in the dry." And then when it was learned that Mrs. Barlow had left her young swain a handsome bequest, Abigail was appalled.

Less subtle cases were more frequently the cause of sisterly alarm. These were always instances of what Mary Cranch called "a shameless woman." Such a female, according to Mary, was "a horrid sight." Just down the road from the Cranch home in Braintree dwelt one of many examples in Mary's opinion—a woman who worked for Captain Brackett. "She drinks, you know, to excess—when she can get enough to make a fool of herself." Life was full of risks for a female, Mary announced, and the "critical period" was "from sixteen to twenty-one." For the woman this was "the most dangerous of their whole lives—especially if they are very gay."

Mary's views hardly needed the reinforcement they received from alarming bulletins sent to her by Abigail from England and France between 1784 and 1788. These reports displayed Abigail's nearly perpetual state of shock over the contamination of European morals. Nor did virtue seem much stronger in the United States when Abigail became first lady. To her sisters she mailed indignant descriptions of female fashion, recounting particularly the style which revealed all of a lady's charms. "You might literally see through her," a disgusted Abigail reported, and then turned her wrath upon those whose faces were painted with rouge.

The first lady was convinced that American women had capitulated to ideas drawn from a French harlot's brain. Why could not the female be content "with the show which nature bestows?" Instead, stylish women in the nation's capital were trying to outdo each other in seeking to "look like nursing mothers." These typical calls to alarm sent by Abigail to her sisters confirmed what the trio suspected, that modesty and restraint in females were highly essential. These attributes could both awe and enchant a male, while the impudent stare and the immodest form led to disaster. No matter how worldly-wise a woman was, said Abigail, in the presence of men she should profess ignorance.

Thus arose the doctrine Abigail repeated often to Elizabeth and Mary: "Chastity, modesty, decency, and conjugal faith are the pillars of society." Without these, "the whole fabrick falls sooner or later." It had fallen in Europe, she conceded, where 60,000 known prostitutes were found in one city alone. And yet many of these women were among the most beautiful Abigail had ever seen. Even the strongest marriage might not survive against these temptations to husbands, Abigail predicted.

Elizabeth could be nearly as stern toward the faltering female as her sisters. She advised young men in her care of the unfortunate necessity to be on guard when talking with females, among whom always lurked the potential "libertine." Be delicate and dignified, Elizabeth's charges were told, when they were with young women. Particularly they should beware of using the double entendre, that subtle corruptor, Elizabeth called it, as well as the "unguarded look or gesture" which might "excite familiarities." Like Abigail and Mary, Elizabeth recognized how unfortunate it could be when a man found himself with a woman whose desire had been unleashed.

Elizabeth did not linger over these cases as Mary and Abigail seemed to, however, for the youngest sister always preferred to write about the happiness conjugal affection could bring. But she too could be a realist. When Abigail's daughter Nabby was preparing for a London wedding in 1786, Elizabeth sent her niece a formula for "female character." Above all, Nabby must keep "a proper reverence for yourself," along with dignity and a sweetness of temper. Never seek ascendancy over one's husband,

Elizabeth advised, even if she had "superior qualities." Domestic contention was scrupulously to be avoided, allowing the aunt to cite as excellent examples the marriages of Mary Cranch and Abigail Adams. These were instances of an ideal unity between man and woman, Elizabeth claimed.

Was it possible, the sisters wondered, that at heart men feared women? If so, the implications for history and society were enormous. Since men dominated the political arena, the sisters agreed that males might seek to give themselves even more control over females, should their fear increase. Abigail was especially mindful of this threat, given her knowledge of how the political world turned. The precariousness of the balance between the sexes seemed exemplified, to Abigail, in the case of a Miss Mahew, a Massachusetts belle who was wealthy but also aggressive, with a strong mind and a bent for sharp satire and ridicule. This talent of Miss Mahew's "terrified" men, said Abigail, adding that "it argues cowardice with gentlemen that she still remains single." Abigail was confident Miss Mahew knew that no prudent woman made her husband an object of ridicule. Yet, despite the wittiness and good nature in Miss Mahew's satire, according to Abigail her example proved once again that "it is a most dangerous thing for a Female to be distinguished for any qualification beyond the rest of her sex." Men grew jealous quickly.

But how could males be made more comfortable with talented females? On this point the sisters admired the insight which Abigail displayed when she said that one way to make the Miss Mahews of any community acceptable was to "increase the number of accomplished women." When it seemed education would continue to be kept out of women's reach, Abigail sensed a deepening insecurity within men. She shrewdly concluded that treading on women might be an unconscious act by men. Still, Abigail could not resist asking her thoughtful cousin John Thaxter a question she felt the new American nation must answer: "Why should your sex wish for such a disparity in those whom they one day intend for companions and associates?" She could not, Abigail admitted, "help sometimes suspecting that this neglect arises in some measure from an ungenerous jealousy of rivals near the throne."

Perhaps the most famous comment by an American woman on the relation between male and female was in Abigail's letter to her husband John in the springtime of 1776. Recently this epistle has been cited in many campaigns for women's rights. The users have forgotten that Abigail's plea to "Remember the Ladies," was uttered when new laws were being created for an independent America and that Abigail's concern was to protect women from men. All males, Abigail reminded her husband, "would be tyrants if they could." To offset this, Abigail urged men to discard the "harsh title of Master for the more tender and endearing one of Friend." Males were designed by nature to protect females, and their strength should be used "only for happiness." Abigail's acclaimed call, therefore, was to protect her sex from the more vicious males who would "use us with cruelty and indignity and impunity." Any man "of Sense," said Abigail, should join women in loathing those customs which made "vassells" out of females.

There was a far different kind of subordination for women which also deeply alarmed Mary, Abigail, and Elizabeth. It was "the sad slavery" imposed on women who bore numerous children. Consequently, when a sister, a daughter, or a friend who had already produced her share of infants experienced miscarriage—typically called "a mishap"—the sisters usually considered the event more "good than ill luck." Nothing in the surviving letters indicates what means, beyond self-control, these sisters considered useful for avoiding pregnancy. Few messages between Mary and Elizabeth and their husbands exist, which tempts one to exaggerate the meaning in Abigail's frequent lectures to the amorous-minded John Adams. To him, as to her sisters, Abigail stressed that married couples should anticipate and welcome a mellowing in their sexual partnership, one in which passion was replaced by the more enduring merits of friendly companionship.

To Abigail's way of thinking, advancing years for a woman should bring important changes in her relationship with her husband. This was particularly so, Abigail contended, for females like the Smith sisters, whose bodily frailty had always made them especially endangered by childbirth. Thus, urged Abigail, let all women take the view that with age "the gratification of sense languishes." Then, too, a great number of children kept a woman, no matter how strong her health, so burdened that she could not properly carry a full share of duty with her mate. Nor could such a woman be the strong figure required by a community.

As these views filled the sisters' letters to each other, they formed the foundation on which the three women built hopes and expectations for their own daughters. By the mid-1780s, the trio had contributed handsomely to the next generation. Abigail had one daughter, while Mary and Elizabeth each gave birth to two. Unfortunately, the lives of these five younger persons illustrated to a dismaying degree how easily the female could stumble into the pitfalls which Abigail, Mary, and Elizabeth feared endangered every woman.

5

Weymouth Again

Of the sisters, Mary Cranch bore the first child, a daughter born 25 January 1763 and given her grandmother Smith's name, Elizabeth, though her relatives called her Betsy. The natural interest in Betsy as the oldest member of the second generation was deepened when her fate led the family to Weymouth again. There, in the familiar parsonage, Betsy's story would turn tragic. Before that occurred, however, Mary, Abigail, and Elizabeth had time to give their attention to two other young women also named Betsy. One was Elizabeth Shaw's daughter, of whom we shall speak later. The other was the child of William Smith, who himself was the only son of Parson and Elizabeth Smith, and who grew up in Weymouth with his sisters.

William Smith's story was pushed into the shadow by saddened relatives who wished to erase his memory. Little is known of him, except that he was born in 1746 and died on either the third or the tenth of September 1787, a victim of alcoholism. As his sisters later reviewed his career, they realized that Parson Smith did little to discipline the lad, and Elizabeth Smith had been unable to intervene.

William had been married on 2 January 1771 to Catherine Louisa Salmon, called Kitty. They began life together on a 140-acre farm near Lincoln, not far from Concord. It was property that Kitty brought to the marriage, but which soon was mortgaged to Parson Smith as William became handicapped by his unfortunate habits. There was at least one creditable feat for which William could be praised. It was he who rang the bell in the Lincoln church to warn his neighbors that British troops were approaching. The date was the fateful nineteenth of April 1775.

Thereafter, William's whereabouts were increasingly uncertain, although stories frequently reached Weymouth and Braintree about his disgraceful behavior around Philadelphia. When the Reverend Smith died in 1783, his last thoughts were fixed upon the son, "whose life has been one continuous error," and his final words became a prayer for the "reformation and salvation of the prodigal." The Lincoln farm was left in trust for young William's family. Parson Smith knew his male offspring would quickly squander an outright legacy. Four years later young William died far from home of what his relatives learned was "the black jaundice."

Nearly a century later one of Parson Smith's descendants, Charles Francis Adams, stumbled across his forebear's letters to the errant William. Before he destroyed them Charles read enough of the epistles to be reminded of "how much that is sad is in every private record." Young Smith had let his vices master him, but, said Charles, "the old minister of Weymouth had compensation in his daughters, which is more than falls the lot of some." The parson's daughters never forgot the story of their brother, especially as they watched his shadow fall across their own offspring. Of the five sons born to Mary, Abigail, and Elizabeth, three died of the same malady that destroyed William Smith.

Even before his death, William's sisters were supporting his wife Kitty, and urging him to stay away from her. Only two of Kitty and William's children survived to maturity, daughters who had to be raised by Abigail Adams and Elizabeth Shaw. Consumption, the family scourge, carried off the rest, two sons and two other girls. The ordeal was instructive for William's three sisters, who sympathized with Kitty, even when the forlorn creature built "enchanted castles" to hold dreams of better days. Most of the time, Kitty was stuck in Lincoln where there was no school, leaving her to try teaching her children.

Times for Kitty were especially bad in the winter of 1785, which brought the harshest weather in memory. The roads around Lincoln remained largely impassable. When spring allowed mail service to resume, Kitty sent word to Mary Cranch of how, after six months of isolation, she felt it was no exaggeration to claim she had suffered more degradation than most women. To Abigail, Kitty complained that women were falling into danger by allowing themselves "to be considered as a species apart from the Lords of Creation." What was worse, said Kitty, while many women might resent their fate, most "have not enough resolution to bust those magick fetters which that tyrant Custom has shackled them with."

Abused as she was, Kitty sought redemption for her husband. "Poor, unhappy man," Kitty conceded, praying that he be restored "to virtue and to his family." If that miracle came to pass, she believed, she might yet have time to lift him through the power of woman as a moral force. Kitty's yearning had classic overtones: "With what a heartfelt satisfaction would

I take the unhappy wanderer by the hand and lead him back to the path of rectitude and to a reconciliation with his God."

There was no penance, however, and soon a widowed Kitty was left to watch four of her children die. She spent the rest of her life under Abigail's protection in Braintree, living on a modest income from Parson Smith's legacy, using her talent for knitting stockings, and relying on aid from her sisters-in-law. Pondering their brother's tragedy, they agreed that "some very capital mistakes were undesignedly made." For Mary, Abigail, and Elizabeth the lesson from their brother's story was painfully straightforward. He was "proof how much the best and worthyest [parent] may err."

William's daughter Betsy was reared by Elizabeth Shaw as a child of her own. Betsy Smith was born in 1771, and grew into a particularly lively young lady. She seemed something of a flirt, which set Abigail and Mary to worrying. Would Elizabeth be able to manage the waif? Surely Elizabeth would remember, as Abigail put it, "that she herself was once young, and possessed a heart as liable to impressions, and as susceptible of the tender passions as any body I can recollect. Betsy has a hereditary spice of the romantic in her constitution."

Abigail need not have fretted. In 1796, Elizabeth sent Betsy to Quincy for the special polishing which Abigail could provide, and also to help during another round of sickness in the Cranch household. Elizabeth had an added motive, as well. Quincy was near Boston, where Betsy might have a chance for a better matrimonial match than was possible in remote Atkinson. Betsy lost no time. She soon had the earnest attention of a prospering upholsterer from Boston, James H. Foster, who braved rain, wind, and snow to ride to Quincy for visits.

The romance had its setting in the Cranch residence, where Mary watched the pair with a mixture of alarm and amusement. Betsy denied there was any prospect of matrimony in all this, saying that Foster's frequent stops were entirely accidental. Mary was not convinced. "She does fib," Mary wrote Abigail in October 1797. "I know she does. They were several hours alone together in our east parlour."

Then Foster vanished for five weeks, so that the Cranches began to believe Betsy's protests—until the swain reappeared in mid-December and the two, as Mary hastened to tell her sisters, "were up long after the family was in bed." Mary stressed that such behavior was not Betsy's custom with anyone else. If Mr. Foster "was not offered honey," Mary speculated, certainly Betsy "has given him opportunity enough to do it, and I would say he had not." Whatever Mary's surmise might mean literally, Betsy refused to budge from her casual stance. There was no romance, she insisted, although Abigail suspected otherwise when her niece wrote in the spring of 1798 to ask about the latest fashions in Philadelphia. The answer, by the way, was that "fashions are as various as the changes of the moon."

In June 1798, Betsy announced she would marry James Foster, but to the dismay of her aunts, she offered no details. Mary was alarmed—the girl had done not "the least thing to prepare for housekeeping." Was it now "the custom to begin [marriage] with wedding clothes [?] She must make haste or they will be out of fashion." Unmoved, Betsy went up to Atkinson to visit Aunt Elizabeth. This was only proper, Mary acknowledged, since Elizabeth had reared the prospective bride. It was Elizabeth who coaxed Betsy to make her plans known, and to set an early date for the wedding, which took place on 15 November 1798 at the Adams residence in Quincy.

While Abigail was feeling frail and depressed, she gave the occasion her full attention, hoping it might "amuse my mind." Only a small group gathered for the ceremony. Mary and Richard Cranch were too ill to appear, but Elizabeth came down from Atkinson, leaving little Abby with Parson Peabody. The Foster family was there, although Abigail had only met the groom a few days before. Also present was Kitty Salmon Smith, the bride's mother. Elizabeth reported to her son Billy that the wedding "was directed by your Aunt's usual beneficence, the blessed effects of which you have so often experienced." To Elizabeth's relief, Betsy behaved with the dignity of "a woman," putting aside the "too exquisite sensibility" which had formerly alarmed her aunts.

Elizabeth returned to Atkinson cheered by thoughts of Betsy Smith's prospect of happiness with her husband. Surely now the niece had found the "tranquility to which her heart and her too anxious mind had been long a stranger." Abigail sent reassuring messages saying that the Fosters were well and happy. "I call her a very fortunate girl," Abigail observed, adding how comforting it was "that in these days of frivolity and licentiousness, she should be united with a man of sobriety, virtue, and religion, with habits of industry and economy." Betsy Smith Foster was indeed more fortunate than most of the younger women in Abigail's circle. She lived a long and healthy life, produced many children, and did much to sustain her husband who was not physically strong and who often had to leave the children and the upholstering to Betsy while he fled to spas for rejuvenation.

It had taken fortitude for Elizabeth Peabody to attend Betsy Smith's marriage ceremony in the Adams house. Only six months before, Elizabeth had watched her own daughter she called Betsy die at age eighteen of that wasting pulmonary disorder, tuberculosis. In Elizabeth's day, the malady was called consumption, and to many parents its name sounded the death knell for a child. However, Elizabeth was determined not to capitulate without a struggle. She fought so ardently to save her daughter that Mary and Abigail feared she herself would succumb.

To avoid confusion with other family members having the same name, Elizabeth had called her daughter by her first and middle names, Betsy Quincy, or, more often, simply Betsy Q. The child, said Elizabeth, had her father's amiableness, his philanthropy, his cheerfulness, and his unreserved manner. After John Shaw's unfortunate end, Elizabeth would add that Betsy's qualities required a special degree of regulation. To attain that, Elizabeth had sent Betsy Q., before she fell ill, to Abigail, so that the young lady might master the finer points of a useful and disciplined woman. However, Elizabeth was actually trying to spare the girl the sight of her father's alcoholism.

In this way, Betsy Q. spent enough time in the Adams home that Abigail felt like her second mother and thus was more than ordinarily alarmed over news that Betsy had entered what seemed to be a consumptive state. The first lady immediately prescribed medication for Betsy Q.'s condition, distressed that she could not rush to Atkinson and supervise the sickroom. Both Abigail and Mary agreed that Betsy Q.'s sickness was such an emergency that they should intervene. Was it not the kind of crisis when sisters needed each other? they asked. True, Elizabeth "had everything in Mr. Peabody that a kind, good husband can be," but, Mary continued, "she wants [lacks] the assistance of a sister." The pair feared especially that Elizabeth might not survive the shock of Betsy's death so soon after her sorrows over John Shaw.

As it turned out, Elizabeth possibly received more aid than she wanted. Abigail asked for a detailed description of Betsy's condition—the grim facts were too familiar, a pain in the right side, the desperate need to take deep breaths, and the "stricture upon the breast." After consulting her friend Benjamin Rush, America's most renowned physician, Abigail mailed instructions to Atkinson. The first lady's reliance upon Dr. Rush stemmed in part from her agreement with him on the value of bleeding as an almost universal remedy. Emetics, bleeding, and the bark were, in Abigail's catechism of health, the holy trinity of treatment. The bark, a form of quinine made from various species of the cinchona tree, was considered especially valuable. When Abigail tried to cure Betsy Q., however, she emphasized blood-letting. Betsy must be bled frequently, and blisters placed on her side, Abigail stressed to Elizabeth.

To Abigail's dismay, Elizabeth chose not to have her daughter bled. The first lady's faith in this practice was unbounded, but only if the blood were taken early and regularly. The results were sometimes amazing; Abigail cited the triumphant effect after she discovered one of her servants had a sore throat. At Abigail's orders, the stricken fellow was bled five times, drawing sixty ounces of blood altogether. Reporting this to Mary, Abigail announced with satisfaction that the victim was soon well, "tho pale." Why, then, must Elizabeth have "the aversion to the lancet," Abigail fumed. By July 1798, Abigail was certain that Elizabeth's tactics had doomed Betsy Q. "Poor girl," said her aunt, Betsy had been "sacrificed by a wrong management."

It is likely that impatience with Abigail's insistence was as much a cause for Elizabeth to put aside letter writing as were worry and grief. At the end of that summer, Betsy was dead. Only to her son Billy could Elizabeth talk of her daughter's ordeal, of "her faltering accents breathing love and gratitude, her affectionate farewell, her soul quivering upon her pale lips." Betsy had died composed in her Christian faith, and Elizabeth was determined to take the same comfort. "I will not sink in despair," she assured her son. "It is a dangerous, thorny, devious, rugged road through which we have to pass." Only faith within a compassionate life would bring the weary pilgrim out of this "gloomy vale."

The bereaved Elizabeth had renewed anxiety early in 1799 when she wrote to Mary Cranch to say that "she in whom my soul too-too much delighted lies there under yonder cold sod." By then, she expected that her second daughter, little Abby, would soon be put to rest beside Betsy Q. Abby appeared doomed by the same disease. Hearing of this, Abigail sent more medical guidance along with the heartening exhortation that Elizabeth must keep busy. A daily round of work would "dispel the weight of grief and the bitterness of sorrow will be healed by the lenient hand of time."

Elizabeth made no reply, waiting until the end of March 1799 politely to ask that Abigail stop sending advice. Then, as if to explain, Elizabeth told of often beginning letters that were soon blotted with tears over Abby, whose condition "looked so much like her sister." Abigail obediently subsided, and left to Elizabeth the long watch over the invalid little girl who badly suffered what her mother described as a "puking" condition. Abigail privately announced that the child could not survive, but Elizabeth never lost hope. Instead of bleeding the youngster, she took her for exercise and for rides into the country. They went as far as they dared without having to stop, for "we hate to go puking about" in the homes of friends, Elizabeth explained. Abby lived to be an old woman.

Mary Cranch's daughter was the third member of this trio named Betsy, and her story was the most revealing and important. Betsy Cranch was reared in the large, rambling house her parents rented in the middle of Braintree, where she began writing the journal that now ranks among the most valuable items in the mass of Adams family papers. It records the heartfelt impressions of a young woman and also documents daily life in Braintree and Haverhill.

Betsy and her sister Lucy often were up and baking before breakfast. Then came the seemingly endless washing, ironing, sewing, knitting, and other chores which took up much of the day. Each season brought special tasks, such as rubbing the furniture and washing the windows. Everyday duties had to be concluded in time to receive callers, or to allow the girls and Mary to "go abroad" on visits of their own. Dinner was a mid-afternoon meal for family, boarders, and guests.

With Mary Cranch looking after the entire village, or so it often seemed, Betsy was frequently left in charge of the Cranch house. Not surprisingly then, Betsy often talked in her diary as much like a matron as her mother and aunts did. She early adopted the patronizing sympathy which women of that era often showed for the male of the species whose physical and social character pushed him close to danger. Betsy liked to ponder the temptations life brought to a gentleman's baser self. When a young school teacher who boarded several times with the Cranches departed to resume study at Harvard, Betsy saw him go in the assurance that he was yet "entirely innocent." Would Heaven keep him that way? She uttered a prayer: "May not the frequent sight of vice make him desire it."

There was no sparing herself when Betsy thought of life's pitfalls. On her eighteenth birthday she wrote, "What am I to be? . . . Has my life been such as it ought to be? Have I done all the good that has been in my power to do?" Temptation had often visited her, she conceded, making her act "contrary to the dictates of science [reason]." Deeply religious all her life, Betsy confronted these falls from grace with the hope that her Saviour would pardon her. Perhaps to assure that only God knew her heart, Betsy kept silent in her diary over a number of episodes, or, as is evident in some cases, pages with potentially embarrassing revelations were later destroyed by Betsy or her descendants.

As an example of her reserve, Betsy wrote very little at the time she gave her heart to a young man who went off to the Kentucky frontier to make his fortune, vowing to return and marry her. This courageous person was Thomas Perkins, a schoolteacher who had boarded at the Cranches' during 1781, leaving in April 1782. His departure, at least, was touchingly portrayed by Betsy in her journal. After describing how her father Richard Cranch bade farewell to Perkins, the older man shedding tears and admonishing him to fight the good fight against vice, Betsy said that he then left her alone with Perkins.

"I wished him a pleasant journey," said Betsy. " 'twas all my lips could utter. But could he have read my mind," she added that he would have seen many personal wishes "I could not express by words." The nineteen-year-old Betsy was disgusted with herself. "When my heart feels the most, it is apt to express the least." Wanting desperately to speak, as her betrothed took his leave, she was nearly mute. And yet "he was my friend, and such a one as I ever wish to have."

The Cranches knew it would take time before Thomas Perkins found success in Kentucky. But when three years had passed, some change of scene seemed needed to lift Betsy's spirits while she waited. It was decided that she should spend the winter of 1785–86 with Aunt Elizabeth Shaw and other friends in Haverhill. Visits were often exchanged between the Shaw and Cranch offspring, although one of this length was unusual. Betsy's journal for these seven months is charming, as well as revealing of life in a New England town. Her jottings also show the struggle of a young woman to remain loyal to a distant love from whom letters were rare.

Betsy passed her twenty-second birthday soon after reaching Haverhill, and her uneasiness about this milestone was perhaps one reason why she found herself delighting in the court paid to her by several eligible Haverhill males. She wished to be true to Thomas Perkins, but his absence was beginning to seem endless. With every report of Indian assaults in Kentucky, there was less hope that Thomas was alive, and if so, that he might survive to return. It was in this difficult circumstance that Betsy's cousin John Quincy Adams found her in 1785 when he returned from Paris to study with his uncle.

John Quincy left a description of Betsy in which she fared remarkably well. Never one to spare his cousins or himself from his own severe scrutiny, young Adams found Betsy, who was four years his senior, very attractive. He had not seen her for nearly six years, and she was now a woman. "Her complexion is dark, and her face, though not beautiful, has a sweetness, and benign candour in it," John Quincy wrote in his diary. Betsy's charm, he said, was much to be preferred over "that insipid thing called beauty."

He grew even more enthusiastic: "Her eye expresses the exquisite Sensibility of her heart. Perhaps this is too great for her own happiness." Still, he conceded, this quality of tenderness and empathy was the one most to be desired in a woman. Naturally John Quincy admired Betsy's wide reading, and her keen imagination which, he was relieved to note, had not been spoiled by "unmeaning novels, or immoral plays." Her studies had been of the sort "to cultivate, and improve, as well as to entertain and delight the mind." Then, a word of highest praise from John Quincy Adams—Betsy "knows how to improve what she reads."

In the privacy of his diary John Quincy seemed to speak endlessly of Betsy Cranch, stressing her affability and her good nature, qualities which he claimed "endear her to those who are acquainted with her, and must always be pleasing to a stranger." Then, pausing to review what he had written, Betsy's cousin said anyone reading these pages would consider he had penned a panegyric unless they knew Betsy; then they would concede he had not exaggerated.

Since the two of them arrived in Haverhill at about the same time during the autumn, Betsy was assigned to live with neighbors, perhaps because Elizabeth and John Shaw were taking a three-week vacation just as the cousins made their appearances in town. John Quincy was chagrined by this arrangement: "I cannot help wishing she was to spend more of the time in this house [the Shaw parsonage], for several reasons." As soon as the Shaws had returned, Betsy did stay overnight with her aunt and uncle, but did not move in with them until John Quincy departed Haverhill to enroll at Harvard in April 1786. Cousin John Quincy was not so busy studying with Uncle Shaw that he could not read, walk, and talk with Betsy. She even looked after his clothing and packed for him as he prepared to leave for Harvard.

Her sessions with J. Q. Adams were not always placid, however. One day late in January 1786, he astonished her by reading aloud from his journal. Evidently John Quincy wished Betsy to hear his observations on feminine nature, the subject to which his attention continually returned. At eighteen, John Quincy was much Betsy's junior, but his fabled travels and his obvious talent made her look at him as more than a younger brother. She tended therefore to take seriously his fulminations against young women. Noting that her cousin skillfully brought to light the foolishness which he believed endemic in female behavior, Betsy was so impressed by these criticisms that she ruefully noted, "I must mortifyingly confess that they are just."

This uneasy outlook plagued Betsy's journal entries during her stay with the Shaws. "I know not what events may yet hide in the book of futurity," she wrote soon after arriving. She obviously felt freer in Haverhill than back in Braintree, and her liberty included, to her discomfiture, a tendency to forget the absent Thomas Perkins. In fact, Betsy worried that she might allow herself to become better friends with the young gentlemen of Haverhill than would be advisable. She would try to keep them at a distance, she vowed, otherwise "I am more apt to commit inadvertence than when I feel an indifference."

As the weeks passed, Betsy's mood lifted, and she worried less about maintaining a cautious distance from her new friends. Her life as a guest also held a good many distractions that assisted in keeping her mind away from Kentucky, with its rumors of Indian brutality. Uncle John Shaw was a talented storyteller, it seems, and the Shaw house, where Betsy spent most of the daytime, had plenty of books. Shakespeare, history, and the new romance stories were her favorites. Evenings, however, seemed to hold the events which dominated her journal.

Betsy greatly enjoyed the winter's social season for young people in Haverhill. After making lace in the morning, and reading or visiting in the afternoon, she devoted her evenings in January and February to dancing, sleigh rides, and other activities which remained as important in village life as when Elizabeth had arrived ten years before. Betsy seemed surprised by the care she took in dressing for these outings, and by the pleasure she found in dancing, although usually it was so cold that every dance was essential to comfort.

Often these evenings closed with Betsy inviting one or more of the very attentive gentlemen to drink coffee with her and Peggy White, a good friend and the daughter in the house where Betsy stayed during most of her Haverhill visit. These late sessions meant that often Betsy retired after two, usually dropping happily to sleep. Then began troubled dreams which may have been caused by Betsy's guilt at taking pleasure in male companionship when Thomas Perkins was far away and striving to be able to marry her. In Betsy's nightmares, snakes were frequently the menace.

One outing which particularly thrilled Betsy was when she joined a group going by sleigh nine miles to a country residence where a fiddler played while the ladies and gentlemen danced. "A most delightful evening," she recorded. "The moon shone with incomparable lustre." Indeed, Betsy added, the "Feast of Reason" was far from their minds. Her lighthearted behavior won her even more masculine attention, for a few nights later, at one of the Haverhill Assemblies where the community met for fellowship, Betsy observed that during the voluntary dances, many men now sought her as a partner.

It was the practice that a lady draw the name of a gentleman who would be her ballroom companion during the evening, except for some dances where other gallants might approach. After relishing such an event and returning home, Betsy faced her journal, usually by offering the lament "alas! alas!" as she reproached herself for having allowed her heart to feel so free that evening. The remedy, she knew, was to think about Perkins and Kentucky until the intoxicating effect of other men wore off. Seeking distraction as best she could, Betsy carefully checked her heart to see that "each pulse was calm and beat in perfect unison." Then she retired for the night, only to have nightmares return. It was, said Betsy, "as if fancy were envious of the power of reason." Fancy won out, Betsy reported, sending "delusive ideas" into her dreams, unspecified thoughts which, Betsy said, "were sufficiently strong to disturb my tranquillity, and her

[Fancy's] impulses remained to prevent my regaining that sweetly pleasing calmness of which she had deprived me."

The main cause behind Betsy's struggle was the presence of her second cousin, John Thaxter, who had moved to the Haverhill area and was one of the locale's most eligible bachelors. Thaxter was only seven years older than Betsy. Dancing, walking, and talking with him became her delight—and her reason for self-reproach. "Ah, who shall pretend to fathom the deep recesses of the human heart?" Betsy asked herself, proceeding to unpack the few letters she had received from Perkins. For a time, she planned to return them as her romance with John Thaxter threatened to become very serious in late winter 1786.

On 13 March John and Betsy had a long talk, lingering over "*one* subject that affects me much and in consequence of it I slept very little that night. *Oh, how frail is human nature!*" The next day Betsy announced she would not attend that evening's dance, telling herself she would do something foolish if she did appear. It is possible that her real purpose was to test the waters, for her absence provoked much comment, and John Thaxter rushed to her side to discuss it. The following morning Betsy was again depressed, staring out the window, weeping that a new lover was pulling her away from one to whom she was pledged but whom she had not seen for four years.

At this point, evidently, Aunt Elizabeth decided it was time to intervene. She was typically helpful, opening her own journal (which later vanished) to the confused niece in order that the younger woman could see her thoughts of ten or more years before when she was experiencing a similar torment. Betsy was impressed by how, despite her youth, Elizabeth had managed to write with a mind "matured by virtue and real piety." Using such adjectives as "soft, amiable, and candid" to describe her aunt, Betsy noted particularly that Elizabeth had seemed to keep strict self-discipline during her days of courtship. "May I be aided to transplant all her virtues into my own heart and life."

Thus edified, at the end of March Betsy and John Thaxter had another earnest conversation, and must have agreed to cool their ardor. It seemed a pity, Betsy implied somewhat wistfully, for that evening Thaxter had paid her the compliment of calling for her in a chaise to attend yet another night of dancing. The conversation between the pair did not begin until after 2:00 A.M., when they left the dance. Afterward, when she finally got to sleep, Betsy said, "My slumbers were those of a heart at ease. Every form of anxiety and perplexity were removed and I was—was—most happy." But Betsy spoke too soon, for the next night she reported that the "horrible" dreams reappeared.

Fortunately, it was almost time for returning to Braintree, and not a moment too soon for Thomas Perkins' cause. Having parted with John Thaxter, Betsy now found herself attracted to Leonard White, back from Harvard where he roomed with her brother William. On 17 April Betsy departed feeling much distressed at leaving Haverhill and the White and Shaw households. Leonard White hovered over her while goodbyes were exchanged. As Betsy put it in her journal, "I had only time to say that one word—Leonard" as he "handed me into the chaise."

Soon afterward, Leonard White discovered many reasons to visit Braintree, usually claiming that he needed to see his great friends, William Cranch and John Quincy Adams, but spending most of his stay in Betsy's company. When they were parted, he enlisted travelers to Braintree to carry his letters to Betsy. All this meant that Betsy was again finding it difficult to stay loyal to Thomas Perkins who, after many months, had sent no message. Just as Leonard White began courting Betsy in earnest, word arrived from Perkins in Kentucky. Conscience-stricken, Betsy tried to exult, insisting in her diary that the epistles brought her the "long wished for happiness." Such bliss did not prevent her the next day from welcoming Leonard White on another visit. In fact they had a delightful time roaming in the woods and along the beach, where they stopped for a long rest while Betsy wrote a letter to Peggy White, her companion's sister, "with *Leonard's knee* for my table."

Her experiences with John Thaxter and Leonard White led Betsy to realize that she held considerable fascination for men, and the discovery apparently pleased her. When Leonard was not at hand, she did not reread the letters from Kentucky, but accepted the earnest attention of a summer lodger in the Cranch household. This was a Mr. Dingley, the same young man whom Betsy had seen leave for Harvard in 1781 with her hopes for his continued innocence. Dingley was now teaching in Braintree. He lost little time in his suit, Betsy noting with amusement that Dingley addressed her as "Betsy without Miss!!!—what presumption!" The pair naturally took long walks, the standard pastime for couples, and Betsy acknowledged that it pleased her when Dingley scrambled to make certain he had the seat beside her at dinner.

By the end of August, the pair was debating topics with a verve reminiscent of Aunt Elizabeth's maidenly discussions with Isaac Smith and Stephen Peabody. One issue explored with Mr. Dingley was, "Which was the more despicable character—a masculine woman or an effeminate man." Said Betsy, "I think the latter and endeavored to prove it, in opposition to Mr. D——who differs from me." By early fall, Dingley and Betsy seemed to have grown even closer. She ironed his clothes, baked pies for him before breakfast, and discovered she was jealous when he paid attention to an attractive cousin from the Palmer family who called at the Cranch residence. That night Betsy reported she had another alarming dream— this one featured snakes again.

Evidently, Betsy decided that once more her life was getting out of hand. "I feel almost a stranger to myself," she admitted, claiming to regret how she had allowed Dingley to draw her from thoughts about Thomas Perkins. She vowed to keep more to herself. "Quiet and reason are friendly to the concerns of the heart. It requires frequent examinations and is always better for it." Thereupon she spent a solitary evening playing the harpsichord kept in the Cranch parlor. Together with her mother Mary, Betsy began to read aloud romance novels, which were becoming increasingly popular. Sometimes these books kept the pair up well after midnight, despite the chores facing them in a few hours. Betsy found their stories very assuring, depicting as they did worthy couples eventually united after much difficulty, and usually with happiness and abundant prosperity.

Betsy, however, had acquired some of Mary Cranch's realism. Despite the simplistic romances she and her mother read, Betsy could be a sharp critic of both men and women. She used this capacity in late September 1786, when the Cranches welcomed as dinner guests Betsy's friend, Nabby Bishop, who was accompanied by her latest swain. "She makes a most ridiculous figure," Betsy said of Miss Bishop. She "talks as if she never *did love* nor ever will." As for her admirer, "He loves most *violently* her Money, and I dare say will, if he can, her person." In Betsy's view, Nabby Bishop's mind was "a mere vacuum," while her suitor, whose name was Archelous Putnam, "was a sensible, agreeable man." He must have one fault, mused Betsy, or he "would never have made such a choice." After dinner Mr. Putnam and Miss Bishop left, unescorted, to pay more calls down the road in Weymouth.

As fall approached in 1786, Betsy resolved anew to keep her mind and affection centered on Kentucky and Mr. Perkins. She wrote to Aunt Abigail in London: "O, 'tis a *comfortable* thing to have one's heart secure, either in our own possession or in the hands of one who will *treat* and *value* it as their own." A short time later, on 30 October 1786, Betsy found that reassuring world shattered. At this point her journal fell silent for two months, leaving no clue as to her feelings when Richard Cranch brought out to Quincy a letter he had picked up in Boston. The epistle was from Kentucky but not from Thomas Perkins. It was sent by a friend of his and described Perkins' sudden death in August from illness.

According to the report, Perkins had been prospering in his career, chiefly as a lawyer, and anticipated returning soon as a success to claim Betsy's hand. John Quincy Adams was present when the tragic announcement was made and observed the display of Betsy's "great sensibility." He applauded how she managed to confine her sorrow to her countenance. Mary Cranch, however, watched her daughter with pity and apprehension. Even if Betsy had not shed tears in public, her "tender heart" had suffered a deep wound, said Mary.

The extent to which Betsy had rekindled her affection for Perkins had escaped even Mary's motherly awareness. Mary did not linger over the tragedy, for now there was a very practical consideration to be faced. Betsy was approaching twenty-four, and had passed up opportunities which might well have led to marriage, all out of devotion to Perkins. The result was that Mary now found herself with two unmarried daughters. She turned to the worldly-wise Abigail for assistance.

Hasten home from London with advice, Mary begged her sister. Betsy and Lucy Cranch were young women of talent, well-educated through the attentiveness of their father, but their mother believed they were socially handicapped, since the Cranches could not afford to go out into the world where suitable husbands might be found. They were much above the capacities of the semiliterate men of Braintree, Mary proudly claimed, assuring Abigail that Betsy and Lucy required men of "taste, learning, and virtue" as husbands if they were to be happily married.

Mary predicted that Betsy's wound would not soon heal, particularly because her daughter felt guilty about the fatal risk Thomas Perkins took in order to make himself eligible for her hand. However, Betsy showed in a letter to Aunt Abigail of January 1787 that she might recover. She made some conventionally melancholy remarks, observing how "disappointment is written upon many a page of my life." There was hope, she ventured, if she could only travel, which seemed a broad hint to her far-away Aunt Abigail, the only person who might make a change of scene possible.

Betsy may have been hinting, but she tactfully added a remark about how life was teaching her "that happiness depends more upon bounding my desires and wishes than in seeking earnestly to gratify them." She must turn anew to religious faith, Betsy conceded, and to cultivating a sense of resignation, which brought a "lenient balm." Her hopes for happiness were crushed, Betsy insisted, and she tried, not very successfully, to believe she was solaced by realizing that Heaven sent these sorrows out of mercy and love.

These painful lines were written on 7 January 1787, just before Betsy began a visit in Weymouth where the family anticipated she would be comforted by time spent with cheerful Uncle Cotton Tufts. The success of this stay exceeded anyone's expectations, and Uncle Cotton could not claim the credit. Betsy arrived in the village just as her grandfather's old church sought a new minister. Having recently lost one fine prospect, the parish now had another in Jacob Norton, who had just graduated from

Harvard. Norton was born in 1764, making him nearly a year Betsy's junior. Since he lodged at the Tufts residence, Betsy saw much of the young parson, and managed, despite grief, to find him pleasing. "Mr. Norton appears to be quite agreeable and sensible—loves philosophical conversation," she reported as she took up her diary again.

It was a good sign. Betsy kept talking with the Reverend Norton, while back in Braintree Mr. Dingley renewed his suit. Betsy still tried to be the mourner, speaking about the danger of sinking into indifference and resignation. She professed astonishment that her empty heart had once been "the seat of lively happiness." Then her diary became silent. Within a year the family considered Jacob Norton the winner over Dingley, and there was talk that Betsy would be married, an especially pleasing prospect for Mary Cranch and her sisters, for becoming Mrs. Jacob Norton would allow Betsy to preside in the parsonage where her mother and aunts had been reared. Even John Quincy Adams approved the match, noting that Jacob Norton "is said to be a young man of good sense and a good disposition."

Meanwhile Betsy and Jacob began to enjoy the leisurely pursuits of lovers. At a favorite wood Parson Norton carved their names on a tree trunk where couples before them had left their mark. Then, in the late summer of 1788, Betsy's old foe, a snake, literally crossed her path. Norton killed it, but apparently it set Betsy to remembering her old love, and led her to question her affection for Jacob. She could not eat or sleep, despite Mary's advice that she was letting her imagination get the better of her. Betsy shared her misgiving with her suitor, who did what he could to strengthen his case. At night she found "no quiet sleep." Then Betsy heard that her friend Fanny Apthorp had committed suicide by poison. The news seemed to calm Betsy and bring her to count her blessings.

In October 1788, Betsy agreed to an engagement and called Norton her "best friend," a designation men and women at that time gave to their mates. Then followed the customary visit to meet the groom's parents, an episode that went well enough, despite Betsy's being so excited that she could not sleep the first night, and had to be put to bed exhausted at the close of the second day. On 11 February 1789, a Tuesday, Betsy found herself standing beside Jacob Norton and before Parson Wibird. It was her wedding day, scheduled so that Aunt Abigail and Uncle John Adams could be present before they departed for Philadelphia where John was to begin his labors as vice president.

What must have been a restrained honeymoon followed as the bride and groom spent the wedding night with Betsy's parents. On Wednesday, the Reverend and Mrs. Norton went for a ride, and on Thursday Jacob returned to Weymouth to tend his flock, leaving Betsy to join him the following Monday. That day she took up housekeeping by welcoming the numerous callers who traditionally appeared at the door of newly married couples. For two days after joining her husband, Betsy had a houseful of company.

Reviewing her first years as a wife, Betsy focused on events which ought to have warned her of what was to come. One month after the wedding, she was depressed again: "I felt unhappy. O how painful to be conscious of giving pain to those we most assuredly love." Mary Cranch made many helpful visits, feeling comfortable at being back in the parsonage where she had grown up. Betsy's journal does not disclose whether she told her mother of the ominous event in late April 1789 when she began spitting blood. Consumption was a family scourge, and Betsy admitted she was frightened. Rest was considered the ideal therapy for those threatened by the disease, but rest was a luxury Betsy could not afford. She became pregnant almost at once, and with no servants to help her meet the endless procession of guests to the parsonage, found herself exhausted at the outset of her married life.

In fact, Betsy became so busy or depressed that she laid aside her journal for nine years. When she resumed, in September 1797, she was the mother of four children, with that many more still to arrive. The relentless regularity of her pregnancies was only one indication of the ordeal which marital life had brought her. She had to struggle with the meager income Weymouth provided its minister, while her husband apparently was little concerned about her situation and of no help. Parson Norton took great pleasure in the number of gentlemen who dropped in unannounced to have dinner or simply to sit and smoke. In a note she made in 1794, Betsy uttered a cry that probably echoed the sentiments of many young wives, weary of being treated as girl servants. She was, Mrs. Norton admitted, "tired of being *Betsy* so long—hope to get some *help* soon."

It was a futile expectation. Soon Betsy's mother and Aunt Abigail were exchanging worried letters as they deplored Betsy's regimen in the Weymouth parsonage. Life for Mary's daughter seemed to consist of little else but laundry, churning, cooking and baking, gardening, child care, and playing hostess at the minister's table. But it was particularly the menace to Betsy's slender strength from repeated childbearing which caused anxiety for her mother and aunts. Abigail was elated by Betsy's first pregnancy—"Does she begin to look stately? I shall want to see her." But when Betsy was with child soon after the birth of a son, Abigail confided in Mary, "I pray that she may not have children as fast as Mrs. Smith [Abigail's daughter]. It is enough to wear out an Iron constitution."

To worsen matters, Betsy's first child, little Richard Norton, was an amazingly strong lad who required a large amount of mother's milk. This duty alone exhausted Betsy. "The poor girl is wasted to nothing," Mary reported to Abigail in August 1790. "She wants [needs] better living than a country clergyman can afford. I made her get some wine and prescribed a glass or two of it every day." The young mother complained of the same "faintness" which Mary recalled overcame Abigail "when you nursed." But there was no respite. In 1798, Betsy once again had what Aunt Abigail delicately called *"her old sickness."* She was pregnant for the fifth time. Since thus far all the Norton children had been sons, her grandparents tried to be cheerful by hoping for a granddaughter. And Abigail sent word that when Betsy "is blessed with a daughter I shall think she deserves well of her country, and need not further aid it with recruits."

In 1802, Betsy's first female infant arrived, followed by two more, the last in 1806, for a total of five sons and three daughters. Each wedding anniversary led Betsy to reflect on whether her life would be spared long enough to rear these youngsters. She had little time, obviously, for her great love—literature. She was careful to keep some history books nearby, and there was no end of religious material, thanks to Jacob Norton's determination to fight, alone if necessary, the rise of unitarian and universalist ideas, dangers so threatening to his severely Calvinist outlook that in time he alienated his parish. In what was perhaps a welcome change from her ususal routine in the winter of 1798, Betsy managed to read a volume called *Matrimonial Preception*, but did not comment on it.

Her written observations concerned instead her fears about the "vicious and profligate habits" that loomed ahead of her sons and were ready to "blast our fondest expectations and make a Mother's heart bleed with keenest anguish." Like her mother and aunts, Betsy shared the view that a mother must hope death would spare her long enough to steer aright the young sons who were her responsibility. Betsy and her female relatives evidently considered guiding young males a woman's task in which fathers were of dubious assistance.

Betsy repeatedly wondered if, as a result of her labors, her sons would "behave in such a manner as to cause me joy . . . but should they so behave as to wound my heart, the days will be clouded and saddened oe'r with sorrow, sorrow which none but a mother can know. May God Almighty shield them from temptation and preserve them from evil, and give them grace to walk uprightly through this world of sin and sorrows." This preoccupation was due, in part, to the approaching death of Betsy's cousin, Abigail's son Charles Adams, from alcoholism. However, Betsy's next ordeal would come from a very different source.

In 1800, her health broke, and near death from weariness and tuberculosis, Betsy had to knock at her parents' door for help. With several small children, she stayed with the Cranches for two months. Mary and

Richard were so certain she could not survive that one day they discussed plans for her burial as they sat beside her bed in the sickroom, unaware that she was conscious and heard them. Mary even selected the attire for her daughter's corpse.

Betsy finally recovered enough to return to Weymouth, however, leaving two children with her parents. When she arrived in the parsonage, her husband announced he was weary and, leaving his wife in charge of the household, the Reverend Norton went off to refresh himself by the waters of Saratoga Springs. "I was very unwilling to see him leave us," Betsy confided in her diary. "But he thought it best to go!" Betsy surprised herself by conceding that it was quite possible to get along without her husband. Soon she felt her strength returning.

Betsy Cranch Norton lived another ten years, during which she had reason to give thanks that her marriage, difficult though it had proved, was luckier than that of her cousin Nabby, the only daughter of Abigail Adams. Nabby's wedding in London had been acclaimed by Aunt Adams as the first step in a marital partnership certain to flourish, so noble was Nabby's husband. It turned out to be a disaster, and filled Nabby's life with sorrows greater even than those clouding the Weymouth parsonage.

6

Wedding in London

Abigail named her first child, a daughter born 14 July 1765, after herself. But this second Abigail was known by her nickname, Nabby. Nabby received the same demanding upbringing as her three brothers—John Quincy, Charles, and Thomas. After her tenth birthday, her father, John Adams, was rarely at home, off first to the Continental Congress in Philadelphia and then to France and Holland as emissary for the new American government. Consequently, Nabby was left without a male parent, and was reared by a dynamic mother who skillfully managed the family and its property. Nabby soon discovered that her relatives expected her to be like her mother, a difficult task even had the two been alike in personality and ability. Nabby, however, was a more ordinary person than her remarkable mother.

The pressure on Nabby issued also from Abigail's belief that her own chief duty was to prepare her children for entrance into a world full of evil. Though a loving parent, Abigail's demands on Nabby and her brothers for excellence in morals, intelligence, and deportment sometimes obscured her affection for them. At an early age, Nabby became repressed, aloof, and highly self-critical. Much of her authentic personality was suppressed by resentment and anxiety over the expectations placed upon her. She matured into a silent, withdrawn young woman, characteristics that made Abigail impatient.

The bond between daughter and father was more comfortable, but even here Nabby could not escape the intimidating example of her mother. When he was away from Braintree, John Adams frequently sent his daughter advice intended as encouragement, but it often served only to put more pressure on her. Typical of John's misguided efforts was his reminder to Nabby that "it is by the female world that the greatest and best characters among men are formed." John said that when he heard of a successful man he inquired at once about the man's mother. And though Nabby was somewhat reassured by her father's stated regard for her "understanding and consideration," John probably did not appreciate how much less than helpful he was by repeatedly pointing out to his daughter that she had "a mother who was an ornament to her sex."

Nabby needed no prompting on the matter of Abigail's achievement as family leader during John's extended absence after 1774. The more vigorous Abigail became, the more subdued Nabby seemed. Hoping to coax her daughter out of her shell, Abigail dispatched her in 1778 to spend several months in nearby Plymouth, living with the family of Mercy Otis Warren, whom Abigail admired greatly. How fortunate, Abigail thought, that a female of Mrs. Warren's charm and ability could be put before Nabby as an example to emulate.

At Plymouth, and during later escapes from Braintree, Nabby wrote with remarkable candor to her confidante, cousin Betsy Cranch, her elder by two years. Nabby made no effort to hide her pleasure at being away from home, visiting with the Warrens or with Boston relatives. "I have a secret hope that Mamma does not intend to send for me yet," she confessed to Betsy, adding "though I dare not say so." Nabby talked a great deal about personality, a topic which Abigail often brought up. There was a note of envy in Nabby's observation to Betsy, an assured and outgoing individual, that "a good opinion of our selves and our abilities is very necessary in this life, it adds to the happiness of those who possess it, and sometimes raises a person in the opinion of their acquaintances. When there are real abilities it is not disgusting."

But for those who lacked talent, Nabby said, striving to live with oneself carried "disadvantages that no one can have any idea of but those who labour under them." At the same time that she begged Betsy to show these observations to no one—meaning, in particular, no parent—Nabby also confessed that it felt stupid to sit with a group and have nothing to say. "Do you not pity me?" Nabby implored. "Do out of benevolence write me a conversation that I may make use of when I go into company." Confiding in cousin Betsy was a great blessing for Nabby. "You know altho I do not take a talkative part in company, yet it is ever my wish to have one friend that I can with freedom express my thoughts to at the very time." Nabby added, "I have not yet met with one person that I wish should supply your place in every degree." Having said this, Nabby begged that her letter be destroyed.

On other occasions, Nabby found it impossible to write a single line, for instance when Abigail insisted she prepare letters for her father and her brother, John Quincy. Nabby tried to beg off, claiming that her efforts would disgrace her since these relatives were severe judges of correspondence. Her father's and brother's praise of the letters they received from Abigail, left Nabby so intimidated that when she finally sat down to write under Abigail's eye her efforts are as painful to read today as they were for her to write. Nabby habitually confessed to her brother how deeply she felt "her own unworthiness." Consequently, she produced stale imitations of her mother's exhortatory epistles.

Nabby's letters stressed, for instance, that John Quincy must take advantages of his travels to become "an ornament to your parents who watch with attention each improvement and whose hearts would be wounded by a misconduct." This was followed by trite statements on behalf of virtue, all aimed to alert her brother to the fact that, though surrounded by European vice, his mind must remain "the seat of innocence." Nabby's letters to John and John Quincy communicated precisely what her mother would approve, no more and no less.

It was only in a confidential corner, such as her exchanges with Betsy Cranch, that Nabby continued to try to establish an independent self. At age fourteen in 1779, soon after Aunt Elizabeth Smith had gone off to Haverhill as Mrs. Shaw, it dawned on Nabby, as it did on her cousins and brothers, that Elizabeth could be a source of advice, consolation, and affection. Nabby told Betsy that she yearned to see Aunt Shaw: "I have often lamented that I was not older before she left the once pleasant but now solitary Mansion at Weymouth that I might have profited by her good advice." At the same time Nabby talked more ardently of her own wishes for a new life, one with her father, whose plight she drew for cousin Betsy: "No partner to soothe and comfort him in his unhappiness."

Surely, Nabby said, a daughter could substitute as a wife and thus bring to her father the "tender attentions" he so needed. For Nabby, John Adams' life without a feminine companion was distressing beyond words, but Abigail rejected Nabby's repeated requests that she be allowed to go to France and aid her father, although the mother agreed the change might be beneficial to her daughter's personality. By now it was 1782, and Nabby had a prematurely buxom appearance which Abigail told John would surely "grace" his table in Europe. But the mother doubted whether going abroad would prompt the young woman to overcome her main fault, her taciturnity and shyness in public. Abigail exasperatedly reported to John that their daughter was much "too silent."

Abigail's vehemence masked a new worry, she feared that her daughter was discouraging a suitor in whom Abigail took a considerable interest. Not even romance, it seemed, permitted Nabby to escape Abigail's pressure. Too little of Nabby's writing remains to indicate how she felt at the outset about this man, Royall Tyler, but her first reference to him could hardly have been less promising. From Boston, where she was visiting her great-uncle Isaac Smith and his family, Nabby sent an urgent warning to Betsy during June 1782 about Tyler, who would soon arrive in Braintree to practice law and board at the Cranch residence. There was much talk in Boston concerning Tyler, Nabby reported, and many relatives and family friends suspected he was designing to replace Thomas Perkins in Betsy's affection, now that the former had gone off to Kentucky. According to Nabby, Betsy's friends wished her to know that Tyler was considered "the essence and quintessence of artfulness." He might easily manage to "find a way to soothe your sorrows."

Nabby assured Betsy that she had defended her before those who feared Tyler might cause trouble. They need not worry, the loyal Nabby had said, for Betsy would see Tyler as he really was "and that you would despise the attempt, and detest the action." Still, Nabby heard such alarming tales of the appeal of Royall Tyler that she felt it necessary to give Betsy a quiet word of warning: "Perhaps you will laugh at me."

As for herself, Nabby announced she was determined to have nothing to do with Tyler when she was back in Braintree. "Our sex," she reminded Betsy, could not be "too careful of the characters of the acquaintances we form." It was soon apparent that Nabby had underestimated Tyler's prowess, for he dominated her life and Abigail's over the next four years, during which interval the Adamses, Cranches, Shaws, and, it sometimes seemed, the entire town of Braintree debated the worthiness of Royall Tyler. It was an episode of family and village history that was part comedy, part tragedy. Even today some mystery clings to the story.

Tyler was born in 1757 to prosperous Boston parents. His father, successful in commerce and politics, was interested in books and often chatted about literary matters with John Adams. The elder Tyler died in 1771, leaving Royall amply prepared to enjoy a boisterous and spendthrift career in Harvard College. Despite his outrageous behavior, young Tyler nevertheless impressed the faculty and the Boston community with his talent as a man of letters, as a wit, and as an orator. He graduated in 1777 with such distinction that Yale College also awarded him a degree. The recipient wore his honors casually, rejoicing in post-graduate revels, possibly fathering a child out of wedlock, and publicly insulting the dignity of Harvard by affecting indifference when the college prepared to grant him a master's degree, actually a routine matter at the time. But so charming was Tyler's apology that the honor was bestowed in 1779.

After brief service in the Revolutionary War, a period of no consequence except that Tyler met General Joseph Palmer, Mary Cranch's brother-in-law, the young man attempted practicing law on the Maine frontier. This proved much too dull, so Tyler decided in 1782 to try Braintree, which was somewhat livelier and had the advantage of being near Boston. All the townspeople seemed to know Tyler's reputation when he took up residence with the Cranches. Citizens agreed the newcomer was charming, generous, came from a good family, might have outgrown his wild ways, and was the possessor of some wealth. He was twenty-five and made an excellent first impression.

Or so it seemed to Abigail Adams, who soon was welcoming Tyler to her fireside nearly every evening as autumn arrived in 1782. Observers said that Tyler's aim was to woo Nabby, daughter of Braintree's most distinguished citizen. John Adams' long absence in the public's service meant that his legal practice and uncollected accounts needed the attention of an able young attorney, a circumstance Tyler had not overlooked. Yet with all these advantages, Tyler faced a serious difficulty. Nabby was not thrilled by him. Given her earlier warnings to Betsy Cranch, it is hardly surprising that Nabby sat wordless and suspicious on those evenings when Royall Tyler was a guest in her parlor.

When long silences ensued, the suitor turned to the mother. Abigail Adams never denied that she preferred the company of men, and especially those with a literary turn. Abigail was then age thirty-seven, with her attractiveness as compelling as ever, a charm growing particularly from her clever talk and literary enthusiasm. Unlike the daughter, the mother found visits by Royall Tyler very gratifying and his conversation refreshing. He had the cleverness which other village males Nabby's age usually lacked. Like most mothers, Abigail was eager to see her daughter make a good match. But with Nabby's tendency to withdraw, Abigail saw that maternal assistance would be needed. She began to work in Tyler's behalf.

Already weary of her mother's pushing and prompting, Nabby's misgivings about Royall Tyler were anything but overcome by Abigail's making the association a triangle. Since Nabby wrote little about the matter at the time, the extent of her feelings must be left to conjecture, but not so for those of her father. Abigail sent enthusiastic news of Nabby's courtship to John, who saw at once that Tyler had made a conquest—of Abigail! If only Nabby would relent, Abigail told John. She seemed so cool and dignified. What she needed was "a tender passion," an experience that her mother was sure would break down Nabby's "natural reserve and soften her form and manners."

The prospect of such a development in his daughter distressed a father who was aghast at what he considered the shamelessness of most European women. John rebuked his wife for letting herself be the courted party, and urged that his daughter's—and his wife's—capacity for silence be strengthened. As for Tyler, John knew of the talk about Royall which Nabby overheard in Boston, and he applauded his daughter's determination to have nothing to do with any former rake. These paternal objections were raised in early 1783, well after Tyler's appearance in Braintree, but it required that long for Abigail's reports to reach Europe.

By the time John read letters from home, the situation in Braintree was changed. Nabby had insisted on continuing her custom of spending much of the winter away from Braintree, which now had the added advantage of affording escape from the long evenings with Tyler and her mother. She went into Boston, leaving Abigail glumly reconciled to adjourning her campaign for Tyler. In the spring of 1783, Abigail reported to John that the romance had gotten nowhere. "Your daughter has a firmness of mind and a prudence beyond her years," the thwarted Abigail had to concede.

Nabby certainly tried to resist all efforts to manage her life. From the relative safety of Boston she acknowledged that she was guilty of the "independence of disposition" which some persons, doubtless including Abigail, ascribed to her. Writing to her ally, Betsy Cranch, Nabby admitted that she should try to be more cheerful and outgoing, giving as the main reason that it would please "Mamma." Her father, who had not yet received letters telling of Tyler's stalled cause, was bombarding Abigail with his indignation and alarm. John obviously found it difficult to understand how his partner in marriage, whose judgment he so admired, could support Royall Tyler: "He is but a Prodigal son, and though a penitent, has no right to your daughter, who deserves a character without a spot."

By the middle of 1783, well aware of her husband's distress, Abigail sought to reassure John, although she still privately yearned to see Nabby accept courtship from Tyler. Abigail informed her husband that it was now clear Royall Tyler "will never be in any other character" to Nabby "than an acquaintance." Although she announced that Tyler's cause was "wholly done with," Abigail still hoped to wrest victory from defeat. She gambled that behind a solemn exterior Nabby had a secret regard for her suitor. If Nabby could believe that her father might accept Tyler, Abigail saw a chance for a change of heart.

The persistent mother continued to mail across the Atlantic glowing assurances of Royall's steadfastness at work and virtue. His talent and exemplary conduct, she pointed out, were her reasons for showing such "partiality" to him. Meanwhile John urged that Nabby persist in displaying the "reserve" her father admired. For Abigail's benefit, John added, "I wish her Mother had been more so than she has been upon this occasion."

It took months before Abigail's strategems began to succeed. As late as December 1783, Nabby stubbornly held aloof from the romance being arranged for her. "You well know that nature has given me pride enough to balance all my other qualities," she told Betsy Cranch. Even in Betsy's case, where her sweetheart was still far away in Kentucky, Nabby advised caution, saying it was a mistake to fall in love readily, and even more a blunder to show it. Earlier, she had spoken of her own "natural insensibility," by which she meant emotional coldness. Nabby admitted to being human, however, confessing at the close of 1783, "I long to be in love—it must be a strong feeling."

Even as Nabby wrote, however, Royall Tyler and his champions were closing in. Not only had Tyler been steadfastly upright and industrious; he also undertook to purchase one of the finest estates in Braintree, property which became available once it hd been confiscated from its Tory owners. Abigail was impressed and excited, something Tyler doubtless expected. This realty deal was a prudent step, Abigail told her husband, adding that Tyler had taken it in "hope that he may not be considered unworthy a connection in this family." To Abigail's dismay, Nabby remained indifferent. "The forms of courtship, as the world sees it, do not subsist between the young folks," John was informed. Certainly aware of Tyler's valiance, Nabby confided in Betsy, "I have sometimes been at a loss to know whether I have a heart or not." Had she, Nabby wondered, been "deprived of it" by her upbringing?

Then Abigail made a brilliant move. She persuaded Betsy's father, Richard Cranch, to send John Adams an endorsement of Royall Tyler. There was no one in Braintree whom John admired or trusted more than "brother Cranch." So when he read Richard's commendation of Tyler, written in October 1783, Nabby's father gallantly changed his stance. His new outlook was strengthened when another envelope reached him containing Richard's endorsement of an enclosed epistle from Tyler, wherein the latter asked John Adams for permission to court Nabby, but pledging no intent of any prompt marriage should an engagement ensue.

Richard Cranch had proclaimed Royall Tyler a man of "Politeness, Genius, Learning, and Virtue." John was assured that the world could now forget Tyler's "gaiety and sprightliness" at college. Instead, "brother Cranch" envisioned a splendid future for Nabby's suitor. As he capitulated, John shrewdly remembered that this was Nabby's romance, not Abigail's nor anyone else's. With this in mind, he wrote a charming letter in which he announced he would gladly leave the determination about Tyler to Nabby. John pointedly observed that perhaps it was time he heard from Nabby on the subject, rather than from Abigail and other relatives.

If the silent Nabby wished to marry Tyler, John said she had his paternal blessing, adding in a letter to Abigail that he trusted Nabby to make the decision. He said he knew Nabby would first confer with her mother and her aunts Mary and Elizabeth. He even sounded enthusiastic. Nabby and her husband could live in the family's cottage, he suggested, thereby allowing Abigail at long last to join him in Europe. In his most graceful gesture, John made his law library available to Tyler, who, he wished, would be the proper legal instructor for young John Quincy Adams. Summing up his new view of Tyler, John stated, "If he has sown his wild oats and will study and mind his business, he is all I want."

John's consent and his deferral to Nabby arrived after Abigail departed for Europe in May 1784 with Nabby in tow. For several years Abigail had hesitated to make the trip. She had feared that, as a simple woman of the provinces, she might disgrace herself before the courts of Europe. But if she must go, she was determined that Nabby should come along. What Nabby might have done had her father's words arrived before she sailed makes a tempting question. She was devoted to her father, and with his permission to make her own decision with regard to Tyler, she might well have turned him away. However, since Nabby was to leave Massachusetts for an extended time, she was convinced that some arrangement with Tyler was necessary. The record as to what Nabby actually agreed to is unclear, but apparently she allowed Royall Tyler to hope that someday he might have her hand in marriage.

Shortly before sailing, Nabby pushed aside doubts about Tyler, but not as a result of Abigail's campaign for the gentleman. Nabby's sympathy for Tyler may have gone from bud to flower in reaction to Aunt Mary Cranch's urging of caution. Having watched Tyler closely from her vantage point as his landlady, Mary had lately grown alarmed at his habits and decided to warn Nabby against him. She did so as the Adams mother and daughter were packing for Europe, with Nabby under pressure to decide about Tyler. Upon hearing Mary assert her belief that all of Tyler's wild oats had not yet been scattered and that the young man should be viewed skeptically, Nabby bridled. To her dismay, Mrs. Cranch realized that her intrusion encouraged Nabby to side with her mother.

Mary always believed that her speaking out had been misunderstood. It evidently authenticated for Nabby the story going around Braintree that certain persons wanted Miss Adams out of the way so that Lucy Cranch, Mary's daughter, could gain Tyler's favor. There appears to have been no basis for this rumor. The likeliest reason for Mary's warning was her deep-seated fear of dissolute men. Observing Tyler's daily behavior, which now seemed less correct, Mary was reminded of her doomed brother William Smith. Royall Tyler had been raised in a similarly undisciplined way. Mary had also recently learned that Tyler had cut his ties with his mother, who by then had twice been widowed. Probably little of this background was shared with Nabby, so that the latter permitted impulse and desperation to lead her in the direction toward which Abigail had been pointing for two years. After giving an elated Royall Tyler some sort of encouragement, Nabby sailed for Europe with Abigail.

Mary bade them goodbye uneasily, for she was left to guard Adams affairs which now included the awkward task of monitoring the habits of a man who might marry Nabby Adams. Mary was as uncomfortable with the situation as Abigail was pleased. For the next two years, the story of Nabby Adams' romance unfolded in two locations, separated by the Atlantic Ocean. Confusion prevailed because of the many weeks required for messages to travel across the sea. Often the Adamses and the Cranches had only outdated information to act on.

It is best to begin with the European side of the story. Daughter and mother survived the Atlantic crossing, during which Abigail noticed Nabby appeared undismayed that she had left her ardent suitor behind. For nearly a year Nabby attended mainly to her new surroundings and enjoyed the company of her brother John Quincy, until he departed for America and Harvard College. The two saw much of Paris, and relished the obvious pleasure Abigail and John took in the family reunion. Nabby wrote to Royall Tyler, but none of her letters appears to have survived.

Abigail also corresponded with Tyler. Copies of these letters are available. Her advice to him was stern and matronly, emphasizing the danger of vain attachments and trifling passions. "Our happiness depends only on the nature of our inclinations," she said. "I hope you are going on in such a way as to give those who are disposed to assist you no cause to regret their friendly disposition toward you." In lengthy letters describing the family's intimate life, Abigail adopted a tone that made Tyler appear a member of the Adams inner circle.

Abigail told Tyler how welcome his letters were, and she reassured him: "You have a share and that not a small one in the affectionate regards of A. Adams." Nabby was mentioned only when Abigail reminded Tyler that her daughter looked forward to his letters. Abigail's messages suggest she was working overtime to keep the romance alive. There are hints that Abigail feared Nabby's interest in Tyler was forced and superficial, a condition which she hoped time would overcome.

Almost nothing remains of Royall Tyler's responses, except an epistle of respect and gratitude, a model of its type, in which he replied to a message from John Adams warmly welcoming him as Nabby's friend. Never had he felt more at a loss for words, Tyler wrote in late summer 1784. But he managed to find his tongue and proceeded to display some of the talent for which he was famous by giving John a full report on the progress in profession and property which he, Tyler, was making. He expressed gratitude to John for letting him use his library and assured John that he and Nabby would never take a step without the blessing of her parents. He closed with the "hope that our union will afford you and your Lady that enviable satisfaction which Parents do experience when they perceive their children useful, worthy, respectable, and happy."

Nabby's letters to cousin Betsy Cranch, written from France and then England, were limited mostly to comments about how what she saw differed from Braintree and Boston. There was no hint of a young woman in love. Nabby doubtless took pains to reveal nothing personal in a letter to the Cranch household, remembering her Aunt Mary Cranch's warnings about Royall Tyler. Betsy heard much about European life, and received Nabby's promise to tell more when the cousins were face to face. "I wish I could give you some idea of the French ladies but it is impossible to do it by letter," Nabby said. "I should absolutely be ashamed to write what I must if I tell you truths. There is not a subject in nature that they will not talk upon in any company and there is no distinction of sex after they are married." Nabby reported upon one young lady who, though pregnant, spoke unabashedly to John Quincy Adams about her expected child.

In May 1785, Paris was left behind as the Adamses removed to London, where John became the United States' first minister to Great Britain. That assignment brought help from Congress in the person of a secretary who joined the family just as Nabby passed her twentieth birthday, Colonel William Stephens Smith, whose arrival coincided with a sudden falling off of letters from Royall Tyler. With even greater ease than Tyler, Smith won the favor of Abigail Adams, and soon that of Nabby. This was early evidence that the colonel deserved his life-long reputation as a ladies' man. His future sister-in-law, Mrs. John Quincy Adams, remembered, "There was an easy imperativeness in the man and in all that he did that produced a great effect upon the world in which he moved." Louisa also recalled the colonel's monumental self-confidence.

Smith had been born in New York on 8 November 1755, making him ten years Nabby's senior. He was part of a large and undistinguished family, but his personal attractiveness led to his appointment as one of General George Washington's aides, an assignment Smith carried out creditably during the Revolution. Arriving in England with that record, William Smith was certain his country owed him support for his wartime contribution. The handsome officer immediately impressed Abigail as having none of the shadows in his past that handicapped Royall Tyler. She was soon advising John Quincy that he could send his very private letters to her most safely if they were addressed to Colonel Smith, while her messages glowed with the kind of praise for Smith which formerly had been reserved for Royall Tyler.

Nabby's first impressions of Smith are unknown. What is certain is that some months after he took up residence with the Adamses, Nabby broke off her understanding with Royall Tyler. Abigail insisted this was because

Tyler had failed to write, although the Adamses were experienced enough to know how often transatlantic mail miscarried. It is more likely that Nabby's independence had been strengthened by living abroad. Her arrangement with Tyler had never been substantial, and when he neglected to write she had a convenient reason for putting aside any so-called engagement. Meanwhile the handsome and gallant Smith, who paid her considerable attention, certainly helped loosen Tyler's precarious grip on Nabby's affection.

Once again, Uncle Cotton Tufts was summoned for assistance. Nabby asked him to give Royall Tyler a note from her which said, with wonderful terseness, "Herewith you receive your letters and miniature with my desire that you would return mine to my uncle Cranch, and my hopes that you are well satisfied with the affair as is A. A." To strengthen Nabby's hand, Abigail sent word to relatives in Massachusetts that her daughter was not acting hastily, that she had long considered dismissing Tyler but delayed doing so because John Adams had become a convert to the young man's cause. Laboring to show that Nabby had reached her decision alone, without parental pressure, Abigail predicted that now her daughter would "proceed with a caution purchased by experience."

During the time it took for this news to cross the sea and for thunder-struck replies to be received, Nabby's love life became more exciting. Smith began courting her in the summer of 1785, unaware of her pledge to Tyler. It was Abigail who, ever so casually, as she recalled, mentioned Tyler's place in Nabby's life to Smith. Abigail claimed she did not hint that Nabby was inclined to drop Tyler. Learning about Tyler, the colonel offered to make a gentlemanly retreat by going at once to the Continent, ostensibly for business purposes. He pledged he would no longer seek Nabby's favor once he had come back to London.

Off Smith went, reappearing late in 1785 after long overstaying his leave, to the disgust of John Adams. He found that Nabby had not only ended her understanding with Royall Tyler, but that she was willing to accept a new suitor. In Smith's absence, Abigail had warmed to the prospect of having him as a son-in-law, possibly prodded by the realization that, back in Braintree, people might be saying it was Tyler who had broken off with Nabby, as his failure to write could indicate. Consequently, as Smith wandered among the sights of Europe, he apparently received discreet bulletins from Abigail concerning the change in Nabby's outlook. He certainly returned from his travels, not with Nabby erased from his affection as he had promised, but determined to press for her hand at once.

Like Royall Tyler, the colonel found his best ally in Abigail, who was obviously charmed by him. He did not make his proposal of marriage to Nabby nor to her father, the logical parties. Instead he wrote a letter to

Abigail just after Christmas of 1785. She understood him best, he told her, and to her he expressed his hope of eventually wedding Nabby. It was a skillful presentation, in which William Smith conceded that he came from a family with neither fame nor fortune, "but such as I am, I ask your friendship and aspire to your daughter's love."

Colonel Smith was exceedingly vague as to his plans for supporting a wife. For now, however, the fact that a man like Smith wanted to marry her daughter was enough for Abigail. Only later did it occur to her that she would have to explain and explain again that Nabby did not take her new suitor on the rebound, after being rejected by Tyler, and that she had not dropped her distant and less promising relationship with Tyler simply for the grander passion at hand. Abigail would repeatedly insist to relatives and friends in America that both Nabby and Smith had acted honorably. Unfortunately, we probably will never know to what degree Smith's presence in London influenced Nabby's rejection of Tyler.

In the early months of 1786, the friendship between Nabby Adams and William Smith flourished, and Abigail began sending hints to Braintree concerning the fast-moving developments in London. In a long letter to her son John Quincy, which she knew would be shared with Mary Cranch and Elizabeth Shaw, Abigail rhetorically raised the inevitable question about a new romance: "You will say, is not this sudden?" Admitting that it might appear so, Abigail defended Nabby, whose "pensive sedateness" was still a strength. She contended that Nabby had written Tyler letters of reproach and warning before she turned him away. Abigail assured the folks back home that honor had always guided Nabby.

Nabby, meanwhile, was claiming in letters to Betsy Cranch that nothing whatsoever had troubled her after leaving America, except that she regretted being away from relatives like Betsy. Nabby wrote this in February 1786, by which time she could also inform her cousin that now there was "some one individual that may attract my mind and whom my judgment and reason may approve." Nabby then coyly closed her letter, "But I shall confess too much if I don't take care."

Soon after this, Nabby and her parents received a letter from Royall Tyler, written after he had read Nabby's curt message of dismissal. His words have been lost, but we know from Abigail that Tyler's defense and plea had been touching. Abigail assured Mary, however, that she "saw the consummate artistry of it." Evidently Tyler insisted that he had written often to Nabby, that he still loved her, and would cross the Atlantic to make his case in person, if that would change her mind. In fact, all three—Nabby, Abigail, and John—were moved to tears, as Abigail later acknowledged. John was so stirred that he urged giving Tyler a second chance, but Abigail strongly dissented and advised Nabby to stand fast. The daughter complied.

After this William Smith and Nabby Adams soon became engaged. An exultant Abigail could not say enough in praise of Nabby's suitor and paid him one of the highest compliments at her command when she told Mary that Colonel Smith reminded her very much of Richard Cranch. Later this comparison would seem astounding and would often haunt Abigail. But in the spring of 1786 the only dismay Smith caused was when he insisted that the wedding take place immediately. To Abigail's surprise, John Adams was sympathetic, reminding her of the painful wait they had suffered before their marriage. Abigail responded that their delay was necessary since John first needed to be assured of income sufficient to support a family. As for Colonel Smith, Abigail told Mary Cranch that he would always have a fine position serving his country.

Abigail continued proclaiming the merit of her prospective son-in-law: "Delicacy of sentiment and honour are the striking traits of his character." And despite her misgivings about Smith's haste to reach the altar, Abigail assured sister Elizabeth: "I gave her to him with all my heart. He is worthy of her." The ceremony took place at the American minister's residence in London's Grosvenor Square on a Sunday, 12 June 1786. It had the blessing of the Archbishop of Canterbury, who had been persuaded by Abigail to omit from the Church of England service some of what she considered its "grossest" passages. A small group was present, including the American artist John Singleton Copley and his wife.

On the eve of the wedding, Abigail dreamed of Royall Tyler. Later she confessed to Mary Cranch that she had felt twinges of conscience about how Nabby had ended the affair. Surely, she hoped, Tyler's poor conduct would always justify Nabby's action "in the sight of both God and man." The day before the marriage ceremony, Abigail earnestly inquired of Nabby if she had indeed forgotten Royall. Nabby assured her she had. Even so, Abigail trembled during the service. But then it was over, and Abigail had the wrenching experience of seeing her daughter weep when the colonel took her to the fashionable residence he had arranged in Wimpole Street, half a mile from Grosvenor Square.

To Abigail's dismay, early the next morning John Adams slipped away to visit the newlyweds. When he returned near noon, Abigail confronted him. The minister looked sheepish: "Ah, well, I have been to see them." "What, could you not stay till your usual hour?" "No, I could not. I wanted to go before breakfast." John had also noticed his daughter's distress at leaving her parents. In letters after the wedding, Nabby said that the ceremony had made her feel closer to her family. Marriage meant little more than a change in name, she contended. Nevertheless, a difference soon became apparent in Nabby's letters, as she strove for a loftier tone. She seemed to ape the matron's style, which others, she may have believed, including Abigail, now expected of her.

Among Nabby's letters of this period, one is particularly memorable. Having heard from Betsy Cranch about John Quincy's harsh views of women, Nabby dropped her customarily safe and banal concerns and pointedly told her brother, "A gentleman who is severe against the ladies is also upon every principle impolitic. His character is soon established for a morose, severe, ill-natured fellow, and upon my word I think it the most convincing proof that he can give that he feels their power's importance and superiority." This advice to her brother affords a rare glimpse of the Nabby usually hidden behind reserve and small talk. In fact, she went on to warn John Quincy that, like all men, he would eventually be forced to the point in life where he must admit a "dependence" upon women. It was a viewpoint which Abigail, of course, had often defended.

Back in Braintree and Haverhill, efforts to understand Nabby's romance with Tyler had been stymied for long periods because of the exasperatingly slow mail. But even as relatives and friends waited for news, there was enough local excitement caused by Tyler to occupy the gossipers. It was widely known that no sooner had Tyler bade Nabby farewell when she sailed in May 1784 than he rushed back to the Cranch residence, where he boarded, and made a startling scene. First flinging himself upon the furniture, and then lying on the floor, he shouted his grief at Nabby's departure—"I shall never see her again!" In a day or two, however, he recovered and began to absent himself from his lodging, except for breakfast and sleep.

Mary Cranch was convinced that Tyler's excessive grief was bogus. Barely was Nabby out of sight when Mary began detecting signs of faithlessness in this young man who was presumably pledged to her niece. Stories circulated about Royall's "gallanting" of women, including married ones, in the local grog shops. Fretting over these tales and yet not wishing to intrude again—for Nabby had already rebuffed her once—Mary hesitantly started on several descriptions of the situation to Abigail, only to burn them. Meanwhile, Tyler seemed to be writing to Nabby as often as sailing schedules allowed. In due course he was receiving letters from Abigail which urged him to strengthen his resolve by visiting the Adams cottage, "although deserted," for the sight of it would surely recall "to your remembrance what it once was!" Tyler was assured that his prospective mother-in-law sympathized with him and wished that she could send comfort in a more personal form.

And so Mary Cranch held her tongue for a time. Even Elizabeth Shaw was a supporter of Tyler, whom she had come to know from visits to her relatives. His literary leanings pleased her, as did the fact that he sent lovely gifts to Nabby's young brothers who were studying in Haverhill. The close bond between Tyler and Aunt Elizabeth was apparent when he complied with her request for his old cotton stockings which she then cut down for use by her daughter. And even Mary was touched when Tyler reacted to the arrival of letters from Nabby by closeting himself for three days to pen a reply.

Soon complaints from the Adamses began arriving, showing that few of Tyler's letters were reaching their destination. Elizabeth Shaw's heart went out to Nabby: "I really commiserate her situation." Ah, well, said her aunt, "Time may do much on both sides—a state of probation we are all in, if we act our parts with fidelity, we shall receive an ample reward." But given the increasing rumors that Tyler might not be playing his role honorably, Elizabeth thought it best to caution Mary. "Circumspection," said Elizabeth, must be Mary's guide. "You have, my sister, a critical, delicate part to act."

Elizabeth acknowledged that, with all the alarming stories about Tyler in circulation, it would be difficult indeed for Mary to reply in candor and impartiality when Abigail inquired about the young man, especially since "it is not sufficient to hear only upon one side—and know not anything of the merits of the cause." As consolation, Elizabeth assured Mary that "your own prudence and goodness of heart will direct you in the path of duty." Nevertheless, Elizabeth knew how easily Mary could be made to appear again in the role of troublemaker if she took seriously the tales about Tyler. And what both Mary and Elizabeth wanted to salvage out of this confusion was, as Elizabeth put it, "the satisfaction and happiness of all our families."

It was now a year after Nabby had departed. Tyler continued to appear the "lovesick swain," as Elizabeth described him in mid-August. He still created a great commotion about letters from Nabby, staring mournfully at her miniature, which he often wore suspended from his neck, and talking grandly of their future. Yet he did most of his legal business in the parlor of a lady he admired, and kept unseemly hours. The tormented Mary could no longer restrain from passing along at least a hint of misgiving to Abigail, so she wrote to say that she had begun two letters and burned them since the contents needed to be spoken in private.

Meanwhile, now that he was back in Massachusetts, John Quincy was dutifully spending time with Royall Tyler, and clearly enjoying it. Well into the autumn of 1785 they were virtually inseparable, unless business matters or the writing of long letters to Europe detained Tyler. Young Adams was, of course, unaware that his sister's message breaking off with Tyler was en route across the Atlantic. However, since he himself had been with Nabby only a few months before, John Quincy seemed to think that Royall Tyler overestimated his chances with Nabby. Aside from conveying his amusement at Tyler's confident talk of marriage, John Quincy mentioned no doubts in his diary about Tyler's integrity.

Then came the letters from England announcing Tyler's fate. Struggling to be fair, and herself rather fond of Tyler, Mary still hesitated to express any criticism of Tyler to Abigail. Her worry now was whether, if she kept silent and the rumors about Tyler's misbehavior reached John Adams, would he feel that he had been misled by Abigail and by Richard Cranch? And what if Nabby changed her mind and returned to Tyler?

These were good reasons for Mary to intrude by reporting to Abigail on Tyler's lifestyle, or so mused the loyal Mrs. Cranch as she wrote—and destroyed—more letters of warning. Finally, late in 1786 Mary decided to tell Abigail everything. She explained that she had not written because what she had to tell Abigail was mostly rumor. Mary also mentioned her opinion that Nabby had left for Europe erroneously believing that the Cranches coveted Tyler for their daughter Lucy. After these defenses for her silence, Mary proceeded to describe Tyler's behavior and the rumors about him.

Mary urged Abigail to hide these letters of disclosure, for she still worried that Nabby's mind might be changed. At this point, letters acclaiming the advent of Colonel William Smith had not yet reached Braintree or Haverhill, leaving Mary unaware of a new romance. Of course Mary praised Nabby highly, for had she not removed all of them from an awkward situation by her "prudent conduct"? Even Elizabeth Shaw applauded the breakup, much as she liked Royall Tyler. She accepted the charge that he had neglected Nabby by failing to write. And now that Nabby had shown such fortitude and wisdom, Elizabeth acclaimed the dismissal of Tyler as another victory for women. Nabby had shown that judgment must never give ground entirely to passion.

After sending Abigail word about Tyler, Mary displayed her own curiosity. What was the real cause, she asked Abigail, for Nabby's rejection of Royall Tyler? Was it simply his apparent failure to write often, or were there other reasons? Mary tried to phrase her inquiry carefully, but she could not quite disguise her astonishment that an engagement could be overthrown on so flimsy a basis as mail service. As far as could be seen, Tyler had written dutifully, or else he had duped the Cranches, Mary said. She had believed Tyler's claims that he was writing regularly and lengthily to his beloved. John Quincy was also a bit mystified by news of a broken engagement, claiming again that, while there were stories going about that Tyler pursued the ladies and strong drink, he personally could find no fault in Tyler.

To complicate life for the Cranches even more, Nabby's rejection of Tyler was, in theory, known only to him, except that Uncle Cotton Tufts, the message bearer, had let other family members in on the secret. So, with Tyler still her boarder, Mary and her household pretended to know nothing about Tyler's misfortune. It was the young man who, as Mary put it, opened the bag so that "the cat has jumped out." Tyler loudly announced that there had been a misunderstanding which he could set right in half an hour once he reached London, where he proposed to go as soon as business allowed.

Tyler, too, assumed that there must be more reason for losing Nabby than merely failing to write. He began charging that false and alarming reports about himself were sent to the Adamses. Soon everyone knew that he blamed Mary Cranch for bearing false witness. Much of what Tyler was saying reached Mary through the family of her brother-in-law, Joseph Palmer, with whom Royall was on friendly terms and with whom he boarded when affairs took him into Boston. The Palmers were very fond of Tyler, as most persons were, and sought to intercede for him, while trying to keep intact their good relationship with the Cranches.

Tyler's charges against her angered the usually kindhearted Mary, who now was convinced that she had indeed kept silent too long about Nabby's beau. As if to offer amends, Mary began reporting so much about Tyler in her letters to Abigail that the latter ordered her not to mention his name again. And yet Tyler continued to live at the Cranches until 1788, when Abigail and John returned to Braintree. Mary cooked for him, washed his linen, while the two managed to be correctly cordial. Tyler and Richard Cranch were political allies, for such was Royall's charm that he was chosen moderator of the town meeting—" he has popular talents, you know," Mary reminded Abigail. The team of Cranch and Tyler worked enthusiastically to make John Adams lieutenant governor of Massachusetts, a cause doomed by their unknowing candidate's absence abroad.

Perhaps Tyler still had hopes of reclaiming Nabby, for news of her marriage to Colonel Smith did not reach Braintree until the autumn of 1786. To strengthen his eligibility, Tyler built a magnificent windmill which was to produce many things, he claimed, including chocolate. He gave a party for the town when the mill was finished. Mary could not resist wondering if his law business was also intended to run by wind. He took his time about returning Nabby's letters to Uncle Tufts, and he still could be seen kissing her miniature in public. Yet his personal affairs were rumored to be in disarray because of poor management and imprudence. It was said he would not be able to meet payment on the estate he had purchased earlier when he was trying to win the Adamses' esteem.

All of this Mary passed on to Abigail, at a time when her sister wanted nothing to remind her that Tyler might have been treated shabbily. It was true, as Mary had to admit, that there were persons in Braintree and Boston who were eager to side with Royall Tyler, and to contend that young Miss Adams had simply been fickle and allowed the next man in her life to sweep her away. Such public gossip flourished as hints arrived from other Americans in England that Nabby had a new lover. The story spread that she had wed one of two candidates, William Vans Murray or Colonel David Humphreys, known to the Adams relatives as admirable men, and both of whom were in England at the time.

Criticism of Nabby grew so pointed that Mary had to visit with friends of Abigail's to explain that her niece had not been pressured by anyone (including Mary herself), but had moved into a new romance on her own initiative. But to Abigail, Mary was obviously irritated that she had to beg for a clear statement about Nabby's situation. Was she engaged, or perhaps married? Mary needed to know if she was to quell the rumors. Why all the mystery? she asked. Let us have details about this "sudden match." And who was this man Smith whose name was lately linked with Nabby?

Sister Elizabeth Shaw was even more direct with Abigail, clearly resenting that she knew nothing about any engagement until she first heard the story over tea when she visited Mercy Otis Warren. It was embarrassing, Elizabeth complained. And who, indeed, was this Smith about whom there were so many rumors? "Did you think we should not want to know the name of this favoured youth," Elizabeth chided Abigail. "Or did you think we were high priests this year and could divine?" Nor did Elizabeth soothe Abigail's guilty feelings by assuring her that she, Elizabeth, did not for a moment believe all the stories attributing "fickleness and inconstancy" to Nabby.

Royall Tyler first learned of Nabby's determination to wed from a letter carefully left open by the Cranches in a place where he was sure to see it. Lucy Cranch happened to be nearby when Tyler found it, and she reported that he turned to her and said, with studied reference to the summertime weather, " 'Tis a very changeable time, Miss Lucy.' " Others in the household were pleased and relieved when it became clear whom Nabby was to marry. Betsy Cranch rejoiced in her diary, "May all happiness attend her!" She added, "May past troubles and vexations serve but to enhance her present and future enjoyments." The day word arrived confirming the marriage to Colonel Smith, Betsy and her mother spent the evening knitting and chatting about the joyous outcome of cousin Nabby's vexing case.

Mary, however, wished she could have an hour to talk with Nabby herself, convinced that this would allow her to clear up the misunderstanding Mary still believed estranged her from the new Mrs. Smith. "I could convince her how tenderly I love her," Mary told Abigail, certain that her niece refused to believe that Mary had seen, before anyone else, the juvenile thoughtlessness which headed the list of Royall Tyler's less appealing qualities. "I shall leave it to her reason and good sense to determine whether I do not deserve a higher place in her affections than what her civility obliges her to give me as the sister of her dear Mamma."

There is only Mary's contention to suggest that Nabby retained her ill will toward her aunt, although she certainly must have received complaints about Mrs. Cranch's tale-bearing from friends in the Palmer family who had accepted Royall's protests that he had been victimized. Nabby's letters, of which only a few survive, give no clue. The relationship between Nabby and her Aunt Mary never seemed as warm as earlier, which may have been the result simply of time and distance.

Meanwhile Mary took the lead in a plan helpful to Royall Tyler as well as to John and Abigail Adams. Mary recognized that Tyler would not be able to pay for his Braintree estate, so she persuaded Abigail to buy it as a new home for the Adamses to inhabit upon their return to Massachusetts. This was carried out circumspectly, of course, with the faithful Uncle Cotton Tufts handling the transaction. As a result, the property—home to four generations of Adamses and known today as the Adams National Historic Site—came to Abigail and John as a sort of legacy by default from the Royall Tyler affair.

All the while she encouraged Abigail's real estate venture, Mary also sent her sister the latest bulletins concerning Royall Tyler. The latter's life had grown colorful, so there was much to report. In 1787 he had joined in the Commonwealth's suppression of Shays' Rebellion, an uprising in western Massachusetts by residents who claimed they merited more political and economic advantages. During that episode, while serving as aide to General Benjamin Lincoln, Major Tyler found himself in New York City on a military mission. There he had time to write a play which was produced in April 1787 and gained him fame at once.

The Contrast was the first theatrical production by an American author to be performed in the United States. Betsy recorded in her diary that Tyler's play, which comically pitted rural life against high society, received "great applause." Mary told Abigail that she was eager to read this work, which all critics had deemed an "extraordinary effort of genius." It is possible Mary meant to needle Abigail with this remarkable news, even though the older sister closed her letter with an elaborate apology for speaking of Tyler, a subject Abigail had banned. After describing Tyler's great triumph, Mary said, "But hush, hush, this is not keeping my promise. Forgive me."

Thereafter Tyler disappeared from the story of the Adams women. His career remained remarkable, but at the same time increasingly pathetic. He settled in Vermont, where he deepened his relationship with General Joseph Palmer and family, relatives of Mary and Richard. When they fell into destitution, he generously provided money and even found employment for needy members. In 1794 he married Mary Palmer, grandniece of Richard and Mary Cranch, after a romance as bewildering as Nabby's had been. His bride was eighteen, exactly half Royall's age.

Mary Palmer gave Royall Tyler eleven mostly successful children, nursed him through a long terminal illness, outlived him by forty years, and wrote a memoir which praised her husband and established the legend that Mary Cranch had destroyed Royall's engagement to Nabby Adams. Devoted as Mary Palmer Tyler was to her husband, however, she acknowledged that he had always remained something of a spoiled child. He dedicated his life to jurisprudence and writing, although none of his publications, except for his famous dramatic piece, won much attention.

Tyler served on the Vermont Supreme Court, and for several years was its chief justice. He also prepared an acclaimed compendium of Vermont court decisions. After 1813, his health and finances collapsed, and while he continued to produce children and literature, he eventually had to accept public charity. He died in 1826 after a long agonizing bout with cancer. In these circumstances, Mary Tyler proved herself a person of resolution, courage, love, and faith. When the cancer entered her husband's eye, she wrote in her journal, "Support us O God! under this and every dispensation of thy providence!"

Nabby, meanwhile, chose not to face the community where her romances had created such a sensation. She announced her intention to settle with her husband in New York, his native state. It was much easier for a woman to live in a new area, Nabby said, since a female could readily make friends. A man, on the other hand, needed useful connections. Therefore, Nabby said, it was her preference to leave Massachusetts, a prospect which obviously grieved Abigail far more than it did her daughter. As she sailed for America with Colonel Smith in the early summer of 1788, Nabby took with her a son, born ten months after her marriage, and named after his father. Soon thereafter, Abigail reached Braintree, where she took up the residence that had been the admired property of Royall Tyler.

From there Abigail witnessed the tragic result of the London wedding which brought together Nabby Adams and William Smith. What happened to Nabby illustrated for Mary, Elizabeth, and Abigail how, through an unwise marriage, a woman's life could sink into despair and helplessness. Abigail eventually confessed to her sisters that for Nabby the only prospect was "humiliation." Neither Mary nor Elizabeth ever reminded Abigail that she had rapturously praised Colonel Smith's "delicacy of sentiment and honour" when he prepared to marry Nabby in London. Within two years, the virtues which Abigail ascribed to Smith had become a mockery.

7

No Relief

When Abigail and John Adams returned to Massachusetts from London in June 1788, there was new excitement in the lives of Mary Cranch and Elizabeth Shaw and their families. By sharing vicariously in Abigail's next career as wife of the vice president and then president of the United States, the sisters found their existences enlivened and their outlooks challenged. So distracted were Abigail, Mary, and Elizabeth by political issues, that at times they were momentarily freed from what seemed the unrelieved strain of family disappointment, illness, and grief. Nabby's difficulties with William Smith were to account for only part of the darkness surrounding the sisters.

For a time, things went well enough, although the house Abigail had bought for herself and John seemed cramped when they returned to Braintree. Nevertheless, the Adamses were elated to be back in the village, and the reluctance they felt at leaving again was genuine. In April 1789, John took office in New York as vice president. After a year, the federal capital moved to Philadelphia, where Abigail often stayed with John as he completed two terms under George Washington. He then became president in March 1797, serving for four years. Near the close of his term Abigail had to travel even farther from her New England relatives, for the District of Columbia had become the new seat of national government.

Throughout these thrilling years, the letters between Abigail, Mary, and Elizabeth sparkled with the keen interest they shared in public affairs. Their exchanges frequently softened the often unhappy tidings the sisters also exchanged. Abigail so enjoyed sharing what went on in her life with Mary and Elizabeth that John sometimes had to beg his wife to hold her tongue. This hindrance proved doubly essential when Abigail became first lady. She conceded that difficulties lay ahead: "I have been so used to a freedom of sentiment that I know not how to place so many guards about me." Still, she knew that as the president's wife she must "look at every word before I utter it, and to impose silence upon myself when I long to talk."

Abigail felt she could trust her sisters. She gave thanks for their discretion and also for their sympathy when she faced the difficult task of succeeding Martha Washington. The new first lady received what she acknowledged was "a charming letter" of encouragement from Elizabeth: "Surely she openeth her mouth with wisdom and upon her tongue is the law of kindness." Abigail had long since discarded the tendency to be condescending toward her younger sister. Instead, Abigail told Elizabeth and Mary she feared that being the first lady might alter her, and asked her sisters "to watch over my conduct and if at any time they [her sisters] perceive any alteration in me in respect to them, arising as they may suppose from my situation in life, I beg they should with the utmost freedom acquaint me with it."

Once again Elizabeth offered support. Her only concern about her now famous sister, she said, was that the strain might harm her; she was already frail. "That glow in your features which I have contemplated with so much satisfaction," Elizabeth wrote, "I should be grieved to see injured by sickness or any disaster." After assuring Abigail that "nature and grace have both inspired in your favor," Elizabeth closed with the sort of words that made her so beloved: "For that beauty which depends principally upon the mind, upon the Divinity that stirs within, cannot easily be defamed by time, sickness, or any accidental circumstances."

Actually the sisters had more misgivings about John than about Abigail, and expressed them candidly. In 1798 Mary warned her brother-in-law, that in his presidential messages he appeared to be trying "to flatter" the people. Mary urged Abigail to put John on his guard against this unfortunate tactic, and reminded her that when it came to appeasing the public, John Adams "never did know how to do it." Like all Quincy's residents, Mary recognized that John Adams' natural style was direct and caustic.

Elizabeth, surrounded by students of composition in the Atkinson Academy, warned John that his addresses to Congress were much too complex. The ideas he advanced might be clear to him, but he left many lesser minds uncertain, an assessment, Elizabeth added, which was shared by many in her neighborhood. Abigail agreed and pointed out to the unfortunate John that his inaugural address in 1797 had been especially difficult both to read and to comprehend.

While Mary kept saying it was absurd for her to advise the president of the United States on any subject, she continued offering counsel. In mid-

1798, she was pleased to be able to send an encouraging report. John now seemed to express himself "with more ease and clearness," said his sister-in-law, who then added an aside to Abigail, "You see I dare to criticize upon him, great as he is. He will call me saucy, I suppose, but I don't care." Mary assured Abigail that, no matter how many suggestions she might offer, she remained a staunch supporter of the administration. This was also true of Elizabeth. Both sisters, therefore, along with most of New England, were dismayed when John Adams startled his party by avoiding war with France during 1798 and 1799.

It was not France's abuse of American neutrality during the Napoleonic wars that outraged Elizabeth and Mary. What they opposed was the atheistic licentiousness which they believed revolutionary France was trying to spread across the globe. Abigail concurred, indicating to Mary in July 1798 that she yearned to see Congress declare war on France. If it failed to do so, that body "must be answerable for the consequences." When President Adams skirted open hostilities with a foe seemingly bent on destroying chastity, the Bible, and every other element of Christian society, the sisters were indignant.

Mary, Abigail, and Elizabeth believed France's campaign masked an aim to convert the universal body politic into a den of wolves. Abigail summed up what she and her sisters contended: "Liberty which poetry represents as a goddess, History describes as a cannibal." As graphic evidence of the danger caused by supporters of France, Abigail described for Elizabeth and Mary what Francophiles were doing to life in Philadelphia. The first lady claimed the American capital had become more debauched than London. At least in England the lower classes respected their betters, Abigail sniffed. She referred to a postal worker who had somehow annoyed her as a "Blockhead," one of those "underbidden who cannot read the direction upon his papers; such kind of people who want the reigns of government."

Corruption was even making it difficult to run a decent household, Abigail complained. No domestic detail in the life of the first lady failed to interest Mary and Elizabeth. Abigail told them how she arose at 5:00 A.M. in Philadelphia and worked with the servants until nearly 12:00, when she dressed and received callers until 3:00 P.M. After dinner, she took a carriage ride and then retired from public view at 7:00 P.M. This daily regimen was modest, according to Abigail, when compared to the demands made on her when she traveled. For example, in the summer of 1797 Abigail decided she had enough of Philadelphia and wanted to spend the summer in Quincy. She set out amid heat so intense that both she and the horses nearly perished. She halted the carriage often and entered an inn where she could "entirely undress myself and lie down on the bed." At night it was too hot to sleep, even though Abigail stretched out on the floor, hoping for a breeze.

This ordeal was undertaken in part, at least, because of Abigail's disgust with the pride, laziness, and incompetence of her servants, all corrupted by the democratic spirit infecting the city. Her description of the grief caused by her hired help astounded Mary and Elizabeth, even though they had been informed by their sister that Philadelphia's populace constituted "a vile, low tribe." From this community Abigail, in the space of eighteen months, had selected and promptly discharged seven females who filled the post of household cook. "Not a virtuous woman among them," she assured her appalled sisters; most had proved to be drunkards. Finally, Abigail found a woman with excellent written recommendations and installed her in the kitchen. Alas, this latest cook soon became so intoxicated that she had to be "carried to bed" shouting obscene proposals to every male within earshot. Abigail wasted no time shooing the men servants out of the house until the cook could be quieted.

Women in Philadelphia were being degraded, Abigail assured her sisters, because of the infiltration of European females. When Abigail discovered that the black women of Philadelphia seemed to have escaped the contagion, she recruited her servants from among them. Philadelphia might be a den of iniquity but Abigail returned to it, reluctantly, as often as her health permitted, because of her responsibility to John. Philadelphia was the "place which it is my duty to occupy." There "I have a part to discharge."

It also put her closer to New York, where Nabby and Colonel William Smith had settled upon returning from England in 1788. Nabby's life had quickly disintegrated. Her husband proved to be a spendthrift who expected money to fall into his lap either through a political appointment or through land speculation. The dashing colonel was no more than what Louisa Adams later described him as, "a gay, deluded boy" who was "born to be the charm and plague of doating woman." Colonel William Stephens Smith managed all his life to avoid facing his shortcomings, preferring to dream that ease and wealth were his by some vague birthright.

Nabby needed little time to foresee what a wretched partnership her marriage would become. Soon after reaching the United States in 1788, Nabby wrote with uncharacteristic passion to her brother John Quincy of "extravagance, dissipation, and folly." William Smith had been attracted at once to the speculative craze in America, which drew men toward what Nabby called "those very airy fabricks and visionary castles of splendor." Surely, she contended, enough tragic examples of what befell those who sought something for nothing abounded "to deter others from pursuing so fallacious a plan of life." After this outburst, further comments by Nabby were rare, as she became even more taciturn, to the dismay of her

mother, aunts, and cousins, all of whom yearned somehow to rescue her
disappointing marriage.

One likely advantage from William Smith's vagabond career was that
Nabby missed many opportunities to become pregnant. At first it seemed
she might set the family's record for fecundity, or so her mother feared.
One son, William, had been born to the Smiths in April 1787, ten months
after their marriage. A year later, when Nabby sailed for home in spring
1788, she was pregnant with a second son, John, born in November of
that year, and within a short time the Smiths expected a third child, a son
born in August 1790. This lad, named Thomas Hollis Smith, died in
infancy through circumstances unknown today. None of the surviving
family papers describe the baby's death.

The manuscripts only allude to Nabby's next pregnancy, which apparently ended in miscarriage about the time little Thomas died. Then, with
her husband often away from home, Nabby was released from these
relentless conceptions until mid-1794, when she again became pregnant.
Her last child, a much desired daughter, was born in February 1795. This
was Caroline, who became her mother's solace and companion, especially
since the little girl's brothers were usually placed with grandmother Abigail
and her sisters. These older women needed no convincing that Nabby's
sons could easily be corrupted if they grew up near their father.

The Cranches had difficulty feeling sympathy for Colonel Smith himself.
Perhaps it was a preference for Royall Tyler, but Mary and her family
wished not to see much of Nabby's husband. They seemed readily to
forgive Nabby for not writing to them after she was back in America, but
they were insulted by the haughty style Colonel Smith displayed toward
them. He "look'd down," they complained. The Quincy relatives felt only
compassion for Nabby as it grew evident that her husband lived in New
York with "a glitter" built only upon "the hope of wealth."

Abigail had waited expectantly for her son-in-law to pursue some
successful career, but he skirted the subject whenever she brought it up.
When he did not find gold on the streets of the new republic and was
offered no government job, the only recourse was for him and Nabby to
join Vice President and Mrs. Adams in their rented house in New York.
Yet even this advantageous location did not bring Smith favorable attention
from his former commander, George Washington. At last Smith persuaded
some American businessmen to make use of his purported experience and
connections in London by sending him there as their representative.

Wandering from reality was a specialty of Smith's. He left for England
alone late in 1790, saying only that he knew there was wealth ahead.
Nothing came of the venture. Abigail relayed to her son-in-law the rumor
that President Washington was relenting and that a fine federal job was

soon to be his. Smith hastened back, but found no place at the public trough. So he returned to London in 1792, taking Nabby and their two sons with him. He claimed to have a two-year term as business agent for American interests. The Smith family's departure was delayed when the Colonel came down with what was vaguely called a bilious complaint, related to his fondness for food and drink.

Apparently, the one brief period of happiness in Nabby's marriage was this stay in England during 1792. The Smiths spent much time with the American consul, Joshua Johnson, and his family, even sharing a summer house in Brighton with them. Johnson's daughter Louisa was soon to be Nabby's sister-in-law, the future Mrs. John Quincy Adams. She was among the few relatives who had a cheerful recollection of Nabby: "She was one of the most placid, quiet beings I ever saw, cold in her glacial manners, but when she laughed and entered into the spirit of our gaiety, which was very often, she would romp or dance and partake of all the jokes like one of us." During that summer of 1792, Nabby would occasionally unbend, and, Louisa remembered, was "perfectly adored" by the Johnsons.

Louisa always contended that beneath "the appearance of coldness and reserve" Nabby was a very affectionate creature. "I loved her then," said Louisa, "and still better when I became her sister." Louisa thought marriage had plunged Nabby from her high station into "the misery of poverty and obloquy." Yet she endured this with such fortitude and amazing devotion to Colonel Smith that Louisa claimed sainthood for Nabby. Meanwhile, the colonel was writing home to boast about this summer with the Johnsons. "Tho' we are but private people, we cannot help being a little fashionable," he explained to John Adams.

The Smith family debts mounted, and Nabby quickly discovered there was little basis to her husband's role as a commercial agent. The Smiths returned to the United States early in 1793 where the undaunted colonel embarked full-time on speculation. He believed the stories circulating about the quick wealth that could be made from rising land prices. Not hesitating to trade on his father-in-law's name, Smith managed to borrow money. Even John Quincy Adams turned over most of his modest savings to him, joining others who were impressed by his brother-in-law's monumental self-assurance. All these investments were lost, and Smith could not even pay the interest on his debts. By now it was 1796, and Nabby's husband disappeared. Rumor spoke of his being in the west arranging a triumph which would restore him to public grace.

Nabby was left alone with her tiny daughter, for she had sent her sons to the Atkinson Academy where, out of their father's reach, they might mature in the uplifting presence of their great-aunt Elizabeth Peabody and her new husband. To the shame brought by a husband's behavior,

Nabby's response was to become even more withdrawn, though she occasionally displayed her emotions, as when she spoke of her "mortifying situation," and of feeling alone and unprotected in the "wide world."

To her brother John Quincy, with whom she shared her thoughts more than with Abigail, Nabby talked bitterly about President Washington's failure to provide the federal appointment which could have reduced her plight. When her life failed to improve, Nabby's letters became careless, and her spelling and penmanship deteriorated. Her observations, no longer stilted and formal, seemed almost childlike. From the lonely spot on Long Island where Smith had left her before he vanished, she broke down while writing to her father. She told him that now her main grief was the humiliating life ahead for her children, and she prayed that her heart "may be steeled against the misfortunes which await us." She brought John Adams to tears by begging his forgiveness for sharing her sorrows with him when he was so busy. To ease John's anguish, Abigail tried intercepting Nabby's letters.

After the colonel had not written to Nabby in nearly two years, Abigail implored her daughter to accept that he had abandoned her and that she move to Quincy. Nabby resisted, and remained in the rural environs of New York City, rushing into town at the slightest rumor that her husband had been spotted. In 1797, when the colonel's whereabouts had been unknown for many months, Nabby confessed to John Quincy, "I only wonder that I have retained my senses." Nabby was candid to this extent only with her father and brother, however.

During most of this sad story, the old strain between Nabby and her mother seemed to deepen. Abigail's letters were hardly encouraging, even if well-intentioned. Having helped hustle Nabby into Smith's arms in 1786, Abigail now was eager to see her daughter free of him, and often complained that her daughter was "unapproachable" when Abigail tried to bring her into the Adamses' official family in Philadelphia. Nabby's somber reluctance was due in large part to a fear of obliging her beloved father to make embarrassing explanations to friends about his daughter's presence. Yet more than once Nabby had no alternative but to take refuge with the president and first lady.

In Philadelphia, the Adamses lived on the southeast corner of Sixth and Market streets in a residence previously occupied by President and Mrs. Washington, and before them, Robert Morris. Here Nabby grew even more withdrawn. "I could not converse with her," Abigail reported to Mary. "I saw her heart too full." All of which caused Abigail to denounce "the folly and madness of speculation and extravagance" in frequent outbursts that Nabby dreaded. One wonders who regretted more the choice of Smith as Nabby's mate—Abigail or Nabby.

Finally, in 1798, Nabby was prevailed upon to bring little Caroline for a summer at the farm in Quincy. There, far from Philadelphia and the affairs of the state, John could spend time with Nabby. When John reluctantly returned to Philadelphia in November, Nabby was left behind to winter with Abigail, whose health did not allow her to make the trip. Nabby's distress at this prospect was so apparent that Abigail bade her leave and catch up with her father. Nabby was packed and gone within half an hour. Abigail explained to neighbors that Nabby wanted to renew her search for Colonel Smith. To Aunt Mary Cranch, Nabby had confided, "I sometimes feel as if I stood alone in the world."

Finally, William Smith reappeared late in 1798 to be greeted by a silent wife, demanding creditors, and a cool reception from Abigail Adams. Smith used the same strategy that had helped win Nabby's hand—appealing to Abigail. This time he literally begged the first lady to arrange a federal appointment for him. The colonel assured Abigail that, with such a job and his excellent connections, he could quiet the clamor his creditors were raising. He insisted that during his long absence he had written to Nabby, and loudly claimed that the letters must have been miscarried.

In all likelihood, William Smith was more foolish than evil. Many years later, both John and Abigail were inclined to be forgiving, despite the enormity of their son-in-law's sins. He insisted to Abigail that his record as husband and father was spotless, and he expressed astonishment over "the horrid state that I find myself in." Smith continued forever arguing that, given time, he could redeem himself, despite having been "wounded in my honor by the false statements of wicked and designing men." He was tempted, Smith once told Abigail, to "wrap myself in my mantle and retire in disgust from the world."

Abigail heard repeatedly from the colonel that he was just on the verge of fiscal triumph—although he coyly refrained from telling his mother-in-law about his plans lest she deem them "visionary and delusive." Abigail did aid him, out of concern for Nabby and family pride. The first lady seemed always ready to urge President Adams to help a troubled relative by providing a government job, and Nabby's shiftless husband was no exception. John complied reluctantly and tried to get the Senate to confirm Colonel Smith as the army's adjutant general, since the nation was preparing for possible war against France. The Senate scoffed at this recommendation.

Finally Smith had to accept the lowly command of a regiment, with the understanding that he keep his wife with him. Nabby joined her husband in New Jersey, where they lived in a log hut near Smith's troops. Although John Adams had succumbed to family insistence and aided the colonel, the president felt humiliated. Nothing in life, including his alcoholic son

Charles' behavior, had "disgraced me so much as this man," John told
Abigail early in 1799. "His pay will not feed his dogs, and his dogs must
be fed if his children starve. What a folly!"

Still, John conceded, there was nothing vicious or unpatriotic about
Smith, so with the support of Alexander Hamilton (who may actually have
been seeking to enlarge the President's embarrassments) John won Senate
consent in mid-1800 to appoint William Smith surveyor of the Port of
New York. Nabby's elated husband prepared immediately to build a
palatial home, proposing an exact replica of Washington's Mount Vernon
residence. The mansion was never constructed, for Smith, as before,
retained not a penny that came his way.

In 1801 Nabby and her husband were visited in New York City by John
Quincy, who reported back to Abigail that William Smith and his friends
seemed interested only in gaming, hunting, and quick money. Nabby took
her brother away from this clamor and into another room where the two
quietly played chess. These signs that Nabby's husband was unrepentant
caused Abigail to tell Elizabeth Peabody how Nabby's woes were such "as
to become not a parent to relate, but such as bring the gray hairs with
sorrow to the grave."

For a few years Nabby's life was calm, if uneasy. She even came to
Quincy in 1805, after her mother and brother John Quincy pleaded that
she visit. During this stay, Nabby appeared in Massachusetts society, going
with her brother to that annual gala, the Harvard commencement. It
required about two hours to travel the distance between Quincy and
Cambridge, but the Adamses undertook the journey casually and often.
In November 1805 Nabby returned to New York, where she had the
comfort of seeing John Quincy Adams, now a United States senator,
associating with Colonel Smith, even though the latter had never repaid a
large debt he owed to her brother. The two men rode together, did some
visiting, and John Quincy particularly enjoyed studying engravings and
books which the Emperor Napoleon had sent as gifts to the New York
Academy of Arts and which were in the custody of Smith, in his role as
chief of customs.

Such amity was short-lived, for early the next year, 1806, Nabby's
husband was removed from his office and clapped into prison, the charges
being unpaid debts and alleged assistance to South American revolution-
aries said to have used American soil, with Smith's aid, in planning an
invasion of Venezuela. Nabby's husband was indignant. Would his friends,
he asked, "consent that I should be sacrificed and my wife and children
deprived of bread to shelter men in higher station for their want of
consistency, political integrity, and firmness of mind?" Smith, in other

words, charged that Jeffersonian politicians had rigged the indictment against him.

As always, William Smith protested that he was an innocent victim, and demanded indignantly that if he must lose his customs post, it should be given to his brother—whose reputation, by the way, was as unenviable as the colonel's. With both civil and criminal prosecution confronting Smith, Nabby's family once more implored her to leave him and take up residence in Massachusetts. She refused, and actually moved onto the prison grounds, living in a tiny cottage with her husband until he was acquitted of the criminal charges because of insufficient evidence.

From Atkinson, where Nabby's sons had grown up, Elizabeth Peabody wondered what ambition, pride, and avarice would do next to humiliate Nabby. The family had not long to wait for an answer. After the colonel was discharged from prison, he was stripped of his employment and, though penniless, obliged to dodge more angry creditors than ever. Late in 1806 Nabby and her husband faced eviction from their rented quarters and had no place to turn. Not that this seemed to dismay Smith, who continued "to flatter himself with the hope of an appointment—I know not why," as John Quincy reported to his wife Louisa. These circumstances forced Nabby even more deeply into herself, and she no longer wrote even to her brother.

Hearing of Nabby's plight, Abigail writhed helplessly during the cold winter of 1807. In February Nabby roused herself long enough to send a letter, not to her mother, but to her father. The epistle apparently was a vivid description of William Smith's numerous sins. Abigail intercepted the letter and promptly advised Nabby that it was imprudent for John Adams to see it, so great would be his wrath. Once more, Nabby was made to seem like an inept child, no matter that she had turned to her father with a story of husbandly misbehavior worse than anything Abigail dared imagine. Nabby's letter was destroyed, and Abigail refused even to summarize its contents for John Quincy, telling him to use his imagination in conjuring up the dreadful circumstances surrounding Nabby.

The Smiths soon parted, Nabby allowing John Quincy to bring her as a refugee to her parents' home in March 1807. The colonel fled his enemies by hiding in a remote part of upper New York, where some of the Smith clan provided asylum. It was a terrible journey to New England for Nabby, since the stagecoach was an uncomfortable wreck driven by a drunk. To worsen matters, as the vehicle careened around a corner, John Quincy's bags were thrown off and precious books and clothes were dragged through the mud. But they reached Boston, and Nabby seemed happier, living with John Quincy and Louisa as often as she could reasonably escape

Abigail's residence. Nabby endeared herself to Louisa by comforting her during the last months of a difficulty pregnancy, and she pleased her brother by playing chess with him, a game he and Louisa found it wise not to attempt. John Quincy's impatience with his wife was much greater than with his sister.

Abigail, meanwhile, pondered her daughter's prolonged silence. Confiding in Elizabeth, Abigail said of her daughter, "She is a woman of great firmness of mind, you know, from her youth up. She has had ample scope for the exercise of it in the vicissitudes of fortune which have attended her. To herself are confined her troubles. She never makes them a subject of complaint to her most intimate friends." Nevertheless, difficulties obviously bore upon Nabby's outlook: "They silently wear upon her spirits, and produce many a silent tear."

It was expected that Nabby would remain with her relatives permanently, but this was not her husband's plan. To the dismay of everyone, Colonel Smith suddenly appeared in Quincy in January 1808, insisting that Nabby must return with him to Hamilton, New York, where they could live with his relatives. Nabby obediently went along, taking care to leave her sons under the direction of old John Adams. Once departed, Nabby entered a long silence which lasted until early in 1811. Abigail feared she would never see her daughter again, and marveled that such unrelieved disappointment and trouble could afflict anyone in the twenty years since Nabby had returned to America.

But that interval had produced more than Nabby's woes to distress Abigail, Mary, and Elizabeth. For instance, during the 1790s, there appeared to be no way the sisters could prevent Abigail's son Charles from destroying himself. Charles was the second of the Adams sons. Like John Quincy he had a chance to profit from study abroad when he traveled in Europe with his father. Charles longed to return to Abigail, however, and so his stay in Europe was brief. His self-indulgent ways as a student at Harvard troubled his parents. Eventually he married Sally Smith, a sister of Nabby's husband, thereby binding himself to in-laws who were less than helpful in his predicament. Charles' efforts as an attorney and politician were hampered by the same dreams of easy success which hindered William Smith and his brothers, and by relentless intemperance. By 1800, Charles had become a pauper and was nearly dead from alcoholism. His refuge was Nabby's home in New York City, where she cared for him as he was dying late that year. He left two daughters, who, with their mother, came to Quincy and became part of Abigail's household.

These refugees arrived at the Adams residence at a time when Mary Cranch was wondering if her only son, William, would add another tragic chapter to the family annals. Young William Cranch had received every attention and encouragement from his parents and two older sisters, Betsy and Lucy. His father used the greatest patience in teaching William to master Latin, an attainment Richard Cranch considered vital for any career in which discourse with cultivated persons was likely. Painfully aware that their son would not have the enviable and unique opportunities that Abigail's sons John Quincy and Charles received, the Cranches still sought to give William every benefit permitted by their limited library and funds.

Born in 1769, William was the youngest of Mary's children. As a male, he naturally received the most attention, which the astute Mary feared might make him fail to appreciate his sisters. She warned her son that brothers usually did not realize what sacrifices their sisters made to advance them in life. Remembering the tragic results of the pampering her own brother had received, and conscious of the advantages inherent in being a boy, Mary urged her son not to be like other young men. He must recognize and remember the debt he owed his sisters, who, in a few years, "will look to you for protection."

To enhance his opportunities to become "a great and good man," Mary sent her son to Haverhill in 1783 where Uncle John Shaw prepared him for entry into Harvard College. Mary was anxious when William reached the age that she and her sisters feared was so perilous for a young man, the period from sixteen to twenty-two, which the sisters watched prayerfully, hopeful that their sons' lust would be governable. Since every effort must be made to keep the youths in wholesome surroundings, a collegiate career loomed as a great hazard, as Charles Adams' experience had evidently shown.

Harvard seemed a paradox to Mary Cranch. The school offered learning and the credentials necessary for future success, but it also exposed young males in their most vulnerable years to every dangerous temptation. Mary and her sisters were inclined to believe that if a son could pass unscathed through Harvard, his morals could probably withstand any subsequent menace. Thus, while Mary looked to Elizabeth's help in arming William Cranch for the dangers of college life, she did not shirk her own duties, such as explaining that "forward" girls must be avoided. These women, Mary informed her son, were most likely to be found among the "lower classes."

At college William never got beyond Mary's influence. She made his clothes; she worried over his finances. Did he owe money? "I dont chuse you should be in debt to anyone"—so she often scraped together a little cash for him, no matter how scarce it was in the Cranch house. Cleanliness was a special concern. Mary once directed that, when next in Boston, her son should buy a cake of soap (was none to be had in Cambridge? one wonders) "and scour your neck or we shall never get the dirt out of your collars." As it was, Mary complained, she was rubbing his shirts to pieces trying to make them clean. Whether it was a "Nankeen coat," curtains for his dormitory room, or tasty cakes, Mary labored to supply young William's needs.

It was her son's mind and soul that Mary tended with the greater concern. Knowing that the college library was famous for acquiring books which beguiled young believers into infidelity, Mary shipped her son many volumes designed to help him fight Satan. She recommended in particular Adam Smith's *The Theory of Moral Sentiments* and the works of Joseph Butler, at one time the Bishop of Durham, whose *Analogy of Religion* was especially cherished by Mary for its able defense of Christianity against the arguments of the Deists. Mary admonished William to be serious in his study of Hebrew, reminding him that it was his father's favorite subject. Above all, Mary cautioned her son not to stray from fundamental Christianity, even though every "coxcomb" jested at true religion. Meanwhile she persuaded Uncle Tufts to send William eight gallons of good cider.

William Cranch was fifteen when he entered Harvard. He graduated in 1787, then studied law with William Dawes, who sat on the Massachusetts Supreme Court. After this, he settled in Haverhill, claiming to see a much brighter professional future there than in his hometown of Braintree. Haverhill also offered the more cheerful household of Elizabeth and John Shaw. With his cousins, the sons of Abigail Adams, young Cranch shared a great affection for his Aunt Elizabeth, who in the eyes of her nephews appeared as a comparatively young, attractive woman with a sympathy for the outlook of youthful males. William Cranch remained in Haverhill for four years and flourished.

Mary's son was so impatient with his success, however, that he, despite warnings from relatives, submitted to the enticements of quick money. William joined land speculators in the newly formed District of Columbia, where the federal capital was about to relocate. William's decision was nearly fatal, and his ensuing plight overpowered his parents, who were already upset by his decision to leave New England.

The move was an aftermath of William's romance with Nancy Greenleaf, whom he met because she was the sister of Margaret Greenleaf Dawes, wife of his mentor, Judge Dawes. Nancy and Margaret were among the fifteen children of the prosperous Boston druggist and mercantilist, William Greenleaf and his wife, Mary Brown Greenleaf. Another daughter, Rebecca Greenleaf married Noah Webster, the man of letters and lexicographer. These sisters had a brother, James, who ranks among the most enterprising of early Americans. It was he who caused the downfall of William Cranch.

Mary Cranch and her sisters admired the Greenleaf family, so that

William's marriage to Nancy was welcomed. The Cranches had a quite different reaction when Nancy's brother James offered William an alluring opportunity to make money quickly by exchanging the safe and proper life in Haverhill for the District of Columbia, where William was to aid Greenleaf in developing three thousand building lots which Greenleaf and his partner, Robert Morris, the financial hero of the Continental Congress, had purchased on credit from government agents at reduced prices by pledging to improve the land. Through this sort of speculation, Greenleaf and Morris momentarily owned one-third of the newly created capital city. The prospect bedazzled William Cranch, who hastened to enlist in the scheme.

William and Nancy moved to Washington in 1795. Two years later, the enterprise was bankrupt, leaving young Cranch destitute. The entire Greenleaf family was also ruined, for James had persuaded all his relatives to back his venture. There were also major losses to many Boston friends. The ambitious team of Greenleaf and Morris was imprisoned for debt in Philadelphia, a fate Mary Cranch's son barely escaped. The Cranch family was devastated. Not only was their promising son apparently implicated and disgraced; James' brother John Greenleaf, a blind musician who had recently married William Cranch's sister Lucy, had also lost everything. Mary Cranch suddenly had a son and a daughter who were penniless.

This tragedy particularly distressed Aunt Elizabeth Peabody since she had sought to discourage young Cranch from following the lure of city riches. "All in life is vanity," Elizabeth reminded Abigail. "Man is born to trouble as the sparks fly upward." Having watched Colonel Smith's deluded career, Abigail was especially fervent in her condemnation of "this spirit of speculation." One feature of William Cranch's plight, however, consoled both Abigail and Elizabeth.

They admired the courage being displayed by Nancy Greenleaf Cranch, William's wife, as she exemplified the strength women often had to show in marriage. When her husband's misfortune left him in a seriously depressed mood, Nancy displayed her own version of the Greenleaf family's mettle. Abigail Adams, who was not easily impressed, informed her nephew, William Cranch, that he had a mate of whom they were all proud. Nancy now ranked high in Abigail's "esteem and regard" for "her prudence, her discretion, and many other excellent qualities."

Back in Quincy, Mary and Richard Cranch worried themselves into illness over their far-off son, whose extravagant ventures were beyond his parents' understanding. The only hope of saving William seemed to involve Mary's perpetual benefactor, the first lady. "What do you think?" Mary asked Abigail. "I know so little myself." Abigail proceeded at once to the rescue. First, it was necessary to rouse young Cranch from his "melancholy," as Abigail described it. She shared her concern with Elizabeth, and suggested she not even hint to Mary how dangerous William's mood was. But Mary recognized what was happening and announced that William was destroying his usefulness "for want of fortitude and resolute spirit."

Positive thinking was Abigail's remedy, so she tried to convince William that he still could succeed. All he needed to do was "think himself the most sensible and capable man with whom he is acquainted." This was a tactic Abigail had dependably employed with her husband and sons when they lost self-esteem, a frequent malady among Adams males. William Cranch also received much practical counsel from Aunt Abigail, usually concerning the needs at hand. Ought he not, Abigail asked pointedly, accept his brother-in-law Noah Webster's offer of a position in a Massachusetts publishing venture?

The rescue of William Cranch was suspenseful, and ended thrillingly. Time was short, for Abigail's capacity to help required John's continuing as president, already an unlikely prospect in 1799. The first lady tried immediately to have her nephew selected as clerk of the U.S. Supreme Court. The plan failed early in 1800 when an undeniably superior candidate was chosen. This left direct presidential intervention as the last resort. William's Uncle John bowed to Abigail's prodding and named his nephew to be a District of Columbia commissioner, a position calling for the supervision of property and buildings. While not particularly glamorous, this job seemed the best Abigail could manage. Then came President Adams' decision in the last moments of his administration to appoint twenty-three federal judges. Thanks to Aunt Abigail, William Cranch found himself taking a seat on the District of Columbia Circuit Court in March 1801.

William did not disappoint. The opportunity provided by his Adams relatives was all his naturally hardworking nature seemed to require. He recovered his spirit and performed so well in his new post that the next president, Thomas Jefferson, appointed him chief judge of the District judiciary in 1805. William Cranch served in this capacity for fifty-four years, becoming one of America's most respected practitioners and authors in the field of jurisprudence. With Nancy, he also received another reward. Thirteen children were born to them, which did not keep Nancy Greenleaf Cranch from living to 1843, famed till the end for her happy, playful nature. William died in 1855, at age eighty-six, totaling one year more than his father, Richard, whom he came to resemble in certain respects, particularly in his deeply religious and tender nature.

William was not the only Cranch child entangled with the Greenleaf family. After her son's deliverance, Mary fretted over her daughter Lucy, who seemed bound in as difficult a marriage as Betsy Norton's. The family's ugly duckling, Lucy had remained in the background until the age of twenty-eight, when she married John, the blind brother of James and Nancy Greenleaf. Before that event, Lucy's only notable accomplishment was to be the recipient of Aunt Abigail Adams' best statement about women's place in the scheme of life. Intending probably to arouse her niece, whom she considered much too passive, Abigail informed Lucy in 1787 that women must move "beyond the limits of the drawing room and kitchen to which even some men of sense have been illiberal enough to wish us confined." How, Abigail wondered, could men not wish to see women rise above "the present pernicious modes of fashionable levities and polite accomplishments"?

For plain Lucy's benefit, her aunt emphasized that a cultivated mind did wonders to improve the female appearance. A woman simply needed to bestir herself, Abigail insisted, and her countenance would improve along with the mind. If she sought to be amiable and useful, a woman would find her appearance "ennobled as her heart is elevated," and she would become, said Abigail, "a pleasing companion to the man of science and of sensibility." Elizabeth Shaw was more optimistic about Lucy, for she admired what she considered the niece's excellent temper. "Her constitution will never be impaired by any violent agitation of spirits, for she is sensible enough, gentle, tranquil, not greatly elated or depressed." But it was true, Elizabeth conceded to Abigail, that Lucy was far less engaging than her sister Betsy, and thus "rather withdraws than obtrudes upon your notice." Among others who sensed that Lucy might have hidden resources was Nabby. Writing in 1790, when her own troubles were mounting, Nabby congratulated her cousin Lucy for possessing "the greatest of all blessings," which was "a contented mind."

Unfortunately, Lucy's surviving letters are so few that no one can discover whether her placid exterior covered a similar spirit within. Years later, however, when Lucy was very elderly and still living with John Greenleaf in the old Cranch house, her cousin Charles Francis Adams observed that Lucy's life had been one of unvarying calmness amid meager circumstances. The little money John Greenleaf had was lost in his brother's debacle, but somehow Lucy and John managed to raise a large family. John taught music and served as a much underpaid church organist, at least in Abigail Adams' opinion.

Even Mary marveled at Lucy's spirit amid adversity. No matter how severe matters got, Lucy and John remained cheerful and hopeful. When they began to have children, Lucy's mother disapproved—because of John's blindness—much as she enjoyed her grandchildren. The Greenleafs had seven youngsters in all, none of whom seems to have brought grief to their parents and grandparents, surely more than Mary, Elizabeth, and

Abigail could say about their other offspring. When Abigail was dying, her principal nurse was Lucy Cranch Greenleaf, whose gentle, durable nature comforted not only the patient but all the Adamses. Lucy lived to within a year of her eightieth birthday, and proved to the satisfaction of her family and community that she was a worthy successor to her mother, Mary Cranch.

Abigail could have used Lucy's strength when John Adams was defeated for reelection in 1800. The first lady could not visualize a way to save the American Republic from degeneration. According to her, the new nation was falling from the high estate to which early leaders like her husband had taken it. When she and John were young, his bleak opinion of human nature seemed overly harsh to her. But by 1801, she was more pessimistic than her mate. John left public life badly bruised and unappreciated, but in remarkably good humor compared to Abigail.

What especially dismayed Abigail was the rise of political parties and their appeal to voters' passions. Proof of how easily humankind was deluded came when her once-trusted friend Thomas Jefferson, vice president during the Adams term, emerged not only as leader of the opposition but, in her view, as an advocate of the licentiousness practiced by the French nation during its revolution. For Abigail, Jefferson's victory meant the beginning of mob rule in America. In Abigail's opinion, America was sinking into languor, supineness, effeminacy, luxury, and unreason. What the nation needed, she told sister Mary, was "severe and repeated scourging." Only thus might it be restored as "that happy people saved of the Lord."

Returning to Quincy with this glum outlook, Abigail sank into depression, and after many weeks wrote only one letter. Further, there developed an interesting reversal in her marital role and John's. While she continued to feel outraged and angry about the course taken by the Republic and by John's electoral repudiation, tranquility and good spirits now characterized the ex-president.

Reporting to her son Thomas that his father "bears and sees all these things with a total indifference," Abigail added that "he is not embittered by them, but views them with calmness, pity, and compassion." She conceded that her mood was different. Even the amazingly cold spring of 1801 delighted her, because the freak season was dubbed "Jeffersonian weather" by her neighbors. Meanwhile, to her utter astonishment, John Adams took up reading romance novels. "I think he enjoys them as highly as a girl in her teens," Abigail concluded.

It was only natural that Abigail showed her indignation to her sisters, who agreed with her views. Up in Atkinson, Elizabeth's dismay seemed even to exceed Abigail's as when she claimed that governance under

Jefferson was guided by "imbecility." And when a new war with Britain broke out in 1812, the Peabodys sent word that this catastrophe arose wholly from the "fraud of party and the lies of state." It warmed Abigail's soul to hear Elizabeth say about the American scene, "My heart sickens, and I turn from it mortified and with disgust."

Abigail's vexation after returning to Quincy was aggravated by her health. It became as poor as Mary's. For a time it was feared that Abigail, not Mary, would die first. The two sisters often exhorted each other to be ready for the last summons, so frail did they seem by 1801. In the autumn of 1798, Abigail felt so close to death that she directed her relatives to assemble so she might take leave of them properly. Even Nabby arrived to help with the nursing. The malady perplexed Abigail's physicians, who saw it mostly as a bilious fever, which she had suffered from frequently. Once the fever receded, another foe of many Adamses, rheumatism, took command, along with Abigail's usual complaint of insomnia. She favored a treatment involving a compound placed behind her ears to raise blisters. Only Abigail seemed surprised that this painful remedy limited her sleep to only one night a week. It must be an "agitation of the nerves" that caused her sleeplessness, Abigail insisted.

Yet another disorder plagued Abigail, St. Anthony's fire or erysipelas, which caused severe inflammation of the skin, particularly on the head. In 1809, Abigail complained that St. Anthony had "scourged me most cruelly," leaving her face so swollen as nearly to blind her. "It seemed as though my blood fried," she reported to Elizabeth Peabody. "If such are the penances of saints, I hope to hold no further intercourse with them." Elizabeth, always sympathetic, replied with soothing comments, such as "Sick beds are searchers of the heart."

Elizabeth also sought to persuade Abigail to reduce her exertions as ruler of house and hamlet. But no one, not even Elizabeth, had much luck in this effort. At Christmas in 1811, Abigail gave a dinner for many gentlemen from the town, and was thereafter led off to bed ill. Admitting for once that she had overtaxed herself, Abigail told Elizabeth, "I am really so self-sufficient as to believe that I can do it better than any one of my family." Thus, she acknowledged, "I am punished for my self-conceit and vanity."

Abigail found distraction by playing her favorite role as manager of family, relatives, and village. So astute had she been at handling the property she and John owned when he was away after 1774 that he still gladly left much of their affairs in her hands, preferring himself to read books, plow fields, or tend his livestock. Abigail had made only one major fiscal blunder; she purchased a sizable amount of land in 1781 located on the northern frontier, "the woods of Vermont." She acted in the belief that John would want to retreat there once his public service ended. But she was disappointed on two counts: the investment did not swiftly rise in value, and John refused to have anything to do with Vermont, saying he could never bear to be out of sight of the Atlantic.

Much more successful had been the aftermath of Abigail's decision to move into the house Royall Tyler had briefly owned. She soon decided the structure was not large enough to afford John a study fitting for a retired head of state, so she arranged to add a new parlor below and a library and writing chamber above. Her scheme was discovered by John before the project was completed. To her relief, he was enthusiastic, fearing only that her plan might not be commodious enough. Abigail always made it clear that, if she were left alone, the family's affairs would prosper more than when John had time to take a hand.

Even in retirement, John could easily be tempted to buy more land in the Quincy area, mostly purchases which Abigail considered imprudent. She urged investment in public securities, but on these matters, she admitted to sister Mary, "I have always been so unfortunate as to differ from my partner." John should have listened to his wife, for Abigail skillfully handled the assets she had inherited from her Smith and Quincy predecessors. In 1809, for instance, she found herself with $1,700 in paid-up stock to be reinvested, a sizable amount in those days. John, on the other hand, was land poor and desperate for income. The family's liquid capital had practically vanished in 1803 with the failure of the English investment firm to which John had entrusted the funds. The event produced Abigail's most terrifying year. Losing much of the family's resources was a blow so staggering "I could scarcely realize it." Abigail confessed that "to suffer want is a new lesson." It was particularly woeful for her since "I dread debt."

An additional cause of distress for Abigail was knowing she must now be less generous with her relatives and neighbors. Her charitable spirit was well known, and while her style of assistance was much more regal than sister Mary's Samaritan compassion, it was no less real. Abigail rejoiced in aiding others, particularly kinfolk, even if their needs made heavy demands upon her resources. After 1808, however, the troubles besetting her sisters and herself were not the kind money could help. In fact family sorrows grew beyond the capacity of even Abigail's sturdy spirit.

8

Death and the Sisters

From the time she and John had returned to Quincy in 1801, Abigail rarely had a day without concern for Mary Cranch and her family. Richard was seventy-five and Mary was sixty, an attainment in years which agreeably surprised their relatives since on several occasions both had narrowly recovered from illness. But it was their daughter, Betsy Norton, whose state was most alarming. She continued to bear children and her husband seemed nearly oblivious to how her burdens had weakened her. Even when some of her youngsters were looked after by Mary and Abigail, Betsy's condition seemed to deteriorate. For Mary and her sisters there was a special pathos in Betsy's plight, as they watched it worsen in the parsonage where they had grown up so happily.

In 1807, Betsy briefly resumed her journal, adding only terse comments, such as "I have had a good deal of care upon me and have laboured hard, but I still hold out. Hope buoys up my spirits generally, but sometimes I think I must yield to the pressure of cares." Often her entries consisted of a clipped "working day" and the notation that she had gone to bed early. On her forty-fourth birthday Betsy wrote, in an obviously painful scrawl, "How swiftly shall I slide down the declivity of life." The last entry occurred on 15 August 1809. The following June, a distressed Abigail informed Elizabeth that Betsy had entered "a confirmed consumption."

The only hope for Betsy, in Abigail's opinion, was "if she could be entirely free of care, and [had] her kind mother for a nurse." But since "she must return to her family," there was "no chance" for Betsy. "She is now a shadow," strong enough only to be out of bed for half days. Domestic life doomed her. In January 1811, Betsy's years of toil and illness were closed by death, an event greeted by her mother and aunts with Christian fortitude. As was so often the case, Elizabeth Peabody best expressed the sisters' feelings. She urged that they remember how no cries or tears can "avert the fatal arrow, when commissioned by the sovereign Arbiter." It was "a hard, bitter cup, but it must be drunk—and let us strive from the heart to say: thy will be done!!" Elizabeth brought two of Betsy's youngsters to live in the Atkinson parsonage, while Mary Cranch, though often bedridden, took four of her grandchildren home after Betsy's funeral.

Without delay, Mary sought her sisters' help in assisting Betsy's husband, the Reverend Jacob Norton, to remarry. The trio agreed it would not be easy to locate a new wife willing to be a mother to all of Betsy's offspring and to toil all day in the Weymouth parsonage. Still, it was the sort of challenge which especially appealed to Elizabeth Peabody, who retained her eagerness to spread romance. Doing Cupid's work was delayed, however, for in the months after Betsy's death, New England suffered through an unusually cruel winter. In Atkinson, the snow was so deep it required eighteen yoke of oxen to clear the post road.

As the cold weather continued, a housebound Elizabeth reviewed the prospects who might become the Reverend Norton's next partner. Many women were eager to marry, Elizabeth observed, but not many were experienced mothers. An ideal choice, in Elizabeth's opinion, was someone who preferred to do good in her own way, "rather than be devout to any man, however *devout* he may be." Betsy's successor, in other words, should stand her ground against Jacob Norton. Even so, Elizabeth acknowledged that some selfless and courageous female, by agreeing to be Jacob Norton's wife, would do more to illustrate the nature of benevolence than any theologian could.

No such woman had been found by the spring of 1812, leaving Elizabeth still searching for the inspiration that might lead to Norton's remarriage. Every possibility occurring to her had some disadvantage. As Elizabeth summarized the problem for Abigail: "A but and an if is attached to every being." It seemed each nominee who came to mind was disqualified because of what she expected, especially in her style of life, or else she was too humble, too young, too old, too enthusiastic, or "without principle." Elizabeth finally proposed Betsy and Sarah White, sisters who lived near Haverhill, although it discouraged Elizabeth that Betsy professed no religion and had once refused matrimony.

Amid this bustling help, the Reverend Norton found his own second wife, Hannah Bower, whom he married in 1813. Reassembling his children, Norton remained in the Weymouth parsonage for another decade until his stubborn theological views created such controversy that he was compelled to resign in 1824. Thereafter he continued his long ministry in the congregation of Sharon, Massachusetts. He died in 1858 at age ninety-three, outliving all the children Betsy had borne, except two daughters.

Abigail, meanwhile, found she had little time to think about a new mother for Betsy's youngsters. A few months after Betsy's death, an alarming letter reached Quincy from Nabby, who reported that she had discovered evidence of mammary cancer. Abigail acted at once. She conferred with the best physicians in Boston, then turned to the nation's most famous man of medicine, her old friend Dr. Benjamin Rush of Philadelphia. All agreed that Nabby should not hide in frontier New York, but must come at once to Boston for treatment. Nabby resisted this advice, telling her mother she was reluctant to leave the colonel. Abigail was not deceived, confiding to her sisters, "The real truth is, I believe, she thinks the physicians would urge the knife, which she says the very thought of would be death to her."

Eventually Nabby capitulated and made the six-day journey to Quincy in July, traveling in an open carriage of a style new to Abigail, who hurriedly inspected Nabby's afflicted breast and wrote at once to Elizabeth that Mrs. Smith suffered from "the most to be dreaded of all complaints." At first the doctors disagreed, saying that it possibly was not cancer but an obstructed gland. They prescribed hemlock pills. Abigail reported this to Colonel Smith who, for once, replied soberly and directly, despite the dismay he had shown at being left behind by Nabby. Smith urged that Nabby be further examined, and cautioned that delay would allow the disease to spread through his wife's system. He even spoke of the dangerous side effects of hemlock medicine.

The colonel proposed coming to Quincy as soon as he was summoned, although he recognized that Nabby did not want him present. He said he was willing to settle in Quincy, an option rejected by Nabby, since for her the ultimate degradation would have been for the disgraced William Smith to be surrounded by relatives and friends who remembered Royall Tyler, whose career was then at its pinnacle, for he sat as Vermont's chief justice. As for Smith's counsel against delays in Nabby's treatment, Abigail brushed it aside for the moment. She desperately wished to believe the doctors' encouraging diagnoses. The colonel, twice rebuffed, curtly replied that he would hereafter keep silent, "conscious of having fully discharged my duty to you and my dear wife."

Soon, however, any hope that Nabby's disorder was not cancer evaporated when Abigail sent a full report to Benjamin Rush. He hesitated to prescribe treatment at a distance, but indicated that what he was told convinced him that removal of the diseased breast was essential. Only this grim procedure, he said, would save Nabby's life. When she received this terrifying verdict, Abigail undertook to persuade Nabby to accept surgery. Nabby agreed and called upon her astounding fortitude to endure the operation calmly. The ordeal took place in Abigail's residence on 10

October at a time when anesthesia was still unavailable. Abigail was so shaken by the sufferings of Nabby that she avoided writing about the mastectomy, preferring to emphasize how well Nabby was healing and how the four surgeons agreed that all the cancerous matter was now removed. Colonel Smith was permitted to visit Quincy briefly, and he announced that Nabby might stay indefinitely with her parents.

Smith returned to New York, leaving behind a pathetic scene. Soon after Nabby's operation, Richard and Mary Cranch had died after sickness and infirmities so unremitting that Abigail could only say to Elizabeth, "What a wreck does age and sickness make of the human frame." By the time Nabby had arrived in Quincy, Mary was so weakened by consumption and age that she no longer could hold a pen. Her zest for conversation was as great as ever, however. "She cannot bear to be left alone," Abigail observed. Unfortunately, during that summer, as Mary sank and Nabby suffered, Quincy experienced hot weather worse than anyone could recall. The heat did not prevent Elizabeth from journeying to Quincy to see Nabby and make a final visit with the Cranches.

As the Cranches' condition deteriorated, Abigail managed the teams of relatives and neighbors who nursed them. At home, in addition to Nabby, Abigail had John to worry about, for he received a terrible wound when he went out in the dark to watch a comet and tore his leg on a sharp stick. Moving between her residence and the Cranch home, Abigail kept both hospitals under her command and planned for the inevitable. Garments were selected in which to dress Mary after death. One of Abigail's bonnets was put aside for Lucy Greenleaf to wear at the funeral. While life flickered, Abigail brought such luxuries as oranges, lemons, wine, and beef to the Cranch home, and sent a stream of encouraging messages to Mary's daughter Lucy, who was serving as chief nurse: "Your call is great for firmness and fortitude."

Somehow the torrid summer of 1811 passed into the cool of autumn, and Mary still lived. When her venerable uncle, Dr. Cotton Tufts, himself now bent by age, advised Mary that she must soon die, she refused to accept it, and actually seemed offended that anyone should make such a suggestion. Then, on 16 October, five days after Nabby's surgery, the impasse was broken by the surprising and sudden death of Richard Cranch, who had appeared in no danger. This news about "my dear partner," as Mary had always called Richard, was brought gently to his widow. Immediately, Mary announced that now she was ready to expire, for she had clung to life rather than see the hapless Richard left without her guidance.

The Cranch children and grandchildren were assembled. Tears flowed, both for Mary and for her deceased husband, who lay in the next room.

Thinking that Mary would linger for a time, Abigail went home to look in on the sickrooms there and to supervise dinner. When she returned to the Cranches, Mary was dead. It was 17 October, one day after Richard died. Mary expired calmly and cheerfully, claiming she had "held converse with superior beings" and thus was no longer an inhabitant of this world. The death scene had been most solemn, Abigail reported to Elizabeth. Imagine, she said, seeing "two dear relatives sleeping in death at the same moment."

Both Abigail and Elizabeth repeatedly used the words "together freed" in describing the miracle of this united departure. Elizabeth yearned to be present, wishing particularly that she could have seen Mary's glimpse of Heaven while awaiting death. Indeed, she said, the Cranches were "joint heirs of the grace of God." Elizabeth had to miss all this, however, for Stephen Peabody had suffered a severe fall and his wife felt she could not leave him. With a touch of pride, Elizabeth reported that lesser men would have been killed by the tumble which left the Reverend Peabody with a badly cut leg, a blackened shoulder, and a bruised hip. Elizabeth confessed she had been so concerned for her partner that she had not shed a tear over the deaths in Quincy.

Tears aplenty were reported during the joint funeral for Mary and Richard on Saturday, 19 October, when the church was crowded with mourners for the pair whose guidance and comfort had blessed the village for forty years. The ritual was presided over by the Reverend Peter Whitney, the same Cranch protégé from those exciting days when Mary had led Parson Wibird into retirement. Abigail was impressed by the size of the audience and also by the funeral sermon, later published in pamphlet form. Choosing a passage from the Psalms, "The righteous shall be in everlasting remembrance," Whitney portrayed Richard's life as a striking example of the virtues precious in God's sight. In fact, so exemplary was the deceased that custom governing funeral sermons was put aside while Whitney emphasized Richard's interest in ancient tongues and prophecy. The minister was careful to stress how this learning had been employed to foster Richard Cranch's extraordinary piety.

Finally turning to Mary, Whitney exclaimed that her mind had been "above the ordinary level," and had abetted a life dedicated to being useful to her neighbors. "Habitually serious and devout," Mrs. Cranch's last hours revealed that heaven had "already begun in her soul." Closing his funeral oratory, Peter Whitney urged Abigail and the absent Elizabeth to hasten to their Saviour for consolation, and to be ready themselves for death's approach. Uplifted by this excellent advice, the congregation formed a procession which carried the bodies of Mary and Richard across the road to the burying ground. The venerable partners were laid side by side in the Adams tomb; they had no cemetery plot of their own, their estate being comprised mostly of debt, although Abigail confided in Elizabeth that Jacob Norton had owed his former in-laws $900.

Many commented on the manner in which the Cranches died. As John Quincy Adams observed of his aunt and uncle, "Their union was too perfect to be separated even by Death." Abigail found particular comfort in the simultaneous demise of her dear Richard and Mary as she struggled with her worry about Nabby. Abigail told Elizabeth that the Cranches "lie down and rise in my thoughts daily," for "I can dwell with delight upon their lives." With this inspiration, Abigail went through the winter of 1811–12, hovering over Nabby, believing she saw signs of improvement.

Nabby and her daughter Caroline had planned to stay in Quincy indefinitely, to the great delight of the Adamses. Everyone was gravely disappointed when William Smith turned up in July 1812 to claim his wife and daughter. Reluctantly, Nabby and Caroline accompanied him to Lebanon, New York, where Smith was actively campaigning against the party of Thomas Jefferson and James Madison. Smith spent a term in Congress, but in his imprudence he was charged with favoring the British in the War of 1812, and his brief public career ended.

Smith's difficulty was trivial compared to his wife's. Barely back in New York, Nabby was once again abandoned in a remote area while the colonel went off to Washington, boasting he would salvage the wreck of his political life. He took what money there was, leaving Nabby destitute, worrying about medical bills, and insisting it was only rheumatism that was causing the excruciating pain she began suffering soon after departing Quincy. Finally, in May 1813, Abigail learned from Colonel Smith's sister that Nabby was being consumed by cancer. The shock was immense, for Abigail believed the disease had been defeated.

Hearing this news, Elizabeth sent letter after letter of encouragement and consolation to Abigail, even though Atkinson was now a sorrowful place, for Stephen Peabody had suffered a stroke. While she nursed her husband, Elizabeth urged Abigail to seek assurance from God in the face of these endless afflictions. Through their Heavenly Father, said Elizabeth, the greatest good could come "out of what *we* deem evil." He would never forsake his beleaguered children. Elizabeth urged that Nabby be moved to Quincy, a plea fulfilled in a stirring manner after Abigail was notified that her daughter had but one wish, to die "in her father's house." In order to reach Quincy in July 1813, Nabby summoned her son John from New York City, where he was floundering as a lawyer. With his assistance, Nabby submitted to a jolting trek by carriage across three hundred miles of trails and crude roads. After fifteen days of unremitting agony, Nabby reached her parents' home on 26 July. Abigail could only murmur to Lucy Greenleaf: "How she got here is a marvel to me."

Abigail foresaw at once that Nabby must die. The only questions were how long it would take and how much she would suffer. The prospect brought Abigail near to collapse; she feared she lacked courage to nurse her dying daughter through such a terrible ordeal. "My heart bleeds," she said. Nabby survived just over a fortnight, but in that time proved herself the strongest woman in the house. Only John Adams managed to approach his daughter's fortitude and composure as he provided the comfort she had traveled so far to find. Abigail acknowledged that she could not bear to watch the final days of Nabby's life.

With pain so intense that her frame doubled in contortion, Nabby was unable to take any nourishment save some Indian meal and water. Opium provided only slight relief. But Heaven spared Nabby weeks of prolonged suffering, as Abigail reported to Elizabeth. On Sunday morning, 15 August, Nabby died, her father beside her. A few hours earlier, in a tableau whose inspirational benefit the family cherished for a generation, Nabby announced she was ready to die and dispatched her father to bring a hymnal. Opening it, Nabby found her favorite song, and asked that her relatives sing with her. The hymn was "Longing for Heaven," and its first lines reduced the family to tears as they tried to join in: "O could I soar to worlds above/That blessed state of peace and love!/How gladly would I mount and fly/On angels' wings to joys on high!"

After this moving scene, not even Abigail needed convincing that it was for the best when Nabby expired at noon. She was forty-eight years old. To the end, she had hidden behind the "armour" which her mother rarely penetrated. As Lucy Greenleaf heard about it from Abigail, Nabby had simply released her spirit "to join those of your dear parents and many others of the just made perfect." Thank God, said Abigail, that Nabby's sufferings were cut short.

The uneasiness between mother and daughter evidently remained to the end, and it was left to Nabby's favorite parent, John Adams, to be her main source of final comfort. Abigail had demanded much of her only daughter and intruded often in her life. Nabby's response displayed a combination of resentment, indignation, and—perhaps mostly—guilt and shame that her accomplishments fell short of Abigail's expectations. No one can say how much blame, if any, for her disappointing existence, especially her marriage with Colonel Smith, Nabby may have assigned to her mother. Nabby's courage ultimately won over Abigail, however, who said that she remembered her daughter with admiration, as she "treasured up her patience, resignation, and submission as a solace for my woes."

Nabby's corpse was placed in the Adams tomb, next to Aunt and Uncle Cranch.

Colonel Smith reached Quincy just before Nabby died. His display of grief caused even John Adams to relax his scorn for the hapless son-in-law. Thereafter, William spent the remaining three years of his life as an exile in upstate New York, sponging off his brothers. He retained his bravado and charm, adopting the guise of a heroic Revolutionary War veteran. He died in 1816 at age sixty, leaving debts exceeding $200,000. His remains were interred at Sherbourne, New York, in a plot his brothers owned. During the 1880s, a monument was erected at this spot to announce that Colonel William Stephens Smith, George Washington's favorite aide, rested beneath. This exaggeration turned into deceit when the marker trumpeted that the daughter of the second president of the United States, Smith's wife, lay beside him. In death as in life pretense shrouded Nabby's mate.

It was two weeks after Nabby's death before Abigail found the composure to take up her pen and write letters. One of the first she wrote was to Thomas Jefferson, with whom she and John had recently resumed a fond relationship. Aware of the sadness in Jefferson's own life, including the loss of a wife and daughter, Abigail announced that she knew he could "feelingly sympathize with your bereaved friend." Then, pouring out her sorrow into "the bosom of sympathizing friendship," Abigail acclaimed Nabby's purity, patience, and resignation, telling Jefferson that her daughter adorned the Christian religion.

Abigail considered Nabby's illness "the most trying affliction of all I have ever been called to endure." John Adams announced that Nabby's manner of dying was "the most magnanimous that I ever witnessed." From Atkinson, Elizabeth told how she wished she might be in Quincy to help soothe the Adams family's sorrow. "Our rebellious sighs" must be stifled, she advised Abigail, as she thrilled at the story of how Nabby came to choose a final hymn. After all, Elizabeth asked, what was the worth of this world? Recalling the death of her daughter Betsy, who also had been courageous in her final hour, Elizabeth gave her benediction to Abigail: "May angels whisper peace and calm resignation to all your anxious, troubled minds. Adieu, adieu."

The deaths of Mary, Nabby, and Mary's daughter Betsy forged an even stronger bond between Elizabeth and Abigail. The Peabodys and Adamses exchanged visits annually. While Atkinson was a dull place for ex-president Adams, who missed his beloved books, it had one merit: a neighbor of the Peabodys produced what John and Abigail considered the best cheese in New England. Travelers from Atkinson who passed through Quincy often carried quantities of this product to leave at the Adams residence. The cheese was so delectable that Abigail complained only mildly at its relatively high price—two cents per pound—and wished there was something from Quincy of similar quality which could be sent to New Hampshire.

Actually, Abigail easily found ways to please Elizabeth. Abigail had a splendid wardrobe, and she gladly shared it with her sister. In 1812, for instance, Elizabeth saw that her black silk dress, once adequate for special occasions, could now serve only as "a common gown." Having just bought a new black dress, Abigail sent its slightly used predecessor to Elizabeth. She knew that her younger sister always tried to be attired in the high style Haverhill and Atkinson judged appropriate for the minister's wife.

Abigail also aided Elizabeth by skillfully overseeing the farm in Medford which the two had jointly inherited from their father. Rent from the estate brought Elizabeth the only money she received, and it became essential as Parson Peabody's great physical strength waned and he could no longer toil in the field and garden. There was a lesson in this for Elizabeth's shrewd eye. In 1814 she explained to Abigail how real estate rather than personal property should be most prized by a woman, because a female was instinctively loath to give up any landed holdings, whereas she might be coaxed out of money or jewelry. Realty would more likely be at hand to help a woman in her old age, the time of greatest need.

Elizabeth showed her prudence in many ways. On one occasion her family and the Atkinson community wanted a portrait painted of her. Elizabeth's response was to seek a competent but uncelebrated artist whose name would not command the fee received by Gilbert Stuart. Parson Peabody agreed that such frugality would suit his own portrait, but he insisted that if Abigail Adams could be painted by Stuart, so should her sister. Elizabeth's son William Shaw joined this campaign, so that, while John Johnston painted a workmanlike resemblance of Stephen Peabody, Elizabeth sat for Stuart, with much misgiving, in October 1809. Both the ordeal of posing before a famous painter and the extravagant cost worried her. She urged her son to see if Stuart did not have several prices, and if hers could be painted in his least expensive style. Not realizing that her son was paying for the portrait, Elizabeth believed that she must compensate the artist from her Medford farm income.

Finally consenting to the portrait, Elizabeth told her son, "I have no ambition but that it should be expressive of my benevolence to creation and my maternal affection for my beloved children, for these are sentiments which ever glow in my bosom and I hope illumine my countenance." She dreaded "to be looked at, or to look up in a stranger's face," and was certain that her true appearance would vanish under Stuart's gaze. It is not certain whether Elizabeth ever saw the finished product, for William

Shaw did not pay for it until after his mother's death and Stuart was notoriously slow. As it turned out, Elizabeth enjoyed posing for him. Like John Adams, she found the artist exceedingly entertaining, an opinion Abigail found very strange.

William (or Billy) Shaw was a concern of both Elizabeth and Abigail in their older years. After serving as John Adams' secretary, Shaw had settled in Boston, but suffered so badly from rheumatism that he frequently had to be brought out to Quincy for care. That Abigail was tending her son gave Elizabeth inexpressible comfort, since the young man's bachelor life made her uneasy. Abigail was hardly reassuring in her reports, one time informing Elizabeth, "I could have been almost angry with William. Tho so handsomely supplied with clothes, do you think he put them on?" The unfortunate fellow had turned up at a Harvard event in what Abigail described as old traveling garb, and then had the courage to tell his Aunt Adams that he deemed them "proper enough." "It mortified me," said Abigail.

Some relief came from Abigail's assurance that William still seemed "free from vice." And for a time, life went well enough for Billy Shaw, except for his being too miserly and shy to let anyone find him a wife. He was an attorney, serving for years as clerk of the U.S. district court in Boston. Like his mother, however, William's heart was in books, both as a reader and as a collector. When Boston's Anthology Society voted in September 1805 to establish a reading room, it was William Shaw who rose to second the motion of the Reverend William Emerson, Ralph Waldo's father.

The early years of what became the Boston Athenaeum, one of America's great libraries, shaped William Shaw's life. He served as secretary and librarian of the Athenaeum from 1807 until 1823, posthumously receiving the title "Founder" when the institution celebrated its centenary. In his lifetime William became known around Boston as Athenaeum Shaw, and it was he, mindful perhaps of his mother's outlook, who helped the author Hannah Adams become the first woman permitted to use the library. He also brought the collection instant success when he persuaded his cousin John Quincy Adams to deposit his six thousand-volume library with the Athenaeum in 1809 when Adams departed for Russia.

Shaw himself was an idefatigable collector, so much so that it became impossible to determine where his own possessions ended and the Athenaeum's began. He never charged the library for his services. As his Aunt Abigail said, he was "enveloped in science, a promoter of literature with all his heart and soul and strength." Well and good, but what of his person? Ah, his aunt sighed to his concerned mother, "a man whose mind is so engrossed with great objects cannot descend to the minutiae of an odd sock, a ragged wristband, etc."

As the years passed, Athenaeum Shaw's bedraggled appearance was not what distressed the community. It seems doubtful that Elizabeth realized before she died just how afflicted her son was with the alcoholism which humbled his father and his uncle William Smith. His devoted friend and kinsman, John Adams, sought to help him, without success. By 1818, William needed assistance at the library, due to his "ill health." In 1824 his duties had to be reassigned, but the affection and gratitude of his associates paid for Gilbert Stuart's painting of Shaw, made shortly before William died in April 1826 at age forty-eight. His brother-in-law and executor Joseph Felt reached agreement with Athenaeum officials over the tangle of Shaw's personal collection with that of the library. As a result, Elizabeth's son is today acclaimed as the Athenaeum's greatest benefactor.

A tactful tribute to Elizabeth's son was offered in 1826 by his cousin Charles Francis Adams, who said, "Had his fate been kept a little more in his own power by himself, he might have been if not a distinguished man, at least a very respectable one." It is difficult to know William Shaw himself in midlife; most of his letters have vanished. Enough of a glimpse is available to suggest that behind his passion for the well-being of literature was something of his mother's humble desire simply to be helpful.

After Elizabeth's death, William offered aid to his sister Abby, saying, "I desire to bless my God for his infinite kindness to me, in giving me the means." Fortunately, he took time for special kindness to Elizabeth a few months before she died, leaving her with the impression that he was *"better every way,"* as his mother put it to Abigail, with such emphasis as to hint she knew her son was tempted as his father had been.

Working with the Academy students still brought pleasure to Elizabeth, even when she was over sixty. Abigail received regular reports on the dinnertime conversations her sister and Stephen conducted with the young people in their care. In the spring of 1811, the topic "What is Beauty?" was popular, but it made Elizabeth glum, because, as she confessed to Abigail, her thoughts had necessarily turned to the grievous effect of age on the female's appearance. Time had taken all the attractiveness she ever had, Elizabeth lamented, and she was left trying to find consolation in Addison's reminder that true beauty was only in the mind. There was more discouragement when Elizabeth's daughter Abby, now a grown woman, kept saying, "Oh Momma, how you look!"

Age did not diminish Elizabeth's supply of affection and compassion, and she had plenty left to lavish on Abigail. After Nabby's death, when Abigail was especially frail and worn, Elizabeth's letters were filled with tenderness. Abigail grew increasingly prone to observe that Elizabeth's epistles were unsurpassed in quality. In replying to one, Abigail said, "Your imagination was so glowingly alive in your last descriptive letter that mine lags after it in vain. From the vivid warmth of the closing I should fancy that the cold north wind had not blown rudely upon you this season." After Elizabeth's death, Abigail reminded Abby Shaw, "Few pens were like hers. She guided and governed the heart (of her readers) as she pleased." It was high praise from a woman whom America has come to acclaim as one of its greatest correspondents. But Abigail was in earnest when she yielded first place to Elizabeth Shaw Peabody.

Elizabeth did not rely entirely on her pen. She visited Quincy in order to examine Abigail's condition and offer advice. After one encounter, Elizabeth wrote, "Your lungs appeared more easily affected than I had ever known them before." She also tried to distract Abigail from her woes by seeking her advice on how to handle the various problems resulting from Parson Peabody's entering "decrepit age." By 1814 Stephen was seventy-three, and a life of unceasing labor was showing its effects in rheumatism and mild strokes. He now walked with a cane and found it difficult in winter to trudge to church through the deep snow. What tactic might best persuade Stephen to accept a younger pastor as helper? Elizabeth asked of Abigail. Both of them recalled how difficult the situation had been in their father's advancing years.

Parson Peabody had the capacity to rally, as he did later in 1814 when Elizabeth herself fell ill. The couple still shared a bedroom, so that Stephen could be with his wife constantly. The chance to aid her caused a remarkable improvement in the old clergyman. Obviously touched, Elizabeth reported that when she was bedfast, it roused her husband "to spring about as if nothing had ailed him." Yet Stephen Peabody was as mindful of old age as Abigail and Elizabeth were. The last surviving entry in his journal was made in 1814, when he ruminated about how mortals must stand prepared to meet the final judge. He hoped to do so with a peaceful heart "when I shall have done with time!"

Elizabeth fought time's encroachment as best she could. She began to joke about looking old, saying it put "all my courage and resignation to the test" to look in a glass. "Humiliating, faithful mirror, I will forgive thee." Having done so, Elizabeth reminded Abigail that age brought other graces, "til we roam with celestial lustre." She was more distressed by her advancing deafness, and she suffered such severe attacks of weakness that she felt it would be too great a burden to hold a grasshopper. She ingeniously devised ways to keep from asking people to repeat themselves. The more she failed physically, the more Elizabeth managed to find spiritual comfort for herself and Abigail.

The Mount Wollaston farm was the ancestral Quincy family seat for Abigail and her sisters. Scene painted by Eliza Susan Quincy in 1822 shows the harbor where Louisa delighted in fishing. *Courtesy of the Massachusetts Historical Society and the Boston Athenaeum. Photo by George M. Cushing.*

From this rented house Mary Smith Cranch cared for her family and the citizens of Quincy. She and her husband Richard died here in 1811. Sketch is by Mary's grandson Christopher P. Cranch. *Courtesy of the Quincy Historical Society.*

Cottage in the foreground is where Abigail lived in Braintree as a bride, and where Nabby was born. House in the background is where Nancy Harrod Adams struggled with her husband from 1810 to 1819. Photo from the 1880s. *Courtesy of the National Park Service.*

Abigail Smith Adams in 1766, two years after her marriage. Pastel by Benjamin Blyth. *Courtesy of the Massachusetts Historical Society.*

Elizabeth Smith Shaw Peabody dreaded sitting for Gilbert Stuart in 1809, fearing her "benevolence to creation" would not show through. The artist did not fail her. *Courtesy of the University Art Collections, Arizona State University.*

Elizabeth knew the Haverhill parsonage without the portico and pillars. The house witnessed many bittersweet experiences of Elizabeth, her daughter Betsy, and her niece Betsy Cranch. *Courtesy of the Trustees of the Haverhill Public Library and the Massachusetts Historical Society.*

The Atkinson Academy building as constructed by Elizabeth and Stephen Peabody in
1803 after the original burned
to the ground one cold January night. Here Louisa's sons
attended school, along with
the grandchildren of Mary
and Abigail. *Photo by Dorothy
Wrigley.*

The original of John Singleton Copley's portrait of Nabby Adams was destroyed by
fire. The artist captured this likeness in 1786, the time of Nabby's ill-fated marriage.
Copley was a guest at the ceremony. *Courtesy of the Massachusetts Historical Society.*

Eliza Susan Quincy painted this view of the mansion and farm in Quincy in 1822. The property was purchased by the Adamses from Royall Tyler after the collapse of his romance with Nabby. It became a peaceful refuge for both Abigail and Louisa. *Courtesy of the Massachusetts Historical Society and the Boston Athenaeum. Photo by George M. Cushing.*

Long talks between Abigail and her sisters occurred in this sitting room of the Adams mansion. It was also Louisa's favorite spot for serving tea to John Quincy in their old age. *Courtesy of the National Park Service.*

Three generations of Adams women slept with their husbands in this room. It was also the chamber where births and deaths took place. Here Abigail died in 1818 and little Fanny was born in 1830 and died in 1839. *Courtesy of the National Park Service.*

View within the old Quincy cemetery. In the foreground is the burial vault where many of the Adams women are interred. Beyond is the Quincy church which houses the crypt where Abigail and Louisa rest with their husbands. *Courtesy of the Massachusetts Historical Society.*

Grave of Elizabeth Peabody and her daughter Betsy. The Rev. Stephen Peabody also reposes here. Setting is the old burial ground in Atkinson, New Hampshire. *Photo by Dorothy Wrigley.*

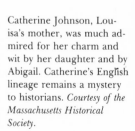

Catherine Johnson, Louisa's mother, was much admired for her charm and wit by her daughter and by Abigail. Catherine's English lineage remains a mystery to historians. *Courtesy of the Massachusetts Historical Society.*

Quincy November 10th 1818

My ever dear, ever affectionate, ever dutiful and deserving Son
The bitterness of Death is past. The grim Specter
So terrible to human Nature has no Sting left for me.
My consolations are more than I can number.
The Separation cannot be so long as twenty Separations
heretofore. The Pangs and the Anguish have not been
So great as when you and I embarked for France
in 1778.
The Sympathy and Benevolence of all the World, has been
Such as I shall not live long enough to disorder.
I have not Strength to do Justice to Individuals. Louisa Susan
Miss Harriet Welsh have been with us constantly. The
Three Families of Greenleafs, Mrs John Greenleaf, has
been (your Mother said it to me, in her last moments
"a Mother to me"). Mr Daniel Greenleaf has been really
the good Samaritan.
        Louisa Harriet and Mrs John Greenleaf have been
above all praise, Mr and Mrs Quincy have been more
like Sons and Daughters than like Neighbours, Mr Shaw
and your Sons have been all you could desire.
        Your Letter of the Second is all and no more than all
that I expected, Never was a more dutifull Son, Never a
more Affectionate Mother. Love to your Wife. May you never
experience her Loss.   So prays your Aged and Afflicted
J. Q. A   Father John Adams

Holograph letter containing John Adams' sentiments at the time of Abigail's demise in 1818. "The bitterness of Death is past. The grim Specter so terrible to human Nature has no sting left for me. . . . Love to your Wife. May you never experience her loss." From the original in the Adams Papers. *Courtesy of the Massachusetts Historical Society.*

This portrait of herself by Charles Robert Leslie delighted Louisa, who considered it a good likeness. It was painted in 1816 during the happy years in London. *Courtesy of the Massachusetts Historical Society.*

Chester Harding painted this portrait of Nancy Harrod Adams in 1835, after she had recovered from the ordeal of her husband's life and death. *Courtesy of Mr. and Mrs. L. M. Polan.*

Photograph of Mary Hellen Adams in her middle years, before the death of her last daughter whitened her hair and led to her own premature end. *Courtesy of the Massachusetts Historical Society.*

Abby Brooks Adams, shown here in profile, mastered the tribulations of her early married years and had by this time become a comfort to Louisa in her old age. *Courtesy of the National Park Service.*

Abby arranged her parlor in 57 Mount Vernon Street with an eye toward Victorian style. *Courtesy of the National Park Service.*

This building on F Street near the White House was Louisa's home during many of her years in Washington and the site of her death. Earlier, it had been the residence of Dolley and James Madison. The property remained in the Adams family until 1884. This photo was taken by Mathew Brady during the Civil War when the house was rented by Lincoln's government. *Courtesy of the Library of Congress.*

The only impressive feature of the residence at 57 Mount Vernon Street on Beacon Hill was its entry. Abby raised her large family here, including her son Henry Adams, who was moved into this house just after he had barely survived scarlet fever in 1841. *Photo by Jeff Nagel.*

This daguerreotype shows the Adams mansion in Quincy when Louisa last lived there in the summer of 1848. Thereafter, Abby became its mistress until her death. Built in 1732, the house was home to four generations of Adamses, and today is the crown jewel among the National Park Service's historic sites. *Courtesy of the National Park Service.*

This interior view of the crypt beneath the first parish church in Quincy shows Abigail's sarcophagus at center. In the foreground is John's resting place and behind Abigail lies John Quincy. Louisa sleeps in the sarcophagus at the rear of the photo. *Courtesy of the Massachusetts Historical Society.*

Each of the three sisters had kept their deep religious faith, but Elizabeth was best able to express it. What she tried to convey, particularly to the often-beseiged Abigail, was the Christian outlook "which makes us smile in grief." Every death, Elizabeth told Abigail, "should increase our zeal in the service of our heavenly Master," so that when "our day is far spent, may we be found with our lamps trimmed and burning, ready to attend our final summons."

Abigail was confident that Elizabeth would outlive her by many years, and expressed the hope that her younger sister would attend to John, whom Abigail also expected would survive her. But on 9 April 1815, Abigail received a heartbreaking message from Stephen Peabody. At 4:00 A.M., he had lost "my dear companion and best friend." Only the day before, Elizabeth had taken up a volume of commentaries on the Bible, announcing that she intended reading the Scriptures through. She studied two sermons before retiring, and then awoke at about 2:00 A.M. chilled and feeling a very heavy weight upon her chest. A doctor was summoned, but when he arrived Elizabeth was dead. "So tranquil was her exit," Stephen wrote, that those gathered around her bed assumed she slept.

The grief-stricken Parson Peabody could only cry, "My loss is irreparable!" To Abigail he begged, "Let me have your prayers," and signed himself "your distressed brother." In Quincy, housebound by poor health and terrible weather, Abigail seemed to surpass in her grief what she had experienced at the time of Mary's and Nabby's deaths, both at least expected. To Stephen she said, "By the agony of your own bosom, you can judge of the affliction of mine."

Abigail's eulogy for her sister occupied her for days. She called Elizabeth "the best of wives," and the "most tender and affectionate" mother. Indeed, "her sex are deprived of one of the purest examples of conjugal, maternal, and sisterly affection," whose life was "one continued series of useful services." She described the Peabody marriage as one in which hearts were truly entwined. Of Stephen, Abigail observed, "She had done him good all the days of her life, she was his pride, his glory, and his crown."

Abigail never quite recovered from losing Elizabeth. Grief had "broken me down," she confessed to John Quincy. Now she was solitary. "I stand alone, the only scion of the parent stock—soon to be leveled with the rest. Would to God that I felt myself equally worthy with those who have gone before me, but I fear I am but an unprofitable servant." She wondered why she had been spared, and tried to find a message in Elizabeth's unexpected demise: "May the warning not be in vain."

The sermon preached over Elizabeth's corpse was sent to Abigail, who was particularly touched that the address was given by the Reverend Samuel Gilman, once Elizabeth's favorite student. Only Elizabeth would have insisted that Gilman exaggerated when he told the mourners, "Her whole life was a constant admonition to all around her to go unto Christ." Mrs. Peabody was a "departed saint," "a perfect Christian," who blended "inspiring dignity," "winning affability," and "tender charity."

Afterward, the coffin was taken to the nearby cemetery, where Elizabeth was interred alongside her daughter Betsy and near Stephen's first wife. Space was left between them for the old parson's eventual burial. The inscription above Elizabeth can still be read today: "She was eminent for strength of mind and the acquisition of literature. She lived not for herself but for the benefit of others, and the honor of her maker. The religion she professed was exemplified in her life." To all of this Abigail sobbed "amen," joined by a host of New England men and women who had lived and studied with Elizabeth. Stephen Peabody lingered for four years, lost without Elizabeth. When he died in 1819, the parish did not choose a successor until thirteen years later, preferring to call upon ministers in the area who had been taught by the beloved Peabodys.

Though devastated, Abigail continued to display her talent for management. She took an interest in Elizabeth's daughter Abby Shaw, and reminded her that her mother's "whole life was full of instruction" as she distributed moral nourishment to old and young. Lest her namesake lack for such sustenance, Abigial kept Abby amply supplied with counsel, particularly as the young woman prepared for an oft-postponed wedding. In 1815, Abigail Adams Shaw was twenty-five. Even her mother had doubted the girl would survive to become an adult—until 1805, when Elizabeth believed her prayers were answered by Abby's suddenly becoming vigorous. Thereafter she played her part fully at home, and aided the Cranch household when Mary and Richard were dying.

Before Elizabeth died, Abby had been engaged for several years to a graduate of the Atkinson Academy, Joseph Barlow Felt. Felt was slow to establish himself happily in life, veering between commerce and divinity. He finally turned to the latter, and Abby at last married him, despite having often claimed "she would never make a minister's wife!"—or so Elizabeth had confided to Abigail. After the mourning for Elizabeth ended, a wedding date was set for autumn 1816. Abby resisted Aunt Adams' prodding that the ceremony take place in the ex-president's home in Quincy, a location Abigail claimed would have pleased the bride's mother. When her niece did not write about this or other matters, Abigail was indignant. She urged that Abby become a regular correspondent: "It is a talent you ought not to hide, and one in which your dear mother was distinguished."

What distressed Abigail most about her niece's independent approach to marriage was that she might enter wedlock without proper advice. At this delicate time, Abigail told the prospective bride, "the countenance of a female friend and relative would be most desirable." If Abby sought counsel about marriage, it was not from her Aunt Adams. Nor did Abby send any messages to Quincy for a year after her wedding.

In 1818 Abigail had time before she died for one last plea to her niece for letters. Referring again to Elizabeth's talent, Abigail presented Abby with the perfect epitaph for her mother: "Few persons held so eloquent a pen, or could find such ready access to the heart. I scarcely ever received a letter from her which did not draw involuntary tears from my eyes. Her imagination was brilliant. Her heart warm. Her affections pure and ardent. Her wit and playfulness full of good humour, unalloyed with acrimony. To know her was to love her. To know her was to respect her." Above all, Abigail emphasized, sister Elizabeth had planted such good seed in young minds, "which, I doubt not, will be her crown of rejoicing."

Despite the illness, grief, and disappointment which besieged her last years, Abigail never quite lost her liveliness. Her grandson Charles Francis Adams saw much of Abigail in her final year, and remarked how, despite the problems, she continued to display "her sunny spirit," enlivening her household and the larger community. No one recognized this blessing more than John Adams, who often marveled at Abigail's capacity for wit and good cheer in the face of adversity. Since she sensed that she had not long to live, Abigail cautioned her family that "many a taper brightens up just before it is extinguished."

In her final vigor, Abigail relished looking after husband, home, and village, a weight which often kept her old enemy, insomnia, nearby. Sleeplessness was her most consistent physical complaint throughout life, but Abigail claimed it brought one benefit. Wakefulness gave her more time to write letters, she said, confessing to John that she was still "a talkative wife." She was more than that, for Abigail was not content merely with handling her own correspondence. She also tried to shape John's letters. As late as 1815, Abigail was for John a source of caution and restraint in those moments when public dispute over his career led the former president occasionally to lose his tranquility and draft an indignant defense. Abigail admitted that John still "submits his letters to the inspection of the old lady for her approbation or dissent, altho," she added, "he will not always alter."

On 22 October 1814, she and John celebrated their Golden Wedding Anniversary, at which time Abigail announced that the only unhappiness in their marriage had been her separation from her husband for so long during the Revolutionary years. John later exclaimed to John Quincy, "Bless my heart! How many feet have your mother and your father in the grave? And yet how frolicksome we are!" Abigail, meanwhile, thanked

God "that I have not yet lived to those days in which there is no pleasure." Each Sunday she opened the Adams home to the community, and the rooms filled with neighbors and friends.

One of those often present was a youthful cousin, Josiah Quincy, one of many to bear the name. This Josiah graduated from Harvard in 1821. His description of Abigail in old age made her seem a bit intimidating compared to John Adams who, young Quincy said, "had not the smallest chip of an iceberg in his composition." He recalled Abigail's rich silks and laces, adornments appropriate for "her dignified position in the town." To this he added, "If there was a little savor of patronage in the generous hospitality she exercised among her simple neighbors, it was never regarded as more than a natural emphasis of her undoubted claims to precedence."

Age prevented Abigail from attending the local clambakes and dances, but she tried to be good-humored about enfeeblement. Once she recalled a retort she made many years before to Parson Wilbird's injudicious doubts about the usefulness of the female who had become "old, withered, feeble, and most good for nothing." "The only answer I could give," said Mrs. Adams, "was that she could do as a set off against an old man!" At other times, she liked to argue that having young persons around brought an elderly lady new life. This was Abigail's experience as her house filled with grandchildren.

Nabby's daughter Caroline remained in Quincy after her mother's death, and was Abigail's favorite granddaughter, partly because she worked so hard to make a pleasing disposition outweigh her homeliness. Abigail had expected to have Caroline with her permanently, but in 1814 she fell in love with a Columbia College classmate of her brother, John Peter deWindt, whose prosperity included an estate of two thousand acres in the Hudson River valley. Abigail wanted the marriage postponed, until Elizabeth Peabody, Cupid's veteran friend, begged her to relent. "Of what benefit can delay be?" Elizabeth asked, adding that it would be easy enough to discover if Caroline, at nineteen, was genuinely in love. "Enquire at the damsel's mouth. If she smiles, consent." As for Caroline's plain features, Elizabeth was not discouraged, saying that she was certain Abigail's granddaughter would soon learn the "thousand ways a woman could make a man's home his chief delight."

Abigail gave in, arranging a handsome wedding on 11 September 1814, though she claimed to be inconsolable at losing Caroline. All of Quincy remembered the ceremony, for the town soon heard that the Reverend Peter Whitney had received $50 from the groom for officiating, in exchange for which an amused Abigail reported that Whitney provided an "inimitable" ceremony. Afterward, the bride's grandmother served a cold supper to twenty-six guests, the fare including ham, "chickings" (Abigail's way of spelling chickens), pies, puddings, custards, whips, cheese, melon, and other fruits. The next morning Mr. and Mrs. deWindt rode off in an impressive carriage and four, which Abigail told Elizabeth was not for show but was young deWindt's accustomed conveyance.

The pair resided in Fishkill, New York, where Caroline gave birth to eleven children and undertook to assemble carefully selected portions of Nabby's letters and journals for publication. Her loyalty left her determined that her parents' lives be pictured as prosperous and happy. Caroline pleased her grandmother in September 1816 by bringing a great-grand-child to Quincy, the first of four in that generation which Abigail lived to see. Abigail was gratified, but nevertheless inclined to brood over the hazardous lineage of any infant descended from Colonel William Smith.

Abigail did not have far to look to turn up a Smith to whom she had a distressing blood link: her brother William Smith had died from alcoholism thirty years before. William's daughter Louisa Smith, who never married, was a mainstay of Abigail's old age, living in what the family called "single blessedness," taking much pleasure from all the grandchildren and great-grandchildren who passed through Quincy, and from the family of her sister Betsy Foster, whom she visited regularly in Boston. But it was to Abigail Louisa Smith clung. And Abigail cared for Louisa in death as in life, leaving instructions for John Quincy Adams, who had borrowed $1,200 from Abigail, that the repayment should go to Louisa.

Other grandchildren also were present, some for tragic reasons. These included Susan and Abby, the two daughters of Charles Adams, Abigail's son who had died pathetically in 1800. Then there were John and George Adams, sons of John Quincy and Louisa, both were left with Abigail and Elizabeth for six years after 1809 when their parents served as diplomats abroad. Other nieces and nephews occasionally sent their offspring to Abigail; more than once she served twenty-two relatives at dinner.

These youngsters lived more casually with their grandmother than her own children had. The granddaughters were allowed, for example, to enjoy blowing soap bubbles with their grandfather's pipe, a pleasure Abigail and John recalled from their childhood, but which they had denied their own progeny. Now Abigail could see a useful lesson in these bubbles, so she urged the children to learn as they played. The bubbles, Abigail told them, were as fleeting as life's hopes and ideals. Only sound morality was eternal. The youngsters were advised that "all the rest is balloon and bubble from the cradle to the grave."

Thoughts of death sent Abigail again to the mirror where she said she could witness "what all must see and all know—that this earthly fabric must fall to decay before this mortal can put on immortality." What Abigail now dreaded was lapsing into the helplessness of senility. Not to be in command—of herself and others—was clearly the fate which Abigail dreaded more than death. She pitied friends who, as she put it, "are prolonged to try the virtues of those around them, their filial gratitude." How ironic, she thought, that an elderly woman should linger ineffectually, cared for by those who once "hung upon the breast, incapable of helping themselves." Abigail was spared this.

She took care to prepare her will in January 1816, unable to resist making her last testament into instructions for her family. Especially did she urge equity and amity among them. She also made a stirring plea for the care of Louisa Smith, but the document was dominated by a description of Abigail's huge collection of clothes, the distribution of which she directed in careful detail, overlooking no one, not even the widow of her brother William, who received some garments and $50. In addition to clothing, Abigail assigned items of jewelry, stock in bridge companies, cash, and real estate to a host of female relatives—males now required little attention. When the names of granddaughters, nieces, cousins, and other females were called to receive something, Abigail's concern for womankind was never clearer.

The summer of 1818 brought unprecedented heat, spreading disease through Quincy. In early October, Abigail fell into an "alarming illness." By the eighteenth, it was clear that she was stricken severely with typhoid fever. The distinguished scientist Benjamin Waterhouse himself came to examine her, and confirmed for the family that her condition was grave. It was a case, he said, of "Typhus fever with that affection of the biliary system that has given it the name of bilious fever." Once before, this enemy had nearly snatched Abigail from John. The cause of her illness probably was contaminated water or food, plausible enough in the torrid weather which the town had been experiencing. For an aged adult in Abigail's weakened state, the chances of surviving the inevitable several weeks of fever were small. The kidneys of older victims were particularly vulnerable.

Abigail knew she was likely to die, but this did not prevent her from commanding the household and all who entered to provide assistance. John remained in the sickroom, watching Lucy Greenleaf and other relatives nurse his wife. One of these was Harriet Welsh, daughter of Dr. Thomas Welsh, whose financial collapse had been the sorrow of the family twenty years before. After Nabby's death, Harriet had approached the status of daughter for Abigail. It was Harriet who recorded the details of Abigail's last days. About 20 October, it seemed the patient might survive, thanks to faithful care by Dr. Amos Holbrook, who prescribed much bark, one of Abigail's favorite remedies, and also old Madeira wine, which William Shaw quickly brought out to Quincy.

On the twenty-third, John relaxed enough to leave the sickroom and allow himself to be read to. Three days later Abigail seemed weaker, though she remained conscious and still directed the family's affairs. Then, on 28 October, Abigail suddenly lost her remaining strength. John was called for, and the old gentleman, suffering from acute palsy, heard from Abigail that she must die. The old president's tearful wish was to lie beside her in death. When she told him how much she was beginning to suffer, John grew more reconciled to her approaching end. Abigail then conferred with her nurses about what needed to be done after her death. That accomplished, she decided it was time to summon the minister. For once, Peter Whitney failed her by not being at home when the call came.

With none of her children present, Abigail bestowed her final blessing on Lucy Greenleaf, who had nursed her so lovingly. Then, at 1:00 P.M. on 28 October 1818, Abigail dropped asleep and died quietly. Her last words were that if she could not be useful, she did not wish to live. Thinking as always of others, John put aside his grief and led Louisa Smith away to comfort her. He permitted himself one outburst: "Blessed are the dead who die in the Lord!" The news spread immediately through the neighborhood, and the Adams house filled with friends who simply wanted to be there. All of Quincy was soon dressed in black or wearing crepe on their sleeves.

The funeral took place at 2:00 P.M. on Saturday, 31 October. The preceding evening John Adams enthralled callers with stories of Abigail's prowess. He then led the family and walked behind his wife's coffin to the church, half a mile away. Among the pallbearers were the governor of the Commonwealth and the president of Harvard, John T. Kirkland, who also delivered the funeral address, drawn from St. Paul's first letter to the Corinthians, chapter seven, verses 29–31. Kirkland stressed Paul's words, ". . . for the fashion of this world passeth away," reminding Abigail's mourners that "the tomb may open under every step we take." Thus, said Harvard's president, let all learn from Abigail Adams to walk in faith and patience.

After Kirkland finished, the coffin was carried across the road and placed in the family tomb beside Nabby and the Cranches. Next day was Sunday, and Parson Whitney took his turn to preach about Abigail, and uttered the admonitions that were staple fare for any congregation: let the prospect of death encourage in everyone a disposition to look steadfastly toward the final judgment. No matter that Mrs. Adams had a mind of unusual capacity and attainment, it was more important that she had a soul without pride. "She was always the same meek and humble and obliging Christian."

Whitney's sermon pleased the community. But Abigail's absent son,

Secretary of State John Quincy Adams, elevated the level of praise, announcing that his mother was now "purified from that little less than heavenly purity which in her existence here was united with the lot of mortality." John Quincy listed his mother's virtues: she rose with the dawn and labored until night—a pattern the son set for himself; she had been cheerful but not frivolous; she had a profound but not obtuse sensibility; she possessed neither gall nor guile; she relished politics, conversation, and nature; and she had a delicate sense of propriety. In short, John Quincy claimed, "Her price was indeed above rubies."

John Quincy and his wife Louisa read all the newspaper notices of Abigail's death. These "puffs" were unworthy of Abigail, said Louisa, for they "blazon virtues to the multitude who feel and respect them as if they had never existed and by whom they are no sooner read than forgotten." No public utterances would do justice to the deceased, Louisa contended, for Abigail's "excellencies were engraved on the hearts of those who knew her." With a deft touch that would have pleased Elizabeth, Louisa added that Abigail's qualities "will dwell in the mind and operate on the heart as the evening breeze which succeeds a sultry day soothes the soul to peace."

No one captured the nature of Abigail Adams better than Louisa. First she said that her mother-in-law was "the guiding planet around which all revolved, performing their separate duties only by the impulse of her magnetic power." Then, in a poem of farewell, Louisa enlarged the tribute in charming lines which especially touched old John Adams: "Depart thou Sainted Spirit, wing thy happy flight/To the bright realms of everlasting light./Yet fondly hover oe'r thy lonely friend,/In nightly visions resignation send,/Cheer his great mind, Attune his soul to peace,/Till in this world his hopeless grief may cease,/And when his spirit quits this mortal clay,/Lead him to heavenly bliss and guide him on his way."

Louisa sensed that even in death Abigail Adams would wish to remain busy. What more characteristic service could she perform than that of being a loving wife and partner still directing and aiding her husband? In fact, the lines Louisa penned could as well pay homage for each of the sisters—Mary, Elizabeth, and Abigail—whose lives and marriages had been profound partnerships with their mates.

9

Enter a Fine Lady

In 1818, the tribute which Louisa Adams paid to her departed mother-in-law bespoke affection and admiration. Abigail had died holding Louisa in similar regard. Only two decades before, however, when Louisa entered the Adams family as a bride, Abigail's hostility toward the newcomer made future amity between them unlikely. To Abigail, Louisa Catherine Johnson was a weak and spoiled creature, a "fine lady" wholly unworthy to be the wife of a son in whom Abigail saw greatness. This early view of Louisa proved one of Abigail's great miscalculations.

Not only was Louisa far more talented than Abigail perceived; the younger woman continued to grow during her long life, more so than Abigail, who seemed little changed at death from the strong creature who left the Weymouth parsonage as John Adams' partner. When mutual respect eventually linked these two very different women, it meant a great deal to Louisa, who took courage from having become acceptable to Abigail. Even so, Louisa never wholly forgot those early days when she lamented about Abigail: "She forms a most striking contrast to poor me."

Born in England on 12 February 1775 to an American father and a British mother, Louisa Catherine Johnson passed through life feeling she belonged nowhere. A third of her days were spent outside the United States. She believed herself particularly unsuited to be an American, a charge sometimes leveled by her husband's political foes. Louisa's father, Joshua Johnson, was born in Maryland in 1742, and came from a large family which included a brother, Thomas Johnson, who served as Maryland's first governor after Independence and also sat briefly as a U.S. Supreme Court justice. Avoiding politics, Joshua Johnson entered business in 1764, did well and came to London in 1771 to represent his firm, Wallace, Davidson, and Johnson.

Joshua prospered until the outbreak of the Revolution, shrewdly buying commodities such as cloth, hardware, and silk for American customers, while also representing colonial tobacco interests. A charming but volatile person, Johnson preferred to keep his private affairs to himself; hence little is known about how he met Catherine Nuth, whose background remains as murky today as it was for Louisa's descendants. Catherine was evidently born in 1757, making her fifteen years her husband's junior. She was sixteen when her first child, Ann, whom her parents called Nancy, was born on 22 December 1773, and probably not quite eighteen when Louisa Catherine arrived early in 1775. Catherine bore seven more children, all but one of whom lived to maturity. All were female, save for Thomas Baker Johnson, whose eccentric ways eventually caused his sisters much alarm. Of the group only Louisa had a memorable career. She also seems to have been the only Johnson child with much talent.

After marrying, Joshua Johnson began a style of life which alarmed his partners and acquaintances and which must be ascribed to his devotion to his wife. There apparently was no luxury or attention which he did not lavish on Catherine, whose beauty and wit Louisa always admired. Joshua went deeply into debt so that his wife and family could be surrounded by elegance. Eleven servants were regularly part of the household, and the family dined and entertained in a grand manner. Louisa once conceded that much of this luxurious existence came about because her mother wished it, and that her father never had the courage to ask the family to be prudent.

At distressing points in her life, Louisa comforted herself with memories of her youth, and the loving and attentive presence of her parents. She came, in time, to deplore the foolish path her father pursued, but praised to the end his unfailing attentions to his wife and children. Catherine Johnson apparently ran the household, and was a valuable hostess, while her husband showed great pride in her. The Johnson marriage thus was another example of a true marital partnership, similar to what Louisa would also see in the union of John and Abigail Adams and other marriages of the late eighteenth century.

During the War for American Independence, the Johnsons lived in France. Joshua did not become a loyalist, so life and business in England were not easy for him and his family between 1778 and 1783, the first years Louisa remembered. She recalled living in Nantes, where she became quite French, acquiring a fluency in the language which she never lost, and imbibing a Roman Catholic outlook from her convent teachers. In time she gravitated toward Anglo-Catholicism, but remained devoted to the language and literature introduced to her during her French exile.

After returning to London, where Joshua became the first American consul, the Johnson residence was the gathering place for Americans who arrived in England after the war. The consul's home offered the finest food and entertainment in impressive surroundings. Abigail Adams knew the Johnsons from 1785 to 1788 when she lived in London as the American minister's wife. She came away with a dislike for the extravagance she observed under Joshua's roof, blaming it on the damage American males suffered by marrying European women.

Louisa attracted her parents' notice as the single offspring of great promise among their brood. She received every possible encouragement for development, particularly in her musical and literary interests. From this experience, Louisa acknowledged that she drew many false inferences about what life held in store. She took for granted that husbands and wives were attentive to each other, that children could expect only sympathetic understanding and encouragement, and that days should be passed amid music and sprightly conversation among sophisticated people. It produced a world in which Louisa foresaw women taking a vigorous role, one of equal importance to that of men. For the rest of her life, Louisa searched for such a setting.

Even as a youngster Louisa was something of a paradox. She gave signs early of being highly critical of herself and others, and of demanding excellence. She remembered her father warning that this outlook would cause her disappointment and unhappiness. Her sisters and brother teased Louisa for her so-called pride, which was actually excessive modesty, for she hesitated to speak, perform, or even appear for fear that she would not measure up to her own expectations. An uncompromising critic of herself, Louisa made another discovery: she sensed in herself a "warm and affectionate" nature that held "deep and powerful" passions. Louisa always contended it was well that her parents kept her safely apart from dissolute London society, for otherwise, she said, she might easily have become "a very vicious woman." Later, she took pains to stress to her sons that she came to her marriage a virgin.

Given Louisa's demands upon the world and herself, along with her wit and talent, her sensuality, and her volatile and sensitive personality, only an extraordinary male could appreciate and share fully her capacity for life. Louisa undoubtedly married an unusual man, but he was precisely the sort of husband she should have avoided. John Quincy Adams appeared at the Johnson residence in London during 1795. So different was his style that neither Louisa nor her family recognized that he was interested in Louisa rather than her older sister Nancy.

Long before he entered the Johnson salon, there had been many signs that Abigail Adams' oldest son would distress any but the most passive female. Born on 11 July 1767 in Braintree, John Quincy spent his first ten years mostly under the supervision of Abigail, since his father was busy with his legal practice and with politics. Carrying such parental responsibility, the talented Abigail was an even more awesome force in the lives of her three sons than she was in Nabby's youth. The horrid example of her brother William Smith's failure was always before Abigail as she strove to rear worthy men.

Abigail's sons were never allowed to forget the temptations confronting the male body and mind. Falling victim to them, John Quincy understood, would bring as much shame to his mother as to himself. Dominated as he was by a woman of great ability and strong personality who sought to make him worthy before God and herself, John Quincy remembered Abigail's practice of ceaseless admonishment better than moments such as when she took him to a high place in Braintree on 17 June 1775 so that he might watch the Battle of Bunker Hill in the distance.

As an adult, John Quincy recognized he had a bleak presence, and that he was a bumbler around women. Even when he passed the age of fifty, he conceded that he was still "cold" in the society of females. This ineptness he laid to Abigail's insistence that he should keep silent in company, lest he blurt some comment which might embarrass the family. Matronly concern dominated Abigail's letters to her son when he went to Europe with his father. They rang with hopes for John Quincy's purity and success. She graphically pictured for him many of the pitfalls life presented to even the best-prepared male. As a result, the well-intentioned Abigail did much to deprive John Quincy of confidence in himself, and to make him a fanatic about work and achievement. She also convinced him inadvertently that females should accept a subordinate place in marriage and in society.

Both Aunt Elizabeth Shaw and Cousin Betsy Cranch were dismayed by the attitude toward women which John Quincy displayed after returning from Europe in 1785 to live with the Shaws before attending Harvard. Writing to Nabby, Elizabeth said, "Upon my word, I never was half so afraid of a young man in my life." Both in journals and casual conversation, John Quincy continually censured women's manner and nature. "To *our sex*," Elizabeth noticed, "but little mercy is shown them." Confiding in her sister, Mary Cranch, Elizabeth Shaw spoke of John Quincy's "curious notions," as well as his "tenacious" adherence to them. In a statement which Louisa would echo many times over the years, Elizabeth tried to soften her nephew's Olympian perspective of women, telling him "that I had seen people, while they thought they were possessed [of] and adopting the most liberal sentiments, grow contracted and illiberal."

John Quincy's diary and letters reveal that he was both drawn to and repelled by the female body and mind. Lust, about which he had been warned so often, was a force he usually believed he could manage, if only women would cooperate through calm and reticent behavior. What alarmed him was that he sensed the strength of female desire and the skill with which it could be used to overcome male resistance. When John Quincy left Haverhill, where young men and women were encouraged to mingle, he took refuge at Harvard College, whose masculine atmosphere encouraged sober thought about the opposite sex.

His conclusions took the form of two presentations before the Harvard chapter of Phi Beta Kappa in the spring of 1787, when he was twenty years old. His first address contended that, whenever possible, money rather than passion should be the basis for marriage. This was because love, so-called, was mostly physical desire. John Quincy claimed that, once animal needs were gratified by regular sexual congress, the married couple would, in astonishment, discover that love had been a compound of "*Lust, and Vanity.*" This realization would leave them "chain'd to eternal strife."

It therefore followed that if a man could marry a wealthy woman, esteem and gratitude "will induce him to treat his wife with complaisance and affection." Consequently "no disappointed passion" would divide them, and, as good friends, the couple would have no reason "to regret the absence of that extravagant passion, which like the Sirens of ancient fable, charms but to destroy." Lucky was the man with a woman who appreciated "mutual esteem" over "Love." The first was based on reason and the second "is diametrically opposite."

This hymn to reason was offered on 5 March 1787. Three months later, on 5 June, John Quincy arose before the Phi Beta Kappa fellowship to claim that rationality called for a change in the status of women. Cautiously, he proposed that women should be allowed to initiate courtship without incurring doubts about their chastity. His premise was not one that his mother, his aunts, and his future wife would endorse, for John Quincy argued that woman's duty in life was to acknowledge that she dwelt in a man's world. The only place for her was domesticity. The "inferiority" of woman made acquisition of a mate her only hope for a useful, admirable existence. An unmarried female became a burden and was often ridiculed and despised; a married woman was a mother and helper, earning her way.

Furthermore, according to John Quincy, a female's circumstances were complicated by the fact she had "warmer passions" than the male. Men could divert their desires through business and other masculine outlets, but women had only marriage as an avenue of release. Thus, while the sexes were created for each other, and marriage was the acceptable basis for union, women depended upon matrimony more than men did. The upshot was that, since women desperately needed marriage, they should be allowed to announce their interest to men they favored, without the disgrace imposed by current mores. John Quincy never saw in marriage the partnership arrangement advocated by his parents and his Aunts Cranch and Shaw. At heart he seemed to fear the opposite sex, and eventually most of his anxiety took the form of disregarding and disobeying his wife.

If the imposing figure of Abigail was the initial cause of her son's attitude, she added to the damage by forbidding his marriage after he entered the amorous passion he had argued against at Harvard. In 1790 John Quincy fell in love with a young Bostonian named Mary Frazier but lacked the means to support a family, his career as a lawyer having just begun. While the contest between his rational outlook and his physical desires frequently left John Quincy depressed and immobile, Mary Frazier helped him over his anger and frustration.

Little is said about Mary in John Quincy's diary, but it is a tribute to her that he stopped penning such caustic comments as, "Indulgence is the defect even of the most accomplished women." We gather that Miss Frazier was educated, but know nothing else. Young Adams was attracted to her so strongly that Abigail felt drastic means might be needed to end the romance. It is likely she urged her husband, then vice president, to arrange an appointment in the diplomatic service which would honorably take the lovelorn John Quincy far from Boston. In 1794, President Washington conveniently nominated John Quincy American minister to Holland. The romance with Mary Frazier was closed sadly and by mutual consent, John Quincy announcing that thereafter he would keep his heart to himself and never marry.

The following year, official business took John Quincy from The Hague to London where, like most other Americans, he turned up in Joshua Johnson's popular household. Louisa paid little attention to him at first, but the young diplomat was soon a fixture, since his stay in England was extended to six months. He appeared at the Johnson residence punctually every afternoon and remained frequently until 2:00 A.M. Louisa thought her father was correct when he decided that young Adams had romantic ideas about her older sister Nancy. This left Louisa free to be natural and relaxed, where she had every advantage, given her wit, beauty, literary knowledge, and talent for music. Louisa had a perfect ear for melody, and played the harp so agreeably that even the young diplomat was impressed. She also sang charmingly, and performed George Frederick Handel's arias with consummate artistry.

Louisa, in turn, could see how brilliant was young Mr. Adams, whose father was vice president of the United States. Louisa later told her children that it was John Quincy's superior abilities which first drew her to him when, in early 1796, the Johnsons realized Louisa was being wooed by this person. Her father was at first opposed, hoping that his favorite daughter might find a better man than a narrow-minded and unprosperous Yankee. Catherine Johnson, however, favored young Adams, and so the romance proceeded. Louisa had precious little time alone with her suitor, for her mother and sisters seemed always eager to take walks or play whist with the pair. Yet even in those few, brief moments with one another, there were quarrels, misunderstandings, and certainly glimpses of John Quincy's scorn for feminine capacities. While he wished to marry, his nature compelled him to pursue the goal gracelessly.

After four months, Louisa and John Quincy became engaged. He returned to The Hague in May 1796 and was not back in London for thirteen months. Louisa suggested that they wed before he left, but young Adams claimed his finances were as yet insufficient. When Louisa pointed out that she could remain in England with her family for a time after marriage, he did not budge, and Louisa consequently had to live with her future husband by letter, which proved a trial since John Quincy's epistles were cheerless exercises in admonition. They warned Louisa about marriage's grim reality, and hinted at indefinite delays before a wedding could take place. Louisa dreaded hearing from John Quincy because she was uncertain how to reply.

She did repond, however, and in messages that returned love and patience for pride and grumpiness. Louisa's talent and charm were evident from the start in her letters, which, at this early point and throughout her life, were the equal of those written by Abigail Adams and Elizabeth Peabody. So appealing were her messages that, unbeknownst to Louisa, they may have been responsible for holding John Quincy when Abigail undertook to break the engagement.

For a time Abigail was in the dark about her son's intentions, although friends in London told her he was spending long hours at the Johnson residence, in Abigail's memory a place of glitter and waste. Lest any of Joshua Johnson's lovely daughters attract John Quincy through his sensual weaknesses, Abigail sent him reminders that both passion and beauty soon faded, and that a good marriage must be founded upon friendship, the doctrine he had advanced at Harvard not long before. But enduring friendship, Abigail pointed out, required compatibility, which, she sternly stressed, arose from similar values and tastes. Few of these, Abigail hinted, were shared by the Adamses and Johnsons.

When she learned from acquaintances that her son was wooing Louisa Johnson, Abigail did what she could to inform John Quincy of Louisa's shortcomings. Louisa was not an American, and had been brought up in circumstances alien to Massachusetts. Even more important, Abigail wrote,

Louisa would have a temperament very different from John Quincy's. Remembering Louisa from ten years before, Abigail reluctantly complimented her: "She has classical looks as Virgil styles them. Heavenly blue eyes and plays music delightfully." Yet this must not blind her son, the mother stressed, to the young woman's inexperience and to the fact that she most certainly would be spoiled for life in the United States.

Abigail did not add, though she implied, that a wife with Louisa's background would hinder the career of a rising American statesman. Even John Adams was pressed into service, suggesting to his eldest son that marriage to a daughter of Joshua Johnson meant that John Quincy would have to post a close watch upon his purse. Louisa never fully realized that Abigail's pressure probably helped keep a stubborn John Quincy determined this time to marry the woman of his choice. He had not forgotten how he had been obliged to surrender Mary Frazier.

John Quincy disclosed little to his mother about his plans, which infuriated Abigail. Her wrath enlarged when her son announced that he intended to retire from a public career and give his life to literature, perhaps settling in the American South—where Joshua Johnson claimed to have a huge plantation in Georgia. He seemed in no hurry to have a wife, however, so long as the English Channel kept the attractions of Louisa at a distance. He tried to postpone the wedding, even suggesting that Louisa travel to America with her family when the Johnsons left England in late summer 1797. The reluctant groom still contended that he was not yet able to support a wife, by which he may have been hinting that he could not pay for a mate accustomed to a glamorous style of life.

Louisa, for her part, kept sending reassurances, even insisting that she go to The Hague, accompanied by her father, and be married there. When John Quincy replied stuffily about the impropriety of such a plan, Louisa finally lost her temper and accused John Quincy of humiliating her. Let her be the judge of what was proper, she suggested, adding that she was "perfectly satisfied" with her proposal's "appearance to the world." Being engaged to him was one long lesson in restraint and philosophy, Louisa announced. Yet her admiration for John Quincy's undoubted talent still ruled her. She freely told him so, and mentioned that she desired to earn his esteem. This was what her fiancé longed to hear. John Quincy commended her for displaying "a kind of spirit that I admire, a resolution that I most cordially approve, and which I am sure you will carry into effect."

Louisa later told her children that she was well aware of their father's "unnecessary harshness and severity of character" before she married him. She knew how determined he was to bow to no woman, remembering how he announced during their engagement that "*his* wife" must never interfere, even with his style of dress, one of the subjects about which Abigail made the most commotion. Louisa also had noted that John Quincy could not endure teasing and that he could be selfish and cruel. But when she offered to end their engagement, John Quincy hastily dismissed the suggestion. Louisa was left to defend herself by sending him letters that were affectionate but also sometimes mocking. Obviously, she hoped by such a tactic to persuade his clever mind of the justice of her point of view.

If John Quincy read between the lines of Louisa's subtle letters, he gave no sign, not even when she told him that she was reading Lord Chesterfield's writings and heartily disliked his condescending view of women. "Never, my beloved friend, let my weakness lessen your affection for me," Louisa wryly told her future husband, and made his cup overflow by asking that he "teach my rebellious heart gently to acquiesce without murmuring." Meanwhile, as he directed, Louisa prepared to emigrate to America without him. She left a touching pledge: "Remember, that there lives not a being who loves you as well as your faithful Louisa C. Johnson."

Then, abruptly, events made marriage unavoidable for John Quincy. Just before he retired to Mount Vernon, President Washington switched the young diplomat's assignment to Portugal, where the pay was much higher. Abigail did not wish her son to live in Lisbon unmarried, so she reluctantly capitulated to his plan to wed Louisa. But John Quincy continued to balk. Louisa's father then stepped in. Either because he pitied his daughter and wished to be Cupid's ally, or because he saw advantage in having a child married to the son of the new president of the United States, or out of a mixture of these motives, Louisa's father shrewdly campaigned against John Quincy's determination to delay marriage. Joshua Johnson demolished every reason young Adams offered for deferring a wedding. He even supplied a ship to carry the lovers to Lisbon, after hearing the prospective groom complain that he could not afford to transport his bride.

Meanwhile, the Johnsons prepared to go to the United States. It was now mid-1797, and Joshua's luck was exhausted. He knew he must give up his extravagant life, and take refuge in America from his English creditors. In the New World he expected to replenish the family finances with his investments in land around Savannah, hopes not unlike those of Colonel William Smith and James Greenleaf. Joshua Johnson intimated to John Quincy that he was hard-pressed financially, and the latter acknowledged that Louisa's father told him the Johnson fortunes were at the moment insubstantial. It meant that Louisa's dowry would be limited to £500, with John Quincy assured that more was to come.

Arriving in London for his wedding, John Quincy demonstrated how resentful and cruel he could be. At first he ignored Louisa, finally calling on the Johnsons toward the close of his second day in town. Louisa never forgave this snub. Despite the wound, however, the twenty-two-year-old Louisa Catherine Johnson married John Quincy Adams, age thirty, on 26 July 1797, in one of London's oldest structures, the Church of All Hallows by the Tower, sometimes called All Hallows Barking. Founded in the year 675, it had a Saxon cross and doorway, and Romans were buried in the crypt.

The wedding day and a few days thereafter were happy, even by Louisa's standards. The young couple seemed blissful, so much so that John Quincy let his rigorous schedule collapse, conceding grudgingly to his diary that "an inevitable cause" made him arise much later each morning than usual. Even after two months, the pair was rarely up and about before nine, and John Quincy had to admit that "several circumstances occur to frustrate my intention of steady early rising." After breakfast, the couple read and wrote past noon. Then they took walks, visited friends, or haunted the booksellers. Dinner was at five, after which they enjoyed an hour of leisure. In the evening, Louisa's husband read aloud until ten, when they supped lightly and retired, usually by eleven.

In the United States, the Adams circle had no details of John Quincy's wedding plans, so secretive had he been. Abigail learned of his marriage at the same time as everyone else. She disgustedly reported to Elizabeth Peabody, "My son, you will see as I do by the papers, is married." Only after the ceremony was behind him did the groom inform Abigail that from "an amiable and respectable family," he had taken a charming daughter to be his wife. He was confident, he said, that she would adorn that role. Louisa added a postscript to the letter, saying that her ambition now was to win and deserve the Adamses' esteem and affection. John Quincy quickly regretted his praise of the Johnsons, however, for just after the letter was dispatched, Joshua and Catherine had to flee their creditors, departing London before dawn on 9 September while the bridal couple slept.

They left a mortified daughter and a son-in-law who found that not even the first £500 of dowry was to be paid. Joshua Johnson went to America a pauper, leaving Louisa and John Quincy to face a flock of angry bill collectors who gathered at the pair's hotel looking for money. There were even unpaid family servants who cursed Louisa. The honeymoon was abruptly ended, and the early autumn of 1797 was a time Louisa tried to forget. Finally, on 18 October she and John Quincy escaped London, heading not for Lisbon but Berlin, where John Adams had decreed his son could best serve as the eyes of America in Europe, possibly overlooking that the post in Germany would pay his son considerably less than the Portugal assignment. Louisa barely got away from her troubles in England, for John Quincy showed her that good management was not among his strengths by neglecting to arrange for their passports. When they finally set off, Louisa quickly discovered how seasick a Channel crossing could make her.

In this dismal fashion, Louisa began her first four years of marriage. The strange surroundings of Berlin did not help. If she had enjoyed better luck, her cheerfulness, energy, and determination could have overcome the language barrier, alien customs, and the limited housing John Quincy's meager pay allowed. Instead, she had to battle illness, miscarriages, and the knowledge that an unforgiving Abigail showed no sign of relenting. John Adams was the first to accept Louisa, for he sent word that he was "already prepared to love you." Louisa's father-in-law said that on all sides he heard reports of her "amiable character." Another relative pleased by encouraging reports about John Quincy's bride was Mary Cranch. These opinions, of course, were immediately relayed to Abigail. Mary informed the first lady that her new daughter-in-law "appears to be just such a woman as you would have wished for your son."

Since the Joshua Johnsons had settled in the District of Columbia, it was easy for Louisa's mother to share with Abigail letters which the Johnsons had received from Berlin. These glimpses of Louisa soothed Abigail somewhat, particularly a letter in which Louisa insisted she was meant for domestic existence and not for the wastefulness of court life. Abigail kept her distance, however. When her letters to Berlin persisted in coldly calling Louisa "Mrs. Adams," John Quincy was moved to join in his wife's protests. Eventually, Abigail apologized.

Even John Quincy showed satisfaction with the results of the first twelve months of marriage, remarking in his diary that, although it had been a difficult time, "from the loveliness of temper and excellence of character of my wife, I account it the happiest year of my life." It was not easy for Louisa's husband to display this cheerful mood to his wife. His mother-in-law, Catherine Johnson, knew this and sensed that Louisa's high spirits might lead to conflicts with her domineering husband. She sent her daughter some stern advice, reminding Louisa how a wife must learn to modify herself to suit her husband's "temper." It was disagreeable counsel, but Catherine insisted that such a stance was "the only basis on which we women ought to build." This comment was easily made when a woman had been married to a man of Joshua Johnson's deferential ways. Accommodating John Quincy Adams' temper was quite another matter, as Louisa knew. Doing so proved at times even to be humiliating.

Harsh feelings erupted once when Louisa and John Quincy prepared to go out for the evening. Louisa decided to apply rouge to her cheeks, an acceptable practice in Berlin society, although one she knew her husband deplored. She was pleased with the effect, but decided not to show her face to her husband. As they started to leave the apartment, Louisa asked John Quincy to put out the light and precede her. At once, he became suspicious. Taking Louisa to the lamp, he saw the rouge and ordered her to wash her face. Louisa said no. Later she reported what happened: "He took a towel and drew me on his knee, and all my beauty was clean washed away." At that point, she suppressed her anger, accepted a kiss, "and we drove off to the party where I showed my face as usual."

Louisa was not always so easily governed. The next night out, she put on rouge again and, when John Quincy demanded she remove it, "I with some temper refused." The American minister to Prussia found his wrath unavailing, so he turned on his heel, dashed down to the carriage, and rode off without her. Left alone, Louisa wept in vexation for just a moment. Then, with her face still decorated, she went to the party on her own. After all, as Louisa knew, not only was she the beautiful wife of an admired diplomat; she was also the daughter-in-law of the president of the United States, a role which counted for much in Berlin's court society. Louisa did not have to depend on her husband's attention during social outings. She was often escorted by Thomas Boylston Adams, John Quincy's brother and secretary, who liked nothing better than to look after his new sister-in-law. This was fortunate, since Louisa enjoyed dancing, while John Quincy felt time was better spent talking politics with male members of the diplomatic corps.

The king and queen of Prussia were much taken by Louisa, to the discomfiture of John Quincy. He feared that his spontaneous and clever wife, who was fluent in French, the language of diplomatic society, might say something to embarrass him and the United States. Louisa knew that John Quincy "terribly dreaded some indiscretion on my part." She was as interested in people and affairs as her husband, but when she sought to discuss issues of the day with him, John Quincy insisted they were not fitting subjects for females. "Women had nothing to do with politics," he told her, a view John Quincy knew would have made his mother indignant.

Even more distressing for Louisa was her husband's discovery that the admirable John Wesley, the founder of Methodism who had died earlier in the decade, customarily arose at 4:00 A.M. At once John Quincy strove to emulate Wesley's ascetic practice, thus ending the pleasant early morning occasions with which their marriage had begun. These and other stern measures were indications to Louisa of how her mate worried that he might falter in his high calling. He grew increasingly dour and repressed, limiting the ways Louisa could seek to be his companion in Berlin. For friendship she turned therefore to the family of an English doctor named Brown. It was a lively group which welcomed her and provided something of the conversation Louisa had enjoyed in her parents' home. All of this was not lost upon John Quincy who, in his self-centered way, increasingly loved and admired his wife. There was more than a hint of this in his comment to Abigail that, should he praise Louisa as he was inclined to do, his mother "would imagine that the lover had not yet subsided into the husband."

Louisa's mate had good reason to respect her as she valiantly strove to bear him what he yearned to have, a son. It is impossible to say who suffered more, Louisa or John Quincy, as these Berlin years were marred by the physical and emotional trauma of four miscarriages. Louisa had already conceived when the couple arrived in Europe, and thereafter spent most of her time trying to bring several pregnancies to full term. Her failures devastated both would-be parents, although clearly Louisa was stronger; John Quincy was left unable to read or think.

When he finally fell ill from worry, Louisa arose to help, grateful for any circumstance that forced her husband to depend on her. "She nursed me," he admitted, "with all the tenderness and affection which women only can display and which she possesses in a degree so eminent even among her own sex." In this manner Abigail learned through her son that Louisa displayed admirable strength which the mother-in-law had not expected to find in her. In these early years, however, Louisa knew better than to share confidences with Abigail. She turned instead to her own mother and sisters with lamentations of how ill and "ugly" she had been most of the time since her wedding. Meanwhile John Quincy recorded in his diary the dreadful days of pain and suspense as Louisa fought to avert what came to seem inevitable, yet another miscarriage. The pair began to fear theirs would be a childless marriage.

Such a prospect seemed not to alarm Abigail, who believed that any births should await the couple's return to America, an event she eagerly anticipated. When she heard of a fourth miscarriage, Abigail sent John Quincy an almost lyrical message: "My love to Louisa. No little Johnny. No little Louisa. All for the best, be assured." Abigail was much brisker when she discussed the sad situation with Louisa's mother; something must be done to save what strength might remain to Louisa, so that the young woman could survive to reach America. Abigail implied that imprudent behavior on Louisa's part accounted for the failed pregnancies. The last such loss, Abigail knew, had occurred after Louisa exerted herself at a party to aid the Spanish minister's wife who had fallen, breaking a leg.

In the late summer of 1800, Louisa and John Quincy traveled to Leipzig on a holiday during which they discovered that once again Louisa was pregnant. Despite the familiar heart-stopping alarms, this time Louisa went full term and gave birth to a son on 12 April 1801. Here her good fortune stopped when she was mishandled by a drunken midwife. Although the new mother was so weak and bruised that it took her a fortnight to recover, she proudly provided such abundant milk that another child was brought to share the nourishment. The Queen of Prussia asked daily after Louisa's progress, while the King banned all traffic on the street where the Adamses' residence stood, lest the noise disturb his good friend Louisa.

Louisa was exultant and John Quincy's report to Abigail was not as self-centered as it sounded, even though he viewed a male offspring as very much a father's property: "The day before yesterday, at half past three o'clock afternoon, my dear Louisa gave me a son." He decreed that the child should be christened George Washington Adams, and the new parents prepared to take the infant back to America—John Quincy had been recalled just before his father's administration closed.

Knowing that she brought a grandchild did not prevent Louisa from being intimidated by thoughts of Boston and Quincy. Not only did Abigail lie in wait, but on the voyage home John Quincy thought it best to inform Louisa of his former love for Mary Frazier. He bumbled the effort, leaving Louisa feeling inferior to this creature whose beauty and attainments she heard her husband praise. Nor were Louisa's spirits lifted when, after disembarking in New York, John Quincy put her and their baby on the stage to travel alone to Washington while he hastened to a reunion with his parents in Massachusetts. Abigail immediately commented on what she thought was the change wrought in her son by marriage. Where, she wondered, was the son who used to smile? Maybe he should begin to eat between meals, Abigail advised, lest his stomach "fill with wind."

Abigail welcomed Louisa to America by expressing fear that her daughter-in-law might behave in ways harmful to the Adams family's reputation through carelessness about what she said. "Every syllable she utters will be heard not with ears of candor, but carping malice." Nor was Louisa cheered by Abigail's reminder that the Johnson family was an embarassment to the Adamses. Then there was the terrible shock which greeted Louisa when she reached Washington in September 1801. Her father was so broken in spirit and body that he did not recognize her. Joshua Johnson's life in America had been disappointing from the moment he and his family arrived during the autumn of 1797. They were coldly received by Joshua's Maryland relatives, who knew he was a pauper before he did. From them Joshua learned that his involvement in Georgia land speculation had failed completely, possibly because he was betrayed by associates.

With unflagging loyalty, Louisa never doubted that her father's difficulties in Europe and America were the fault of unscrupulous persons who took advantage of a kind and generous man. Yet even Louisa's mother apparently entertained doubts about her husband. Writing to Louisa of the accusations leveled against Joshua, Catherine Johnson said, "You know your father's heart. I will not I trust be easily led to believe that he is a villain. I will however drop the subject, leaving it to God." She noted, however, that the arts of slander and calumny were as skillfully practiced in America as in Europe.

To observers in America, Joshua, Catherine, and their children were refugees in flight from debts left in England. They were reaping as they had sown. These critics blamed Louisa's mother for much of the plight, since her reputation for costly style had preceded her. Little help was offered to Joshua by his kinsmen, and this once-glamorous figure in London society landed in American a broken old man. The crisis tested Catherine Johnson's capacities. In what proved to be a tactical triumph she visited the Adamses in Philadelphia, causing Abigail to change her mind completely about Louisa's mother. "Sensible, discreet, prudent, lively, sedate, judicious, impressive, elegant, all that constitutes a fine woman" was the tribute an astonished Abigail paid to Catherine Johnson. The latter was still comparatively young, only forty when she sailed to America. Abigail immediately informed John Quincy that she felt more kindly toward Louisa now that she really knew Mrs. Johnson.

Although it is likely that Abigail urged her husband, as president, to aid these afflicted immigrants, Louisa had reason to believe her mother-in-law advised against a federal job for Joshua Johnson. Nevertheless, John Adams did help in the spring of 1800. He sent Joshua's name to the Senate for approval as superintendent of stamps, a position recently created by congress and carrying an annual salary of $2,000. The recommendation received a tie vote, broken favorably by Vice President Thomas Jefferson. In spite of his frail condition, Joshua still held this post when Louisa reached Washington, although the Jefferson administration soon removed him.

When Louisa was reunited with her parents, her father was desperately ill. An enlarged prostate gland left him in misery throughout Louisa's visit. An added worry for the family had been the necessity of withdrawing Louisa's brother Thomas as a student from Harvard, and putting him under the tutelage of an Annapolis attorney, a step which astounded Abigail who, while considering Harvard a source of evil for the souls and bodies of young males, still believed a degree from the college was essential for the men who would lead America.

Catherine Johnson had no money to pay her son's tuition, however, and she also realized that preparing for a legal career in Maryland—the state where his family had lived for generations—was the quickest way for Thomas to help support his relatives. There were other far-sighted moves made by Louisa's mother. She put aside the habits of a pampered wife, and set out to establish her family by using a valuable resource, her charming, cultivated, and unmarried daughters. Even before Louisa appeared in America, Catherine had brought about the marriage of the oldest girl, Nancy, to a cousin, Walter Hellen, who was already prospering as a tobacco merchant. His residence in Washington became the refuge for Catherine and her brood.

The Walter Hellen house was the scene of Louisa's reunion with her family, and she could talk there free from the gaze of her apprehensive husband. Only the pathetic state of her father saddened these otherwise joyful days for Louisa. At the close of 1801, Joshua Johnson's torture from the "gravel" was so extreme that his brothers showed mercy. One of them, Baker Johnson, took him home to Fredericktown, Maryland where, on 21 April 1802, Louisa's father died. This was a few months after Louisa's visit with her relatives ended and her own troubles began.

In late October 1801, John Quincy arrived in Washington to bring Louisa to Quincy, although he had asked her to make the trip alone. Only when she insisted did he agree to escort her. Before they departed, courtesy required that President Jefferson invite Mr. and Mrs. Adams and the Johnsons to the executive mansion for dinner. It was an occasion "of chilling frigidity," all agreed, even if James and Dolley Madison were present, along with Meriwether Lewis. The next day, Louisa and her husband visited Martha Washington, now widowed at Mt. Vernon, where they found a much more cordial reception. Mrs. Washington charmed Louisa, and persuaded her and John Quincy to spend the night.

On 3 November Louisa and her little son George were hustled off to New England by an impatient John Quincy, who dreaded the winter which might descend at any moment. The trip was unrelievedly miserable. Louisa later commented that by comparison her famous journey alone from St. Petersburg to Paris in 1815 was a pleasure. She had a dreadful cold as they set out, and little George, whom she had been persuaded against her will to wean, suffered from diarrhea, as unpleasant a disorder as one might carry on a bumpy and interminable stagecoach trip. Louisa remembered feeling more dead than alive when, at noon on 25 November, she was presented to her Adams relatives in Quincy.

Louisa appeared to these New Englanders as, in her words, "a maudlin, hysterical, fine lady not fit to be John Quincy Adams' wife." Louisa could hardly speak for coughing, so severe had her cold become, and to Abigail, a racking cough was the sound of death. She announced to relatives that Louisa's "frame is so slender and her constitution so delicate that I have many fears that she will be of short duration." Louisa wondered if she would survive the wholly different sort of existence these Adamses and their neighbors were accustomed to.

What startled Louisa most about Quincy and Boston was the life a woman was expected to lead there. Most females devoted all day to feeding and caring for their children and husbands. Massachusetts women were little better off than the Indian squaws she had seen in the neighborhood of Washington. Everything she encountered in her husband's native community seemed hostile. Not even her son George was received as Louisa had hoped: Abigail was displeased that the lad had not been named after John Adams. The ex-president proved the only sunshine in the dark Massachusetts landscape, giving Louisa such an obviously genuine and affectionate welcome that a bond was created between them which lasted for a quarter of a century.

The maid Louisa brought with her from Germany loudly and unfavorably compared life in New England to that in England and Germany. John Quincy hurried to discharge this embarrassing woman for what he termed reasons of economy. Even without her servant, Louisa was eager to move into Boston in late December 1801. There she hoped to handle life in her own way. She set up housekeeping with furniture mostly obtained when Uncle Norton Quincy conveniently died a few weeks before. Only occasionally did she join John Quincy in his dutiful weekly pilgrimages to Quincy for conferences with Abigail and John.

Instead Louisa awaited the pleasure of a long visit her mother paid in 1802, soon after Joshua's death. Catherine brought with her one of Louisa's sisters. Thereafter Louisa kept at least a sister and sometimes two with her. They were helpful as allies in Louisa's campaign to keep house as she preferred, and their stay in Boston relieved Catherine Johnson's financial load. Most important, these sisters were companions for Louisa when John Quincy slipped away into politics, where he hoped to make a living and to redeem the family name after his father's defeat for reelection as president. Louisa was prepared for this and continued to establish her own life, refusing to stay housebound. She attended legislative sessions as a spectator, and, with her sisters, found pleasure in a growing circle of friends.

In early January 1803, Louisa demonstrated the talent as a hostess for which she eventually became famous. She gave a party for forty Bostonians which succeeded marvelously despite the cramped size of her residence. The guests frolicked past midnight, with the crowning achievement being John Quincy's admission: "I danced myself the whole evening." A week later, Louisa took her husband and a sister to the grand ball marking the opening of a new legislative session. There the Adamses played whist and danced into the early morning. Louisa encouraged John Quincy to bring home gentlemen from his social clubs, and she also entertained ladies.

Louisa studied the Yankee world closely. It intimidated her less than

Abigail did. There was the time, for instance, when she sought a nursemaid to help with her newborn son in 1803. What did she discover in "this land of good or bundling habits"? The twenty applicants she interviewed each confessed to being the mother of a bastard. Finally, one of Louisa's Boston friends, Mrs. Harrison Gray Otis, recommended a "staid-looking" older woman, whom Louisa immediately sought, only to find that she had a baby whose father was a black man. The next girl employed proved impossible since she was "constantly in hysterics because she could not see her sweetheart."

In the fact of these revelations, Louisa noted with dismay how Boston smugly maintained its false modesty. On 1 July 1803, while entertaining the daughters of Dr. Thomas Welsh, Louisa began labor pains. Immediately, she said, the two young women jumped up and "ran away from the tea table." A very different reaction was displayed by Louisa's sister Carolina, who was visiting. When a midwife put Louisa's second son on the drafty floor, Carolina "ran into the room almost undressed, to assist and took the child immediately." The infant was named John Adams.

Unimpressed by Louisa's accomplishments, Abigail continued to insist that John Quincy had blundered badly in his choice of a wife. True, she said, a person married for better or worse, but if her son had used sound judgment, he would have found a wife with "a healthy and good constitution." Abigail did not hide her disappointment, and as time passed Louisa felt more estranged than ever from her mother-in-law. She admired Abigail for being "equal to every occasion in life," and desperately desired to be similarly endowed. Abigail's letters contain enough sarcastic comments about Louisa to support the latter's belief that her volatile spirits, delicate health, foreign manners, and outspokeness continued to make her seem an alien, or, worse still, "a fine lady."

Aware of the disapproval of her new relatives, Louisa tended to remain silent around them, which immediately brought the charge that she was proud. During Louisa's pregnancy with little John, Elizabeth Peabody wanted to offer suggestions about easing that condition, but since she had not met Louisa, and knew her only through Abigail's eyes, she hesitated to advise Louisa about New England remedies for the discomfort of childbearing. "I suppose she will think it, like the King of Israel, too small a thing to submit to," Elizabeth said to Abigail, who merely shook her head over "Madam's confinement," and the attention Louisa seemed to believe John Quincy owed her.

With the birth of a second son, Louisa took heart and renewed her effort to gain Abigail's respect. Surely, she told herself, being mother of "two fine children" should count as a substantial achievement. Louisa went out to Quincy "as soon as I could crawl," to visit Abigail, who was then desperately ill. The gesture made a favorable impression, giving Louisa hope that there might be a comfortable place for her in life with the Adamses.

This prospect was disrupted when Louisa was moved into yet another world, national politics. John Quincy was elected United States senator from Massachusetts, and late in 1803 Louisa found herself in Washington. There she saw even less of her husband, but at least enjoyed the company of her mother and sisters. Louisa had persuaded John Quincy that they should board in Walter Hellen's large house located on what is now the 2600 block of K Street Northwest. The economy of the arrangement appealed to John Quincy, and Louisa was thrilled to be with her family.

Washington was still the muddy village Abigail had despised. But it had a lively if small social circle, which meant that wives of cabinet members were happy to welcome Louisa since few senators' wives accompanied their husbands to Washington in those days. Another benefit for Louisa was that in Washington, more than in Boston, she could ride horseback, one of her favorite activities. She even coaxed John Quincy into an occasional canter with her. She had less success converting him to another of her pleasures, the race track. John Quincy preferred studying and writing, which Louisa could tolerate now that she had ample opportunity for conversation with her relatives. Consequently, Louisa thrived as a senator's mate while her husband grew more taciturn and troubled by politics.

Louisa was remarkably sturdy, despite her seeming frailness. Once, to John Quincy's astonishment, she arose unharmed after being thrown from her horse because of a poorly secured saddle. He, poor man, was shaken for days by the sight. It was Senator Adams' health, in fact, which obliged Abigail to communicate with Louisa, the older woman being zealously interested in her son's digestion, slumber, and apparel. At first her letters to Louisa took the tone one would ordinarily use while addressing a ten-year-old, but when Louisa replied maturely and enthusiastically about the subject so dear to his mother—John Quincy's disregard for his health and person—Abigail's messages began to sound more like herself. The older woman was pleased after Louisa took the initiative in December 1804 to buy a horse for her husband. Louisa figured that his health and their marriage might both improve if they rode daily together.

When John Quincy announced he was unwilling to take the time for these excursions, Louisa conspired with Abigail, asking her help in urging Senator Adams to change his mind. This was the sort of enlightened wifely strategy which pleased Abigail. While John Quincy continued to evade his horse, Louisa slowly ascended in her mother-in-law's esteem. Soon specific instruction about John Quincy's diet, clothing, and habits were regularly mailed by Abigail to Louisa. John Quincy may have resented the alliance created by concern over his personal habits. At any rate, in 1804 he announced that financial shortages meant he and Louisa would have to cease living in Washington part of the year and the remainder in Boston. Funds were available for only one household, and he assumed that Louisa would return to live in Massachusetts.

To John Quincy's surprise, his plan backfired. Louisa announced she would remain in Washington, a decision which meant that her home would no longer be in New England. This was unthinkable in John Quincy's view, and he spoke bitterly to Louisa, since he did not know how else to cope with a strong-minded woman. Louisa retorted with equal heat, even remarking on her husband's frigid nature and on his disdain for her family. She acknowledged that she was repelled by Boston and Quincy. These disclosures, said John Quincy in a letter written after he had returned alone to New England, were "painful and unexpected," particularly in their personal implications. "Of coldness and unkindness to you at any time, I am not conscious," he replied.

Reflecting on how his idea had failed, and finding himself very lonely for Louisa, John Quincy began writing letters to her which contained signs of humility. He conceded that his yearning for her happiness was more than he was able to put into words and deeds. Their life should be spent together, but he would abide by her choice. As for her remarks about his family, John Quincy loftily said he would ignore these, and observed only that he honored his bonds in Massachusetts just as she preferred hers in Washington. He now had the wisdom, however, to add that he had discovered something about himself: "I never can be happy distant from you."

As if to prove his point, although he spent the summer of 1804 in the presence of Abigail, John Quincy suffered from sleeplessness, inability to concentrate, and general depression. When he complained, Louisa's reply was rather stern. She reminded him that their separation had been his choice since he told her she must live either in one place or the other, though she added that being apart from him was no pleasure for her. As the summer wore on, John Quincy agreed that Louisa had been correct when she tried to show him it would cost no more to have her with him, whether in New England or in Washington. Louisa then took her turn at reconciliation, assuring her husband, "I shall know no happiness or peace till you return."

It was Louisa, rather than John Quincy, who identified the weakness in their marriage, the constant struggle between love's attractions and the divisiveness caused by competing interests and temperaments. "My head and my heart are constantly at war," Louisa admitted to her mate. It was a refrain she would repeat many times in their marriage. For Louisa, it seemed impossible to live with John Quincy or without him. The crux of the problem, she pointed out, was that her husband's outlook and his political worries led him to show little respect for her or willingness to share time with her. Yet Louisa yearned for John Quincy as a lover, and did not wish again to be separated. In October 1804, a letter Louisa sent from Washington to Quincy spoke rapturously of how she would clasp John Quincy to her when he returned. Upon receiving these words, Senator Adams promptly departed for the federal city, leaving Quincy much sooner than planned.

10

St. Petersburg and Back

When her husband reached Washington, Louisa welcomed him warmly. There was a brief season of amity between them. They agreed to a plan for the care and education of their sons, both having heard Abigail express concern that George and John might grow up in what she scornfully described as the atmosphere of a Washington boardinghouse. There certainly were disadvantages to living in Walter Hellen's residence, but they were not what Abigail imagined. Louisa's brother-in-law's property was near somewhat isolated Georgetown and thus inconvenient. In fact the women there were alone on Christmas Day 1805 when a band of Cherokee Indians, visiting the capital, stopped at the house and refused to leave. Louisa had the presence of mind to play the piano for them and give them ribbons. Pleased, the braves departed.

Louisa reluctantly agreed that her sons would be better off in New England. Since keeping a house in Boston was now financially impossible for John Quincy, their summers would be spent with the children in Quincy, living in the cottage where John Quincy was born. When Congress resumed, Louisa would go south with her husband, the two sons, George and John, remaining with Abigail and the Cranches. From the start, the separation imposed by this arrangement distressed Louisa. Despite Abigail's careful reports on the state of her grandsons, including graphic details about their bowel activity, Louisa was obviously guilt-ridden at leaving the lads. She feared she would lose their affection, and complained to her mother-in-law that she had been compelled to leave her boys, the sort of self-pitying assertion that Abigail pounced upon.

Life became more awkward when Louisa discovered she was pregnant. By early 1806, she was safely beyond the months when she might miscarry, a familiar disappointment and one she had experienced the previous year.

With the baby due in early summer, Louisa decided to remain in Washington while John Quincy went north to be with their sons. Also, he had become a professor of Rhetoric at Harvard University, and had classes to teach in the summer. (In those days, members of Congress often had other employment.) Left with her Johnson relatives and with time to think, Louisa decided to send Abigail a statement which she hoped might strengthen the tie between them.

The remarkable letter came directly to the point. Louisa explained to Abigail that she did indeed covet "your good opinion." She acknowledged, however, that trying to please the Adamses "may have given a harshness to my character which does not naturally belong to it." Although Louisa addressed the letter to "my dear Mother," rather than using the customary and chilly "Madam," she was not abjectly surrendering. Abigail was informed that, difficult though Louisa often found life in America, she would struggle to maintain her own character. She was determined to do so, Louisa emphasized, even if it gave her an unladylike outspokeness, or harshness. Apparently Abigail made no direct reply.

After Louisa's laments to John Quincy about the "dreadful insipidity" of pregnant life in which her main diversions were long walks, her child, a son, was still-born. This physical and emotional ordeal was accepted calmly by Louisa, who soon hastened to Boston where, thanks to his Harvard position, John Quincy had the money to buy a house. He even talked of leaving the Senate, a prospect that now pleased Louisa, who said she would welcome settling down, even in Boston, if that was the way to keep her husband and boys together. She was only slightly annoyed when, without consulting her, John Quincy chose a house located in a remote neighborhood no one had even heard of.

Pregnant again, Louisa willingly remained in Boston during the winter of 1806–07 along with her sister Carolina. The two women enjoyed the community's social life. They even went out to Quincy for one of the first dances held in the town. It proved a great success, and Louisa and Carolina remained until 3:00 A.M. When two fires broke out in the house John Quincy had secured, Louisa could make a reasonable argument for changing residences, and she moved to a much better dwelling situated on the corner of Nassau Street and Frog Lane.

In no location could Louisa escape quarrels with John Quincy over the discipline he insisted she must use with their sons. Louisa was much gentler, and preferred giving the lads lessons in French instead of the Latin their father cherished. Above all, she resisted imposing the severe punishments he demanded for misdeeds. Contemplating what such differences in their outlook implied, Louisa once again found herself telling John Quincy that she could not live happily with him or without him. It was a paradox her husband claimed "I do not fully understand," for by then their separation was making the couple eager for each other.

The mood led Senator Adams to compose a poem for his wife: "*Louisa!* thus remote from thee/Still something to each *Joy* is wanting/While thy *Affection* can, to me/Make the most dreary scene enchanting." Louisa's charming reply stressed how she thought constantly about her husband and described the dreariness of each morning when she awoke to find his space beside her empty. No happiness was possible for her, Louisa told John Quincy, until she could hold him "once more to the heart of your tenderly affectionate wife."

Senator Adams returned to Boston in time to join Louisa in being hosts for the wedding on 21 July 1807 of her sister Carolina Virginia Marylander Johnson to Andrew Buchanan. The dancing lasted until well into the next morning. A few weeks later, Louisa gave birth to Charles Francis Adams after unusually severe labor. The ordeal was considerably eased for Louisa by the comforting presence of her sister-in-law, Nabby Smith, now visiting in New England after her husband's release from prison. No woman in the Adams circle seems to have had more difficulty when her babies were delivered than Louisa, yet she recovered swiftly and seemed eager to bear more youngsters.

In the autumn of 1807, taking her infant with her, Louisa accompanied John Quincy to Washington for his last season in the Senate. Seeing Louisa off on such a journey increased Abigail's respect for what had once seemed such a frail "fine lady." It looked to Abigail that traveling without privacy in a stagecoach while nursing a baby was unthinkable. Louisa attributed her lack of prudishness concerning this and other matters to an outlook formed when she grew up in Europe. Trying to see some good in Louisa's uninhibited determination, the dubious Abigail conceded that this early travel could instill courage in Louisa's infant. "The little fellow seems to be born for deeds of greater hardihood than his brothers," said Grandmother Adams.

By May 1808, John Quincy and Louisa were back in Boston, having returned under a cloud. In Washington, Senator Adams had been voting with the Jeffersonian faction, making it appear that he had abandoned the Federalist position which he was expected by Massachusetts to represent. Actually John Quincy believed that certain Jeffersonian policies, such as the Louisiana Purchase and the Embargo Bill of 1807, were in the national interest. The outraged Massachusetts legislature disagreed and repudiated John Quincy in 1808 by electing his successor a year early. John Quincy promptly resigned his seat, and seemed in earnest when he talked with Louisa of a permanent residence in Boston, where he would teach at Harvard, practice law, and write.

The prospect pleased Louisa, even when she found that the bitterness in Massachusetts toward the now retired senator was so great as to make many social exchanges awkward or impossible. Louisa reported that they faced "a system of persecution painful to our family, but disgraceful to the state of Massachusetts whose citizens are ever slaves to a handful of men." The experience did nothing to stunt Louisa's growing belief that politics was no field for men of principle. Her recommendation was that she and her husband rise above the cold stares, the whispering, and the slander.

But for John Quincy the predicament smacked of personal failure. He suffered indescribable pain knowing that even his mother was dismayed by and suspicious of what seemed collusion on the part of her son with political enemies. Old John Adams was somewhat more understanding. All the Adamses were mortified, though, when John Quincy strengthened the worst suspicions about his apostasy by accepting President James Madison's appointment to be America's first minister to Russia. The news horrified Louisa who, like Abigail, had not been consulted about this abrupt change in John Quincy's intentions.

For Louisa a devastating experience now began. She was informed by her husband that she must accompany him to Europe, leaving their two eldest sons with Abigail. Charles Francis, less than two years old at the time, would be allowed to travel with his mother. These plans might have been dropped if Louisa had avoided miscarriage early in 1809. A baby probably would have caused John Quincy to keep Louisa in Boston with all her children. When the prospect of an infant vanished, Louisa was compelled to part from George and John. Outrage and grief over this cruelty sapped much of the love from Louisa's marriage. She never forgave her husband for what she believed was an enforced betrayal of her responsibilities as a parent.

So angry was Louisa in the days just before she sailed for Russia that John Quincy and Abigail kept her from being alone with John Adams, whose sympathy for her might have persuaded him that she be allowed either to take all her children or to stay in America with them. Although Abigail heartily disapproved of her son's decision to go abroad as a Jeffersonian emissary, she was certain that Louisa belonged at his side, no matter what her daughter-in-law might prefer. Further, Abigail was confident that, between herself and Aunt and Uncle Peabody in Atkinson, Louisa's sons would get as good an education and even better discipline there than in Louisa's care.

Louisa's outrage lingered for years. From that moment in 1809, she said, "to the end of time life to me will be a succession of miseries only to cease with existence." Being wrenched from her children was an "agony of agonies"; even worse, she felt she had sinned in submitting to her husband and deserting her sons at a time when they most needed a mother's influence. Louisa thought carefully about the dilemma that confronted any woman torn between duty to her children and to her husband. In her case, she wished she had insisted on remaining with her children, who were more important than a woman's mate. When she left them, it was "at the expense of every feeling of my soul, and of the sweetest affections of the heart."

Privately Abigail worried about John Quincy. She confided to Elizabeth Peabody that "a man of his worth ought not be permitted to leave the country." Although she realized her son was badly depressed by his political ignominy, Abigail told Catherine Johnson that she knew he could have surmounted the slander if he had only endured it for a time. Of course this had also been Louisa's position, but her advice had been dismissed. And so, at age thirty-four, Louisa started across the Atlantic in August 1809. She would live for nearly six years in Russia, where circumstances did little to relieve her guilt and anger.

Louisa and John Quincy arrived in St. Petersburg just as winter began. The beautiful Russian capital, created a century before by Peter the Great, was situated on a marsh at the head of the Baltic Sea where, for half of each year, the city was surrounded by ice. To Louisa, the isolation symbolized her own plight, cut off for half of each year from corresponding with her sons. To make matters worse, nothing Louisa had seen before in Europe quite prepared her for the sensual, lavish living which prevailed around the tsar's court, the center of existence for diplomats and their wives. Costs were fearfully high in St. Petersburg, which meant the Adamses had to limit themselves to fourteen "thieving" servants, a pitiable number in the opinion of Louisa's acquaintances in the diplomatic corps, who wondered how she managed with so few.

No matter where she might have been forced to accompany her husband, the gloomy and very indignant Louisa would have proved difficult to please. So it was not surprising that life in St. Petersburg infuriated her. "I do not like the place or the people," she reported to Abigail. She begged to be sent home in 1810, but John Quincy refused because of the expense. Meanwhile Louisa noted that her husband was losing sleep from worry that he would disgrace the United States by failing to keep pace with life in the tsar's court. As Louisa described it to Abigail, she and John Quincy were rarely in bed before 4:00 A.M. They arose at 11:00, ate no meal worth mentioning until dinner at 5:00 P.M., followed by tea at 10:00 P.M. and supper at 1:00 A.M.

Small wonder, Louisa observed, that Russian women lost their beauty early, and became "cold and haughtily repulsive in their manners."

Furthermore, women in St. Petersburg were wholly unrestrained in their relationships with men, Louisa had noticed, so that she and her sister Kitty, who had accompanied her, were quickly put on their guard. There was one redeeming aspect of her years in St. Petersburg, the cordial relationship she soon developed with Tsar Alexander I and his wife, Empress Elizabeth. Alexander and John Quincy also became good friends; the learned American minister favorably impressed the monarch and the two often took long walks together.

Louisa's talents demonstrated once again that she was much more impressive than she ever openly conceded. Since French was the language spoken at court, the American minister's wife was quite at home. Her wide reading and musical gifts also were assets rarely found in any diplomat's wife, particularly one from the raw new nation in North America, and endeared her to Alexander and Elizabeth. One of her reports on this relationship includes an exquisite description of the emperor and empress seated for an hour on the floor playing with Charles Francis, whom they found "most charming."

While much of the correspondence Louisa sent back to America asked for reassurance about her children, she wrote often to her Johnson relatives, who stayed in close touch with the Adamses in Quincy. Catherine Johnson delighted Abigail with vivid accounts of politics and society in the nation's capital. (Unfortunately, all these descriptions have been lost.) In exchange, Abigail offered Louisa's mother much counsel, even intervening when Catherine's daughter Eliza proposed to marry an impoverished clergyman. From Abigail came the familiar and sobering advice that had become so characteristic of her. She urged Eliza to contemplate what would happen after love had cooled. Alluding to Betsy Norton's dismal life in the Weymouth parsonage, Abigail said that even with a clergyman, poverty was difficult to bear once passion subsided.

Abigail sent admiring congratulations to Catherine on her success in getting President Madison to appoint her son Thomas Baker Johnson to a $3,000–per annum job with the postal service in New Orleans. Catherine was preparing to move south to share in Thomas' success when the fearful year of 1811 changed everything. First came the death of Louisa's older sister, Nancy Hellen. This was followed by Catherine's own demise at age fifty-four on 29 October and then that of Louisa's brother-in-law, Andrew Buchanan, a few days later. All were victims of a fever epidemic that ravaged the Washington area. From John Adams came a notable tribute to Louisa's mother, who was, said the former president, "a woman of fine understanding."

With Catherine and the eldest Johnson daughter Nancy both deceased, and Louisa out of the country, Abigail undertook to take charge of what was left of the family. The youthful Johnson women freely sought her advice, especially when the youngest of them, twenty-four-year-old Adelaide, was being pursued by Walter Hellen, bereaved husband of the late Nancy. What should they do about their brother-in-law's behavior? A shocked Abigail replied, "I could never reconcile a double connection." Were there not clear biblical cautions against a male marrying the sister of a dead wife? Eventually, the realistic Abigail decided to overlook this, in view of the poverty faced by Adelaide, and reluctantly blessed her union with Hellen.

There was no time to ask questions about another crisis in the Johnson family, one taking place not in Washington, but St. Petersburg. To Louisa's dismay, Catherine "Kitty" Johnson, her sister and companion, found herself pregnant in 1812. The male involved was none other than William Steuben Smith, the son of Nabby, who had pleaded with John Quincy to take the young man to Russia. Kitty's pregnancy was but one of several escapades undertaken by young Smith, who resembled his father, the colonel, in many ways. He was, for instance, frequently seen at St. Petersburg's gambling casinos, where he managed to run up sizable debts. Upon hearing of this latest sin in the life of her grandson, Abigail found a shred of consolation in seeing young William compelled to marry a woman older than he and considerably his superior in ability.

Grievous as these events were to Louisa, she had greater troubles of her own. Affairs in Russia had drawn her husband into being more inattentive and impatient than he had been as a senator. As she reported to Abigail, John Quincy "is even more buried in study than when he left America, and has acquired so great a disrelish for society that even his small family will appear at times to become irksome to him." Louisa refrained from elaborating to her mother-in-law, lest she lose her temper while she wrote. In her diary, however, she was quite blunt about how her mate allowed "the vain projects of this world" to imprison him. His mood left no one to whom she could "open her heart." What could be worse, Louisa wondered, than being thus cut off from her husband, the person to whom she was in theory "bound by the closest ties"?

Louisa recorded almost clinically how John Quincy had changed into a creature increasingly intolerant even of those with whom he was intimate. For a time Louisa endured this in quiet, until one day John Quincy spoke caustically about the way she was teaching Charles Francis his prayers. At this point she lost her patience "in a very unbecoming manner." Was there anything she did which pleased him? she asked. After this exchange, her relations with John Quincy went from bad to worse, so that Louisa confessed the situation made "my temper which was never good suffer in proportion to my grief." Next John Quincy charged her with being suspicious and jealous, not recognizing, she said, that the signs he mistook were actually the response inevitable in a woman who was "naturally warm and affectionate," but who was being treated with "perpetual coldness and restraint."

It would have astonished Louisa to know that recently, on the anniversary of their wedding, John Quincy had spoken in his diary about his good fortune to have Louisa as a wife. "Our union has not been without its trials, nor invariably without dissensions between us," he said, explaining this by the fact that their needs and tastes were very different. Furthermore, he conceded, "there are natural frailties of temper in both of us, both being quick and irascible and mine being sometimes harsh." Yet she was a faithful and affectionate wife, who, he paused to note with pride, had nursed each of their children. He would not want to live in a celibate state.

Obviously not. Louisa had found herself pregnant once again soon after arriving in Russia. She miscarried, however, and had to tell Abigail how "a severe indisposition" had deprived her "of the pleasure of presenting you with another little relative." Then, in November 1810, she conceived once again. This time the condition continued until the birth of a daughter on 12 August 1811. John Quincy showed a bit of the humor hidden within him when he reported the event to Abigail: "I think this will convince you that the climate of St. Petersburg is *not* too cold to produce an American." The tsar proposed himself as the infant's godfather, but was made to understand, with some difficulty, that the American public would not be pleased if a monarch played so prominent a role in the family of a republican diplomat.

Louisa was nothing less than blissful. The child was named Louisa Catherine, and for a time flourished. "Such a pair of eyes!! I fear I love her too well!" said Louisa, who informed Abigail that the little girl resembled her grandmother. The presence of a long-sought daughter inspired Louisa to endure the unpleasantness of life in Russia. Unfortunately, her delight lasted exactly one year. On 15 August 1812, John Quincy reported in his diary, "Mrs. Adams weaned the child." He did not indicate that Louisa had strenuously objected to this step, which she took on the eve of a short holiday John Quincy planned in the countryside, where Louisa knew milk and water could be even more treacherous for youthful digestions than in the city.

Much against Louisa's will, the vacation proceeded. All the while she recalled how ill little George became when she weaned him just before setting out for Quincy from Washington in 1801. After three days in the hamlet of Ochta, baby Louisa began the dreaded dysentery. There was no relief as the child grew weaker and convulsive. Since she was constantly at the baby's side, Louisa's writing ceased. But John Quincy's diary shows an anguish that must have equaled his daughter's pain. The doctors applied blisters between the child's shoulders, and lanced her gums—thinking that teething was causing the disease. Yet nothing helped.

"Language cannot express the feelings of a parent beholding the long continued agonies of a lovely infant," John Quincy wrote on 12 September. The next day he reported that the patient was tortured, while "my dear wife . . . is suffering little less than her child." After three days in the sickroom, Louisa agreed to rest, returning on 14 September. Early the next morning, little Louisa Catherine Adams died. She had lived a month past her first birthday. Her mother undertook at once to comfort the family, and especially the grieving husband.

As he would so often during their marriage, a stricken John Quincy envied Louisa's "resignation and fortitude." On 17 September, the child was buried on a knoll in the cemetery of the English quarter in the Russian capital. Immediately afterward, Louisa took her inconsolable husband for a walk through St. Petersburg's public gardens. Trying to support John Quincy, Louisa saved her own sorrow for her journal, which for a time had only the brief entry that her babe had gone to Heaven. Within a month, however, Louisa was writing regularly in the diary as part of her struggle to overcome grief and depression.

Louisa received little comfort from John Quincy, who, when he was not caught up in his own emotions, appeared to confine all his attention to his surviving child, Charles Francis, and seemed even more distant from his wife, with the result that Louisa's journal entries mentioned a suicidal wish to lie beside her dead daughter, and rehearsed her guilt at having weaned the child. Louisa sensed that this release of emotions through her diary would help her "avoid dwelling on the secret and bitter reproaches of my heart." She condemned herself for being proud, and for certain "evil propensities." These included sexual yearning, for Louisa could not take her mind from thoughts of women her age who accepted young lovers.

One of Louisa's most anguished comments was made in the first letter she wrote to Abigail after the baby's death. In April 1813 Louisa told her mother-in-law, "My heart is almost broken, my health is gone, and my peace of mind is, I fear, forever destroy'd." For some time Abigail had sought to arrange with President Madison for John Quincy's recall to America. Now she used all her persuasive power in urging John Quincy to bring Louisa home, pointedly suggesting that he allow no new pregnancy. "Family circumstance" was Abigail's delicate term. John Quincy refused to budge. He had earlier turned down Madison's offer of an appointment to the Supreme Court, which Madison arranged after much negotiation with Abigail who, because the circumstances were urgent, had overcome her pride and asked a favor from a Jeffersonian chief executive.

In her journal, meanwhile, Louisa confessed she was faltering in her

Christian faith. There were dreams of her father and of great storms in which the message was flashed across the skies that her petition was granted. Louisa briefly thought this meant she would die and be buried beside her daughter. When that grave site was filled on 9 June 1813 by the burial of a friend, Louisa accepted it as an important sign. Soon thereafter, she began to emerge from her dark passage, appearing stronger than at any time since coming to St. Petersburg. In August 1813 Louisa noted her uplifted spirits in her journal. "I scarcely know myself."

Her mood refreshed, Louisa redoubled her reading, although she ignored a book on mental diseases handed her by John Quincy. She took new pleasure in Sir Walter Scott, but found Lord Byron's poetry less appealing than before. Louisa's journal entries display how wide her interests were and how zealously she pursued knowledge. She wrote at length on astronomy. She analyzed the career of Louis XIV, and found in this subject a cogent illustration of how ambition and lust motivated some males. Not that she thought women were free of ignoble impulses, least of all herself. She took to reading biography and memoirs of women, notably the mistresses of famous men. One of these, by Diane de Poitiers, companion of Henry II of France, especially struck Louisa, although she said she hesitated to put on paper the thoughts it stimulated.

She sought distraction, instead, by collecting a remarkable variety of recipes from women she met in St. Petersburg. One was for plum pudding, which called for ¾ pint of flour, ½ pint milk, 6 ozs. suet, ½ pound raisins, ½ pound currants, a little nutmeg, a little lemon peel, and two spoonfuls of treacle, all to be boiled for four hours. Another was a formula for treating piles. This involved 1 oz. flour of brimstone, 1 oz. strained honey, 1 oz. conserve of roses, 1 oz. cream of tartar, all to be mixed and a portion taken each morning by pieces the size of a nutmeg. No breakfast was to be eaten with this treatment.

She began studying John Quincy in a more detached way, noting once again his relentless ambition, his remoteness, and his failure to open his heart. Not all great men cut themselves off from intimacy. Why must John Quincy deprive himself and her of shared confidences, thus making "unavailing" to them "the greatest blessing" a couple could have? Even as she asked these questions, Louisa found her situation once again transformed, this time by world events. Early in 1814, John Quincy brought her the news that he was to participate in peace talks to conclude the War of 1812 then going on between the United States and Great Britain. The negotiations were to occur in the Belgian city of Ghent. To that location John Quincy was summoned, leaving Louisa and young Charles Francis in Russia.

Just before departing in late April 1814, John Quincy seemed to rediscover his wife. He even took her for a carriage ride. More astonishing yet, he decided she could handle worldly matters, and gave her a copy of his will—which named Louisa as executrix for all his affairs in Europe— as well as a listing of his assets, including property in Massachusetts. She was even entrusted with the key to his trunk filled with precious papers. These new tactics did not prevent John Quincy, once he was away, from scolding Louisa for spending too much money, although she had moved into a smaller house. Defending herself, Louisa said that if she had indulged herself, she was not aware of it. Her ascetic habits were strong, Louisa assured John Quincy. After all, she told him, "You know that when I am with you this gratification is impossible."

On the whole, her husband's new confidence and attention astonished and pleased Louisa, as did the amorous tone of his letters. After telling her to kiss Charles Francis, John Quincy said: "As for you—as the song says, 'that fruit must be gathered from the tree.' Adieu." Louisa replied frequently, sometimes daily. She talked about matters great and small, trying to keep up her spirits, for she deplored having to stay behind in Russia. She often took trips to the country with Charles Francis, but these did not always lift her mood. After John Quincy was away for two months, she announced to him that the most wretched being on earth is "a woman without her husband." Being parted was difficult enough for persons who were middle-aged. She would not, said Louisa, recommend it to the youthful.

A favorite subject for Louisa's letters was the emotional side of men and women. She scoffed at those who claimed rational capacities could master these passions. Ultimately the latter must prevail. But what Louisa regretted was that the struggle between reason and emotion "must end in moroseness or gloom." In one letter she apologized to John Quincy for being less ardent in recent years: "There are some wounds which are not easy to heal, and forgetfulness is not my best quality." But now, she said encouragingly, his letters were causing her "sensibility" to become "most agreeably excited."

Her thoughts often turned to relations between the sexes. One of Louisa's letters addressed the step many men took of abandoning their middle-aged wives for young women. While she claimed to understand a male's doing so, Louisa chuckled at recalling how even Cicero, an author beloved by John Quincy, found he could not live with the demands of a young woman. Any mature and experienced wife knew, said Louisa, that she should be imaginative in devising ways to keep her husband from passing the evening sleeping in his chair. John Quincy recognized Louisa had him in mind, since his rising at 4:00 A.M. meant that he usually dozed long after dinner.

Coping with a male past forty was usually an unspiring occupation, said Louisa, so that women often were reduced to "sinking into absolute silence or gaping [yawning] for want of something better to do." If this was happiness, Louisa said, she lacked "both taste and sense to enjoy it," implying that she could create a livelier existence if her mate would permit. It was a delicate subject for Louisa to follow in her letters to John Quincy, but her lonely frustrations kept her thinking about her marriage. Did John Quincy expect more of her as a companion? she asked. Was she too much his intellectual inferior? Louisa informed him that it seemed impossible to live up to what he apparently expected. What a sorrowful circumstance it was, she told her husband, that the only happiness they had developed was in those periods when they were separated. In letters he treated her as a highly intelligent confidante. Why must he stop doing so when they were together? she inquired bluntly.

Much of the time, however, Louisa's epistles tried to entice and cheer her mate. She said in November 1814, "It seems to me now that I want you more than ever." A few weeks later she wrote, "God bless and speed you soon to the arms and heart of your faithful wife." There were even teasing comments. One subject was the weight he reported acquiring. Was it correct, she wondered, that "at our time of life fat is very becoming?" And since diplomats were supposed to take up mistresses, whom had he chosen? In these matters, "a woman of my age cannot be jealous," she said, particularly when his was a career where temptation was omnipresent. Since John Quincy seemed impervious to worldly beguilement, Louisa knew her badinage was probably harmless.

Louisa continued to pray earnestly for escape from Russia, but felt there was little hope. Apparently John Quincy would soon return, and they would face more terrible winters and more dreadful expense. Consequently, it was with elation that Louisa read her husband's letter of 27 December 1814 directing her to sell everything and meet him in Paris, "where I shall be impatiently waiting for you." It seemed likely, he acknowledged, that they would thereafter be living in London, where he was to be America's minister. Louisa did not dally. Her friend Elizabeth, the tsaritsa, marveled at the lively spirit Louisa displayed. It seemed to some observers that she was not the same woman who had been wife to the American minister.

Handling matters alone, Louisa promptly disposed of all but the family's essential possessions, mostly her husband's cherished books, which she packed and shipped to London. She reminded John Quincy that he must forgive her if she did not strike as shrewd a bargain as he fancied he could have. "My impatience to meet you is really and earnestly very great," she told him in justifying her swift departure from St. Petersburg. "We have both passed through disagreeable scenes and shall only be able to forget them when we meet." It was a reunion "for which my soul pants." On 12 February 1815, her fortieth birthday, Louisa set out on an adventure which would have daunted most mortals, male or female.

Her travels produced the kind of challenge which drew from Louisa the amazing strength so often latent and disguised within her. Now she was in charge, pushing on from St. Petersburg to Paris with an eight-year-old son, a maid, and two manservants. She traveled in the winter across Europe during the closing weeks of the Napoleonic Wars. Her vehicle was a Russian-style carriage mounted on a sleigh, pulled by a double team of horses. More than once Louisa found herself abandoned by a succession of fickle or frightened servants. Sometimes she lost her way and had to use all her linguistic talents to make herself understood in the countryside of Russia, Poland, and Germany.

Louisa frequently required that her party keep on the road night and day. Her young son gradually overcame his fearfulness and took courage from his mother's unfaltering example. There was a happy respite in Berlin, where Louisa was reunited with friends left behind in 1801. Most of the time, however, she proceeded toward Paris, always against warnings and advice that she turn back. Everywhere she met incredulity that this lone woman was headed where no man dared go unless compelled as a soldier. She even directed the carriage's dangerous crossings of ice-covered rivers. What troubled her most were fields covered with thousands of corpses, the remains of recent battles.

Louisa reached the Franco-German border just as reports arrived that Napoleon had returned from exile. But drawing nearer Paris she relaxed, stopped for luncheon, and calmly ordered champagne. Assured that none of Napoleon's troops was near, Louisa set out again, suddenly to find her obviously Russian carriage surrounded by members of the famous French Imperial Guard. For them anything even faintly Russian was the enemy. These were troops who remembered the savage defeat Napoleon had suffered during the retreat from Moscow in 1812. Their female camp followers were the most enraged, demanding that their men put to death the woman in the Russian vehicle. In the face of this, Louisa pluckily stepped from the carriage and led the crowd in cheers for Napoleon. It was immediately evident that no Russian could speak French so beautifully.

The danger passed, but to make doubly sure Louisa instructed her driver to spread the rumor that she was Napoleon's sister en route to meet him. There were no more delays; near midnight on 23 March Louisa lumbered up to Paris' Hotel du Nord, still in her sturdy Russian carriage. It is easy to imagine her disappointment when she was told that John Quincy had not returned from the theatre. They were soon reunited, and

John Quincy, while not astonished to see her, was amazed by how robust and self-assured Louisa was. He listened with horror to the story of the dangers she experienced during the forty-day trip. Life had been placid in Paris, he admitted, and he had calmly envisioned Louisa enjoying an easy ride. He had awaited her by spending his days in carefree searches for books, and his evenings at concerts and plays.

There was clearly pride in John Quincy's report to Abigail of what Louisa had accomplished. The vigor she displayed throughout her ordeal seemed nothing less than a miracle, a judgment upheld by the fact that Louisa's maid, recruited partway through the trip, collapsed with "brain fever" upon reaching Paris. Louisa's feat made her the toast of the Paris diplomatic corps, but she passed off her accomplishment lightly. She responded to Abigail's congratulations by saying "I have really acquired the reputation of a heroine at a very cheap rate," and hastened to talk instead of how life at the negotiating table had made John Quincy fat.

Twenty years later, in 1836, Louisa was willing to acknowledge that her trek was an amazing story. She wrote a "Narrative of A Journey from Russia to France 1815," recognizing that someday her achievement might be remembered. If so, Louisa said, she wished her experience to show "that undertakings which appear very difficult and audacious to my sex, are by no means so trying as imagination forever depicts them." Louisa contended her ordeal demonstrated "that energy and discretion follow the necessity of their exertion, to protect the fancied weakness of feminine imbecility." Let women use their abilities, Louisa proclaimed, and closed her recollection with what she intended as the motto for any woman's life: "Under all circumstances we must never desert ourselves."

The triumph opened what was perhaps the happiest interval in Louisa's life, the two-year period before she returned to the United States in the summer of 1817. For several weeks in Paris she and John Quincy had a blissful time together. Until they went to London, he had no duties to distract him. They attended concerts, went to the theatre, wandered in galleries, and took in the sights. While conceding he enjoyed all this activity with Louisa, John Quincy had to confide in his diary that it was "a fearful waste of time, but I hope the days of industry will soon return again."

And they did, for the Adamses arrived in England on 24 May 1815, and Dover officials gruffly ordered them to wait in the customs house. Louisa again astonished her husband by refusing to accept such treatment. As wife of the United States minister, she announced she would proceed to the hotel. No one stopped her. That night she was reunited with her sons George and John, who had been sent to meet her by their grandmother Abigail. The happy family lived for a time in London hotels, giving Louisa a chance to go about the city where she had grown up.

On 1 August Louisa supervised a move to the residence John Quincy had found. It required two carts and a wagon to carry their goods out of London seven miles in a westerly direction to Ealing, near Kensington. There, for nearly two years, Louisa presided over her most precious possessions, her husband and children. Their dwelling, known locally as Boston House, afforded Louisa opportunity to worship again in her preferred style—a pew in the village Anglican church came with the house rent. Parish members usually saw Louisa daily, for the death of her daughter had ultimately deepened her already earnest religious commitment.

The setting in Ealing gave Louisa what she most desired: respect and affection from her family. The duties of John Quincy's office were light and carried out in London. Thanks to the success of the peace negotiations at Ghent and his promotion to the London post, John Quincy's twin torments of doubt and zeal receded. With Louisa so obviously happy, her husband spent much time with her and their sons, who went to school nearby, boarding most of each term, but home for weekends. The school provided a close friend for Louisa in Ellen Nicholas, daughter of the headmaster. She shared Louisa's musical talents, and the two gave concerts with piano, harp, and song.

Life with Louisa so charmed John Quincy that he took up writing poetry. Louisa was pleased and touched by this, but drew greater satisfaction from overseeing her husband's daily routine. In the autumn of 1815, he suffered a serious eye infection that deprived him of sight and gave him such pain that he could not sleep. Louisa soothed him through the difficult nights, and he finally allowed her to consult a physician. The latter directed that six leeches be applied to the swollen eyelid. Of these, four "bit keenly" and clung for an hour. Afterward, Louisa kept warm applications on the eye so that her husband bled freely for another five hours.

John Quincy felt considerable satisfaction at not crying out even when the pain was most intense, but the treatment did not reduce the infection. His face grew swollen, leaving a sensation which was, he described to Louisa, as if "four hooks were tearing that side of my face into four quarters." This misery persisted for nearly a month, so that John Quincy had no choice but to accept help from Louisa. She read to him, took dictation, and wrote his letters. He was astonished at her skill. "From this day she will write for me long and often," he vowed. Every evening, she either read to him or sang, sometimes aided by Miss Nicholas. When John Quincy recovered, there were exquisite moments when he joined Louisa to "sit in conversation by the fireside." For Louisa, Boston and Washington had never been so pleasing.

There were other satisfactions. Louisa managed the household, even going into London to select new servants. She not only encouraged John Quincy's poetic efforts, but tried her hand at the art. Her husband acknowledged, again with some amazement, that "with a little practice she would write very beautiful verses." Louisa's joyful mood inspired a poem she wrote to John Quincy upon the twentieth anniversary of their wedding. Her lines spoke of love and admiration, to which John Quincy responded in the same spirit. Louisa's poetry at this time shows how transformed she was from the wretched creature who just a few years before was suffering in St. Petersburg. Who would have recognized that the cruel male described in her Russian journal was now the husband in whom, Louisa wrote, "sense and sweetness joined with ease/Shine forth in evr'y feature"?

At the request of Louisa's brother Thomas, who was still with the postal service in New Orleans, Louisa and John Quincy had their portraits painted by the rising young American artist, Charles Robert Leslie. Louisa was elated by the results—"most striking likenesses"—and notified Abigail that they would be exhibited in Philadelphia. Louisa also informed Abigail that she was now enjoying the best health of her life: "I am only afraid of growing too fat." For a short time, Louisa's contentment was so great that she was undismayed by the occasional moment when her husband was lured into politics. At one of the many parties they attended, John Quincy lost himself in business talk, forgetting that he had summoned their carriage and that Louisa was waiting for him in it. She sat patiently for ninety minutes, then she asked a servant to summon an abashed John Quincy, who confessed he had been thoughtless.

Louisa later perceived an omen in this episode, for soon afterward, in January 1817, word arrived that the Adamses would be recalled to America, where John Quincy would serve as secretary of state in the cabinet the new president, James Monroe, was assembling. Recognizing how this would affect her life and her husband's mood, Louisa moved at once to prevent a repetition of the misery of John Quincy's senatorial career. She forced him to agree to a home in Washington, from which they would make only brief summer visits to Quincy and Boston, places where memories of defeat and disgrace lurked to bedevil John Quincy. Louisa knew these were her greatest enemies. She also feared that in New England Abigail would poach on her claim to John Quincy's allegiance and that of their sons.

Louisa was back in America by mid-August 1817, much to Abigail's relief. She had heard rumors that the return would be delayed because Louisa had become pregnant. "I never had an intimation that such a manufacture had taken place," Abigail informed Harriet Welsh. "I hope it will be of the feminine gender." There was no such delicate condition, and on 18 August, Abigail and John greeted their son and daughter-in-law after an absence of eight years. Abigail was impressed, less with John Quincy, who was now portly and middle-aged, than with Louisa, who, said Abigail, was "looking better than I ever saw her, and younger, I think."

It was soon apparent to Louisa that a bond of affection and candor had been formed between Abigail and herself. The letters they exchanged during Louisa's years in Russia had helped allay the early doubts Abigail had about the "fine lady" John Quincy had married. Abigail chose during the happy reunion in 1817 to apologize for having so misjudged Louisa. This gesture comforted Louisa, who hoped that Abigail could help her retain her courage and self-respect when John Quincy once again buried himself in public affairs.

This happened soon enough. Within a short time Louisa was back in Washington, which had changed little, as she soon realized after persuading John Quincy to join her in paying calls on old friends. Leaving the house, the pair stepped in a large mud puddle and had to go back inside. It was not the primitive city, however, but the political capital which Louisa disliked. But John Quincy had left Washington a disgraced man in 1808; now he was returning in glory. At least this transformation promised a modest improvement in Louisa's prospects, so she was determined to take an interest in what went on.

This curiosity brightened Louisa's long letters to Abigail and John. Filled with Washington lore, these journal-like epistles brightened the old couple's life. John Adams called them "a delicious repast." Their satirical flavor was especially relished by Abigail, who also was eager for Louisa's visits to Quincy. These seemed impossible when Louisa, now forty-three, thought she was pregnant early in 1818. But it was a false alarm, and Louisa had a last, peaceful reunion late that summer with the frail Adams matriarch.

Soon after she returned to Washington in the autumn of 1818, Louisa learned of Abigail's death. Her new ally was gone, leaving Louisa alone to face life with John Quincy, who was daily more distracted by his duties and by his hopes for advancement in the public's esteem. Louisa mourned the loss of Abigail; who, as she put it, "possessed the art of softening the asperities of grosser nature, and in some measure of moulding them to her will." Louisa eagerly hoped to acquire some of this talent. And now, as she observed in her journal, she could only regret how she had mininterpreted Abigail's early efforts to instruct her. Too late, Louisa lamented, she had discovered what "a kind and affectionate mother" Abigail could be.

Yet in some ways Louisa was now much like Abigail, which was one reason why John Adams begged that she continue sending him letters from Washington. The younger woman's experience taught her to interpret life much as Abigail had. One would have thought it was Abigail speaking, when Louisa wrote near the time of her mother-in-law's death, "Every day that I live my opinion of mankind is less and less exalted and I am sure they are capable of almost any meanness to gratify a selfish ambition."

Mary Cranch, Abigail Adams, and Elizabeth Peabody would have been comfortable with Louisa's philosophy. In one of her last messages to Abigail, Louisa spoke of humankind's uncurbed passions, of "vanity and presumption," and of the arrogance which only humility before God could stifle. Thus, despite her very different background, Louisa took a compatible place beside the three sisters who grew up in Weymouth's parsonage. In the decade after Abigail's death, the period which Louisa would partly spend as first lady, events served to strengthen this spiritual kinship.

11

Sisters-in-Law

After the death of Abigail and her sisters, Louisa became the leading figure among the women associated with the Adams family. Not that her eminence went unchallenged. Abigail had left another daughter-in-law, a woman who had married an Adams in the hope of advancing in the world. This was Nancy Harrod, wife of John Quincy's youngest brother, Thomas Boylston Adams. Nancy's aspirations were disappointed, and for many years she resented and envied what seemed to her the good fortune and happiness surrounding Louisa. Friendship between the two sisters-in-law came only when they were older and much bruised by their experiences. Neither could then claim that life had been kinder to the other.

The career of Nancy Harrod Adams was one of failed expectations. She grew up in Haverhill, where her family was known to Elizabeth and John Shaw. From their first appearance in the Boston area in 1649, the Harrods had lived by skillful use of their hands. Joseph Harrod, Nancy's father, was an innkeeper with a talent for making bracelets and other simple jewelry. Nancy's mother was Anna Treat, whom Joseph Harrod married in 1771 when he was twenty-four and she twenty-one. Anna claimed among her forebears an early governor in the colony of Connecticut.

The inn which Joseph and Anna operated was situated in the center of Haverhill and there ten children were born. The eldest of these was Nancy. Rarely called by her proper name—Ann—she was born 25 April 1774. With so many brothers and sisters arriving after her, Nancy often found more attention in the nearby parsonage, where she was welcomed by Elizabeth and John Shaw. The bond between Nancy and the parson's wife grew stronger with the years. In 1799, Elizabeth said, "I feel very maternally interested in her welfare. She was my children's intimate companion and friend. She partook of our pleasures and deeply felt our grief."

Descriptions of the youthful Nancy show her growing into a woman with feelings, taste, and sentiments admired by Elizabeth Shaw, who observed that Nancy had charm of temper and person—"one of the loveliest of her sex." It was under Elizabeth's auspices that Nancy first met Thomas Bolyston Adams in 1784 when he came to Haverhill to study with his uncle John Shaw. Thomas' birthday was 15 September 1772, less than two years before Nancy's. For the next ten years Thomas lived in Nancy's neighborhood, except when he was enrolled at Harvard College.

Thomas' happiest memories were of his times in Haverhill, where his patient and sympathetic Aunt Elizabeth encouraged him but also let him follow his inclination to be a quiet, good-natured fellow. Thomas had trouble withstanding life's pressures, which seemed less severe in Haverhill than in Braintree. Since Thomas was a great favorite of his Aunt Elizabeth, it was natural that she should suggest "my friend" Nancy Harrod when Abigail began thinking of a wife for Thomas. The choice was apparent to Elizabeth, who sensed that from an early age Thomas was interested in the young Miss Harrod whom he had so often seen in the Haverhill parsonage. After removing to Atkinson and marrying Stephen Peabody, Elizabeth kept her enthusiasm for an eventual marriage between Nancy and Thomas.

This plan was endangered for a time by the possibility that Thomas might marry while abroad. In 1794, he had gone to Europe as John Quincy's secretary in the legation at The Hague. To Abigail's alarm, her youngest son had an insidious example before him when John Quincy chose Louisa Johnson as his wife. Thomas distressed his mother by filling his letters with praise for Louisa, causing Abigail to command that Thomas must "choose a wife whose habits, tastes, and sentiments are calculated for the meridian of your own country." At that time, Abigail was convinced Louisa would fail to be an acceptable American.

To Abigail's dismay, her youngest son chose to be as close-mouthed about his romantic intentions as John Quincy and steadfastly resisted his mother's demands to know everything. Thomas' letters to Abigail show how he could be good-natured and teasing while remaining uncommunicative. Fretting that another fine lady like Louisa would ensnare Thomas, Abigail took more interest in her sister Elizabeth's hints that Thomas was fond of the Haverhill maiden, Nancy Harrod.

With Elizabeth's backing, Abigail decided to see this young woman for herself and invited Nancy to visit Quincy. The young woman passed the test, and Thomas' mother assumed command of the campaign on Nancy's behalf, although she admitted privately that the Harrod clan was not of the caliber of those families whom she considered worthy of a marriage alliance with the Adamses. Still, said Abigail, Nancy was far better than a

European female. "I think her a very amiable, accomplished girl, and was much pleased with her," she said in her report to Elizabeth.

At the end of 1798 and still single, Thomas returned to America, seemingly less willing than ever to cooperate with his mother's plans for him. Not only did he keep silent about his love life; he insisted on settling in Philadelphia. He remained there, over his parent's objections, after John Adams' term as president had ended. Thomas made it clear that he wished to be independent, even if it meant he must practice law, an occupation he disliked. That was all Abigail knew until, one day, she accidently saw a letter addressed to Nancy in Thomas' hand. Abigail immediately begged her son to bare his feelings. Was there anything to the rumor of an engagement to Nancy? If so, said Abigail, that was fine with her, although there must be no marriage until Thomas could support a wife.

Early in 1803, affairs between Nancy and Thomas were still a mystery to Abigail. So she invited Miss Harrod for another stay in Quincy. Afterward Abigail wrote to Thomas with praise about "a very charming young lady" who had just been visiting. Nancy was not mentioned by name, although Abigail now hinted that she suspected Thomas' intent. She told her son, "You will never meet with any obstacle from me when ever you see your way clear to support a family."

Unfortunately, that route for Thomas always seemed cluttered with obstacles. He suffered from poor health, in particular severe rheumatism, and also from melancholia. He may have developed a dependence on alcohol by this time. These were among the reasons why none of Thomas' professional efforts in Philadelphia proved fruitful. To his cousin and close friend, Aunt Elizabeth's son Billy Shaw, Thomas confessed, "I am sometimes half distracted at my cursed hard fate." Thomas' prospects worsened in 1803 when any funds John and Abigail might have used to assist him were lost in the failure of an English bank in which the elder Adamses had invested heavily.

Late in 1803, a badly depressed Thomas Adams had to give up his independence and take refuge in Quincy. Since he had no choice but to live with his parents while trying to start a law practice in the area, Thomas found it difficult to keep secrets from Abigail. She soon knew that her son and Nancy were betrothed, although Thomas assured his fiancée that letters to him were seen by no one else and were carefully destroyed. His messages to her were melancholy reports on his impoverished state and the need to postpone even longer their marriage. Most distressing about this story, however, is that not a scrap of paper remains to reveal what Nancy thought about her situation.

While Abigail was assuring relatives of how ardently but prudently

Thomas desired to wed Miss Harrod, Nancy's seemingly endless engagement dragged on. The delay in marriage was now embarrassing to everyone. Surely a son of the former president of the United States could do better than keep his beloved waiting past her thirtieth birthday, which Nancy had reached. Early in 1805, she again visited Quincy. This stay with the Adamses brought life to the stagnant romance. There is indirect evidence that when Nancy returned to Haverhill from visiting Quincy, she gave Thomas an ultimatum. Their engagement must either move ahead or end.

In a touching letter Nancy received after reaching Haverhill, Abigail asserted how she yearned to have "a legal right to call you mine." "I both love and esteem you," Abigail wrote, recalling how much they had enjoyed sitting together by the fire and reading Robert Burns' poetry. Finally, Thomas' mother spoke of the delicate feelings she knew Nancy kept in her heart, adding that she sensed those emotions might be wounded. Nancy's pathetic departure left Abigail so alarmed that she and John dropped the requirement that Thomas be self-sufficient and he was told to take Nancy as his wife and bring her to live with his parents.

During mid-March 1805, Thomas proposed to Nancy that they be wed promptly and settle in Quincy. Abigail read the letter approvingly and added a few lines of her own, which stated that, if Nancy would accept this less than perfect arrangement, "I shall do all in my power to render your situation agreeable to you and hope that you will feel that you have only exchanged one parents' home for another." She prayed that Nancy and she would be "mutual comforts and blessings to each other." Nancy agreed to this way of becoming Mrs. Thomas Boylston Adams. She had been patient for more than a decade, and by then any basis for the marriage probably seemed better than waiting into middle age.

It remained to devise the appearance of worldly success for Thomas, so that neighbors in Quincy might believe he had met his family's requirements for marrying. This was done on 6 May 1805, when Thomas was elected Quincy's representative in the state legislature. Propped by that token achievement, the couple lost no time. Within a fortnight, Nancy welcomed Thomas to Haverhill, where they were married on 17 May 1805; the bride was thirty-one and the groom would soon be thirty-three. They returned to Quincy, and by November Nancy was pregnant, a condition which did not prevent her from accompanying Thomas to Boston, where he would serve in the legislature.

While in the city, the newlyweds stayed with Nancy's younger sister Frances, who had recently married Phineas Foster. The Fosters lived in comparative prosperity and independence. This contrast with Nancy's own modest prospects must have made a vivid impression on her. She already could see that Thomas was unlikely to serve more than a year as a representative and that his law practice was negligible. In frustration, Nancy wrote to Abigail from Boston, seeking the assurance her mother-in-law had pledged. Not much was forthcoming; Abigail replied with remarks about how life was full of disappointment and trial. Nancy was informed that those who courageously faced adversity could display "more graces and virtues than prosperity usually exhibits." It was hardly the consolation which Nancy anticipated, but it was all that the realistic Abigail could offer.

In her life with Thomas Boylston Adams, Nancy Harrod had no end of opportunity to develop those "graces and virtues" described by Abigail. Marriage brought her more grief than any other of the Adams women, save Nabby. And Nancy did not have Nabby's fortitude. As a result, her unhappiness and disappointment were rarely disguised. Even the main success of her marriage proved a liability. Despite waiting until she was past thirty, Nancy soon did not lack in what was acclaimed woman's greatest blessing—babies. She had seven children, of which the first, named Abigail Smith Adams, caused Louisa and John Quincy considerable amusement before she was born. It seems that Nancy followed the fashion of the time, which was to pretend there was no such condition as pregnancy until the baby had arrived.

Left behind in Washington during the spring of 1806 to await the ill-fated birth of her own child, Louisa had to be content with her husband's reports from Quincy about how Nancy's rumored pregnancy was getting on. Since Louisa always displayed a motherly silhouette early in each term, John Quincy assumed that a still slender Nancy must not be expecting. By mid-July, with the birth of a child to Nancy said to be near, she still showed no signs. "I have not ventured to ask the question," John Quincy confessed in a dispatch to Louisa, "and I am not connoisseur in shapes enough to decide upon external inspection."

As July was nearly over, and Nancy should have delivered by then, John Quincy announced a small masculine triumph to Louisa: "I believe I made a more accurate calculation . . . than she made for herself." Abigail put such flawed prophecy differently, remembering an old observation about the overdue expectant mother who "had not counted her cobs rightly." Finally, on 27 July 1806, little Abby Adams was born, and Nancy soon carried the infant proudly to Haverhill, where Elizabeth Peabody in nearby Atkinson joyfully welcomed her "dear Nancy."

Thereafter, Nancy regularly succeeded in becoming pregnant. Children arrived in 1808, 1809, 1811, 1813, and 1815. The last one appeared at the close of 1817 as Nancy approached her forty-fourth birthday. One baby daughter lived less than a year, dying in 1812 a short time before the death of Louisa's baby in St. Petersburg. The most remarkable moment in this series of births occurred when a son, christened Isaac Hull Adams, was born precisely nine months after news had reached Quincy of Captain Isaac Hull's great naval victory. Hull defeated an English vessel while commanding the U.S. frigate *Constitution* off Nova Scotia in August 1812, thereby causing one of the few celebrations available to the United States during the War of 1812. There was special jubilation among the Adamses because John claimed to have created the American navy. Amid the excitement, Nancy and Thomas apparently devised their own private salute to Captain Hull's attainment.

As Nancy's family increased, Abigail and John tried to help by encouraging a degree of independence in Thomas. He and his brood were allowed to live in the cottage where John Adams had been born. Furthermore, it was arranged in 1811 that Thomas would become one of the judges for the Norfolk County circuit of the Court of Common Pleas. This bench heard cases of modest importance. Taking Nancy into a residence of their own had been Thomas' ambition. "I shall be, on many accounts, better to live by myself, with my own little family," he had assured John Quincy in 1807. Living with Abigail and John made him feel like "a pensioner," a milder version of how Nancy saw their plight.

As she prepared to move her family into the cottage and away from John and Abigail, Nancy wrote privately to her in-laws in 1810, saying she was grateful beyond words for their help, and apologizing for any difficulties her presence and that of Thomas may have caused. She insisted that she and Thomas were still "happy in each other" and would find contentment in a simple, independent life. Then, referring vaguely to occasions when she had run away from family gatherings formed around Abigail and John, Nancy begged their sympathetic understanding, knowing they would "draw the veil of charity over those [failings] you have discovered in me."

By then, compassionate observers like Elizabeth Peabody were calling Nancy a woman "not wanting in courage," while Abigail, who had no illusions about Thomas' weaknesses, acclaimed Nancy as a "prudent, industrious, excellent wife and mother, making small means appear handsome." Soon, however, Nancy allowed her new independence to encourage her to undertake more than the family considered wise. She decided to help the elder Adamses by welcoming into her home as boarders the two sons who had been left behind when Louisa and John Quincy went to Russia in 1809. Both Abigail and Mary Cranch acted to prevent these youngsters from living with the dangerous example of Thomas Adams, and though Nancy had already announced her plan in a letter to Louisa, Agibail ordered that the scheme be abandoned. In the care of their Uncle Thomas the lads would be "too much indulged," as Abigail delicately put it.

In a letter to Nancy, Mary Cranch went so far as to express fears about the influence of Thomas on young George and Johnny. Nancy shared this letter with Thomas, perhaps to show her husband how serious his situation had become. Deeply hurt, Thomas told John Quincy and Louisa what had happened. He said he would put the Cranch letter in a safe place, and someday it would reveal what Thomas said were "my excuses if not my justification" for his self-doubt. The few other letters of Thomas which survive from this period show him alternating between dreams of independence and explanations of why handling even the financial affairs of his father and brother caused him to falter. He began to gamble, losing money left in his care by relatives. His alcoholism worsened.

It had become painful for Elizabeth Peabody to think how Nancy's marriage had turned after she had worked so ardently to unite Nancy and Thomas. The unfolding tragedy brought to mind her own experience with an intemperate husband. Shortly before she died, Elizabeth was visited by Thomas. It was "melancholy" to observe his condition. He was now increasingly troubled by rheumatism, bouts of which seemed both to encourage his drinking and to explain periods of inebriation. Abigail was no less disappointed than Elizabeth. Near the time of her death, Thomas' mother said she was unable to trust herself to comment on Nancy's plight. One could only "feel" for the couple.

For a time, Nancy managed to keep up appearances, despite the strain of bearing children and putting up with a worrisome husband. In 1814 she and Thomas called on the Peabodys in Atkinson. Elizabeth was surprised by how "handsome" Nancy was, and how seemingly fit. By 1820, however, Louisa and others were describing Nancy as deeply unhappy. She could no longer disguise her disappointment in life, and began to show her feelings by publicly reminding Thomas of the successes achieved by others, particularly his brother John Quincy. What seems finally to have broken Nancy's hopes for better times was being forced to give up her own residence, such as it was, and to retreat to the Adams mansion.

This came about soon after Abigail died. By then, Thomas' circumstances were so deplorable that there seemed no alternative for Nancy but to move her husband and children in with John Adams where the latter could support them. From early in 1819 until 1832, when Thomas died, each day was devastating for Nancy. She sought to fight humiliation with bravado, spending money she did not have and making elaborate attempts to succeed Abigail as Quincy's social leader. She undertook a pathetic campaign to keep John Adams' home the community center it had been under Abigail's supervision.

At first Nancy thought it might be possible to enlist her father-in-law in the effort to reform Thomas. This soon proved futile as Thomas' behavior worsened. Nancy became so desperate over his drinking that she interceded in a curious way with his increasingly irate parent. She attempted to distract John by describing the latest alcoholic degradation of the unfortunate William Shaw, Elizabeth's son who was almost as dear to her father-in-law as Thomas. Her plan failed, making John even more angry and frustrated by Thomas' behavior and leaving Nancy more embittered. The idea of marriage as a fruitful partnership, as it had been for Abigail and her sisters, had become a mockery in Nancy's case. Louisa fought successfully against a different form of female subjugation; Nancy was broken by burdens neither she nor anyone could shoulder.

Thomas did have improved moments. At such times his relatives tried the therapy of giving him responsibility. His old friend Louisa, for instance, asked him to handle the spending money allotted to her sons during their Harvard careers. The benefit of any such largess was shortlived. After only six months under his father's supervision, Thomas fled for several days in September 1819, chased away, perhaps, by the stern gaze of John Quincy, now secretary of state, and visiting from Washington at the time.

Leaving word that he would never return, Thomas vanished without saying goodbye to Nancy. Louisa and her sons went into Boston to search for him, while Nancy wept in her room. She demanded that if her husband was found, he must thereafter be followed constantly. Nancy suspected Thomas of falling in with evil companions, females as well as males. Louisa and John Quincy, meanwhile, recognized that Nancy's reproaches put Thomas on the run. They wondered if perhaps Thomas could join the crew of a merchant ship or find some other occupation that would remove him temporarily as a grief to wife and parent. Several days later, Thomas reappeared, dreadfully hungover and contrite.

Nancy's humiliation increased when she and her family became dependents of John Quincy and Louisa, for by then John Adams was himself without resources, except for real estate, which yielded little income. Thomas owed his father and his brother large sums of money, on which not even the interest had been paid. Charles Francis Adams, observant at age seventeen, noted in 1824 that Aunt Nancy Adams "writhed" while her husband was usually "under the influence of this fire which he perpetually takes." Yet in spite of Thomas' disgraceful behavior in public, Nancy continued inviting guests to what had once been Abigail's house.

Members of the Harrod family visited from Haverhill. This frequently proved catastrophic, for seeing Nancy's relatives often made Thomas uncontrollable by dinnertime, a mid-afternoon meal. Undeterred, Nancy encouraged the young people to dance, and tried to keep up conversation until Thomas lurched off into the evening alone. The inexperienced Charles considered Nancy's attempts to be oblivious hypocritical, not realizing how important the appearance of a successful life under the Adams roof was for her and her children.

When frustration and grief drove Nancy to speak slightingly of the Adams family, she distressed Louisa. Nancy would pursue this line of talk at mealtime, for John Adams was usually absent, taking dinner in his room. At these moments, even Louisa had difficulty remembering that it was a miserable marriage that made Nancy so defensive. Louisa's son Charles left the saddest description of the cause for Nancy's desolation. Nancy's husband, said Charles, was "one of the most unpleasant characters in this world." He depicted his Uncle Thomas as "a brute in his manners and a bully in his family." Some of the exchanges between Nancy and Thomas made Charles pity his aunt's sufferings, but Charles was equally severe in his assessment of Nancy as of his uncle.

In June 1824, less than twenty years after Nancy entered the Adams family, Charles had this to say while watching his aunt reproach her husband: "She is a woman whose equal will seldom be found. I see so much to blame that I can see nothing to praise. Extravagant without the means and knowing that she plunges her husband deeper in his wretchedness, at every step she takes, she does not mind it, cunning and deceitful, hypocritical in a degree beyond belief and malicious as a serpent." This judgment Louisa might have softened by gently reminding her son that he had grown up in Russia and England, and had not known his aunt in her hopeful days.

Charles claimed that Nancy had done more to harm the family Abigail left behind than any other individual. The most he could say in her behalf was, "She is kind to her children and attached to her blood relations, however, and has some deep feeling for her husband—at least has had for it is now pretty nearly gone." To understand Nancy, Charles asserted, one must realize she possessed "a mass of pride" which "would dignify the most immense lady in the universe." Louisa, however, could probe with a woman's insight, knowing how much Nancy had expected from her marriage to Thomas Adams. What seemed pride to Charles was, in his mother's gaze, Nancy's bitter struggle with disappointment, capped by jealousy.

Only Louisa could appreciate how fickle the world must have seemed to Nancy, who during visits with Abigail in 1799 and 1800 saw a grand life beckoning. In those days the young guest from Haverhill would have heard Abigail deploring John Quincy's choice of a fancy foreign lady as bride. Nor did Abigail disguise her anticipations that, as a daughter-in-law, Nancy would be doubly welcome as one who brought desirable qualities to the Adams family, in the view of Abigail and others who shook their heads over Louisa's first pathetic appearances in Quincy after 1801.

As it turned out, Nancy's finest hour in the Adams circle was the interval before she married Thomas. Louisa, in contrast, reached her fulfillment only after long and painful years of marriage. Much of Nancy's despair following 1818 came as much from watching her rival Louisa rise to become the nation's first lady as it did from observing the ruin of her own marriage. In addition, after Abigail's death, Nancy was forced to witness as first place in John Adams' heart was given to Louisa. Louisa prized nothing more than this bond with her father-in-law. As for the glitter that came with being wife to a secretary of state and president, Louisa would gladly have passed it on to Nancy. What Nancy could never assess was the price which fame exacted from Louisa as a woman.

While Louisa was in Washington with her husband, Nancy had to sit in the Adams mansion, fuming as she overheard neighbors mockingly greet Thomas as "Judge." It was difficult for her to endure what became a family ritual as John Adams listened to someone read aloud every letter sent by Louisa from the federal capital. Each epistle portrayed anew for Nancy what she considered to be Louisa's thrilling life, an existence, by the way, which Louisa generously shared. As Nancy's children became teenagers, they were regularly welcomed in Washington for long visits with Louisa, who also brought the latest dance steps to Quincy from Washington, teaching them to Nancy's two admiring daughters.

Louisa's lively descriptions of Washington life hid her own discomfort, for the letters were meant to amuse the old president. Rarely did they show how returning to politics caused Louisa's marriage to lose the ground gained during the English stay. Buoyed by that recent blissful interlude, Louisa courageously tried to be John Quincy's ally in the political wars of Washington. As she observed this scene, few details escaped Louisa. Even her own behavior was depicted in Louisa's journal-letters to John Adams. In turn, he sent many grateful replies which breathed a pleasure that must have been all too evident for Nancy.

Louisa made the residents in Quincy chuckle by describing John Quincy's irritation during the cold weather of 1817–18 when he felt all of Washington staring at the winter clothing he had worn in St. Petersburg. Nor could Louisa resist pointing out how John Quincy craved public attention more than he would ever concede. An instance was the time Louisa and the Secretary of State had stopped in New Haven while traveling from Quincy to Washington. John Quincy coaxed Louisa to be seen with him as he walked the streets while the boat was loaded with freight. To Louisa's mixture of dismay and amusement, her mate grew so absorbed in greeting citizens that the vessel departed without them. With it went all their luggage. Much later, the couple arrived in New York, having no change of clothing and money barely sufficient for one hotel room.

The dominant features of Louisa's life as a Washington politician's wife were paying and receiving visits, and giving or attending dinners and balls. Louisa had been in Washington only a few months when she invited three hundred persons to a ball in the residence rented by the Adamses at the corner of C and 4½ Street. For such a party, Louisa usually dismantled the house furnishings, including beds, in order to make room for guests, an experience that helped "youthify" her, she said, comically employing a word popular in Washington slang.

Louisa told John Adams that her theory about entertaining called for a relaxed approach. She tried to make guests feel comfortable through an understated style. Thus, on 4 March 1819, when Louisa prepared to give a large dinner at which General Andrew Jackson was a guest, she took a long walk in the afternoon, returning in good spirits which helped lift the mood of Jackson, who was glum at the time. The Tennessean was being investigated for his tactics in the recent Seminole War, during which he executed two British agents, Arbuthnot and Ambrister. Louisa and John Quincy were Jackson supporters, and Louisa believed that the abuse of the general displayed the shabby state of American politics.

Social demands did not deny Louisa the pleasure of reading. In March 1820, she fell captive to Sir Walter Scott's *Ivanhoe*, which had recently been published. So engrossed was she that her preparations to dine at the French minister's residence were entirely forgotten. Somewhat more embarrassing was the time Louisa saw that a meal was served to a group of John Quincy's male guests, after which she excused herself for a bit of reading before dressing for a ball later that evening. Louisa became so absorbed in her book that she forgot not only to dress, but to return and light candles in the dining room where the gentlemen sat around the table with wine and cigars. Louisa did not lift her eyes from her book until she heard "their excellencies tumbling over the chairs in total darkness," while John Quincy groped his way to his wife for help. "Instead of relieving him from his great distress, I was seized with such a convulsive fit of laughter that I could scarcely stand and continued incapable of giving any orders for sometime." However, Louisa assured her father-in-law, she hastened into the dining room and apologized handsomely to the guests. John Adams found in this amusing narrative a glimpse of how America's great men often left dinners so tipsy from the constantly flowing wine that they had difficulty getting home. He warned Louisa that her husband might tend to be "rather too profuse in replenishing his decanters—you must have great care not to make the grave legislators unsteady."

For Louisa's fortitude in Washington life, John Adams had only adoring praise: "Wonderful woman, wife of a wonderful man, how is it possible for you with your delicate constitution and tender health to go through such a living of visits, dinners, and parties?" Louisa admitted to being gratified when John Quincy was pleased with her contribution to his career. After one of her entertainments had clearly been a special triumph and the last guests had departed, her husband, to her delight, "joined in a reel with the boys and myself, and you would have laughed heartily to see the surprise of our people [servants] and the musicians who were the only witnesses of the sport."

Successful though these events were, they were mere preludes to Louisa's greatest effort, the most celebrated society event of nineteenth-century Washington. It came after Louisa gave in to John Quincy's begging and agreed to host a ball for Andrew Jackson on 8 January 1824, the ninth anniversary of Old Hickory's victory over the British in the Battle of New Orleans. Louisa recognized that an affair honoring Jackson was part of her husband's political scheming in a presidential election year, and she took the occasion seriously. The campaign itself was another matter. Louisa confessed to her father-in-law that "I never speak of the great question [the presidential election] for I am so tired of it that I endeavor to forget it is stirring."

By 1824 Louisa could entertain Jackson in a large residence that today is numbered 1333–1335 F Street N.W., just around the corner from the White House. Between 1801 and 1809, it had been the home of James and Dolley Madison. A huge, three-story building, it boasted a ballroom large enough for most of Washington society to assemble there. Louisa put the entire family to work, including her sons, who were home from Harvard for Christmas. Louisa herself made many of the decorations, items to be much admired by the more than a thousand guests.

Finally, all was prepared, and at 9:00 P.M., General Jackson arrived and was escorted about the rooms by Louisa, whose self-possessed manner made her the envy of most women in Washington, not to mention poor Nancy back in Quincy. Louisa was not even fazed when, just as Jackson was proposing a handsome toast to her, a suspended lamp fell and spilled its contents over her shoulders and back. The crowd, she told John Adams, roared that she was now anointed with sacred political oil, to which she retorted that she was sure only of a "spoilt" gown. She changed and returned to reign until the multitude departed at 1:30 A.M. The town talked for days about the attention Andrew Jackson paid to the gracious Mrs. Adams.

Much of what Louisa had to endure in the name of society taxed her sense of humor, however. A special annoyance was the feeble musical talent possessed by many of the women who insisted on performing in public. Possessed of considerable ability herself and being, as she said, a "travelled lady," Louisa struggled to keep a composed countenance while hearing a lovely composition ruined by an inept performer. She was struck by the enormous confidence of these women, and the appearance of complete satisfaction they displayed after concluding their pitiful efforts. Would that she could so deceive herself, Louisa commented to John Adams.

John Adams was much amused by this, as by other goings-on in Washington which Louisa recounted with inimitable irreverence. John confessed that at times he yearned to be back in Washington, although he begged her not to reveal this secret wish. He particularly enjoyed the delightful stories Louisa told about herself. One favorite was an episode involving the Washington's Birthday Ball of 1821 when boredom, perspiration, and hunger were nearly too much for her. She was desperately chatting with the noted political editor, Joseph Gales, when the long-awaited summons to supper was announced. Grabbing the hand of Gales, she "gallopped" to the table, leaving behind an astonished George Canning, with whom she had also been talking. The elegant Canning, soon to be appointed Britain's foreign secretary, must have thought, Louisa surmised, "that the house was on fire and that I was endeavoring to escape with all my might."

Of all Louisa's chronicles, the one John Adams perhaps appreciated most was her commentary on the problem created by the congressional practice of welcoming ladies to the floors of both the House and the Senate. In 1820 large crowds of women flocked to the debates over admitting Missouri as a state, and showed particular interest in speeches by Senator William Pinkney of South Carolina, who was reputed to be quite a man-about-town. Louisa reported that the South Carolinian "has attracted the attention of a part of the fair sex who, if the tongue of scandal says true, out of gratitude must naturally be desirous of affording their admiration and of bestowing it in as public a manner as possible on one who is so ready to distinguish them."

Other solons were said to find this embarrassing, for, as Louisa put it, "the grave fathers of the Senate are supposed to be *old and steady* enough to set a good example for the lower house." Consequently, it was decided that henceforth ladies could appear on the Senate floor only when accompanied by a member of that body. Unfortunately for Vice President Daniel Tompkins, some of his friends among Washington's feminine community, "ladies of a very public character" as Louisa described them with elaborate understatement, managed to slip onto the floor and take seats "on either hand" of poor Tompkins. "He has been subject to some jests for having been thus supported."

Louisa attended debates when the great Pinkney spoke in January 1820. His fulsome style did not stir her, she reported to John Adams. "So heavy a tax was laid upon poor common sense that to those who have passed the age where imagination kindles and blazes at each electric spark, it produced the effect of a fine epic poem which we take up occasionally with delight but which exhausts and fatigues if we attempt to pursue it at one reading." On 24 January Louisa related that Pinkney had finally ended his speech, "and it is said great was the fall thereof." For Louisa, "there is something unnatural in excessive splendor."

Such extravagant oratory was no more absurd, in Louisa's view, than the extremes men went to in their pursuit of public office. Even as early as 1820, her husband was in the chase for the office of president, which would not become vacant until 1825. Louisa promised John Adams he would smile if only he could but see his son, the secretary of state, "every morning preparing a set of [calling] cards with as much formality as if he was drawing up some very important article to negotiate in a commercial treaty." "Thus it is," Louisa added, "he has been brought to it by absolute necessity."

Inevitably Louisa's independence, cynicism, and worldliness colored her chronicles of Washington, a community she disliked as she observed its detestable politicking. Increasingly, her letters grew sarcastic and unhappy, as she watched John Quincy become absorbed in his quest for high office. Louisa considered partisan politics a squalid business, unworthy of her husband, whom she contended possessed more intellectual power than could be found in all the other men in Washington combined. This wifely boast was less exaggerated than it sounds.

Most distressing for Louisa was her certainty that once John Quincy attained the presidency he would become so occupied that he would no longer need or even notice her. Even after a quarter century of marriage, John Quincy still condescended to her, as she once complained to John Adams: "If Mr. A. instead of keeping me back when I was a young woman, had urged me forward in the world, I should have better understood the maneuvering part of my situation." To Harriet Welsh in Boston, Louisa was even more direct, asserting that marriage to a great official placed an indignity upon his wife. No affectionate man would consider his wife inferior, but public affairs encouraged this attitude in politically-minded males.

While she usually managed to keep her letters to John Adams cheerful, by early 1820 Louisa was confessing in her diary that "My life is made so miserably uncomfortable and I am so thoroughly unfit for so exalted a situation, that I think the wisest thing I can do is to retire to some quiet place where I may at least spend my life in peace." While prominence might change her husband, "I am precisely the Louisa Johnson when I married Mr. A. The same romantic, enthusiastic, foolish animal so unfit for real life and so conscious of all my defects which as I rise become more striking." Louisa then added the wistful comment, "How strangely is a woman's mind constructed."

Recalling a recent White House dinner with President and Mrs. James Monroe, Louisa said, "I cast my heavy eyes around the splendid room and as the gay throng passed by me I thought with Solomon 'that all was vanity and vexation of spirit.'" What she needed for contentment, Louisa admitted, in a mood reminiscent of her wretched time in St. Petersburg, was a little "real tenderness." This theme came to dominate Louisa's writings as John Quincy, despite his pretenses to the contrary, stepped up his pursuit of the presidency. Though she admired her husband and remained fiercely loyal, Louisa was aggrieved to confess that her mate was captivated by the vainglory, hypocrisy, and corruption—sins created by democracy: "If such is public virtue, may my sons have nothing to do with it."

Fighting against moodiness, there were times when Louisa left the family circle in order not to infect it with her gloom, a practice she had acquired from her mother, Catherine Johnson. She became alarmed by her own "strange, exaggerated ideas," particularly since once again John Quincy did not take her problem seriously. "I am told I am very whimsical and fanciful." When her husband forgot their wedding anniversary in July 1821, Louisa tried to recall how the two of them once celebrated the day: "Alas, old age has come and all attraction has flown forever."

Actually, Louisa's volatile outlook probably was due, in part, to the onset of a long menopause. The early irregularities of this experience briefly convinced her that she was pregnant at the start of 1822, as she neared her forty-seventh birthday, a time when Louisa most needed a mate of the sort John Quincy had been in England for two joyful years. But now he seemed deliberately to distress and hurt her, or so Louisa believed. For example, despite her remonstrance, John Quincy made a larger show than ever of his early morning baths in the Potomac, boasting how he experimented by paddling with his clothes on, and of his achievement in swimming for eighty minutes without stopping. He ignored her protests that his family and the nation deserved a more cautious style.

Personal and political conditions were almost unendurable by the summer of 1824, so Louisa fled Washington amid whispered suspicions of poor health. She went to Bedford, Pennsylvania, for a month alone at the spa. A startled John Quincy watched her go, admitting, "I was deeply affected at parting with her." She had been suffering from dejected spirits, he noted, a mood he attributed to nervous irritability. Even so, Louisa's husband took time from official duties and politicking to consult her doctor, who assured him that his wife's disorder was caused by peculiarities of the female anatomy. It was not a dangerous condition, said the physician, but it would put her in an excited state from time to time.

For Louisa and for her sister-in-law Nancy back in Quincy, the six years since Abigail's death had brought increasing torment to their marriages. Try though Nancy might to brighten her lot by entertaining friends and spending money, she could not escape the agony of her plight with Thomas Adams. Louisa, on the other hand, yearned to draw her husband into a closer union, but was thwarted by his character and ambition and by their public prominence. The visibility she shared with John Quincy forced Louisa to behave unnaturally, with the result that she came to despise herself. It was discouraging for these sisters-in-law, Nancy and Louisa, to contemplate what their marriages, begun so promisingly, had become. Unfortunately, the worst was still ahead.

12

The Worst of Times

In 1825, Louisa and John Quincy moved into the White House amid protests that the election had been decided by underhanded means. In the preceding campaign, several candidates had sought the presidency; none had secured the required majority in the electoral college. Accordingly, the choice devolved upon the House of Representatives, where, on 9 February 1825, John Quincy Adams was selected over Andrew Jackson, despite the latter's plurality of both popular and electoral votes. Henry Clay, whose share of votes had fallen short of making him eligible for consideration, had urged his supporters in the House to vote for Adams. After he was chosen, John Quincy named Clay secretary of state, an appointment which predictably invited disgruntled Jackson supporters to raise the cry of corruption and to oppose the Adams administration. Thus was born the Democratic party.

No observer of this scene was more distressed than the new first lady, who dreaded that America was coming to be rent by factionalism. Like Abigail, Louisa believed that political parties appealed to voters' emotions rather than to their minds. For John Quincy, the low road he took to power was one he ordinarily shunned, and for the rest of his life he remained silent about the price he paid for becoming president. Louisa never hid her disappointment and anger over the election of 1824. While the hijinks of politics scarcely surprised her, she had expected loftier behavior from her husband. Louisa entered upon her career as first lady dismayed about more than the bottomless March mud of Pennsylvania Avenue.

As she began life in the executive mansion, Louisa's emotional and physical ailments worsened. She underwent the severest part of her menopause, and what she deplored as her physical decline frequently darkened her thoughts and her "scribblings." Louisa wrote often and with regret of how society seemed to sentence older women, after their youthful beauty and childbearing duties were finished, to lives of futility and loneliness. She professed not to be shocked by the portrait Gilbert Stuart submitted for inspection in 1825. The likeness may have revealed "too much of inward suffering and a broken heart"—at least Louisa thought so—but Stuart caught the intensity of Louisa's spirit in her eyes and mouth. To prepare her sons for the portrait, Louisa sent them a poem: "Go fetter'd image tell the tale/Of years long past away/Of faded youth, of sorrow's wail/Of time's too soon decay."

Death would be welcome, the first lady insisted. With her beloved mother interred in Washington's Rock Creek Cemetery, Louisa thought longingly of resting beside her. She put this wish into another poem: "There where my Mother lies I seek/A shady spot to lay my head./Near to the humble Rocky Creek/I fain would make my lowly bed/In solemn calm repose to sleep./And God whose mercy vast and deep/Shall raise my Soul to die no more." The most serious disease Louisa suffered, like her emotional turmoil, was hardly life-threatening. It was the inflammatory disorder that had vexed Abigail, erysipelas or St. Anthony's Fire, which had the habit of erupting when Louisa became upset.

Daily life in the White House was, of course, poor therapy for Louisa, who called the mansion "that dull and stately prison in which the sounds of mirth are seldom heard." She emphasized that from "merit and service," John Quincy assuredly deserved the presidency, "but in point of happiness we are better off without it." It would have been beneficial for both of them to have gone abroad on another diplomatic mission, Louisa claimed, remembering once again how happy she and John Quincy had been in England.

Louisa even felt more kindly toward St. Petersburg once she entered the White House. Looking around the mansion after the Monroes had departed, she found the rooms filled with rubbish. The place would shame an almshouse. Determined to put an end to rumors that the Adamses had moved into grandeur, Louisa ordered the doors of the executive residence opened for public visitation, to the dismay of John Quincy's political associates. When told her strategy might discourage a second term for John Quincy, Louisa replied that she would not grovel to assure another four years in "this desolate city."

"There is something in this great, unsocial house which depresses my spirits beyond expression," Louisa wrote, adding that in the mansion it was "impossible for me to feel at home or to fancy that I have a home anywhere." Requirements for entertainment, the sort of parties she had formerly put on with such flair as wife of a cabinet officer, Louisa now dreaded. Even so, she saw to it that dinners were served frequently to thirty or more guests, although the first lady often did not join the groups. Her good humor of a few years ago was obviously missing in late August 1825 when she welcomed General Lafayette, who was concluding a triumphal tour of the United States. Ordinarily, Louisa would have been thrilled to entertain the venerable hero of Revolutionary days. Still, while her heart was not in it, her reception succeeded better than she probably expected.

Lafayette became so fond of life in Louisa's White House that, with his entourage, he talked of lengthening his stay. Louisa grumbled that she would "hail with joy" the day the general returned to France. "I admire the old gentleman but no admiration can stand family discomfort," the chief result of his visit. "We are all obliged to turn out of our beds to make room for him and his suite," the first lady complained. Her sixteen maids and other staff members were inadequate to the challenge, obliging Louisa to recruit several more servants so that the guests could be properly looked after.

Louisa's strain was made even heavier once it became apparent that John Quincy was to pay for his disputed election with four beleagured years as chief executive. His administration was mostly stymied in its domestic and international plans by the relentless opposition led by vengeful supporters of General Jackson, an experience that helped make Louisa's husband more assertive than ever when he entered the domestic quarters of the White House. This release of presidential frustrations caused suffering mostly for Louisa, a tribulation she usually did not bear in silence. It infuriated her when John Quincy behaved as if he was determined to lift his spirits at her expense. An example of this occurred soon after the couple was established in the White House.

Disregarding Louisa's pleas that he observe prudent habits, the President of the United States trotted off, early on the morning of 13 June 1825, to his favorite place of exercise, the Potomac River, where he was accustomed to swim with his valet, Antoine Guista. Alone in her writing chamber, Louisa soon heard a commotion raised by a messenger running toward the White House from the river. Observers of this drama concluded that the president had drowned, an outcome the first lady had long predicted. Witnesses hastened to spread the news, and gullible travelers were soon carrying the mournful tidings to other parts of the nation. After the rumors had spread in all directions, it was discovered that President Adams was alive, if embarrassed and wet.

Instead of dashing to the White House to report a fatal accident, the emissary had been sent to fetch dry clothing for the chief executive. Louisa's husband had been swimming nude from a boat in midstream when the skiff suddenly sprang a leak and swamped, taking presidential garments down with it. John Quincy grabbed his pantaloons, a hat, and a shoe and swam to the far shore, then ordered his valet, Antoine, to don the sodden garments and go for help while John Quincy occupied himself by swimming and, as he recorded in a rather abashed diary entry, "sitting naked on the bank."

After learning what actually had happened, Louisa was not amused, although vastly relieved. "The affair is altogether ridiculous," she said. John Quincy was more somber: "By the blessing of Heaven our lives were spared." As for Louisa's stern reprimand and her claim that the president owed it to the nation, if not his family, to stop his "swimming expeditions," she had no success. The next morning her mate was in the Potomac again. Until the close of life, John Quincy made fearful demands upon himself in body and mind, continuing to swim in rivers until he neared the age of eighty.

Ruefully comparing her treatment as woman and wife with that enjoyed by her mother, Catherine Johnson, and her mother-in-law, Abigail Adams, Louisa entitled the major portion of her journal "Adventures of a Nobody." The contents were hardly that, as Louisa occasionally had to concede. Nonetheless her surviving manuscripts, which, in addition to journals and diaries include poems, many letters, and other compositions, vividly reveal Louisa's indignation at the lot befalling American women. She contended, as had Abigail Adams, that men and women should be partners. From her vantage point at the White House, Louisa could see that the trend in America's economy, politics, and social arrangements was to disregard the old-fashioned collaboration between the sexes.

None of this seemed to worry John Quincy Adams, for like most men of the time, he rushed out of the home and into a male-dominated superstructure. No matter that Louisa was America's first lady, she could only watch as men moved freely and alone amid politics, money, and excess, while women were left behind. She recognized the hollowness when this newly evolving society began to praise an ideal of domesticity which patronizingly venerated the female for being meek and dutiful in her alloted realm of kitchen, nursery, and marital chamber.

As Louisa hid away at her desk in the White House, "scribbling, scribbling, scribbling," manuscripts piled up which contained her thoughts about the decaying relationship between the sexes. This first lady always preferred the biblical term "helpmate" to describe both spouses; the spirit of this term had governed the marriage of her parents as well as that of John and Abigail Adams. According to the modern outlook Louisa charged that a wife was "made to cook [her husband's] dinner, wash his clothes, gratify his sensual appetites," and for this he expected her to "thank him and love him for permission to drudge through life, at the mercy of his caprices."

Was this, Louisa asked, the interpretation of "helpmate" intended by "the creator, the Father of all mercy?" She denounced the contention that woman became the moral inferior of man after Eve played temptress in the Garden of Eden. Inciting male lust did not result in women being condemned to eternal subordination, Louisa insisted. Eve's transgression was absolved when she undertook "the curse of pain in child birth and the cares attendant in the rearing of wayward children." This was all the penalty God had applied, and He surely did not intend woman to endure "the undermining scorn of her companion, who deliberately partook of her sin while he is said to have possessed the Master Mind."

Not that Louisa was blind to feminine faults. She candidly addressed the dangers of female allure and prowess in a world where sexual drives easily overpowed reason. But in Louisa's judgment sensuality need not deprive a woman of full partnership with a man. Like the male, the female received special talents from nature, while society imposed specific burdens on both sexes. Each gender was meant to complement and respect the other, although at times Louisa became so disgusted by male behavior that she awarded superiority to the female.

Louisa's militancy was at the heart of a play she wrote in 1826 entitled *Suspicion, or Persecuted Innocence*. In it, as in other dramas she composed while in the White House, Louisa stressed the strengths of women, and showed men to be playthings of their emotions. The plot was a trivial imitation of Shakespeare, but Louisa made the lines sing with her conviction. "Men ever dread the weakness of our softer sex," says the heroine, modeled after Louisa herself, "but 'tis in the hour of peril that woman displays the energy of her nature and proves herself the noble helpmate of creation's lord."

As Louisa pondered men and marriage from the White House, she thought often of her mother-in-law, the other Adams first lady. Louisa foresaw that Abigail's letters ought someday to be published. Reading them, Louisa predicted, would "gladden the hearts of many a timid female whose rays too feebly shine, not for want of merit but for want of confidence in the powers and encouragement in the exercise of those capacities with which the Almighty has gifted them." If women could emulate Abigail Adams, the sex at large "might thus redeem the reputation to which it is entitled." With more Abigail Adamses, dormant respect for womanhood would be awakened. The world would rediscover that the mind of woman, "clear, full, and vigorous in its perception, is as capable of solid attainment as that of man."

A little over a year after her White House imprisonment began, Louisa lost her dearest friend and confidant, John Adams. The former president died on 4 July 1826, full of life to the end of his days. Neither Louisa nor John Quincy were present at the old man's departure, but Nancy and Thomas were on hand, worrying about what would happen to them. Their fate suddenly was in John Quincy's hands, as Louisa recognized when she read John Adams' will. In effect, John Quincy acquired his father's unproductive landed estate, but with the responsibility of maintaining a trust from which John Adams had decreed that support must be paid to Nancy, Thomas, and their children.

Louisa saw at once what her father-in-law had done. With the best intentions, he had placed a back-breaking load on John Quincy, unless the latter somehow managed to derive income from Quincy property which had never really supported Abigail and John. When Louisa described this prospect to her husband, he brushed aside her concern, then and later. John Quincy had no head for business, while Louisa seems to have been financially astute. It disgusted her when she was unable to prevent John Quincy from going ever deeper into debt, all for the dubious privilege of retaining the family acreage.

After John Quincy refused once again to discuss their finances, Louisa had the last sarcastic but futile word: "I beg your pardon most sincerely in having as usual foolishly imagined myself of more consequence than I ought to be." Louisa alone looked ahead to the question of where she and John Quincy would live after they left the White House. She emphasized one point to her husband: she would not share the same house in Quincy with Nancy and Thomas. John Quincy, however, talked calmly of doing so, convincing Louisa that even in this important matter her mate would disregard her interest.

For some reason John Quincy never explained to Louisa that he wished to have a new home in Quincy, constructed near his parents' old wooden mansion, but built of stone, which would make it a fireproof repository for the huge libraries he and his father had acquired, as well as a haven for the family manuscripts. Kept in the dark, Louisa was left to expect she must exchange her miserable existence in the White House for subordination in Quincy to her drunken brother-in-law and his shrewish wife.

Ironically, then, it was this misunderstanding over her future in Quincy, a consequence of John Adams' will, which pushed Louisa into the worst phase of her marriage. During the late summer of 1826, Louisa refused to join her husband when he vacationed in Quincy. Instead, she roamed up the Hudson River Valley and over to New Hampshire. This latest estrangement between the president and the first lady lasted nearly three years. Louisa's son Charles, who had reached age nineteen, could not comprehend what compelled his mother to wander "about the country with no fixed purpose and with no intent."

As sympathetic as Charles was toward his mother, not even he could appreciate how unhappy and forlorn Louisa felt, starting in that summer of 1826. The next year, when John Quincy visited Massachusetts, Louisa chose to remain in the White House, and rarely exchanged letters with her husband. Those she did write sounded stilted and cold. Hostility was alien to Louisa's nature, however, and when John Quincy had displayed no sign of accommodation by mid-1828, Louisa finally broke under the strain and became alarmingly ill. Her symptoms were mysterious, but frightening enough to bring John Quincy and her sons rushing back to Washington from their summer holiday in Quincy. During her White House years and afterward, Louisa frequently fell sick in sudden and dramatic ways, recovering almost as quickly once she captured the attention of her husband and family.

Then, from late 1828 through 1830, the tide turned in Louisa's favor. Grievous developments showed John Quincy how much he needed a strong mate beside him, a partner to whom he could come for help and solace. Louisa, in turn, put aside her melancholy and illness, once again responding to a role in which she felt valuable and respected. It began when she was able to reassure the president as he recognized that he faced defeat for reelection in 1828. Louisa pointed out to her husband the delights of retirement and also busily planned the family's removal to rented quarters in Washington. For these services she received the only reward she wished, the pleasure of saying that her husband was being "as kind as possible," and actually sought to do "everything in his power to make me comfortable."

When she and John Quincy had to vacate the White House, it was Louisa who had the courage to insist that her husband banish Thomas and Nancy from the Adams mansion in Quincy, the old house being the only refuge available to the defeated and impecunious president. Nancy packed everything, including most of Abigail's furniture, and took her family to what was the oldest house standing in Quincy. Built in 1641, its rent was affordable. Before vacating the Adams mansion, Nancy made sure it was clean, which Louisa took as an encouraging sign as she and John Quincy prepared to spend the summer of 1829 in Quincy.

A terrible blow crushed these plans. George Washington Adams, the son who had been born in Berlin, died, either by accidental drowning or by suicide. This news reached Washington late in April 1829, just as Louisa was succeeding in bringing John Quincy out of the despair of defeat. George's death was grievous to Louisa, but it left John Quincy helpless.

Their firstborn son had embodied his father's hopes for an offspring of great talent and enterprise. Not only did George lack these; he broke under the strain of parental expectation. Both Louisa and John Quincy had counted on working together for the young man's redemption, but he escaped via death. Louisa put aside her own grief to sustain a heartbroken John Quincy. There was some comfort in knowing that, if only for a time, her husband wished for nothing more than to sit in her presence.

Not until August, when she finally undertook to visit Quincy, did Louisa's own sorrow overcome her. Having held her emotions in check for the sake of her family, Louisa's outburst was distressing. Not surprisingly, it occurred as she traveled to Massachusetts, the scene where twenty years before and almost to the day, she had been forced to abandon George and accompany her husband to St. Petersburg. As long as Louisa lived, she believed that when she left her son, she sealed his doom. Guilt as much as grief was her enemy as Louisa rode to Quincy.

Midway in the journey, Louisa experienced what her son Charles described as "one of those violent attacks which she is subject to with all the family and servants up and trying to assist her in her distress." This time Louisa complained of a coldness about the breast, and seemed so gravely stricken that an alarmed Charles "went downstairs and recovered myself." It was decided to return to Washington. The next morning Louisa was fully recuperated, obviously relieved at not having to face Quincy and its memories.

By the next summer—1830—Louisa had regained her equilibrium and seemed to welcome exchanging Washington for Quincy. Arriving at the Adams mansion, Louisa immediately showed her old sparkle, helping her husband in the library and the garden. In the evenings her music and conversation delighted the family circle. On frequent outings Louisa enjoyed her favorite sport, fishing. Almost no one escaped her insistence that they throw out a line beside hers. She made a point of inviting the sons of Nancy and Thomas, who, like the rest of the family, acknowledged that Louisa was the champion angler.

Beneath this happiness, however, Louisa suffered anxious moments watching John Quincy try to live with defeat. He found the transition to private life more painful and monotonous than his father had. John Quincy proved unable to fulfill a pledge to Louisa that he would spend the rest of his days writing the history of John Adams' career and editing the second president's papers. Although Louisa had argued convincingly that retirement was the only plausible route for her husband, as well as for their family to find happiness, John Quincy grew restless. In the fall of 1830, Louisa's comfortable interlude ended when her husband an-

nounced he would accept election as congressman, which meant a return
to political life in Washington. This time Louisa's dismay was shared by
other family members.

As John Quincy noted in his diary, Louisa had no sympathy with the
sensations which drove him back on the public stage. Particularly, he said,
his wife did not appreciate the feeling of abandonment and loneliness that
had swamped him since his defeat for a second presidential term. Louisa's
husband understated the case. What John Quincy interpreted as lack of
sympathy was Louisa's outrage that even after the humiliation he had
experienced, her mate still so craved the excitement of politics that he
would shove aside the wishes of his wife and family.

Her husband's decision left Louisa facing a choice. On one side was a
wife's duty, defined by the standards of feminine subordination. On the
other there was fidelity to her own nature and interests. Briefly in October
1830, she stood for herself, announcing that John Quincy must live his
new life alone. She would never return to Washington, "the very focus of
political machination." Louisa used this latest decision by her husband as
a lesson for her sons. She urged that John and Charles review their own
marriages and keep in mind that no earthly greatness gave half the benefit
or pleasure as "one devoted heart."

It was true, she conceded, that since women were considered the weaker
half of a marriage, they usually had to sacrifice their preferences to those
of their mates. Never, Louisa argued, ought this to mean that wives should
give up their opinions and comfort. Her sons were then reminded of what
it had already cost her to stand by John Quincy as she pointed to "the
grave of my lost child" and spoke of how often "grasping ambition" had
been the "insatiable passion" of her husband. Surely, Louisa rhetorically
asked her sons, this record was no inducement for going with him again.
When her son John had the temerity to chide his mother for this decision,
Louisa's scorn was withering. Where was he when she had needed comfort?
She would listen now only to those who might know how it scarred a
woman's heart to be abandoned by a husband to hopelessness and
loneliness.

Still, it distressed Louisa to be pushed to the point where she must part
with her husband in order to save herself. As autumn turned into winter,
Louisa began to reconsider. Her own disappointment and pride were
comparatively trivial when weighed against the benefit that would come
to the nation if John Quincy served in Congress. Largely because of her
impartial admiration for her husband's talent, Louisa changed her mind
and followed John Quincy to Washington. Another reason, probably, was
that her son Charles had shrewdly reminded his mother that winters in

Quincy could be harsh and that the old Adams mansion was often so cold that letters must be written near the fire lest the ink freeze in its well.

For the next several years, Louisa's life in Washington was as melancholy as she had foreseen. Not only was she widowed once again by politics, but renewed domestic difficulties seemed impossible to overcome. Chief among these were the responsibilities imposed on John Quincy by his father's will. Louisa's husband had the honor of owning the family properties around Quincy, but the land yielded little profit. For the privilege of this proprietorship, he had to pay Thomas and Nancy a quarterly allowance of $315 from the $21,000 which John Adams' will had required John Quincy to establish as a trust for Nancy and his youngest son's family. In consequence, the ex-president and first lady lacked the cash to pay travel costs between Quincy and Washington, and their own unpaid bills piled up in both locations.

Unfortunately, as their impoverishment increased, Nancy and her husband seemed to demand more and more from their brother-in-law, who they believed had limitless resources. Louisa tried to be compassionate, recognizing that the expenses of Nancy's large family rose as the children grew up, while her husband's only capacities were for whining, drinking, and welcoming the town's ne'er-do-wells into his residence. Louisa could not help noticing that the more squalid Thomas' life appeared, the more extravagant Nancy's tastes became. A typical plea of hers was for John Quincy to pay tuition so that Nancy could realize a dream of having a son attend Phillips Exeter Academy.

In sober moments, Thomas was aware of this unhealthy situation; once he even whispered to John Quincy that he planned to leave Nancy and start life over. He must, Thomas said, escape Quincy, and possibly Massachusetts, and begin a business or establish a law practice. These were what Louisa mournfully called poor Thomas' "fanciful" dreams. They invariably evaporated when John Quincy did not come forward with money to pave the way for his brother's new career. Left to lament his fate, Thomas called Quincy a town "where no good fortune has ever attended me." He even sought loans from Joseph Felt, who had married Aunt Elizabeth's daughter Abby. Thomas complained to Felt of worldly cares that were now overpowering, "greater than I have ever known, with the least ability and disposition to attend to them." Turned down everywhere, Thomas had only John Quincy and Louisa as a source of mercy.

Nancy's begging was inevitable, Louisa realized, and consoled herself with the discovery that Nancy's children had inherited their father's youthful interest in music. Summer evening concerts at Nancy's or Louisa's home were so pleasant that these sisters-in-law could hardly avoid becoming friendlier. There were soon other causes to stir Louisa's compassion for Nancy. It became evident by mid-1831 that Thomas' habits had hopelessly damaged his health. He was drinking with greater determination, leaving a distraught Nancy to share her dire predictions with whomever would listen.

As it turned out, affairs worsened much as Nancy foresaw. The last few months of Thomas' life were ghastly for his family. His unhappiness with his failure practically unhinged him, as his few surviving letters, not to mention his behavior, often attested. On one occasion, Thomas went to Boston intoxicated and rented a chaise which he drove furiously through the city's winding streets until it overturned. Although the wheels ran over him, Thomas was found unhurt, although he had been given up for dead and carried out to Nancy. She and others marveled that he escaped destruction.

Life with Thomas Adams became so difficult in 1831 that Nancy's daughter Lizzie took refuge with Louisa at the Adams mansion. "Poor thing," Louisa sympathized, "her home appears to be so wretched that any place is preferable and her best prospects I fear are miserable." Nancy's oldest child, Abigail, was more fortunate, breaking away in 1831 by marrying John Angier, who operated a boys school in Medford. The sobering requirements for a proper dowry led Thomas to join Nancy in wheedling for more money from John Quincy, who listened to Nancy cry that without financial help her daughter would have to work as hard all her life as Nancy had. Louisa noted with satisfaction, that this scene finally caused John Quincy to see Thomas and Nancy for the sponges they were.

Thomas' alcoholism triggered a fatal liver disorder, so that by late October 1831 he was described as being at death's door. He lingered into 1832, however, and observers wondered whether he suffered more from physical trauma or from remorse. Louisa had returned to Washington, where she received detailed reports on the crisis from her son Charles Francis. On 12 March 1832, to everyone's relief, Nancy's husband died. He had become helpless, and his memory had failed. On the eve of his death Louisa sent Nancy a touching note of sympathy addressed to "my dear Sister," in which she acknowledged that Nancy had passed through "long and almost unwearied affliction." These tribulations, Louisa wrote soothingly, were extreme among "the many and severe trials to which suffering humanity is called." It was a beautiful statement, in which Louisa urged Nancy to remember that comfort was found before God's throne. Evidently Nancy replied gratefully and at once, but her letter is missing.

Thomas Boyleston Adams' funeral was held at his house; last rites which were missed by Louisa and John Quincy, since Congress was in session. After the service, Thomas' remains were deposited in the Adams family tomb, next to his sister Nabby, and near the coffins of Aunt Mary and Uncle Richard Cranch. Not long before, the vault had been opened to receive the corpse of another woman in the Adams story, a person whose life, like Nancy's, had been ruined by an alcoholic mate. The tragic coincidence must have struck some of Thomas' mourners when they peered into the vault to see the coffin of Kitty Salmon Smith, the widow of dissolute Uncle William Smith.

Absence from this melancholy scene did not spare John Quincy the burden of Thomas' funeral expenses. With Louisa's encouragement, John Quincy sought to assure Nancy that she and her children would live comfortably. Although the real estate Thomas had inherited had long before been mortgaged to John Quincy, and now reverted to him, Louisa's husband pledged that all income from it would be paid to Nancy for life. Thomas' widow seemed to take this for granted, and awaited further generous gestures. Louisa struggled to be patient, remembering what marriage had done to Nancy: "Her situation is so truly pitiable I feel for her with all my heart and would wish to show her all the kindness and respect in my power."

Always realistic, Louisa was obliged to add, "I have known enough of this lady to be convinced that enough is always a little more than she has." Charles Francis agreed, calling Nancy "a woman without any energy of character. Her life would have been a very pleasant one if she had married a wealthy, showy man." For several months after Thomas' death, Nancy implored everyone to appreciate that she was on the brink of poverty. Louisa tried to reason with her, but found her determined to be "perfectly miserable." Her behavior proved the rule, said Louisa, that "extreme selfishness destroys the kindly affections and turns us into brutes." Meanwhile John Quincy was so short of funds that his determination to be considerate of Nancy and her children obliged him to substitute interest-bearing notes for his quarterly payments to them.

Gradually, Nancy must have sensed that she could rely on Louisa because for several years she lived as handsomely as she could, visiting relatives in New England and elsewhere. In the autumn of 1835, she had her portrait painted by the popular artist, Chester Harding, inspired to do so after spending the previous winter with Nabby's daughter Caroline, who lived grandly along the Hudson in the deWindt mansion, which was filled with family likenesses. The next year Nancy went to Washington for a long stay with Louisa. With the painful presence of Thomas now departed, the two families got on remarkably well, the bond between Louisa and Nancy growing ever stronger.

Any social event in or near Quincy was sure to attract Nancy. She accompanied her Adams relatives to Hingham in August 1836 to bury the last of Abigail's Thaxter cousins. When a "funeral tea party" was announced after the last rites, Nancy insisted on remaining, demanding that someone make another trip from Quincy to take her home that evening. It was not just her freedom from the embarrassment of Thomas that kept Nancy on the go. Her children had begun to cause her worry, and it was a pleasure at times for her to escape from home. Nancy liked to boast about her offspring. When they disappointed or grieved her, she realized her troubles had not ended with Thomas' death.

Nancy's eldest son was an army officer and the only child to offer much hope. Unfortunately, he had a short life. Lieutenant Thomas Boylston Adams—he was named after his father—died of typhoid fever on 14 December 1837 while on military assignment. Since he was clearly the most promising of the sons, Louisa felt special sadness, even composing a poem to his memory which stressed a mother's anguish. Nancy had three other sons. There was John Quincy Adams II, who proved to have what his famous uncle called "an invincible repugnance and incapacity for learning." John entered the navy where, as a midshipman, he pestered Congressman J. Q. Adams to arrange softer berths for him. With monumental patience, Uncle Adams called upon the secretary of the navy on behalf of his nephew, and was not surprised at the reply. The secretary preferred to hear from the sailors themselves rather than from their relatives in Congress. This nephew was lost at sea in October 1854 aboard the *Albany*.

Another of Nancy's sons, Joseph Harrod Adams, also joined the navy, whose discipline did not inhibit him from passing bad checks written against the account of his congressman uncle. After sobering admonitions from John Quincy, Joseph apparently reformed and lived until October 1853 when, shipboard on the China Sea, he too died of typhoid fever. Nancy's remaining son, Isaac Hull Adams, lived until 1900, a bachelor all his life. Like his father, he fought the demon of alcohol, but with somewhat better results. Hull was particularly dear to Louisa for his fine singing voice. She also was touched by his timidity with women. His general ineptitude worried everyone, however.

Shortly after his father died in 1832, Hull entered West Point, thanks to the efforts of Uncle John Quincy Adams. En route to New York with $100 in expense money on his person, Hull had his pocket picked. "The poor fellow is in despair and considered it so bad an omen at his setting out that he has almost lost his hopes of success," Louisa reported. Replacement money could be found only in John Quincy's purse, "a heavy stroke," Louisa acknowledged.

The episode may well have been the omen Hull dreaded, for failure soon besieged him. He was dismissed from West Point in 1836 for deserting a guard post, the second such infraction he committed. Somehow he had managed to be forgiven for the first. The discharged cadet came to Washington hoping John Quincy would aid his plea to President Jackson for reinstatement. The effort failed and Hull thereafter lived much of his time with his Aunt Louisa; occasionally he used his training from West Point to earn a few dollars as a surveyor.

In the family's view, Hull was "irredeemably unfit for West Point, the army, or the world," a judgment to which the young man calmly agreed, seeming to be "perfectly cool," as John Quincy despairingly described his nephew. Nancy, however, refused to believe any of these revelations about Hull's limits. Louisa learned not to report to her about his behavior in Washington, where he habitually brought disturbing guests. Hull's easy ways and his pleasure in food and drink probably saved him from an early demise when, with President John Tyler and others, he joined the throng aboard the frigate U.S.S. *Princeton* in February 1844 to watch the firing of its new "peacemaker" gun. When the announcement came that a repast and beverages were being served below, Hull rushed down just before the wrought iron gun was fired. It burst, killing and wounding many on deck.

This may have been the most exciting episode in Hull's career, for he spent his last fifty years living in Quincy with his spinster sister Lizzie, who kept him sober as well as she could. It was not a fate Lizzie had expected, nor had Nancy, who had briefly found distraction after Thomas' death in the prospect of Lizzie's marriage to a rising attorney who had come to board in Nancy's house. The romance began in 1831 when Lizzie was twenty-three and concluded in 1835, after it was discovered that the suitor, John M. Gourgas, was himself overly fond of the bottle.

That, anyway, was the explanation Nancy gave for the termination of the affair after it had given the family four exciting years. Louisa observed the romance closely, predicting to her son in 1832 that Gourgas would never marry Lizzie, though "he rules her like a tyrant." Hoping she was wrong, Louisa was eager to see Lizzie, whom she liked, freed from her complaining mother. "I cannot think of what is to become of the poor girl." When Gourgas gave no sign of wishing to marry, Lizzie suffered a succession of nervous collapses which necessitated trips to various relatives for recovery. She even went to New Orleans to visit with Nancy's brother Charles Harrod, in the hope of curing a fancied pulmonary complaint. Apparently the Louisiana air healed Lizzie's wounded heart, for she reappeared in Quincy during July 1834, determined to dismiss Gourgas. He would not accept her return of gifts he had made to her, however, thus technically continuing the engagement.

At this point Nancy chose to intervene and created an uproar in the community. She sent Gourgas a letter which his father opened by mistake, to discover that the widow Adams threatened to expose his son's problem with alcohol, an affliction apparently unknown to the elder Gourgas. Nancy said she would remain silent if Lizzie's suitor decently concluded his engagement to Lizzie. When the alarmed senior Gourgas confronted his son, the latter publicly announced his intention to sue Nancy for slander. Louisa followed all of this, jotting down descriptions of how Lizzie fainted for embarrassment and how Gourgas went around the town in a rage over Nancy's attempt at blackmail.

Eventually, Nancy's tactic succeeded, and Lizzie was allowed to remain unmarried. John Gourgas continued to practice as an attorney in Quincy, and Lizzie devoted much of her life thereafter to preserving letters and memorabilia of her famous grandparents and other relatives. She carefully pruned the manuscripts left by her parents, in the hope that by burning letters she might brighten history's memory of Nancy and her unfortunate husband. She also took pains to see that John and Abigail's furniture, removed from the Adams mansion by Nancy when she was evicted in 1829, was eventually returned to its proper place.

Soon after the exciting close of Lizzie's romance, Nancy began her last ordeal. She confessed to Louisa that she had not bothered to tell anyone about a lump in her breast she had noticed some time earlier. At the end of October 1839, Nancy underwent surgery in the Adams house, with only Louisa nearby, since Nancy did not want her children to know about the operation. She bore it, said Louisa, "with heroic fortitude." The cancer was not halted, however, and as Nancy advanced toward death, the link between herself and Louisa grew stronger. Nancy needed this support, for even as her own condition worsened, her oldest child, Abigail Angier, died of typhoid fever on 4 February 1845, just when her talent with water colors promised a successful career.

Nancy outlived her daughter by seven tortured months, which must have seemed a lifetime to her and to those who sat with her. Opium brought her little relief. Louisa had prayed for her sister-in-law's swift escape from "such dreadful lingering sufferings, almost too trying for mortal endurance." Nancy begged her sister-in-law to stay by the bed, which Louisa did through all of August, while the patient awaited death. When Nancy finally was released, an exhausted Louisa wrote in her journal, "On the 3rd of September Nancy Adams, the widow of T. B. Adams, departed this life after a long and dreadfully suffering illness of five months." For Louisa the sad story closed triumphantly since Nancy died "in the full hope of that blessed future which our merciful Savior has promised to believing Christians in the full forgiveness of sin."

Two days later, after a funeral at her home and with no pallbearers, Nancy was placed next to Thomas in the Adams vault, where the pair rested for thirty years. Louisa's son Charles Francis eventually bore the expense of having their remains removed to a plot in Quincy's new Mount Wollaston cemetery. There, having at last achieved a degree of independence, Thomas and Nancy have for over a century lain near the graves of their offspring. The last of these, Elizabeth Coombs Adams—Lizzie— who was childless, like the rest, died on 13 June 1903 at age ninety-six.

It would have pleased Louisa to know that her grandson, the second Charles Francis Adams, sat at Cousin Lizzie's bedside watching her "flickering out in extreme old age." Recalling the 168 years stretching from the birth of John Adams to Lizzie's death and particularly the disappointing end for Nancy's once-hopeful marriage to Thomas, Charles offered an epitaph: "It was a barren branch of the tree, and now the last leaf has fallen from it."

13

A Young Widow Ages

Not long before she began a vigil at Nancy's bedside, Louisa observed her seventieth birthday. This reminder of time's flight, along with the death, two years before, of her brother Thomas Baker Johnson, led her to reflect on her Johnson relatives. Four years Louisa's junior, Thomas Johnson clearly needed his sister's ministrations and increasingly depended upon her. When John Quincy's imperious ways stifled her, she often rescued her self-respect by trying to brighten Tom's life. It was a challenge larger than even Louisa could handle, for her brother's existence was troubled until he died in 1843. Throughout his life he shuddered at the memory of his father's financial disgrace. His anticipation that he too would die in penury was joined by the still more pathological fear that blacks in America were about to butcher the whites.

In spite of his emotional problems, Thomas Johnson, until the age of forty, employed his considerable talent toward making a small fortune in New Orleans, where his work for the postal service drew praise from Albert Gallatin, the astute secretary of the treasury to Presidents Jefferson and Madison. Louisa's brother also was briefly a director of the New Orleans branch of the National Bank. But by 1825 his psychological difficulties, including his conviction that he was mortally ill, forced him to retire to what his family called a life of "self-cankering idleness." Tom's finances permitted him to travel in Europe, where he went from one physician to another, seeking assurance that he had some terminal disease. He craved the company of young men who claimed noble descent and titles, including one Count "Gortschakoff," as a skeptical Louisa tried to spell it.

When he was in America, Tom concentrated on avoiding the numerous Johnson relatives who might wish a handout. He had the good judgment to ask Charles Francis Adams to manage his modest wealth. Louisa's son had a shrewd business head, and he handled his Uncle Thomas' affairs so astutely that the "invalid" investor was pleased. Consequently Charles, along with Louisa and John Quincy, were the only mortals whom Tom Johnson trusted. Even when he had been comparatively well in New Orleans, Tom confided in Abigail Adams that Louisa's letters from Europe were all that sustained him during his fearful suffering in Louisiana.

This pitiful bachelor invited all the loving attention which life with John Quincy kept pent up in Louisa. She admitted that Tom was "cracked," but she generously avoided giving any explanation except to say her brother's mind "has been severely buffetted by the shocks of this tempestuous world." When John Quincy's presidential campaign began to upset her life, Tom Johnson's ailments amply justified Louisa's spending time away from Washington. She took him to Philadelphia for a stay that lasted from May to October in 1822. "I cannot bear to have him out of my sight," Louisa announced. Under her guidance, Tom underwent treatments by the notorious Dr. Physick, who proclaimed that removal of hemorrhoids would cure most of humanity's ills.

Unfortunately, Tom's was a stubborn case, obliging the disappointed medic to tell Louisa that her brother was merely an "inveterate dyspeptic." Even Louisa lost patience with Tom, although staying away from Washington with him was more balm for her than any prescription the good Dr. Physick might make. The physician, of course, urged Louisa to submit to his knife, but Louisa resisted. Instead she suggested that John Quincy hasten to Philadelphia and be examined, secretly hoping that the gentle, considerate ways of Dr. Physick might be a good example for her mate, to say nothing of what might result if the surgeon dealt with the secretary of state's rectal problems.

Louisa's letters to Washington purred with the happiness she had found under what she called Dr. Physick's "unwearied kindness and attention." Even Tom showed some slight change for the better, Louisa informed John Quincy, although this progress was probably due as much to Louisa's piano playing—she had an instrument placed in their rented quarters— as to Physick's nostrums. Finally, Louisa triumphantly announced to her husband that Tom Johnson was "a new man, and I think he is likely to become a strong and hearty man." Louisa herself was so refreshed by her removal from politics that she ventured to offer her husband some advice: if he must seek office, then he should greet the public with a pleasant countenance, thereby blunting the complaints she had heard in Philadelphia of John Quincy Adams' "aristocratic hauteur, and learned arrogance."

Louisa met with typically poor results in her attempts to counsel her husband, and enjoyed no more success with her brother. John Quincy's style remained unaltered, and Tom was scarcely back in Washington than he was again convinced a horrible end was approaching. To escape, Tom went abroad, where his travel journal recorded the results of his visits to European physicians, one of whom in 1837 finally told the patient what he craved to hear. Emerging from the doctor's consulting room holding a list of ominous sounding ailments, Tom exulted, "I must be incurable!" He notified Louisa that he was coming home to be near her as he prepared to die.

Tom eventually did return to Washington and allowed Louisa to exercise some command over his life. She had her own physician examine him, and received the assurance that nothing ailed Tom. Nothing, that is, which medicine might help. Her brother, Louisa learned, was "whimsical and flighty, but not of unsound mind." Louisa wondered if Tom's eccentricities were not getting out of hand, however, when, in February 1842, he sent word to her late one evening that she should bring John Quincy to his bedside. Convinced that death was moments away, Tom wished to prepare his will. Two sessions, each lasting nearly all night, were required before John Quincy produced a document that Tom would sign. He did so eagerly, and went on living.

Louisa thought her brother was so much improved that she felt comfortable spending the summer of 1843 in Quincy, where she comforted Nancy as the latter's cancer worsened. Louisa was absent from Washington when Tom suffered a series of strokes and died on 14 October, filled with gratitude to have escaped the slave insurrection he had never tired of predicting. His will disclosed that Tom left an estate of $45,000 to be divided into trusts of equal shares for his sisters. Louisa's son Charles served as executor, a task he fulfilled until 1877 when Adelaide Hellen, the last of the Johnson sisters, died. Wanting a personal memento of Tom, Louisa paid $275 for his carriage when his personal effects were auctioned. She also bought his piano.

Thomas Johnson was interred in Rock Creek Cemetery next to his mother and near other family members. Except for Thomas and Louisa, the children of Catherine and Joshua Johnson had died young or gone on through impoverished and difficult lives. Louisa's sister Eliza Johnson had married Senator John Pope in 1810, and died eight years later at her husband's home in Kentucky. Harriet Johnson was determined to marry George Boyd, despite the concern of her relatives. He had a minor government position in Washington which, soon after his wedding, he resigned, confirming the misgivings of Harriet's relatives. According to Louisa, Boyd gave up his job "in a fit of passion" in order to become an Indian agent in northern Michigan. Even Harriet, the bride, pleaded against this step, and Louisa contended that "surely madness must have seized the man." Dragged away to the frontier, sister Harriet saw none of her family again. Thirty years later, she informed Louisa that she had become a penniless widow in Green Bay, Wisconsin. Louisa did what she could to help, observing that Harriet's case showed "what an evil choice in marriage will produce." Harriet died in 1850.

One of the sisters who remained in Washington was Carolina, whose marriage to Andrew Buchanan had been solemnized in Boston with Louisa looking on. Buchanan died, and Carolina took a businessman, Nathaniel Frye, as second husband. He proved ineffectual, especially after Louisa asked him to be financial assistant to John Quincy and herself. He was much more harm than help. Carolina, however, was one of Louisa's great comforts in old age. She outlived Louisa by ten years, dying in 1862, and was interred in the Johnson family plot at Rock Creek Cemetery.

The sister whom Louisa especially loved and tried to help was Kitty (Catherine), with whom she shared an astonishing physical resemblance. Kitty had joined Louisa in the perilous trip to Russia in 1809. She returned to America with an infant after a hasty marriage to William Steuben Smith, Nabby's eldest son, who put more energy and time into indulging himself than into his assignment as John Quincy's secretary. Kitty's child soon died, as did a second baby. Thereafter, nothing but disappointment and tragedy seemed to follow the Smiths.

Kitty and her husband settled in Washington, where "Billy" specialized in bad checks, debt, and intemperance. The couple usually were dependent on Louisa and John Quincy. Nabby's daughter Caroline, who had married into the wealthy deWindt family of New York, kept aloof from her rascally brother, occasionally sending a five-dollar bill for his support. Kitty's husband served several terms in prison, the longest being a two-year stint for bad debt beginning in 1839. His visitors included regular calls at the jail by John Quincy and Louisa.

Louisa was so distressed by Kitty's plight that she could say only that it was "too miserable!!!" Yet Louisa found a rewarding side to this misery— Kitty's "inestimable kindness and affection." Everyone could profit from her sister's example, Louisa announced. In contrast to Louisa, Kitty did not allow the wretchedness of her marriage to change her happy ways. She spent her time "fluttering about like a little butterfly in all the delights of busy nothingness," Louisa observed, adding, "Oh, how I wish I was like her and could pull flowers from a thicket of thorns."

Loyal and loving, Kitty took her meals with her husband at the jail, a scene which reminded the Adamses of Nabby's faithfulness to Billy's father, when the colonel had been imprisoned. As had been the case with his parent, release from confinement tempted Billy to abandon his wife. He took his dishonest ways to Philadelphia, where more disgrace and failure ensued. Billy died in 1853, a destitute alcoholic and a sad footnote to his mother Nabby's wedding in London. When Billy left her, Kitty settled in for good with Louisa, serving as her companion and later her nurse. Her wit and charm were always welcome among the Adamses. Kitty outlived Louisa by many years. She died in 1869 and was laid to rest next to her sister Frye in Rock Creek Cemetery alongside so many other disappointed Johnson women.

Kitty's troubles, and those of her sisters, were another outlet for those strengths and capacities of Louisa's usually thwarted by John Quincy's aloofness. Louisa found satisfaction in being the strong figure among her Johnson siblings: "Though very imperfectly, I endeavor to keep the family together," she said. She admitted that these sisters and their men were such failures that they invited contempt from "the mocking and scrutinizing public." Even so, "however injudicious the conduct of my family may be," Louisa pledged, "I must ever take an interest in their welfare and deeply regret the results of their inconsequences." The children of her sisters sometimes treated Louisa ungratefully and talked behind her back. Nevertheless, she remained determined to live "in peace and love with my unfortunate relatives." Louisa advised Charles Francis to be thankful he was not "troubled by the anxieties and troublesome affection of obtrusive relatives."

Louisa's comment to Charles Francis reflected most clearly her experience with the children of her older sister Nancy. Soon after coming to America with her parents, Nancy married Walter Hellen, her first cousin, and the son of Joshua Johnson's sister Mary. Seven years Nancy's senior, Walter was a successful tobacco merchant in Maryland and the District of Columbia. It was with the Hellens that Louisa and John Quincy lived between 1803 and 1808 when John Quincy was a U.S. senator. Nancy bore four children before her death on 30 December 1810; three survived childhood and were joined by a stepbrother when Walter married Nancy's and Louisa's youngest sister Adelaide in 1813. Walter Hellen did not long survive this union, which had brought consternation to Louisa and others who believed a widower should not marry his late wife's sister. Losing a lifelong battle against consumption, Walter died on 30 October 1815, astonishing his relatives by the large size of his estate, which was valued in excess of $60,000.

Walter's survivors were also surprised by the manner in which he bequeathed his fortune. His will compelled Adelaide to sue for what everyone conceded was her widow's share. Otherwise she would have been left with hardly enough to rear the baby her brief marriage had produced. It was clear that Walter's purpose had been to guarantee financial independence to his older children. Others in the family feared that these youngsters, already spoiled by an indulgent father, would need careful supervision until they finished growing up. As the eldest surviving sister and the one best prepared to do so, Louisa took over the role of parent to these Hellen offspring when she returned from Europe in 1817.

Louisa's charges included one girl and two boys. The former, Mary Catherine, in time became a companion and helpmate to Louisa, who described her as dearer than any daughter could have been. Mary's brothers, Johnson and Thomas Hellen, amounted to nothing but grief for Louisa. With some help from John Quincy, Louisa set out to improve these lads, particularly since the eldest, Johnson Hellen, a tall, thin person, resembled his mother. But after graduating from Princeton, and reaching his majority in February 1821, Johnson settled back to enjoy what his Aunt Louisa called "the most pernicious indolence." He did bestir himself to dally with a distant Adams kin from New York, a young woman who was described by John Quincy as having the "appetite of a shark for lovers."

A few years later, living in the executive mansion with Louisa's family, Johnson disobeyed his aunt by sharing intimacies with her chambermaid, Jane Winnull. This young woman, in Louisa's opinion a "bold and cunning minx," manipulated Johnson into marrying her in 1829. Thereafter, her nephew wasted his life in what Louisa described as "self-degradation." At one point, Louisa sought reconciliation with Johnson by sending word that she "freely and cordially" forgave him for causing so much pain. Johnson made no acceptable response, and went on his way, pursuing "the sport of his own violent passions." He died in 1867, after he and Jane had given issue to ten children.

The second son of Walter and Nancy Hellen had a brief, wretched career. Thomas Hellen was sent to Harvard, where he evinced interest only in strong drink, an enthusiasm which never left him. "If you choose to ruin yourself, I cannot help it," Louisa sadly remarked to Thomas, but she insisted he stop trying to cadge money from his sister. Thomas died a drunkard's death in 1833, at age twenty-four, leaving his sister Mary as the only child of Nancy Hellen to welcome the eager parental attentions of their Aunt Louisa.

At first, Mary's prospects seemed no better than her brothers'. She was allergic to discipline, lazy, and inclined to spread exaggerated accounts of her wealth. But Louisa did not give up, sensing Mary had the potential to become "a very fine woman," but not, the aunt added, "a heroine of romance." Louisa offered her best advice to Mary. For instance, the young woman was urged to learn that her letters should be written openly and fearlessly, conveying what she really thought and not what she felt ought to be said. Louisa's letters to Mary, like those she sent to everyone else, were models of just such writing.

By 1821 Louisa suspected she was losing ground. Mary seemed to join her brothers in a "natural tendency to grossness" that threatened to make Mary "what I most thoroughly despise," said Louisa, "a woman of loose conversation, of coarse and impure mind." This fear put new life in Louisa's exhortations to Mary, one of which stressed that "delicacy through every stage of life" was "the greatest charm a woman can possess." Perhaps "the uneasy obstinacy" of Mary's character for a time made her disobedient. Louisa noticed that when Mary was told to follow a good example, the admonition succeeded only in "souring her disposition." Mary had romances with each of Louisa's sons, causing the aunt to lament that she had no faith in Mary's morals.

Mary first accepted and then broke an engagement with George, eldest of the Adams brothers. Following this, Charles Francis claimed that Mary introduced him to the delights of the flesh, after which she discarded him to pursue Louisa's middle son, John. Charles said his cousin Mary taught him how difficult it could be for a male to restrain the physical passion a female aroused. "There is magic in a petticoat to a young man," Charles asserted. So much so, according to Charles, that bodily desire could lead a man to think himself in love with almost any woman.

Mary's rebelliousness reached its extreme in 1827 when she announced her determination to marry cousin John Adams over the objections of Louisa and John Quincy. The prospective groom himself was a source of grief to his parents, having been dismissed from Harvard for participating in a student uprising and then reduced to living in Washington under the close supervision of his parents. Not close enough, it seems, for John developed the same dependence on alcohol that ruined his older brother George.

The news that Mary intended to marry John came at one of the most miserable points in Louisa's marriage. The first lady decided to send her niece a stern warning. Marriage, Louisa told Mary, had brought her to look forward to death, "where sorrow and treachery are no more." Louisa's point was made with brutal clarity. Men like John Quincy Adams, who possessed superior talent, no longer considered women as colleagues. Although she had a right to expect tenderness and sharing, Louisa confided, she harvested only scorn and contempt. Except when she was trotted out for social purposes, she was now treated as useless baggage.

The point was that marriage could bring unutterable suffering, and she wished her niece to bear that in mind as she hastened toward matrimony. Louisa followed this by assuring friends that there were no plans for a wedding. Congressman Edward Everett and his wife reported to their family in Massachusetts that the first lady had emphatically denied any such prospect existed. When a wedding seemed inevitable in February 1828, there was no commotion, no announcement until just before the ceremony, which struck acquaintances as strange. These persons, of course, knew less about Mary's fickleness and about the unsteady state of John Adams II, conditions which, up to the last moment, Louisa expected would avert a marriage. President John Quincy Adams took the likelihood of a wedding so casually that he lost himself in political affairs on 25 February 1828, and had to be reminded that the rite was about to take place.

The morning after the wedding a vigilant Louisa observed that nothing magical had occurred, for Mary was "as cool, lazy, and indifferent as ever." Louisa noted, however, that one night of marriage left her son looking "as if he had all the cares of the world upon his shoulders." To her son Charles, Louisa wrote, "My heart tells me that there is much to fear." Indeed so, for Mary became pregnant at once, and announced that she was unhappy. To Louisa's dismay, Mary's "mind dwells much more on future cares than on the strengths of maternal affection." The more Louisa tried to help her, the louder Mary railed against being married. She absolutely refused to take any exercise, a practice Louisa strongly recommended. Louisa was "horrified" to think of what sort of child so recalcitrant a woman would produce.

The birth of Mary Louisa Adams, Louisa's granddaughter, on 2 December 1828 introduced an infant of great size and robustness. Since the mother was unable—or unwilling—to take the chores of maternity seriously, Louisa found herself caring for the baby, a task which mostly pleased her, in spite of head-shakings over Mary's behavior. The baby grew so rapidly that Louisa soon found it difficult to lift her. Meanwhile Mary's husband supervised the construction of a residence in Washington, paid for by the inheritance from Walter Hellen which came to Mary on her twenty-first birthday in 1828. Mary remained determined to live in Washington, despite her father-in-law's defeat for reelection.

This decision worried Louisa, who felt Mary and John should live in Quincy, where morals were presumably purer than in Washington, whose taverns attracted her son John. But since Mary wished to stay in the capital, there was little likelihood of persuading her husband to oppose the decision. John, said Louisa, was "completely under her [Mary's] control." Mary's husband explained his preference by arguing that he had to remain in Washington in order to operate a flour mill purchased by John Quincy. This business had been acquired without consulting Louisa, who was outraged when she learned of it and correctly predicted the investment would fail. John was so eager to avoid the dull scenes of Quincy that he was in Washington on 10 September 1830 when a second daughter was

born to Mary. She had accompanied the Adamses to Massachusetts so as
to have the care and comfort of Louisa when the infant arrived.

Mary was prudent in this decision. Her labor was brief, the baby appeared
before the doctor did, and everyone was grateful for Louisa's skillful
management of the delivery. The infant was named Georgiana Frances,
after her father's two brothers. Since the baby's parents could not attend
little Fanny's baptism in the Quincy church, Louisa and John Quincy stood
together and presented the baby girl for christening. It was a happy time
for Louisa. After the ceremony, she returned to the Adams mansion,
where she took pleasure in caring for the new mother and her baby.
Mary's firstborn, Mary Louisa, was also there for Louisa to look after. She
suffered from cutting teeth, and her grandmother happily rocked her all
night.

The presence of these granddaughters helped Louisa accept John
Quincy's decision to serve in Congress. The family settled in the Washington
house Mary's inheritance had built at 1601 I (Eye) Street N.W., situated
just north of Lafayette Square, a tactful distance from the White House.
Unfortunately, the residence on I Street soon was the setting for another
family tragedy. Mary's husband John broke down under alcoholism.
Somehow, Louisa managed to control her own sorrow by working to keep
Mary from depression as John became increasingly helpless. Louisa tried
to coax John to visit Quincy by pawning her silver bread basket to raise
money for his fare. If he and Mary would let her do this, Louisa said
these silver objects would "yield me more pleasure and solid wealth than
they ever have since I owned them."

By this time, John was beyond help, and he left Mary Catherine a widow
on 23 October 1834. He was thirty-one years old. At the time of their
son's death, Louisa and John Quincy were summering in Quincy. When
word reached Quincy on 18 October 1834 that John was dying, Louisa's
guilt was as strong as her grief. Was this destruction of her second son a
renewed punishment, she wondered, for leaving her two boys and accompanying John Quincy to Russia? Now vexation came again when John
Quincy ordered Louisa to stay behind as he hastened to John's side. Louisa
was angry and desolate, believing she should also be in Washington, playing
her part.

Sitting in Quincy, Louisa wrote about the "almost hopeless anxiety which
rends my heart." As the October rain pelted the Massachusetts coast, she
indicted herself once again for deserting God's "precious trust" and going
to St. Petersburg. In so doing she had broken "the sacred pledge which
every mother should fulfill to the helpless beings entrusted to her charge."
But how much punishment would Heaven impose? Was it now God's

intent that she be prevented from being with another dying son, just as she had had been absent from George in his death? Surely she should be allowed to take the lead "in soothing [John's] Soul to peace in his last moments of mortal agony."

Only the comforting presence in Quincy of her sister Kitty Smith helped Louisa over the guilt and disgust of having submitted once again to her husband, who, with the backing of a doctor, had told her a hurried trip to Washington was too much for a woman. Had John Quincy forgotten that only twenty years before she had made the legendary journey alone from St. Petersburg to Paris? This enforced absence during her son's final hours produced an important change in Louisa's behavior. Believing that she should have overruled the male decree forcing her to stay behind, Louisa thereafter openly rebelled against every effort to keep her in the passive pose expected of a proper woman.

The experience of losing his son also stirred John Quincy momentarily into new appreciation of his wife. He called Louisa the "dearest partner of my life" and for a time spoke to her as with a comrade about new duties they must share in caring for Mary and her two daughters. He suggested they approach God together. Such husbandly talk was balm for Louisa. John Quincy even paid homage to the surprising strength Mary had shown since John's death. Louisa's husband never failed to be amazed when females mustered fortitude equal to or exceeding that of males.

At twenty-seven Mary was a widow. She never remarried, devoting herself to her children. Always sympathetic with forlorn women, Louisa set out once again to curb her dissatisfaction with her own life and tried instead to help Mary find some happiness. The question was how long the new widow's "nervous irritability" would last. Charles Francis still considered Mary a self-centered person. "If I judge her character right," he observed, she would soon be over her husband's death. He was correct. Two years later, Mary was markedly restored in spirit, causing Louisa to rejoice that her daughter-in-law was now "so attentive, kind, and affectionate." Said Louisa, "She is not like the same being and this makes up to me for much of the vexation which I otherwise endure."

Here, of course, Louisa was referring to life with John Quincy. His more thoughtful behavior, brought on by the shock of his son's death, had soon subsided. Once more, Louisa complained about being ignored: "My situation is peculiar . . . never listened to. I sometimes sink into despair and indulge dark and desponding thoughts." Now, however, Louisa more easily overcame these moods, especially after she struck on an idea which she felt might cheer everyone. In 1838 she decided that Mary's smaller house in I Street should be let for rent while the entire family moved back to the larger building on F Street which John Quincy had bought when he was secretary of state and then turned over to tenants when the Adamses moved to the executive mansion in 1825.

The F Street residence was where Louisa had triumphed in 1824 with the great ball for Andrew Jackson. Now she brought John Quincy back to it for the last ten years of his life. The huge building was a welcome haven for several reasons. Wherever Louisa was, many of her Johnson relatives were sure to seek her out for refuge. A second and happier purpose was that Louisa now had space for entertaining a growing circle of friends drawn to the brilliant former president and his wife. As Louisa hoped, Mary soon mingled with the Washington social set.

The improvement was brief. Another great sorrow was in store for Mary, one which apparently affected her more than the loss of her husband. After his death, she began living for her daughters, Mary Louisa and Fanny, children who were also the joy of Louisa and John Quincy's life. The busy congressman took time to train the girls in such useful subjects as Greek and advanced mathematics. Louisa would rarely allow Mary and the children from her sight, taking them with her to Quincy each summer. In 1835, the notable American artist Asher B. Durand completed portraits of the two girls—the likeness of five-year-old Fanny was especially successful and touching. Four years later, at age nine, Fanny had become an extraordinarily beautiful and winsome girl, who Louisa and John Quincy agreed had "so much of the angelic in her already that she seems all fitted for a better world."

Their observation seemed a presentiment. While the family was still in Quincy, Fanny was stricken with diphtheria, and at six o'clock in the evening of 20 November 1839, after a long and painful illness, she died in the bed in which she had been born. During the youngster's final "tortured spasms," Louisa knelt at the bedside leading other family members in prayer, although John Quincy found Fanny's "shrieking groans" unendurable, driving him from the room crying, "Oh! My God!"

For the next day, as grief crushed both Mary and John Quincy, Louisa was the source of consolation. The episode recalled her power in 1829 when she supported John Quincy after they learned of George's drowning. Only after Fanny's funeral, when the child's small casket was laid on her father's coffin in the family tomb, did Louisa go to bed with her sorrow. She was so bewildered by what seemed the cruelty of Fanny's last days that for a time she drew little consolation from prayer. "I am ashamed of it, but suffering has subdued my spirit." Surely, Louisa said, the blessed "balm" would come.

Fearing that Mary would now become "a perfect recluse," Louisa was soon up and strengthened. Taken aback by Louisa's fortitude in a crisis that immobilized John Quincy, Mary blurted out that Fanny's grandmother had no heart. Louisa patiently overlooked this and shepherded the family back to Washington, where she sought to rebuild its strength: "The loss of that lovely child has been too heart breaking to us all, and every coming hour seems to add to the bitterness of our affliction." But Louisa persisted until John Quincy recovered and busied himself with congressional matters.

Aided by Louisa's example, time also healed Mary's sorrow. She gratefully accepted invitations to social events. Such attention made her "wretchedly happy," Louisa reported. Most of Mary's life now was devoted to Mary Louisa, the surviving daughter. Recently, a fragment has been discovered of the journal which Mary Louisa kept during the summer of 1841 when she was twelve. A diary must have seemed as natural as breathing for a young person living in the old Adams mansion at Quincy. Grandmother Louisa wrote steadily, as did Uncle Charles Francis Adams in his residence just up the hill. Most impressive, however, for Mary Louisa must have been the sight of John Quincy Adams adding installments to what would become America's most famous diary. The old man was always writing when the young lady entered his chamber early each morning for her lessons.

That summer Mary Louisa was concentrating on logarithms, a subject, along with algebra, which she found "difficult." She reminded herself that "Grandpappa" assured her (with impeccable Adams reasoning) that "if I attend I shall be able to conquer." She soon found a more practical example of what persistence would attain. One day when she was sent to fetch some cream for the family, Mary Louisa discovered her path blocked by three bulls. Undaunted, she hailed a passing gentleman who helped her drive them out of her way.

Mary Louisa usually arose at 6:30 to make the fire in her room. She spent most of each day reading the classics, studying math and French, sewing, drawing, walking, and at "play." After all this exertion, she retired punctually at nine, usually taking a book to bed—Molière was a favorite author. Some of each day she sat with Grandmother Louisa as the latter read the manuscript letters of John Adams, her project for that summer. The two also went fishing, and, of course, to church. One Sunday, Mary Louisa reported that Quincy's new minister, the Reverend William P. Lunt, had "preached and preached." Evidently he exhausted his parishioners, for the youthful diary announced that, although it was communion Sabbath, no one lingered to partake. For Mary Louisa, there was, of course, no shortage of edification at home. Her grandfather often put her to work copying items he felt would nourish a youthful mind, such as an "Ode to Fortitude."

As for Louisa, whether in Washington or Quincy, she seemed invincible as she coped with a household often filled with needy relatives. Some astonished observers recalled how, a dozen years before, she had been an emotional invalid in the White House. Now, the increasingly enfeebled John Quincy was less inclined to brush off her care and concern, and Louisa was at last able to take command, as her resourcefulness was acknowledged as essential. A typical incident occurred one night in 1846 when she was awakened with the news that Mary was ill. While a frightened John Quincy cowered in bed, Louisa diagnosed the complaint as tonsillitis, summoned the doctor, and nursed her niece until morning.

Mary apparently learned from Louisa's example that women need not hang back. In late October 1843, Louisa and Mary were returning to Washington, traveling by boat through Long Island Sound, accompanied by Charles Francis. Fire broke out during the night. By his own admission, Charles Francis panicked in his effort to assist Louisa from her stateroom. Mary took over with great self-possession, seeing to everyone's safety. After the fire was put out, Charles noted in his journal that Mary "behaved with coolness and decision so as materially to lighten my labours." It was, he said, "the most fearfully memorable night of my life." Louisa was elated by Mary's strong actions. "How delightful it is to praise those whom we love and admire," Louisa said to Charles. She made the remark rather pointedly, since Charles, like his father, tended to belittle the abilities of women.

Both Louisa and Mary hovered over Mary Louisa as the surviving granddaughter passed through the dangers of teenage. One reason they did so was that by age sixteen Mary Louisa was alarmingly developed as a woman. Perhaps recalling her own unbridled behavior at that age, Mary became very protective, refusing to permit her daughter to mingle with people her own age. Louisa tried to support Mary's policy, recognizing that Mary Louisa could become "too much of a belle for her age." On the other hand, Louisa mused, keeping the young lady sitting at home and sulking might encourage disobedience and rash behavior. Louisa advocated that Mary allow her daughter to go out in formal society: "better to bring a girl out under proper auspices than to *risk chance acquaintance*."

This counsel was not heeded. Mary Louisa stayed close to her mother until she was nearly twenty-five, when the "chance acquaintance" ironically appeared in the person of William Clarkson Johnson, a third cousin who arrived in Washington to woo Mary Louisa in a whirlwind romance. Johnson, whose first wife had died a short time before, was descended from Abigail and John Adams through their unfortunate son Charles, who had married Colonel William Smith's sister. Johnson remembered Mary Louisa from a chance meeting in Quincy years before. In June 1853, a year after her grandmother died, Mary Louisa announced her intention to marry this man who wanted to change her life so suddenly.

Some of the bride's relatives thought the wedding was a "rather hasty proceeding," although Mary had no choice but to accept the extraordinary development. Mary Louisa became a resident of Utica, New York, where her husband lived. She gave birth eight months later to a daughter. Soon there were two more grandchildren for Mary, who was known to these youngsters as "Grandma Duckie." The scene promised Mary a happy twilight, with much of each year spent in Utica. And then her existence broke apart again. An attack of "brain fever" killed Mary Louisa on 16 July 1859. She was thirty.

In her misery, Mary sent word to her cousin Charles Francis, her nearest relative. She told him how she prayed he would be spared "the share of grief and sorrow" which life had brought her. Alas, Mary's woes were not yet finished. She intended to remain in Utica with her son-in-law and her three grandchildren, although her relatives in Quincy were uneasy about this decision. They knew of reports that Mary's son-in-law had squandered his first wife's property, and that he proposed doing the same with Mary Louisa's small estate.

By now Mary's close companion in the Adams family was Louisa's other daughter-in-law and Charles Francis' wife, Abby. It was she who foresaw what would happen to Mary. "William Johnson is nothing," announced Abby. "He is as selfish as can be. . . . The Johnsons are a mean set." With remarkable accuracy, Abby predicted that Mary's son-in-law would soon marry again, which he did, and that he would dismiss his former mother-in-law, which he also did. In August 1860, William Johnson ordered Mary out of his house, and humiliated her by denying her access to her grandchildren.

At that point Mary was fifty-three, although her gray hair made her appear much older. She lived another ten years, residing mostly in her Washington house on I Street where she looked after Louisa's surviving sisters. Mary died of a stroke on 31 August 1870. Her body was brought to Quincy, where she was buried in the Adams tomb, resting next to her husband and little Fanny. Abby arranged the funeral; it was held in the old Adams mansion on 3 September.

14

Wedding at Mystic Grove

Abigail Brown Brooks—everyone called her Abby—was part of the Adams family for sixty years, beginning with her marriage to Louisa's son Charles Francis. Abby's role was far different from that filled by Mary Hellen since she brought to the Adamses an alliance with a Massachusetts family of great wealth. She mastered the trials of life in the Adams clan and bequeathed to the nation three sons who rank among America's finest historians and writers. Finally, and not least, Louisa found in Abby a valued cohort in the campaign to sustain the power and dignity of women. A bond was knit between the two which never weakened.

Abby's father was Peter Chardon Brooks, who in his day was reputed to be the richest man in New England. The exaggeration, if any, was slight. His money had been carefully accumulated through insuring maritime businesses and through judicious investment. Account books for 1829 show that at the time Abby married Charles Francis Adams the Brooks fortune exceeded $1.5 million. The Brooks family resided in Medford, where Peter owned a four-hundred-acre river estate called Mystic Grove which had been in his family since 1660.

Peter Brooks was born on 6 January 1767. He seemed a success at everything, including his marriage in 1792 to Anna Gorham, daughter of Nathaniel Gorham, a Massachusetts political leader and first president of the Continental Congress. From this union came thirteen children, three of them daughters. Apparently Peter Brooks delighted in women, particularly in his daughters, but his displays of affection toward them, his generosity, and his good humor were somewhat misleading. The Adams men who visited the Brooks home could not miss seeing the sculpted figure of a naked woman on her knees. This bit of art may have unintentionally represented Brooks' true attitude toward women. Peter emphasized that the female's interests properly should be babies, clothes, parties, and gossip, topics that dominated the letters he wrote to his daughters.

Yet Peter Brooks was serious when he said he preferred the company of women. When women traveled, he noted, "they make fewer complaints than men—always." Thus, he asserted, women deserved the best of everything. The merchant in Brooks emerged when he claimed, "I would sooner wait on ten ladies than one man." Yet his wife Anna broke under the strain of thirteen pregnancies, and much of her adult life was darkened by depression and poor health.

The eldest daughter of Peter and Anna Brooks was Ann Gorham Brooks, born 19 February 1797. She was followed by Charlotte Gray Brooks, called Lotty, whose birthday was 4 November 1800. The youngest, Abigail Brown Brooks, was born 25 April 1808. Abby appears to have been her father's favorite, evidently because of her lively and spontaneous ways. Each of the three Brooks women participated in the Adams story, but only Abby played a paramount role.

At age twenty-one, Ann Brooks married Nathaniel Langdon Frothingham, minister of Boston's First Church. Five children issued from this union, including the writer Octavius Brooks Frothingham. Ann's marriage seems to have been a loving one. Romance flourished between the Frothinghams, as can be seen in letters Nathaniel sent to Ann in 1826–27, when he forsook his pulpit for a year to see the sights of Europe. Nothing the Reverend Frothingham saw seemed to take his mind from his wife, who was to him "my dearest" and to whom he sent poetry which emphasized the "throbs of an anxious breast" while he entertained "thoughts of my wedded love."

Nathaniel conceded that some persons might find it "odd" that "a man should be writing verses to his wife nine years after marriage, but it would never seem so to you and me." In a last letter to Ann from Europe, Nathaniel closed with the suggestion, "Comfort yourself with thinking that before you have time to read this over many times, you will be in the arms of your lover and husband."

The Frothingham manse was a gathering point in Boston for the three Brooks sisters, who often made a lively trio. One Sunday in December 1829 these women decided to attend two sermons preached by the future historian John Gorham Palfrey, who chose that day to make what the sisters agreed were "very singular" addresses on the duties wives owed to husbands. That evening, the Brooks daughters, each now married, visited the Palfreys, where they "paid Mr. P. with interest for the advice he had so freely given us thro' the day." Since the minister had stressed the importance of obedience by wives, the trio notified him that "he should not have touched upon that point at all, as it was a subject that had been exploded long ago."

Ann Frothingham was much admired by Louisa Adams, who recognized in her a woman of great strength and amiableness. She praised Ann for being as good a nurse as Louisa herself was. When Charles and Abby's tiny son Henry Adams barely survived scarlet fever in 1841, it was Ann Frothingham who nursed him during the critical early days of the illness while his parents were visiting in Washington. For this, the Adamses remained forever grateful to Ann, who had selflessly persuaded the doctors to keep her younger sister away from the danger and strain involved in the battle for young Henry's life. Invariably, when a female friend was about to give birth, she turned to Ann for supervision.

The second Brooks sister, Lotty, never earned the respect which came to Ann, who was generally conceded to have "twice the substance" of Charlotte Gray Brooks. Lotty's story would intrigue a psychobiographer. For example, in her youth, Peter Chardon Brooks, by his own admission, would "slap" her in order to break her from being left-handed. Whatever drove Lotty's ambitious nature may also account for the melancholia that early began to afflict her, although the condition was more likely a genetic legacy from her mother.

Lotty became Mrs. Edward Everett on 8 May 1822. The groom was born 11 April 1794 and soon impressed New England with his precocity. He took the highest honors when he graduated from Harvard in 1811, the youngest member of his class, and was pastor of Boston's fashionable church on Brattle Street before he was twenty. He stayed only one year, leaving to accept an appointment as Professor of Greek literature at Harvard. He studied further at Göttingen University, becoming the first American to be awarded a Doctor of Philosophy degree.

Troubled by such intellectual zeal, Abigail Adams had Everett in mind when she warned her overly industrious son John Quincy during 1814 of the dangers of insatiably seeking knowledge. Edward Everett, she predicted, would likely be cut down in the morning of life. Instead Everett went to Congress in 1825, and stayed there ten years. Later he was governor of Massachusetts, U.S. minister to England, president of Harvard, briefly secretary of state, then U.S. senator, and finally nominee for vice president on the Constitutional Union ticket in 1860.

Edward Everett excelled in none of these callings, and seemed rather more ambitious than talented or persevering. Those who wish to understand him should begin by reading the letters he and Lotty exchanged. In these epistles Everett sounds stuffy and uninspired, while those from Lotty, often spirited, well-written, and affectionate, express her determination that he continue as a public figure. Some of the Adamses believed that Everett's career was the result of his wife's prodding.

Possibly so. Lotty preferred to have her husband away, in Washington or anywhere, for when they were together, she seemed invariably to become pregnant, a condition she wished to avoid. Many of Lotty's surviving letters to her husband preached the need for him to be stern with himself and overcome his desire to see her. What he termed homesickness, she preferred to call fatigue. At times Lotty talked with a tinge of envy about women who had passed the age when sexual activity was supposed to be necessary, and she ridiculed the tendency of society to disguise the horror of pregnancy by using such euphemisms as "slow fever" or "sickness." In September 1832 and already a mother four times, Lotty feared she was pregnant again. When she discovered there was no cause for alarm, Lotty told everyone how elated she was. This attitude appalled Louisa Adams. Having always been glad for pregnancy, and now yearning to welcome more grandchildren, Louisa was shocked when any healthy woman recoiled from giving birth. According to Louisa, the case of Mrs. Edward Everett, who "cannot bear the thought of increasing her family," was pathetic.

Lotty did not always try to keep Edward at a distance, however. If their separation was prolonged, she wrote passionately, speaking of how she longed to press him to her heart and of kissing his portrait. At those moments Lotty vowed to be a better wife. If he were with her, she assured him, she would make him very happy. She told him of reading romantic novels, and picturing him as the hero.

Before she reached fifty, Lotty's mind began to deteriorate. In 1849 she was still able occasionally to send a few lines to Edward, in which she told him he need not write much, only enough to assure her that he was thinking of her. In the late 1850s, Lotty no longer was capable of knowing whether her husband was near or far. She died on 2 July 1859 at age fifty-eight. For whatever reason, Charlotte Brooks Everett had felt pushed by life, and came to dread existence. This outlook represented an important difference between herself and her younger sister, Abby.

Abigail Brooks' lightheartedness dismayed Lotty. In 1828, at a time when she seemed particularly depressed, Lotty wrote, "I hope Abby may never have any thing to damp her spirits, but I greatly fear that she will not be able to go through life the same happy creature she is now." Fortunately, not even Abby could anticipate in 1828 what was ahead as she prepared for marriage into a family which then included the president of the United States. Louisa Adams, the mother of the groom, could foresee what confronted Abby Brooks.

Musing about this lively young woman who would soon become a mate to an Adams, Louisa wrote a remarkable letter to her son Charles in which she warned him that Adams males were "peculiarly harsh and severe" in approaching women. They lacked "sympathetic tenderness" and were devoid of appreciating how a woman was differently constituted in body and mind. For a woman, whom nature and society sentenced to face "almost unmitigated anxiety and suffering," having an Adams for companion worsened a bad situation. Louisa urged Charles to learn that "even a little tenderness of manner and appearance of affection" would be of immeasurable aid to a wife as she experienced the rigor of bearing and rearing children.

Eventually the bride-to-be and Mrs. Frothingham inquired of Louisa about Charles' dour manner, for it was a disposition not apparent in Abby and Ann's father or in the Reverend Frothingham. Louisa made the best of it in her reply, saying that "the Adamses had a manner of speaking and writing that appeared harsh, though in fact it meant nothing more than the common style of other people." Louisa sought to be reassuring, for she was charmed by Abby Brooks' vivacity and coveted a daughter-in-law with such an outlook. As part of the Adams circle, Abby, with her buoyant spirit, would seem, as Louisa put it, "an exotic."

There was another and more important cause for Louisa's determination to see Abby wed her son. Like Elizabeth Peabody, Louisa wanted love to command everyone's life. It stirred her deeply to know that Charles Francis had been rendered helpless by Cupid. While she never said as much, Louisa could hardly have avoided remembering how she, a lively creature like Abby, had once adored the handsome and brilliant John Quincy Adams. She did her best to encourage the romance between Abby and Charles.

Peter Brooks' wealth seems to have had nothing to do with Charles' sudden and complete captivation by Abby when the eighteen-year-old woman appeared in Washington to spend the winter of 1826–27 with Lotty and Edward Everett. (The latter was then a congressman.) Abby brought with her the sweet, open, and spontaneous personality that was her distinguishing feature. She had no more education than most young ladies of the day and, unlike Louisa, she showed no marked intellectual strengths or talent. She was not even beautiful. But whatever Abby had, it was ample. Charles Francis Adams was hers for life, and virtually from their first encounter.

Washington was a small town in 1827, and President Adams was obviously well acquainted with Representative Everett, so it was natural that Abby should have met Charles at the executive mansion and in her sister's home. By mid-January 1827, Charles was asserting in his diary that, having nothing better to do, he was staying in the presence of Miss Brooks whenever social occasions permitted. This was not lost upon Louisa, who noted that Abby was "a great belle here and a wonderful favorite with the family." She was, said the first lady, "quite an oddity."

Abby's attractiveness grew on Charles each day, which puzzled him, since usually he found proper young women tedious. But after a party in the home of Secretary of State Henry Clay, where Charles was "engrossed" by "Miss Brooks," he announced in his diary, "This young lady's character is so singular that I am much struck with it." How aware Abby was of her conquest is unknown, but by 10 February Charles confessed to himself that he was miserable when not in Abby's company. That night, during a dance given by the French envoy, Baron de Mareuil, Abby's appearance overwhelmed Charles, and when she took his arm for a quiet walk, she received a proposal of marriage.

Although not yet twenty, Charles Francis Adams was a remarkably poised and well-spoken person. Still, he managed to botch his proposal, for Abby mistook his meaning. All she heard was him wondering if she would permit his attention in the future. Seeing her confusion, Charles prompted her by saying that surely she knew what he had in mind. Abby was so startled and Charles so chagrined over stumbling at such a moment that both parties found the occasion "too painful." After Abby said she must consult her family, Charles left her with Martin Van Buren, the widower senator from New York, while he hurried off to find Lotty Everett and confess what he had done.

Charles' dashing about the ballroom must have drawn considerable attention, so that Lotty advised him to stop making a public commotion over so delicate a matter. He was very young, she warned him, foreseeing Peter Brooks' misgivings. Then, relenting a bit, Lotty invited Charles to the Everett residence the next day to pursue the matter. Delighted, the young man rushed back to the White House, where he could share all this with his diary. There he offered avowals of love and also explanations, typically Adams, of why the sudden step was prudent. Charles reasoned it was enough that he and Abby did not suffer from uncertain prospects.

The next morning was Sunday, and Abby saw Lotty and Edward Everett go off to church, leaving her to welcome an impatient Charles, who appeared as soon as the coast was clear. They were together for a blissful two hours, during which Abby told Charles that she returned his love. The problem would be her father, Abby predicted, warning Charles that Peter Brooks had his own ideas about whom she should marry, and when. The best strategy, Abby suggested, was for Charles to seek advice from her brother-in-law. Just as the Everetts returned from worship, Charles was called away by his brother John for horseback riding, a most inconvenient interruption. The excursion over, Abby welcomed her suitor again and sent him in to Edward Everett, who stressed the disadvantage of Charles' youth so strongly that the young man went home ill.

The next day Charles sought comfort from Louisa and told her how he had fallen in love. His mother offered complete support, despite what must have been her astonishment at the impulsive nature of her son's decision. Even Charles was amazed at himself, noting that he had "not been romantic at all during the course of my life." He simply had been captivated by Abby's warmheartedness, he concluded, and rejoiced in recollecting how swiftly she responded with equal fervor to his avowals of love. "There is a frankness, a simplicity about her manner which is much more engaging than the studied elegance of an accomplished belle," said Charles. He recognized that the two of them were very different, for he was usually suppressed and grave while she was outgoing and affectionate.

Charles confessed to Abby that her qualities were especially admirable because, as he put it, "they are out of my reach." He marveled that she could prefer as restrained a nature as his when she was so animated and frank. The couple knew this rapport would be for nought if Peter Chardon Brooks would not surrender his favorite daughter. And, in fact, for a time Mr. Brooks did block Abby's wish to marry. When news about Abby's proposed engagement was sent to Medford by Edward Everett, the proper person to transmit so delicate a message, Peter Brooks was shocked: "I declare it did not come into my mind that any thing of this kind would occur—I will say no more at present."

Soon, however, Abby's father decided he should express his concern to Charles' parents. It was embarrassing to doubt the match, Peter asserted to the president and first lady, but Charles Francis was so very young. An astonished John Quincy, who had been too busy for Louisa to interrupt him with news about the romance, called Charles in for a conference. After this session, Charles' father joined Louisa in approving the engagement, provided no marriage occurred before August 1828, when Charles would come of age. This news was conveyed to Peter Brooks, who thereby was made even more disconcerted, since Edward Everett had indicated Charles would be twenty-one in August 1827.

Abby's parents grew more opposed to any betrothal, though Peter Brooks conceded it made them appear to lack feeling when others seemed to praise the match. Since Abby's side had been presented by Congressman Everett, her father decided it was time to hear from her. He wrote to Abby suggesting she share her feelings with him and advising that all talk of engagement be halted until she returned for a long discussion with her parents.

The day after Peter Brooks wrote to Abby, 2 March 1827, he received a letter from Louisa which changed everything. Louisa's epistle is missing, but it must have been a moving description of two young people in love, and a statement of why she believed it would be a good marriage. She evidently implied that despite their good intentions, the Brookses were causing Abby and Charles much anguish. Always a man of action, Peter Brooks responded immediately, sending word to Edward Everett: "We now give our full consent to Abby to act her pleasure." He also recommended that reports of family opposition to the match be suppressed. Had he been on the scene instead of far away in Medford, Peter Brooks contended, he would have approved an engagement at the outset.

While Edward Everett let his father-in-law believe that these parental hesitations were secret, the congressman had not been able to keep the original opposition to himself. All along, Abby and Lotty had demanded to hear the viewpoint from Medford. Before Peter Brooks' capitulation arrived, which took ten days to reach Washington by winter mail service, Edward Everett learned he had upset two women and caused all Washington to talk about the situation. Abby and Lotty felt their withdrawal from town would now be prudent, and chose Harper's Ferry, not far from Washington, as the place to await the results of additional thought in Medford. And besides, Abby considered it best not to see Charles for a time. This anguish and separation continued until 13 March, when the blessing from Abby's parents arrived, making everyone rejoice. There was also a letter to Louisa from Peter Brooks wherein he explained that, had he known how much his daughter was in love, he never would have ordered delay. "I ought to have known better," he said.

Soon after this happy upshot, Abby returned to her parents' home, leaving the romance to proceed by letter. She had scarcely departed when Charles began congratulating himself on having at last found pure love: "Other women have acted upon me by a voluptuous manner, to which I am unfortunately peculiarly susceptible." Abby was a person whom he could both love and respect. This prospect seemed to relieve him, for even at nineteen he reported, "I have seen so much of their [women's] bad shades of character that I had doubted whether any could create a different effect on me."

Charles may have had in mind his Washington mistress. Nothing is known about her, not even her name, only that when his engagement was certain, but not until then, Charles broke off with her in what he called "one of those disagreeable scenes which occur sometimes in life." The romantic letters now reaching him from Abby led him to observe, "No man of sense will ever keep a mistress. For if she is valuable, the separation when it comes is terrible, and if she is not, she is more plague than profit." He was grateful to have discovered Abby, for now he had the basis on which to "close my licentious intrigues." Charles observed that every generation of males must discover for itself the perils of women who, despite deceptively prudish talk, would look "in that way which a man easily understands."

When Abby returned to New England, Charles could not disguise his impatience for letters from her. She did not disappoint him. In fact, her messages were so winning that Charles felt compelled to explain that his Adams nature prevented his responding in the open style which came so naturally to her. "Our family are peculiar for their sparing use of affectionate expressions," Abby was warned. Charles did not exaggerate. The difference in personality between the two was instantly clear in their letters. Abby's first, dated 29 March 1827, announced, "I have missed you more than I am willing to tell." She wrote easily and charmingly, ardently assuring "my dear, dear Charles" that "my warmest affection belongs to you."

To this Charles responded, "I don't like to tell you how much I love you for fear of making myself extravagant." He humbled himself enough to seek her guidance about an invitation to visit Medford which had been extended by Peter Brooks. She must not tell anyone he sought her counsel, Charles begged, for if she did he would be made to appear "doubtful and afraid to take a step without advice." Abby encouraged her uncertain lover as much as she could. He often implored her to explain why she was attracted to him, and his expectation of a serious and lengthy reply worried her. When Charles told Abby that he loved her because he wished for a gay spirit to amuse him and relieve "the stupidity" of his existence, her tactful rejoinder was that she sought a man who would appreciate her liveliness, yet a husband who was "less gay" and would thereby "qualify to some degree my lightheartedness and folly."

Charles clamored for additional reasons, provoking Abby to ask sweetly why she should say more. Was it not enough that each had fallen so quickly in love with the other? As a diversion, she described how her family was teasing her by saying that Charles had already tired of her and was glad to be away. Abby recognized that Charles was less able than she to endure joking and reasured him that her relatives made this commotion in the knowledge that her love was confident and unshakable.

She worked hard to soothe him in other letters. She described how she relished his words every time he talked of desiring her: "I sometimes have blushed to think how much I have said to you, but why should I be ashamed to confess that I love you better than all the world beside?" Surely, Abby said, it was understandable that she could not think enough about him: "I cannot love you too well." His letters undid her, she confessed: "So you see even at this distance you have complete power over me."

When Charles plaintively asked just what sort of letter from him would most please her, Abby tried patiently to explain that simply what he wished to write was all she needed. Let him just write! Somewhat annoyed, Abby dismissed an implication Charles had made that she required something amusing in his letters. She "should truly feel myself quite a child," if he seriously believed that, she replied. Abby urged Charles to remember "that I am quite a woman." Then, astutely, she distracted him by displaying serious regard for his current interest, usually a book.

Charles was so encouraged by this literary turn that he asked Abby to share with him her opinions of certain authors and their works. Was he in earnest? she chided. "I am pretty sensible how tedious it is to gentlemen to hear ladies discuss those subjects." Yet she welcomed his invitation, telling him that her father now urged her to sit with him and her brothers during their discussions of writers. She also reported that she read books and summarized their contents as requested by Peter Brooks since he was too busy to look at them himself. This helped stretch her memory, Abby said, as she agreed to share literary interests with Charles—if he meant it. Long a petted innocent at home, Abby obviously was a bit startled at being taken for an adult.

As the months passed, Abby's letters lost none of their simplicity and charm. She talked to Charles of his "pretty blue eyes," of how she missed him when he was in Washington, and of her yearning for him. There was space now, however, to describe happenings in New England. One topic of special interest to Charles was the furor caused in July 1827 when Harvard's president, John T. Kirkland, became engaged to marry. No one was actually astonished, said Abby, but nevertheless there was "scandal enough, I assure you." A few months later, Kirkland resigned his post, putting his critics behind him by wedding the lady of his heart, who happened to have sufficient means to provide for their comfort. Charles must have envied his old mentor, for Abby's letters, loving though they were, seemed never to press for marriage. It left Charles suspecting that once again the problem was Peter Chardon Brooks.

Although Charles passed his twenty-first birthday on 18 August 1828, Abby's father seemed to forget about setting a time for his daughter's wedding. He was reluctant to part with Abby, and uncertain about Charles' prospects. The young man was a lawyer with no practice, who gave some attention to managing his father's Boston properties, and the rest to reading. There was little income in this, leaving Charles dependent upon a $1,000-dollar annual gift from John Quincy. When he contemplated marriage, Charles anticipated a handsome allowance would be settled upon Abby by her father—although Charles hesitated to speak of this even to his diary.

Delaying marriage for economic reasons seemed absurd to Charles, and the problem frayed his already delicate spirits. While his letters continued to speak of "my dearest, sweetest" Abby, and his diary showed his thoughts to be always "of the dear kisses of my Abi," Charles began complaining to his sweetheart that it must be she who wished to postpone marriage and that she was not reassuring enough in her avowals of love.

A startled and bruised Abby replied, "Oh, Charles . . . to tell you how much I love you is impossible, but when I read your letters and think of you away so far, in spite of myself the tears will come." He should try more to understand her, she suggested. Charles responded with apologies, saying he could only "congratulate myself upon my lucky stars which led me to you." He was sure their marriage would be one of those made in Heaven; but when, oh when, would they be wed? Keeping up the pressure during the autumn of 1828, Charles hoped that their union would become a matter for serious planning. Was Abby afraid of marriage? If so, she should talk to her sisters, and let them explain the happiness wedded life would bring. Abby replied that she was not holding back and that she would cheerfully becomes Charles' wife at a moment's notice. It was her parents' consent that was needed.

After eighteen months of engagement, and with a father who ignored her wish to marry, Abby decided to seek encouragement during October 1828 when Louisa invited her to visit Washington. Charles was also there, vacationing. Louisa urged Abby to come, not simply because the Adamses "are all anxious to see you," but also to placate Charles. *"You know the cause,"* Louisa said. To everyone's dismay, Peter Brooks forbade the visit. It would appear, he explained, that Abby was making the trip simply to pursue Charles.

This forced the issue, bringing Charles bluntly to ask Peter Brooks for permission to initiate wedding plans. Charles argued that although his income was small, it was adequate, and "delay will do me no good." He then gambled, telling Mr. Brooks that unless a wedding date could be set the engagement must be dissolved—out of fairness to Abby, Charles nobly affirmed. Unperturbed, Peter Brooks insisted on a longer delay; a wedding was unthinkable for at least a year. He cited the poor health of Abby's mother as the major reason.

His bluff called, Charles was unwilling to break with Abby, so he settled on another tactic, even more dangerous. Late in 1828, after he returned to Boston and enjoyed an ecstatic reunion with Abby—"I have never had purer moments of unmingled pleasure than the few hours which passed this evening"—Charles informed Abby that henceforth they must meet only infrequently. He softened the blow by assuring her how painful this sacrifice was to him, for "you are the only connecting chain that I have at present with any kind of happiness."

The strategy succeeded. Abby confronted her father and insisted firmly on permission to marry, and soon. Further delay was hazardous, for Charles had become restless. "My celibacy is likely to be so long that I am tired of waiting for its end," Charles confided to his diary. He vowed to "do as well as I can without being established," and turned an interested eye toward women visitors in the Boston house where he rented bachelor quarters. However, these tempting distractions were quickly shoved aside when, in early December 1828, Peter Chardon Brooks summoned Charles to announce a most generous basis upon which the family would permit Abby's marriage. The date for the occasion was still left vague, put off to sometime the next summer.

Somehow, Abby and Charles survived until their wedding in September 1829, although thwartings and misunderstanding caused them to annoy one another. Charles was particularly impatient to have Abby in the more enlightened surroundings of an Adams residence where she could begin to improve her mind. Abby may have glimpsed the irritation her family caused in Charles, who found it difficult to hide his growing conviction that all Brookses were "immense bores." With them he found none of the talk about literature and politics which dominated Adams gatherings. Abby's own frustration sometimes made her moody and cold, which drove Charles to leave in a huff. Like most engaged couples, the pair quickly became reconciled, and Charles realized anew how eagerly he awaited the end of this "probation." With typical understatement, he announced that "the hot and the cold of lovers is after a certain period distressing."

Louisa was so sympathetic that she confided in Charles the likely reason for Peter Brooks' reluctance to see Abby becoming an Adams. She suggested Abby's father must have discovered that President Adams was relatively impoverished, a plight due mostly to owning much useless land and having numerous dependent relatives. Such reasons would not be viewed sympathetically by a Brooks, Louisa declared. "Real greatness is but little appreciated," she told Charles, because "the penny turns everything." Peter Brooks happily confounded observers in March 1829 by urging a prompt wedding and promising to set the date as soon as he found a Boston residence to purchase for the bride and groom. This handsome prospect calmed Charles and Abby considerably, as did the money Abby was given by her father to set up her own household. The pair would live on Beacon Hill in what Lotty Everett called "one of that pretty row of houses by the side of the State House." The address was 3 Hancock Avenue.

Finally, early in the evening of 3 September 1829, Abby awaited Charles' appearance at their marriage ceremony at Mystic Grove, the Brooks home in Medford. Charles let too much of the day go to reading and other activities, and by the time he put on the "gay and showy style of a bridegroom" and reached Medford, he was late. A small group awaited, including Abby's parents, brothers, and sisters, along with Charles' father, his Uncle Thomas, and a few others. (Louisa was in Washington.) They joined in admiring the bride whom Charles gleefully reported possessed great charm and dignity. She bore up so well during the festivities that Charles announced in his diary, "I cannot too warmly admire her conduct." He was particularly impressed by Abby's calm acceptance of the customary jesting which weddings entailed.

Abby was perfection in Charles' eyes. In fact, he said, on this long awaited day she had brilliantly manifested the superior qualities "which I have always known to be in her, and for which I have married her." After pausing for supper, the bridal couple left a group of spirited guests to more champagne and rejoicing, while they drove to their new home in Boston and "consummated the marriage," as Charles' diary entry described the beginning of the honeymoon.

On the morning after the wedding, John Quincy called on the newlyweds and found Abby surrounded by female visitors. His new daughter-in-law was wearing a beautiful cameo ring which the ex-president had gallantly slipped on her finger the previous evening. Charles had disappeared on an errand to his office, but was not away long. Soon, with Abby sitting nearby and causing him much distraction, Charles tried to write to his brother John: "It is always silly to talk of happiness and all that kind of thing. But I can say with truth that thus far even my hopes and wishes have been more than realised."

The pair was wed on a Thursday evening. By Sunday they were so enraptured that the unthinkable occurred. They remained at home and alone all day, missing the two church services which were the staple of the Sabbath. For Abby and Charles, any interruption of their blissful new life evidently was unwelcome. On Monday, Abby had to propel her husband out of the house at the very tardy hour of 10:00 A.M., just before her morning callers arrived. "How we passed our day it is impossible for me to say," Charles wrote in his diary, "but I can truly say it was to me unmingled happiness or the intoxication of pleasure."

Their love seemed so strong that twelve days after the wedding, Charles decided to tell Abby of his earlier romance with Mary Hellen, who was now Abby's sister-in-law. Charles admitted he felt much relieved by the confession, and by Abby's calm receipt of such unwelcome news. Now, said Charles, he and Abby were indeed "intimately and closely tied." The story of his affair with Mary was also helpful, he felt, as he explained to the ardent Abby what might have seemed an occasional failure of his capacity to keep pace with her romantic needs. "Mine is not a first though a young love," he said, and therefore "I am not fully subject to the impulse of the freshness of feeling which makes the first moments of marriage sometimes so intoxicating."

A few days later, Abby chose to show that she had not attached herself entirely to Charles. The couple went out to Medford for their first visit with the Brooks family since the wedding two weeks before. To the chagrin of her husband, Abby chose to remain overnight with her parents, sending Charles back to Boston alone and complaining to himself that the "delicious current" of their "honeymoon" had been lost. Abby, too, was upset by this separation, and soon reappeared in the house in Hancock Street. Charles was there to welcome her: "Our happiness returned more gushingly than ever, and I remained at home the whole of the afternoon and evening."

Whether Abby was equally blissful cannot be stated, for no scrap of her writing from the aftermath of the wedding has survived. Letters Abby wrote some years later suggest her joy with Charles was warm and enduring. In 1841, while visiting Louisa in Washington, Abby walked in the neighborhood where she and Charles had fallen in love fifteen years before. The experience, she reported to Charles, made her compare her feelings "as a wife" with those of her girlhood: "Much as I loved you then, I love you ten thousand times more now. Indeed, I should make you blush did I tell what I thought and felt today."

1841 brought the couple's first separation, and it pained them both. They wrote often, and with many endearments. Said Abby, "Thanks, thanks for your million kisses. I wish I could have them upon the lips instead of paper." In return she mailed "forty thousand million kisses." Soon after this exchange, Charles gave Abby as a New Year's gift a handsome chest, accompanied with a short message: "Dear Wife. May she ever feel to her husband as he has always felt for her."

Rarely after this experience were the two apart in a marriage that lasted fifty-seven years, until Charles' death in 1886. When family needs or the call of statesmanship temporarily parted them, each was lost without the other. How close the two were even at the start of marriage was noticed by Lotty Everett when she stayed with Abby and Charles three months after their wedding. Lotty was suffering from another bout of depression, and Abby had invited her to visit Hancock Street. Abby's lively spirits once more annoyed Lotty, who complained to her husband that it was very

difficult concentrating on composing a letter since Abby and Charles talked
to one another continually. A disgruntled Lotty was so ignored that not
even a fire was made to warm her room.

Actually Abby was a good hostess. From the start members of the Brooks
family were invited to Hancock Street. Abby saw that "now and then a sip
of some warm Whiskey Punch served to enliven us and chase away care,"
Charles reported with contentment. Abby had found a husband who
enjoyed home life, and much preferred to be with his family and books
than involved in politics or business. Charles therefore made himself much
more of an old-fashioned partner in marriage than his father was. Almost
every morning Abby sent him to the Boston markets to obtain the day's
provisions, a practice he continued throughout his life.

After a year of household shopping, Charles noted, "I recollect that
long before I was married, I used to laugh at this peculiar duty," but
experience had taught him that "it is by no means unpleasant." He would
report to Abby the variation in the cost of essentials, since the two of them
rarely allowed wealth to make them imprudent. The severe winter of
1836, for example, brought the price of beef and ham up to fifteen cents
a pound, and a large chicken cost twenty cents.

In other important ways Abby and Charles complemented each other.
Most significant, at least in Charles' view, was Abby's gregariousness. Her
pleasure in society drew Charles forth from what otherwise would have
been a hermit's existence. In turn, he exposed her to languages and letters.
Abby tried to learn French through many years of instruction by Charles,
who spoke it nearly as well as English, thanks to Louisa's training. And
each evening Abby took great pleasure in listening to Charles read.

He chose as their first fare the classics and other well-worn companions.
Two months into marriage, Abby tired of Charles' ponderous selections
and asked that he read the novels of Sir Walter Scott. Soon Samuel
Richardson's much admired story of besieged female virtue, *Clarissa*,
became a household favorite, and Charles complained that Abby would
never attain "a decided interest in literature." He kept doggedly ahead,
however, trying the works of Ariosto, the sixteenth-century Italian poet,
whom Abby dismissed as "monotonous and a bore." She was discouraged
almost as much by his next project, the memoirs of Goethe. By 1835, Abby
was choosing books for Charles to bring to their evening sessions, after he
had blundered with Juvenal's sixth satire on Roman culture. It had been
a mistake, he admitted, acknowledging that even he did not "admire to
read the ingenuity of woman in making herself a beast, and worse, for
animals are content with the natural enjoyments."

A literary partnership of a sort was shared by Abby and her husband.
Her role was mainly subordinate, but it was she who introduced Charles

to *Uncle Tom's Cabin*, and she proved a capable critic when he began to lecture and publish. While Charles did "not think political squabbles the province of women," around the Adams dining table he and his friends talked endlessly about the public affairs, with Abby an interested witness. In 1837, Louisa visited Abby and Charles in Boston and watched approvingly while Abby aided Charles "with great zeal." He was preparing a lecture concerning searches for the North Pole to be delivered before the Boston lyceum. "Abby thinks the style a little too didactic," Louisa told John Quincy, adding with glee, "It is the family characteristic of his ancestors."

Of course there were qualities of Abby's which Charles sought to smooth and shape. Her irrepressible manner sometimes dismayed him, but he was more eager that she should grow independent in thinking and self-confident, within reason. Since Charles admired Louisa's courage and wit, he used her as a model for Abby, while hoping that she would be spared Louisa's occasional lapses into illness and self-pity.

There was also another embodiment of female excellence which Charles held up not only for Abby's consideration, but also for that of the nation. Both Louisa and Abby were delighted with Charles' determination to publish an edition of his grandmother Abigail Adams' letters. He began this project several years after marrying Abby and to the family's amazement it proved a literary and financial success. Charles' admiration for females, stated clearly in his introduction to the letters in 1840, echoed remarks of Louisa's that he had heard through the years. Her views informed Charles' observation that there was less alloy in the female heart than in the male's, making it easier for a woman to resist "the doctrines of expediency and the promptings of private interest."

Charles' triumph in publishing his grandmother's letters brought Abby to send a note of pride and pleasure to Louisa. Louisa tried not to let her cynicism dampen the younger woman's delight. "I am as much flattered by your husband's success as you are," Louisa assured Abby, adding, "on no account would I crush a just and worthy ambition, either in him or you." What Louisa feared was that Charles would be tempted into politics, and Abby's ideal marriage would suffer. In the event this happened, Louisa urged Abby to be ready to "meet with philosophy and enjoy with prudence the changes and trials which public life may produce." Remember, said Louisa with massive understatement, "The stream of my life has not run smooth."

Slowly the honeymoon spirit faded from Abby's existence, and she faced difficulties that diminished her natural joyfulness. As she sought to encourage Abby, Louisa found new strength for herself. In Abby she had someone who needed and accepted her help. And Louisa soon became essential for Abby. Several years after their marriage, Charles and Abby wandered about the grounds of the Brooks estate in Medford. They recalled the times before their wedding when "life had a golden hue." It was a glow, they agreed, which "reality has rubbed if it has not utterly destroyed." With the arrival of babies, public life, and other distresses, Abby found that "the poetry of life has fallen into prose."

15

A Triumph

As she faced the impositions brought by married life, Abby benefited from a warm emotional tie with Louisa, a relationship which succeeded from the start. By 1832, Louisa was saying of Abby, "I have found her a lovely and charming companion throughout the summer," adding that "it is a real trial to part with her." In the autumn, Louisa marked her return to Washington for the political season by confessing, "When I am away from Abby, I seem to have lost half of myself." Letters from Louisa to Boston always first wanted to know "how my loved Abby goes on."

Affection between the two women had deepened immediately after Abby's marriage, for on 21 February 1830 Anna Gorham Brooks died. In her last years, Abby's mother had been depressed and her mind often wandered. However, she regained her faculties at the time of her demise. With death at the door, Mrs. Brooks had the entire family gather around her bed. She then exchanged a lengthy farewell with each person, showing particular regard for Abby and Charles. The servants were summoned for their own parting with their mistress. Anna then dismissed everyone and died moments later. Her last word was reported to be "Abby." Learning of Mrs. Brooks' death, Louisa assured Abby that she would use affection to ease the younger woman's loss, and she instructed Charles to wipe his wife's tears tenderly.

Abby's mother-in-law seemed always to know how much support to give. Louisa recognized that despite Abby's charming exterior, she was a very uncertain young woman, so she invited Abby to Washington where she could escape the familiar and often smothering spirit of Boston. With obvious elation, Louisa reported that many ladies in the nation's capital considered Abby one of the "loveliest women they ever saw." Lest the significance of such an attainment be lost, Louisa added, "This is no trifling compliment from your own sex, my child."

Louisa enlarged Abby's self-confidence in other ways, as well. For instance, she awarded her daughter-in-law power to arrange the Adams mansion as she saw fit for the family's annual summer stays in Quincy. Abby was advised to use her judgment and ignore the suggestions of John Quincy. "Accustomed to rule with sovereign sway," Louisa remarked, "he is not sufficiently considerate of female comfort which to him has always been a 'secondary consideration.' " She taught Abby how to open a country house soon enough for a timely washing of the bedding, for the very practical reason "that it is necessary to destroy the *creeping gentry* early in the season." Abby was even trusted to select a new featherbed for the former president and first lady. The change "would be very desirable for our old bones," Louisa confided.

By no means, however, did Louisa limit her encouragement to the domestic sphere. One of Louisa's most eloquent defenses of woman's ability was in an 1840 letter to Abby that showed little patience for men, the "Lords of Creation," who had trodden upon women in order to have their own way. There was no natural inferiority in females, Louisa reminded Abby, and she called for women "to preach the equality which God originally assigned to the Sexes as it regards intellectual capacity." Louisa yearned to see women throw off "the thraldom of the *mind*, which has been so long, and so unjustly shackled." Not that certain differences between women and men could be overridden, as some feminists were then demanding. It would be disastrous, said Louisa, if young maidens should lose the "timid delicacy" and the "beautiful blush which indicates the purity of its possessor."

Abby, addressing Louisa as "dearest mother," sent her long journal-style letters filled with news of Boston and Quincy. Those that survive show how completely Louisa had won the confidence of Abby. The pair compared notes on how best to encourage Charles; both took great pride in his rising reputation as an editor, essayist, and political commentator, although Abby said that Charles "would kill me" if he knew how local praise for him was being relayed to his parents.

Louisa was not the only admirer who sought to comfort and encourage Abby. Peter Chardon Brooks undertook to stay especially close to her. Soon after Anna Brooks' death, Peter sent Abby a gift of money "from a Father who loves you most tenderly, and to whom you must always apply, in your little wants, now that one of the best of mothers is no more." Many special tokens came to Abby "for your own dear self," by which Peter meant they were amounts separate from the $3,000 allowance he provided annually. Also, Abby was singled out to receive her mother's watch.

New Year's Day was Mr. Brooks' favorite holiday for presenting Abby with some handsome item. At that time Christmas was only just becoming the occasion for exchanging gifts. Sometimes Abby reciprocated, with comical results. At New Year's in 1836, Abby gave her father a pair of gloves, which he promptly returned "as not being half big enough." After acknowledging kindly that it was difficult for one person to "chuse gloves for another," Peter said he would "beg leave to accept the will for the deed with equal thanks for your remembrance of me."

What Peter Brooks most desired from Abby she was unwilling to give him, however. He wanted to have his youngest daughter with him each summer at Mystic Grove in Medford, and he was equally desirous that she and her family live with him in his Boston mansion during the winters. Abby seems to have sensed the importance of maintaining her independence. Besides, she preferred spending her summers near the sea at Quincy with Louisa and other Adamses. Pained by his daughter's decision, Peter told Abby, "I almost feel myself supplanted in your good graces." Nevertheless, he kept his good humor, and settled for seeing her Sunday evenings when members of the Brooks clan usually assembled at Peter's home.

Meanwhile Charles secured his relationship with his father-in-law. His skill as an investor and business manager so pleased Mr. Brooks that he suggested Charles direct Abby's "fortune," meaning the properties that produced her yearly income. Charles was elated at this tribute from New England's greatest businessman, but he could hardly hope to rival Peter Chardon Brooks' success with Abby's money. And besides, since neither Edward Everett nor Nathaniel Frothingham had been granted this privilege, Charles foresaw trouble if he was singled out.

Louisa Adams developed a great affection for Peter Brooks. She was touched by his wish to have Abby near him, and acted on his behalf, urging her daughter-in-law to please her parent. The shrewd Louisa also advised Abby to see that her father was kept amused and happy, thereby skirting some of the perils that could endanger a widower. These included a special threat from women with designs on the Brooks wealth, a menace so grave that Louisa recommended Mr. Brooks be sent to the comparative safety of Europe, where the widow of Harrison Gray Otis might not find him.

Despite all this backing from her mother-in-law, Abby seemed for a time to grow less confident and to feel unequal to holding her own. Louisa was always at hand to give her a boost: "I think you unjust to yourself and to the ability with which God has blessed you when you deprecate your own talents," Abby was told. Soon, however, Louisa realized that Abby's spirits were threatened, ironically, by one of her strengths. Abby discovered that, like her mother, she easily could have many children.

On this score, Abby had been discouraged at first, for she had confidently expected to become pregnant within days of her wedding. When she did not, she panicked, knowing that her husband considered it a duty to create a third generation of Adamses which would include male offspring. Unaware of the pressure her daughter-in-law felt to conceive, Louisa unwittingly added to Abby's burden by urging that Abby immediately come and see Mary's little daughter, who would give Abby "a very good idea of Grand Mama's good nursing in anticipation of future services."

For over a year there was no sign of maternity, and Abby sank into depression. She kept to her room and spent much time in bed. Her physicians suspected what was amiss, but the only remedy was patience and more effort. It was an especially happy Christmas, in 1830, when Abby discovered she was pregnant. Her liveliness returned, and she enjoyed the next months, even if her figure grew unusually bulky. Louisa sent cheer from Washington: "Keep up your spirits for I have no doubt you will do well, and I shall be near you and offer all the kindness of a mother on the occasion." In July 1831, Louisa was in Boston, ready to assist at the birth of Abby's child. She kept the expectant mother exercising and on the go, the best prenatal therapy, in Louisa's opinion. The mother-in-law was elated to report, "Abby is in fine spirits and does not seem to be at all afraid."

Two days later she gave birth to a daughter, Louisa Catherine. The labor was easy, so much so that even John Quincy mentioned in his diary how "expeditious" Abby had been. No one, however, expressed what lay heavily on the family's mind. There was general dismay that the infant was female, for with Mary having borne two daughters, the Adams line must look to Abby to extend the family name. As if she sensed this, Abby's first child resembled a boy, a "giant" in size, irascible and stubborn in temperament. Keeping up with this daughter, nicknamed Sister Lou, strained Abby during her next pregnancy. Once again, however, Louisa's comforting presence was at hand on 22 September 1833 when at midnight Abby gave birth to a son. This time her labor was extreme. In tribute to his renowned grandfather, the lad was named John Quincy Adams II.

At this point the demands of motherhood took as heavy a toll on Abby as had her earlier struggle to conceive. Her flagging spirits alarmed Louisa, who was prepared at any time, she told Abby, to come to Boston from Washington, thanks to the new railroads which, Louisa said, made travel "inconceivably easy." The railroad had also eliminated one of Louisa's banes, drunken stagecoach drivers. From Washington Louisa sent advice meant to rally Abby. She ought not, in Louisa's opinion, stay at home, since "young people are apt to lose the natural freshness and vivacity of youth if they pass their younger days in too close retirement."

Moving on to shakier ground, Louisa recommended that another pregnancy be avoided for the present. Nature and the young couple paid no heed, for in September 1834 Abby was once more with child. Troubled by this "impediment" to her daughter-in-law's well-being, Louisa hoped for a miscarriage. Abby was "too weak for such a quick succession of shocks to her constitution and the two little things she has are care enough." Louisa advised Charles to be mindful of the strain pregnancy meant for his wife. It was an embarrassing topic, but Louisa bravely brought it up, telling Charles that "the health of your wife is too precious for false delicacy."

Abby's second son, born on 27 May 1835, was named after his father. The lad weighed nearly twelve pounds, and his delivery left Abby "feeble and listless." The parents kept little Charley in their bedroom, causing his mother many "uneasy nights." In June, Louisa received reports about Abby's "thin and poor condition," and about how the "scampers" of the children now were a bother to Charles Francis as well as to Abby. Once so eager for youngsters, the young parents decided to take a holiday from them by spending five weeks in Canada, near Lake Champlain and at Niagara. Louisa suggested they invite their sister-in-law, Mary, recently widowed, but Abby and Charles went alone.

After traveling two thousand miles, the vacationers grew weary as the trip closed, but Abby shrank from returning to her children. She begged Charles to give her some laudanum, the tincture of opium used at the time to relieve stress and pain. It would "carry her on," she implored, gratefully taking the twenty drops Charles doled out. Reaching home, Abby fell ill almost at once, weakened, it was said, by her long trip. Charles himself was weary, and distressed to find that he could not stay alert enough in church to follow the reasoning in his brother-in-law Frothingham's sermons.

Family worry over Abby increased, and Louisa was summoned to nurse her. Charles, dashing around Boston trying to find the unusual food which was all Abby cared to eat, complained that "the season is an unfavorable one for delicacies." John Quincy joined Louisa in hovering over the "drooping" Abby, who remained apathetic even into the autumn of 1836. "Her health and spirits have been among the most precious enjoyments of my life," said John Quincy, "and they have been the exquisite happiness of my son."

With the Christmas season Abby returned to her cheerful, energetic ways. Charles attributed her recovery to rest and to the fact that Abby seemed more vigorous when he stayed with her and tried to keep himself happier. Charles and Abby made a concerted effort to share more time together, with the result that Abby conceived in April 1837. The next nine months brought the family considerable agitation, especially when all the children came down with whooping cough.

The scene at home added to Abby's dread of another baby. She was not yet thirty. Lacking the comforting presence of Louisa, but aided by Ann Frothingham, Abby safely delivered her third son on 16 February 1838. Several of Abby's children turned out to be remarkably successful, but her latest would prove the most famous of all. She named him after her recently deceased brother, Henry Brooks. Not only would Henry Adams become America's greatest historian and one of its finest writers; during his childhood he was Abby's most agreeable youngster.

After Henry's birth, Boston suffered frigid temperatures and deep snow, another reason why Abby shrank from resuming a daily regimen dominated by four small children and a husband prone to worry. She held back from leaving her room, causing Charles to observe, "She seems rather disposed to magnify her own evils, and that almost without any exercise of will." Only after nearly a month had passed did Abby attempt to sit up in bed. Frustrated by being far away in Washington, Louisa filled the mails with her counsel, advising Charles that patience and understanding with Abby were more essential now than ever before. Abby desperately needed "the tenderness and affection of a kind and attentive husband. This was the true balm for the suffering of woman in her grievous peril."

As soon as Abby was able to travel, Louisa demanded that the parents bring baby Henry to Washington. The trio was promised much of that loving attention which Louisa proudly insisted no one else could provide as well as she. Indeed, the trip was beneficial, for the scenes and social whirl of Washington revived Abby. She insisted that Charles accompany her to visit President Van Buren and on frequent appearances in the galleries of Congress. Even after returning to Boston and resuming her household duties, Abby remained in robust health. A puzzled Charles expressed gratitude in his diary pages.

In 1840 the Adams family had much to be grateful for besides Abby's recuperation. That year began a new era for Louisa and John Quincy when the nation repudiated the Democratic party and elected as its president William Henry Harrison, a Whig and, more important, an admirer of John Quincy Adams. Louisa and her husband were suddenly the center of social and political life in Washington. Reverberations were felt even in Boston, where Charles, agreeing to do more for the nation than write political essays, was elected to a seat in the lower house of the Massachusetts legislature. The body met in the State House, across the street from Abby and Charles' residence. When Charles hesitated about entering public life, Abby propelled him forward. She also induced him to bring political cohorts home to dinner. The more lively her husband was, the greater Abby's cheer, it seemed.

Late in 1840, Abby again found herself with child, her fifth, and an experience much like the happiness she enjoyed during her first pregnancy. She faltered occasionally, though. In February 1841, Abby sent a worried letter to her mother-in-law, to which Louisa replied by reminding her that "you have always done so well and had such fine children." There was no reason for her to be anything but "gay and cheerful and full of courage." Keep active, Louisa advised, "go out and forget it and you will pass the time without thinking of it until the birth is happily over."

Louisa wanted this youngster to be born in Quincy under the roof of the old Adams mansion. There Louisa would have every detail of the birth under command. A baby's arrival in the family residence would also be significant, Louisa believed, now that the Adamses were once again receiving favorable political attention. The home of Abigail and John was, after all, for the expected child "the mansion of its two Presidential Ancestors." As for the infant's gender, Louisa could not resist hoping that "it must be a young lady, but either [sex] will be acceptable." Thus supported by Louisa, Abby remained "active and in good spirits" through the ninth month. The happy mood prevailed, Louisa said, even though the mother-to-be was "immense," as usual.

In Boston, on 23 July 1841, Abby gave birth to "another fine fat boy." The event invited curiosity among his siblings, especially Sister Lou, who was ten years old. "The astonishment of the children was very great," reported an amused Louisa. When Sister Lou was told that "the fat nurse brought the boy," she replied " 'it would have been as well to leave it any where else.' " Greater interest was shown in naming the little fellow, with Henry Adams, age three, suggesting "Jim Crow or Harrison." His proposal, said Louisa, "diverted the family amazingly." The baby was christened Arthur, a suggestion of Louisa's. Abby's doctor judged her condition splendid.

Unfortunately, the cheerfulness Abby had enjoyed for many months left her by late August, when she was recovered and facing the daily care of five children. Louisa acted at once, persuading Abby to bring the baby to Washington. The idea succeeded. Abby's letters to Charles were full of tenderness toward the children, and conveyed "a thousand kisses" to him. Charles' replies seemed meant to fortify himself as much as Abby, for he actually worried more than she did about the youngsters, though he recognized the needlessness of his misery. "What is the nature of most of the complaints which we are fond of uttering but the offspring of an exaggerating fancy," he assured himself and his wife. Abby replied proudly that she had not shed a tear since she left him.

While Abby paid calls in Washington, including one on President John Tyler, Charles distracted himself by selecting a larger Boston home for their sizable family. Using money provided by Peter Chardon Brooks and consulting Abby by mail, Charles purchased a house around the corner from their Hancock Street residence, 57 Mount Vernon Street, still near the State House atop Beacon Hill. The move was delayed until Henry Adams recovered from a dangerous illness, after which Abby once again was surrounded by her flock.

The magic of being with Louisa and in Washington lasted for a year. Then, in March 1843, Abby again suffered from sagging spirits. A worried Louisa advised another restorative visit to Washington. Keeping on the move was excellent therapy for a woman, Louisa insisted: "I am in earnest, my dear daughter, not from any apprehension of danger, but from the conviction that change, though often unpleasant, is decidedly beneficial. I attribute my lengthened life to the necessity of this constant exertion; although I candidly confess that it has been and almost always is very painful."

This time, however, Abby would not budge, bringing a stern reply from Louisa: "You must not think that I want to preach to you, but you must allow me to say that a repining spirit adds to the misery of suffering." Louisa was now distressed almost to impatience by Abby's collapse into whining and grumbling about her numerous offspring. These youngsters represented "duties imposed upon us by our heavenly Father," Louisa pointed out, adding that only God could give children to a couple. "You my love are so surrounded by blessings that I can scarcely imagine a motive for complaint."

These messages and admonishments did not help, and by July 1843 Abby's relatives decided it was essential that some novelty be arranged so that she could, as Charles put it, "face the winter." A sea voyage was proposed, but Abby rejected it, not wishing to be so far from the very family which caused her unease. She did agree, however, to join her father and father-in-law in a tour of New England and upper New York, from which she tried to write cheerful letters to Charles and her children. Nevertheless, her symptoms persisted. A worried John Quincy sent Louisa a listing of them—dyspepsia, severe headache, deafness, and incessant noise in her ears. "I believe that the chief, not the only, cause of her complaints was the care of five small children at once," was the opinion of Abby's father-in-law.

The patient wrote home that she was determined to stay away the five weeks prescribed, promising Charles that "if I ever return to your dear arms, you shall never again have so much reason to complain of my temper. I don't say *never*, but I *will* try, indeed I will." No one seemed to recognize that much of the stress Abby experienced at home was unconsciously caused by Charles, whose expectations of an orderly existence and good behavior from his family kept Abby atremble. She both loved and feared her husband, who, though attentive, helpful, and affectionate, could not rid himself of that dour impatience which characterized the male Adamses when they had to deal with lesser mortals. Unlike Louisa, who had the courage to fight John Quincy over issues of household and child care, Abby meekly did as she was told and dreaded Charles' displeasure.

No sooner was Abby returned to Charles' "dear arms" than she became pregnant yet again, but this time she miscarried. When the event was reported to her in late November 1843, Louisa made her habitual recommendation: Abby should visit Washington for restoration. "I have been used to such accidents myself," she reminded Charles; she failed to mention that keeping Abby with her would stop for a time the relentless occurrence of pregnancy. However, Abby found another refuge, one which Louisa could hardly object to—religious faith. Abruptly, Abby joined Charles in the Bible instruction to which he summoned their children each Sunday morning. Husband and wife began private sessions of prayer, guided by their brother-in-law and pastor, Nathaniel Frothingham.

Rejoicing to see Abby's heart "awakening" to faith, Charles proposed "in her company to strengthen my own." The pair wept as the Reverend Frothingham knelt with them. Abby now begged Charles to read sermons to her rather than novels, and both joined the church at Chauncey Place. Abby began to present a radiant countenance, particularly at the dinner she gave for the governor and other leading figures. She was now thirty-six years old, and her new religious interest suggested to Charles that she possessed the means for "strengthening her good dispositions and giving firmness to her determinations."

Instead, for a time Abby's religious outlook seemed to make her more servile. Her letters stressed her contrition not only before God, but also before her husband, to whom she confided a wish to be "worthy of you." There is no indication of what her husband thought when he heard his wife say, "I hope your image is not too nearly connected, in my mind, with God." Just after her birthday in April 1844, Abby assured Charles, "You have truly been an angel to me," and announced that now she hid none of her feelings from him and God. Through divine aid, she claimed to control her irritable moods, and was convinced that prayers were heard.

Pleased by this development, but sensing that further change was still needed, Louisa tactfully suggested to Abby that it was God who spoke through Peter Brooks' generous offer of a trip to Europe. Take this voyage and escape Boston for a time, Louisa advised; she offered to care for all of Abby's children. But Abby stayed home, rushing to her Bible when upset, and leading all the children to church on Sunday. One of these youngsters particularly annoyed her. This was her son Charley, who drove her often to lose her temper. He "is so tiresome and does worry me so with his lessons." Miserable when her anger with a child made her fall from grace, Abby "went and prayed God to forgive me."

Louisa kept looking for signs that a mature Abby would arise from this ordeal and searched for new ways to help her daughter-in-law achieve "cheerfulness and matronly dignity." Abby had these qualities hidden within her, Louisa told the younger woman. She needed only to draw upon them. Charles made the same point, if somewhat differently. He urged that his wife "learn a little more to depend upon herself." Eventually, aided by time, religious faith, and support from Louisa and Charles, Abby not only regained her spirit but advanced to a new independence. In part, this was due to Charles' increased absences. In 1844 he became entangled in presidential politics, joining John Quincy in fighting the expansion of slavery. Abby discovered she could manage the family quite admirably during Charles' excursions. Somewhat astonished, she announced that "I find myself equal to many, many things that once struck me impossible."

Abby gave her husband extensive reports from the home front, of course, including commentaries on the sermons she had been reading. She opened her letters with "my best friend," a salutation Abigail and John had used. Then, when the beloved Charles returned from the political wars, the jubilant Abby became pregnant. This time she was unperturbed, and it was the husband's turn to be, as Charles confessed, "much depressed in spirit but trusting in the mercy of God." Abby continued referring to Charles as "my dearest and best-loved husband." On 19 February 1845, Abby was delighted to have a daughter, named Mary. Of this child, as of all her babies, Abby made the same comment: "not handsome, but *so* good." It was, said Charles, "the sixth edition of the same remark."

A year later came the severest test yet of Abby's deepening maturity. On 9 February 1846, Arthur Adams fell victim to "the croup" and choked to death. Arthur had been the most beautiful of the children, always remembered as "dark-eyed, golden-haired." His loss was something Abby and Charles could never bring themselves to discuss. Instead they wept together on his birthday. Both parents suffered, but Charles was wholly undone, perhaps because he had administered a more severe chastening than usual to the four-year-old just before he became ill.

The circumstances surrounding Arthur's death brought Abby that degree of personal strength which Louisa had long foreseen was possible. The most stirring moment for Abby was when she realized her husband was very human, after all. With Arthur's loss, Charles collapsed into self-reproach and depression, a display of weakness which gave Abby strength. Most of the family papers from this mournful time apparently were later destroyed by Charles. Enough survive, however, to reveal the emergence of a new Abby, while grief left Charles shaken and broken. Several months after the child died, Charles said to Abby, "My spirits do not brace me up much yet, and I don't believe they ever will again."

Charles noticed how Abby had responded to her sorrow. He was consoled by "the remarkable effect which affliction has produced in exalting and refining your character." She had transcended him, Charles acknowledged. From Washington Louisa also took heart, even though she recognized that she now faced a new challenge, rousing her depressed son. She warned Charles against the effect of continued gloominess: "It has caused me so much suffering to indulge in this error that I would if possible guard you against it." Louisa was thrilled to find Abby "gay, ready and active," so buoyant that she worked wonders in teaching John Quincy to smile at the troubles old age was causing him. Whenever Abby visited Louisa, she seemed to know precisely what Louisa wished even before the older woman had expressed a need, demonstrating a sixth sense that, in Louisa's judgment, was proof of maturity in a woman.

Another trial awaited Abby. She discovered late in 1847 that she was pregnant. The baby would be born in June 1848, the year of the presidential contest in which Charles Francis Adams ran for vice president on the Free-Soil ticket. During her wait for maternity, Abby was often left alone with her family as Charles enlisted in the political wars. With much encouragement from Louisa, Abby avoided her old debilities. Seven months pregnant, she wrote to a worried Charles on her fortieth birthday, seeking nothing for herself but trying to comfort him: "It is so seldom I can, or at all events, do give you pleasure that when a chance offers it is not to be resisted." He should be certain of one thing, said Abby: "I love you far far beyond all things else, either in this world or in the world to come."

Two months later, Louisa wrote in her journal, "T'was a heavenly sign of grace, that Charles and Abby Adams's 7th child, a fine large boy was born this morning at half past seven o clock this 24 June St. John's Day 1848." The child was named after his grandfather, Peter Chardon Brooks. The old gentleman was flattered, but he implored Abby that in daily use the name be shortened to Brooks Adams. Not long afterward, on New Year's Day 1849, Peter Brooks died of heart failure. His last request was to know how his investments had fared in the fiscal year just closed. "The ruling passion to the last," an affectionate Charles observed dryly.

On 5 January, in the presence of all the heirs, Peter Brooks' will was read. It disclosed that Abby's share of the nearly $3-million estate could be valued at $400,000, of which one-fourth was paid directly to her and the balance placed in trust. The will referred to Abby's sisters by their husbands' names, but Abby, still special to her father, was listed as "Abigail Brown Brooks, wife of Charles Francis Adams." While her father probably did not realize it, the independent character his will awarded to Abby was appropriate. By 1849, she had established her own identity within the Adams family.

While Abby still faced the normal share of worries, they no longer drained her vitality. She happily spent a holiday with Charles at Saratoga Springs in July 1849, disregarding the nuisance of being in a hotel where the noise usually lasted until dawn, and enjoying the excitement and a chance to make new friends for Charles' career. She found the dinners at Saratoga Springs pleasing, and seemed not to worry that she was putting on weight. A typical meal included two types of fish, black bass and trout, along with woodcock and partridge. There was much wine, and Charles acknowledged that he and Abby "had a very merry time." He was amazed by this seemingly new wife, whom he pronounced "better than I ever knew her."

Letters written by Abby during the 1850s confirm Charles' opinion. They possess a spirit of comradeship and bespeak Abby's sense of equality. Vanished are her earlier abjectness and protests of unworthiness. The pair now often exchanged letters, since one or the other was frequently in Washington with Louisa after John Quincy's death in 1848. With Charles away, Abby was forced to manage the farm properties her husband had inherited. Nearly all of Charles' side of the correspondence is missing, but those letters that survive are uncharacteristically terse. Abby commented in June 1850, "You have certainly reached the perfection of letter writing, if, as you say, you think it consists in brevity. You have curtailed and curtailed your style till it has become an apology for a letter." Could Charles not realize that "a correspondence all on one side is just a little stupid?"

Writing from Quincy, Abby sarcastically told Charles that she would try to adopt his style, but only if he good-naturedly took from others what he gave them to begin with. "I shall confine myself to business and short sentences in the future," a disgusted Abby pledged. It proved difficult for her, there being many interesting tidbits she wished to report. When Charles continued to annoy her with short replies, along with his complaint that hers were still a ramble, Abby lost patience. Clearly, she told him, he did not understand women. He made her feel "constrained" and, worse, egotistical, because of his comments that she talked about herself in her letters. Could not Charles appreciate that in a man's absence, "a thousand things happen to affect a lady's mind and feelings in a manner he can't realize, but every husband should [want to understand] *through* her"?

When Charles was so discouraging, Abby said, "I have but little heart-felt pleasure in writing to you."

It was the newly sturdy Abby who informed her husband, "I don't *need* you—as far as that goes at all." Not forgotten, however, was the old affection: "But I shall rejoice to see you." Taking stock of her qualities, Abby now could conclude, "For myself, the greatest drawback I know is my own bad temper, but there even I feel encouraged, for certainly it is better than it used to be. I bear more and answer less, and I *do have* my trials." When Charles' side of the correspondence still did not improve, in spite of Abby's exhortations, she made her own letters cold and spare. The effect was immediate. Charles begged that she resume her former habit with a pen. Abby gave in slowly, changing what had been her chilly salutation of "My dear Mr. Adams" to "My dear friend," and tormenting him by asking, "There, will that do any better?"

Finally relenting, Abby returned to her loving and vivid style, relaying stories of life at home and imparting her views on various subjects. Louisa knew just what Abby had been trying to teach Charles, that a woman should have a man who sought her opinions and who wished to share her life. But this was a difficult assignment for Charles after 1850. He was preoccupied by political and literary efforts, and by the fear that he was becoming prematurely senile. While Abby kept encouraging him, privately she noticed Charles' diminishing capacity for memory, especially after an occasion when he could not recall what he wished to say while making a public addresss. Shocked by this, Charles was reluctant ever again to be an orator. Abby sought to lift his confidence, and when a young man called late in 1851 in the hope of persuading Charles to speak in Faneuil Hall, it was only the intercession of Abby that made her husband agree.

To her husband's glumness about his health and future, as well as his worries about what would happen to her, Abby replied, "I fully intend leaving you behind me." But should he die first, he need not worry about whether she would take another husband. Most of those females who accepted second mates were *"fools,"* Abby scoffed. Besides, who would want her huge family? She admitted she might be pursued for her money, but "upon that point I am a little sensitive." When Abby had to leave Charles in Boston while she visited Louisa in Washington, he was almost undone by how much he missed her. "I never felt the house so lonely," he moaned in 1852. His cries sounded much like Abby's laments of fifteen years earlier. "Who shall describe the mental agony of such hours," Charles complained. ". . . and to be alone too! With all the care and no word of sympathy."

Once the manager of each household detail, Charles now yearned to have everything under "the superintendance of my wife." On occasions when Charles was absent, Abby could even be comical about her new independence. With him out of town, she told her husband, "Upon the whole I am just as well off and as happy, for there is one less to complain of my temper and be cross at all I do, let me try ever so hard." He should stay away as long as he liked, Abby told Charles. "I wish I could take the two little ones and quit as you can." Abby knew when to soften her tone, however. No less loving than ever, she would close her blunt talk by saying how impatient she was to have Charles with her: "I want you here."

In 1854, Abby and Charles celebrated their Silver Wedding Anniversary. "The day was one of quiet domestic joy than which there is nothing sweeter and purer this side the skies," wrote Charles in his diary. It was a much different scene when their fiftieth anniversary arrived in 1879. By then Abby's prospects were melancholy. Charles was enfeebled by what today would probably be diagnosed as Alzheimer's Disease. His memory deserted him several years before he lost his physical powers. On the forty-ninth anniversary of their wedding, though, Charles was well enough to record in his diary that he and Abby had "slept in each others arms." Soon thereafter he could no longer write, and Abby's partner vanished before her eyes.

Abby's attempts to keep Charles alert were heroic, and reminded her children of the episode in England when Abby had shown her mettle as wife of the American minister. Once, when Abby and Charles were attending a party, the very sizable wife of the Egyptian ambassador collapsed from apoplexy at Abby's feet. London's diplomatic circles admired the way Abby directed the efforts to assist the victim. Charles wrote that Abby displayed "her usual energy and presence of mind in difficulty." Nothing she could do, however, prevented Charles' decay. He died in 1886, and Abby followed him three years later, herself broken by loneliness and infirmity. Mr. and Mrs. Charles Francis Adams are buried in Quincy beneath a single, handsome stone which acclaims Abby as a companion "loved and honored, trusted and true." Those words were the triumph Abby had sought.

16

Peace at Last

Louisa was elderly and frail in 1845 when Abby found independence. After her own life of struggle, the older woman relished her daughter-in-law's success. No one could calculate better than Louisa the cost paid by Abby to earn the respect of herself and her husband. Of the two women, Louisa was the more complex, perceptive, and talented. Only a person of her extraordinary qualities could have reached contentment and dignity after an odyssey whose trials Abby could not even have imagined.

An artistic temperament set Louisa apart from Abby and from all the Adams women, except possibly Elizabeth Peabody; and her powers of discernment and empathy made Louisa wish to put her own experience and reflection in the service of others. Like many artists, she had trouble making herself understood. At times passionate, at times detached, Louisa's style bewildered her family. The Adamses shook their heads over Louisa's "sensitivity," convinced she created most of her own torment. Those "bursts of feeling, which none understand," Louisa called a "sad inheritance." One of her physicians, Dr. Amos Holbrook, said of Louisa when she was fifty-nine that never "was formed a human being of deeper and acuter sensibility."

Among the family, Abby's brilliant son Henry Adams was the one who most appreciated Louisa's unique talent and how it shaped her life. They were much alike, Louisa and Henry. The grandson knew this, for he read many of her letters and journals and spoke of writing her biography. Yet Henry drew back from this task, as eventually he did from life itself. Like Louisa, he wanted to benefit humanity, but also, like her, he came to consider all such efforts futile in the long run. Following Louisa's example, Henry settled for quietly and lovingly aiding those dear to him, while watching the world race toward perdition.

Henry Adams called Louisa an "exotic," and acknowledged that from her he inherited the paradoxical trait of questioning himself while rebelling against the world. As he showed in his *The Education of Henry Adams*, Henry had youthful memories of Louisa seated in the old Adams mansion, serving tea to her tamed husband. He described her as weary, decorative, and delicate, completely at peace. Henry perhaps realized that an aged Louisa wished to foster just such an impression. She had finished the good fight, though the path to victory had not been easy.

Furthermore, Louisa recognized that not even her family could appreciate what an effort it had been for her to reach contentment. If her own dear ones were blind, Louisa knew the world, peering as it did through masculine eyes, could not comprehend a woman's pilgrimage. Louisa died doubting that emancipated women could be understood anywhere on earth, so she fastened her gaze on the life to come. She departed placidly, and Henry's understated description of her would probably have pleased her.

Today Louisa would surely be astonished and possibly gratified to know that her letters and journals are being studied. Through them, the serene figure in Henry's *Education* speaks again for those concerns dear to her, lines of thought which often led her into conflict with her husband, family, and the universe. Louisa's writings mostly address four interests: literature, politics, the status of women, and religious faith. Believing "how superior mind is to matter," it exasperated Louisa to watch John Quincy waste his time in politics. His talent would best be used in writing, she was convinced. And what about female authors? "I ask myself if it is an advantage for a woman to write."

Surely, said Louisa, for anyone "the mere act of writing is certainly harmless." But what of the contention, one Louisa knew John Quincy made, that for "a woman of a reflective turn," trying to be an author would become "a prolific source of erroneous opinions; of propagating inconsistencies; and of betraying the weakness and unsteadiness of mind which is a component part of her sex." Dismissing this view as absurd, Louisa argued that a thoughtful female ought to take up her pen, if only to study the selfishness underpinning most of what was said and done by men.

Louisa zealously followed her own decree. Her "scribblings" were by no means confined to her White House years; her journals, poems, plays, essays, and informal jottings come from many points in her life. Most of what she wrote was done in haste and never revised. Louisa knew the perils of writing in this manner, so that she dubbed one volume of observations her "silly book." However, Louisa usually wrote for a serious purpose, "to fortify my own mind in its convictions of the truth." Solemn though this sounded, she rarely put aside her sense of humor. Her outlook was more agile and clever than it was profound, and her efforts were often prodigious, especially when she was translating Plato and other classics whom she read in French versions.

One of Louisa's pastimes was literary criticism. An example is her careful treatment of the novel *Florence McCarthy*, written in 1818 by the English-woman Sydney Owenson, Lady Morgan. In Louisa's opinion, "There is a great freedom in all her writings, but there is much singularity in her characters which produces a fine effect. Sober reason is so out of fashion that it is the farthest thing from our thoughts ever to seek it. Modern productions and their principal purpose are achieved if they awaken public curiosity enough to meet a ready sale and to amuse the idle half a day." While Louisa considered Lady Morgan's style "inflated" and the book's moral weak, she acclaimed the author as "unquestionably a woman of genius and real genius can seldom condescend to be shackled by common rules."

Certainly John Quincy's prose caught Louisa's critical eye. "It is impossible for you to write otherwise than well," she assured him in 1837. Yet she was obliged to add that "in this day of smooth hypocrisy, the strength and vigor of your expressions partake too much of the old school, when mind predominated over matter, and took a sovereign sway." At present, Louisa observed, "energy is misunderstood, and easy chairs and lounges are more to the taste of our effeminate generation, than the three-legged stools which furnished seats for our brave and hardy forefathers." Louisa always championed old values in literature and politics.

Poetry was Louisa's favorite mode for breathing new life into ancient and moribund wisdom. Her lines deplored the loss of childlike innocence and simplicity and rejoiced when faith triumphed and love reigned, though she believed such moments were rare. She recommended old truths as the lance and breastplate for women in the struggle against those temptations which drew their male associates into a new world of deceit and greed. On another level, Louisa's poetry celebrated the most essential joys of woman's life, as in her lines of 1844 dedicated to an engraving of a child with a flower. "Sweet is the smile of infancy/A flower, a simple toy,/Attracts the gaze of ecstacy/The lovely smile of joy/The crowing laugh resounding shrill/It turns in bright amaze/The mother's heart with joyous thrill/ Whispers the song of praise."

The intensity which Louisa brought to her literary efforts carried over into her writings about politics. Long conversations with John and Abigail Adams taught her much, and she winced under the cruelties experienced by her husband at the hands of unappreciative colleagues and voters. Much as she claimed to detest politics and to deplore her own pugnaciousness, Louisa obviously could not resist taking the offensive against her favorite targets. One of these was the widening gap between republican theories and practices.

At the height of Andrew Jackson's power, Louisa spoke often about the United States as a "perverted nation," one which might blush in disgrace "if she had not apparently lost all sense of shame and thrown herself with open eyes in the arms of the most depraved and abandoned vice." The figures and allusions which recur in Louisa's work were often sensual, even sexual. For her, the Republic was feminine, and its enemy was anything that threatened modesty, affection, and faith. As it happened, the foes of republicanism were, in Louisa's writings, also the main threats to marriage.

Louisa could be deliciously witty when she turned to anecdotes illustrating her gloomy view of human affairs. One of these, told in April 1832, concerned the marriage in Washington of a future president, James K. Polk, a prominent figure in the Jackson circle so detested by Louisa. After the wedding ceremony, Louisa reported that Mr. and Mrs. Polk drove off "in a very showy equipage with four fine spirited horses," accompanied by President Andrew Jackson and his associates. All of these persons, said Louisa, rode in the same singularly undemocratic elegance leaving citizens to benefit "by this most excellent and virtuous display of family tenderness." The bride had broken another betrothal only two months before because she was attracted—"purchased," Louisa claimed—by the wealth of James Polk. "The innocent country lass!!! Who will deny the charms of a carriage and four?"

Louisa watched closely the scramble to replace Jackson in the White House. In addition to the victor, Martin Van Buren, the candidates included Daniel Webster, William Henry Harrison, and Hugh Lawson White. To Louisa, these were nominees of a most inferior quality when compared to the sterling public virtues of John Quincy Adams. Their ascendance and her husband's humiliation brought Louisa to see "the finger of God pointing out the destruction of a country whose beginning was so auspicious and which is now sinking into the lowest moral degradation." Thirty-six years earlier, Abigail Adams had been equally gloomy in her version of the nation's plight after John Adams' defeat.

Rarely losing her sense of humor, Louisa could find a chuckle even when it was clear that Van Buren would succeed Andrew Jackson. She rushed to her composition book with the hilarious news that the next chief executive had a grandmother named Goes, which was pronounced "goose." The result was Louisa's couplet: "For the king of the beasts we find no further use/And the choice of the Nation now falls on a—goose." There was less for Louisa to laugh about in the campaign of 1840 in which slogans exalted birth in a log cabin and the value of a jug of hard cider. Louisa wondered, "What is a People made of?" Answering herself, she asserted, "The catholics are more than half right. Processions and gee-gaws have as good an effect as sugar plums with children."

"Mankind," said Louisa, "cannot be ruled by affection or gentleness and a mild order of government is scarcely ever successful." Observing the trend in American politics gave Louisa the feeling that she was "as new to the world as if I had never lived in it." She was "confounded with its absurdities." Consequently, her irony could be devastating. What would the pilgrims say about "the dignified era to which we have attained?" she wondered, going on to picture the "great forefathers" in some celestial realm looking down with disbelief at "the march of intellect which so happily adjusts the means to the end, in promoting the interests of individual politicians."

Louisa's pessimism concerning American democracy augmented her impatience with John Quincy's addiction to politics. She was proud of what he represented and of what he had sought to accomplish, but embarrassed and baffled by the seriousness of her husband's enthusiasm for the squalid realities of day-to-day democracy. Could he not understand the lesson taught by his own career? Louisa asked him in 1843. "In the history of your father and yourself, the two least selfish and most purely honourable minds that have been brought forward as rulers of this mighty nation [Louisa later inserted 'since Washington']," was it not clear "that the battle between vice and virtue leads to the promotion of the first and to the destruction of the latter"? She made the point tirelessly in verses such as: "Lord, what is man! how frail, how weak/The bauble of an hour?/ Ambition's tool! the little speck/Of momentary power."

Since Louisa's writings on public matters centered on the baseness of human nature, she feared such a bleak outlook might shrivel her effort to be compassionate. She was especially impatient with what she believed was her lack of charity and her vindictive spirit. "Should I preach what I cannot practice?" she asked herself. In this instance, John Quincy proved a help. He assured her that there was no harshness in her character, a notable feat, he told her, when one realized all the trials she had endured. "There is nothing but full and overflowing kindness in your nature now. This is known and felt by all around you." Her husband was obliged to point out again that she caused some of her own problems through an "excess of sensibility."

By touching upon the female mind and nature, John Quincy moved onto Louisa's favorite terrain. Her most valuable writing was about women, for she had a deeper comprehension of society than did such militant contemporaries as Catherine Beecher and Elizabeth Cady Stanton. The former, who was Harriet Beecher Stowe's sister, made a near-religion of domesticity, admonishing women to accept subservience in a world formed for domination by men. At the other extreme, Mrs. Stanton called upon women to seek the vote and to compete with men for places in society. Despite their very different views, both Beecher and Stanton were feminists and optimists. A realist as well as a feminist, Louisa had a more profound understanding. She saw that nineteenth-century progress had propelled American women into a tragic dilemma.

In Louisa's judgment, nature had given women a capacity for more discernment concerning human motives than men possessed. They also had more power to resist worldly temptations, and more strength in the face of life's trials. Despite these superiorities, Louisa pictured females being forced to sit at home and watch as greed, ambition, and lust prodded free-ranging males into misbehavior. It was a fatal social blunder which Louisa was convinced would leave the New World as corrupt as the Old. Louisa's alternative was to exalt former times, where husband and wife collaborated in the home. In that setting there rarely was subservience, but rather a genuine partnership of the sort Abigail and John had enjoyed.

If the modern home was no longer to be the fundamental unit of economic life, Louisa speculated as to women's willingness to remain in domestic roles, even if through some miracle they came to receive genuine respect and their opinions were to be taken seriously. Such a prospect should have seemed sublime, but it troubled the astute Louisa, who suspected that if females entered the business and political arenas, they would eventually fall prey to the baser motives that so easily victimized men. Would this descent be the price of equality for women? Were their superior qualities the result, after all, of their homebound lives rather than a gift from God? Louisa came to fear that America must choose between two evils: woman imprisoned at home or woman unleashed among men.

A possible compromise was to open politics to mature women who had completed duty as mothers and lovers. Age did not change woman's nature, Louisa observed, even if "the fervour of her passions may sleep." Yet society consigned the older woman to the fate of sitting at home, hoping to be satisfied by gestures of respect from a new generation of mothers. Meanwhile the older male could be "the creature of his passions until his death," for while the gratifications of the senses might seem less important, the thrills of avarice, ambition, and politics knew no age limit.

Louisa saw a problem if older women entered public affairs, however. It stemmed from her belief that aged women often sought pleasure as much as men did. Ultimately she rejected a political system based on equal participation of men and women. Since male passions were already too strong a force in matters of governance, Louisa concluded that making older women politicians would still introduce the most tempting and dangerous of emotions into the affairs of state and nation. When a woman stepped out of her limited role, no matter what her age or experience, she became, in Louisa's view, either "an Angel, or a Devil."

Louisa wondered why it was that women and men remained mutually attractive even in old age. She was fascinated by the example of the venerable widow, her friend Dolley Madison, who kept a train of male admirers. "What is this irresistible charm? And why is it so hard to possess it? This is a problem which I fear can never be defined." Alas, it also spoiled Louisa's strategy for allowing women into the public arena; the conclusion to which she returned again and again was that America's pursuit of folly and evil would be slowed only if women were more successful in the home, where they could practice and teach the Christian virtues of love, humility, and selflessness.

This led Louisa to a new stewardship for females. If they rose above the worldly clamor, they might become latter-day prophetesses, decrying the misguided nature of the new economy and government men were designing. She insisted that women must invoke both Scripture and history in calling upon men to repent, while never failing to acknowledge that woman's nature was itself much in need of divine forgiveness. Thus love and compassion, guidance and education should be the concerns of females who, in tackling these responsibilities as respected mothers and wives, might improve the mess men were making of the world.

In addition to the many long and formal passages about women in Louisa's manuscripts, her random jottings often featured a moment's thought about this favorite subject. A typical notation read: "If woman is to be considered inferior to man, why was she made the mother of man after her sin? That the race might depreciate?" Louisa's fascination with this topic occasionally earned her a chiding from John Quincy, who implied that she fretted over issues unsuitable for the female mind. Why should a woman not be concerned with "what constitutes the greatness of moral perfection?" Louisa retorted. Would he bar women from such contemplation because their goals happened to be above the "ephemeral pursuits of political life"?

Louisa also addressed practical issues, including the deprivations caused by economic panics in the 1830s. An angry Louisa portrayed the suffering brought on women and children by a depression which she blamed on political warfare between self-centered men. After an outburst on the subject to her son Charles, Louisa could not resist a sarcastic postscript: "You will I fear think me unfeminine." Indeed, she mused, the sorrow of innocent bystanders "has unsexed me, if the expression of strong feeling

has betrayed me into masculine energy, mayhap unbecoming resentment."
But should it be considered unseemly? Had not society made females the
defenders of weakness while males retained power and property, and
determined the law? "Publick opinion, which was created by man, is always
in favour of himself." Was it really a surprise that women became ill-
tempered?

Louisa could not resist addressing the issue of woman's subjugation,
which often infuriated her. Why should females not be unhappy and
depressed after years of childbearing, domestic labor, sleeplessness, and,
above all, subordinatation to men whose capacities were often inferior to
their own? And then, if a woman spoke out and words were exchanged
between marital partners, leading to the female's being abused and struck,
the final indignity had to be endured. Louisa pointed out that the laws to
which women must turn for redress were designed by men for masculine
advantage. It was understandable, therefore, that females were advised to
be quiet in the face of battering by males. Louisa rejected such a strategy:
"Can a woman who once submits patiently to blows be the honoured
mother of men?"

In 1839, the case of a minister named Jarvis roused Louisa's wrath.
Allegedly, the clergyman struck his wife just before he departed to
administer the rite of communion to his congregation. When his wife
brought her plight before the court, Jarvis was let off on the grounds of
insanity. Appalled by this, Louisa stressed anew that women must not
cringe in silence. As for those ladies who tolerated brutal husbands, Louisa
could only comment sardonically, "I am lost in admiration of their
magnanimity and virtue. I much fear if I had ever been tried, I should
have been found wanting—for I have been found wanting on minor
points. Temper, what a blessing thou art! How has mine failed me in the
trials of a long and troubled life."

Lighter matters surface in Louisa's jottings. To relieve her distress, she
continued the practice of copying recipes and other bits of domestic
paraphernalia. During the White House years, when she saw her feminine
appeal vanishing, she took an interest in one formula: "A little Brazil
Wood and white wine vinegar boiled a minute or two makes a fine and
almost indelible carnation for the lips. It is too deep a colour for the
cheeks." Yet even this modest prescription led Louisa back to difficult
issues. The figure of the painted woman, the harlot, seemed to haunt
Louisa. After a visit in Philadelphia, she denounced the young women of
that city for taking freedoms to the point of "licentiousness."

As her sons advanced through puberty, Louisa tried to remain vigilant
in their behalf as they were sexually tempted. She advised them that no

man could appreciate "how dangerous women become when they choose." It was difficult especially for younger males to resist the "allurements" of a female experienced in such matters. "It requires neither extraordinary beauty nor superior attraction" to be able to stir the masculine senses, Louisa warned her boys, "and I am sorry to say that there are many of my sex who address themselves alone to those passions which are the most easily excited."

Not surprisingly, then, Louisa scoffed at the cheerful version of human nature put forth by American Transcendentalism. In 1838, she studied with interest Ralph Waldo Emerson's famous Divinity School Address, delivered that year at Harvard. His praise for humanity prompted the following lines in her journal: "I have just read the Address of poor W. Emerson!!! It is full of balderdash, and that conceit which makes men mad!!! Again, I say what is Reason! the proud boast of intellectual man." One need only look about and see the need to rely, not upon rational powers, but upon the Deity and Holy Writ. In Louisa's view, sin was tightening its grip on society and only love within families and between neighbors would overcome "that selfish worldliness which confines the spirit and all its petty ambitions to this little sordid and narrow terrestial sphere where man proudly believes himself the lord of all."

In her daily journals, Louisa often examined the heresies that seduced men and women away from what she considered the true faith. Those who believed in fatalism were dangerous foes, for they desired only to follow some "master passion." To Louisa, determinism was a handy way of excusing error and vice and lightening one's conscience. She noticed that many males could never answer directly when she invited them to state their religious belief: "With them it is really a feeling, therefore seldom a fixed principle." Louisa said she did not resent it when acquaintances who had abandoned Christianity chided her for closing her eyes to the truth. "Be it so," she replied. She would not trade her convictions with "the wisest or greatest man, dead or living."

At the time of Louisa's death, her son Charles observed how important faith had been in her life: "My mother's religious feelings were always much greater than her attachment to any form. Yet she respected those forms in which she was brought up without being a slave to them." His father's outlook, on the other hand, "conformed exactly to no church." In her memoirs, Louisa recalled how surprised she was when, after arriving in the United States, she discovered that John Quincy's church preference was actually much different from hers, even though in Europe he had seemed entirely agreeable to her practices. Since John Quincy insisted on ruling their children, Louisa remembered that "I quietly acquiesced to his right of control on a point so material; and I likewise joined in the duties of his religious exercise as a tribute of respect to him, and as an example to my little ones."

Not until 1837 did Louisa seek formal admission into the Anglican communion. On 29 May she was confirmed as an Episcopalian during a service at the little church in Rock Creek Cemetery. Next to the sanctuary Louisa could see her mother Catherine Johnson's grave as well as the resting places of other family members. She chose this setting for receiving church membership, Louisa explained, because it was "in the very presence of my poor Mother." Telling John Quincy about this, Louisa added, "I know that you who were so truly fond of yours [mother] will reciprocate the feeling which made my heart flutter on the occasion."

As a close observer of his mother's life and thought, Louisa's son Charles decided privately that she suffered from too much talent. Betraying a touch of masculine condescension, Charles said his parent's astonishing capacities gave her a "general apathy for the ordinary run of the world, which is as unfortunate a thing as can befall a woman." Perceptive though Charles usually was, this comment supported Louisa's contention that she was misunderstood. She actually rejoiced in household management, even in its most "ordinary" detail.

For instance, Louisa was always an efficient recorder of her expenditures, a quality Charles surely inherited from her rather than from his careless father. Her financial notes show that even in old age, Louisa was as generous as always with her means. One listing of purchases included a breast pin for Mary which cost $10.00, while another for granddaughter Sister Lou was priced at $7.58. Buying several bonnets cost Louisa $3.04, while she paid $15.00 for two scarlet wool dresses for herself. A shawl for Abby came to $2.50. After nearly five decades in America, Louisa continued to calculate her finances using the English style and symbols.

Louisa's special joy was in guiding a household, a task that surely belonged to the most "ordinary run of the world." Her attention to detail was particularly apparent in the summer of 1832 when cholera took many lives in Boston and Quincy. The horrible results caused as much terror in the Adams mansion as anywhere. But Louisa kept her courage and was determined that no one should be lost for lack of precaution. She ordered every member of her household to read the Boston papers for grisly descriptions of what this illness could do to the indifferent.

Louisa suspected that corn and cucumbers were the causes of the disease. She had the stalks and vines on the Adams farm stripped and the produce destroyed. Under her direction, everyone was to pay close attention to their bowels, and to cover their abdomens with special cloths designed by Louisa as a way of drawing out inflammations which she believed were "buried" in the digestive tract. The more Louisa fought the cholera, the more people marveled at how well she seemed.

Despite the epidemic, Quincy had become by 1832 Louisa's preferred place of residence. Had John Quincy enjoyed the house, the farm, the ocean, and the quiet life half as much as she, their marriage might have developed some of the happiness known to Abigail and John. But John Quincy rarely regretted having to stay behind in Washington for congressional business, and on those occasions he willingly watched Louisa head north alone each summer to open the old Adams mansion. For her the house was a capital in its own right, the locus of those values which Washington seemed to mock—simplicity, affection, honesty, and humility.

The trip to Quincy was rarely dull. In July 1844, Louisa and John Quincy were going north on a train that stopped at Jersey City. Although it was after sunset, the elderly couple decided to walk about the station, which, unfortunately, was unlighted. Arm in arm, groping in the dark, Louisa and John Quincy stepped off the railroad platform and toppled four feet to the ground. The former president recorded his thoughts: "While falling I had the distinct idea that I was killed. A shriek from my wife, and the consciousness that she too was killed had in it a thrill of horror which I knew not that the human frame was susceptible." Landing on his rump, John Quincy jumped up at once, "the terror for my wife no pang of death could suppress." Fortunately, Louisa's bulky clothing had broken her fall and she was uninjured, a miracle, the two concluded. The only reminder of their narrow escape was a large black and blue mark on John Quincy's hip.

A few years before this accident, Louisa missed a spectacular tourist sight when John Quincy left a day ahead of her, going by stage to Philadelphia where he was to await her. After she caught up, he told her about an astonishing traveling companion he had encountered in her absence—"a white woman of twelve stone [about 170 pounds] at least, with a baby of proportional size, not in her arms, nor in her lap, but while we sat at the dinner table, literally at the breast. The woman and the baby, both feeding at once with equal voracity. And such a pair of distended udders, my eyes never before beheld. Judge of my relish for the dinner."

On those occasions when John Quincy was detained in Washington and Louisa had gone on to Quincy, she did what she could to tempt him to hurry northward: "Time flies and hope promises your speedy return to be scolded by your wife." She gave him reports on farm life, since even the humble task of counting her chickens gave Louisa great pleasure. At one point, she had as many as forty-six hens. Her letters described Quincy's bracing air, the healthful baths in sea water, the fishing expeditions, the romps with grandchildren, and the comforts of the village social circle.

For Louisa, such domesticity was as satisfying as it had been for Abigail and her sisters. They would have heard their own voices in Louisa's self-assessment: "The natural and strong interest which I take in all that belongs to my family is sufficient to call forth every exertion in my power with a view to promote the welfare of those whom I so sincerely love."

In her later years, Louisa discovered that life's satisfactions were not confined to Quincy. It pleased her when she and John Quincy, as former president and first lady, became admired citizens in Washington after the Whig victory in the presidential election of 1840. William Henry Harrison, who entered the White House in March 1841, went about Washington speaking of John Quincy Adams as his old friend "who had been so unjustly put out." The federal city was a more cheerful place for Louisa when she heard the new chief executive claim that John Quincy was like a brother, and that his counsel was invaluable. After dining with gentlemen at the White House, John Quincy hastened home to tell Louisa of how President Harrison had slapped him on the back and invited him to initiate the toasts. This veneration was all the sweeter since it was displayed before the Adams family's detested enemy, Daniel Webster, who sat glumly through dinner.

Then, in early April, William Henry Harrison fell ill, and Louisa led those who called at the White House with offers of aid. On 5 April, another visit to the executive mansion was necessary, as Louisa and John Quincy went to view the remains of the president. What they saw left Louisa indignant. The coffin stood unadorned and unattended in a drafty hall. No bells tolled, no salutes were being fired. It was one of the few walks they now took together which left Louisa and John Quincy disgusted.

After a season of mourning for Harrison, Louisa decided to improve the capital's social life. She started with a party for one hundred guests, honoring Henry Clay as he left Washington to begin a campaign for the presidency. The evening was so successful—"the dancing was kept up till near midnight"—that Louisa soon entertained another group for music, cards, and dancing. This lively atmosphere infected even John Quincy, who played whist with Louisa's closest friend, Dolley Madison. A few evenings later, as he was on his way home from a political dinner, the ex-president met Dolley Madison and Lord Ashburton, the English minister, and although it was already past 10:00 p.m., he insisted that they accompany him for a late party with Louisa, who was delighted. Even in 1844, when John Quincy was nearing eighty, Louisa often entertained over two hundred guests at events which usually lasted until early morning. She was pleased when these "went off happily."

Nevertheless, such social eminence in Washington only partially distracted Louisa from John Quincy's continued disregard for the comfort of others and often for his own well-being. Once, after traveling to Boston ahead of Louisa, John Quincy reported proudly how long he had been able to go without eating. Louisa promptly sent him a stern reproof, urging that he learn some prudence in his old age. Surely he recalled that God had advised mankind to eat regularly. Anyone with a scintilla of wisdom, she said, knew how important this admonition was, so that "with all your extravagant fondness for new theories, you cannot [here] invent a new idea, therefore I sincerely recommend you to remember that 'I wish you would do as other people do.'"

It was a hard lesson for John Quincy to learn, so that Louisa never quite succeeded in directing her husband. He was still the impatient male she married in London. This side of him persisted especially when the pair struggled to bring some order to the masses of papers and the mounds of books that crowded John Quincy's study in the mansion at Quincy and in Washington. Rarely could Louisa find items or move fast enough to suit her husband. "I am too old and feeble" to keep up with such demands, she complained, returning impatience for impatience. Surrounded by books and letters, the elderly couple accomplished little beyond fussing. They left the library "ill-arranged and so confused" under what Louisa called its "vast and never ending accumulation of papers."

Recognizing how futile it was to try to change John Quincy, Louisa did her best to avoid all "disagreeables" in her effort to keep him vigorous, though it sorely taxed her to suppress "my own quickness of feeling" in the face of her husband's "extreme nervous irritability." On the other hand, as she told Charles, she refused simply to indulge her mate. "He is a man with whom you can not temporise," Louisa reminded Charles, "and the didactic tone is the only one which can be operative. The little attentions which are mere commonplaces in this world are utterly lost upon a man who thinks it a great deal of offence to be asked to change his coat or to put on a clean shirt."

The largest vexation for Louisa continued to be John Quincy's insistence, even in old age, on swimming daily in the Potomac. "He frightens me almost out of my life," Louisa confessed to Abby. "Surely God never intended that Men should be so inconsiderate of those who love [them] as to wantonly sport with their lives and thus inflict such cruel anxiety on those who have already suffered so bitterly under afflictions and dangers of too similar a character." Louisa took pleasure in sending John Quincy a note of protest: "I have a reverence for age in its weakness," she admonished him, "but no sympathy for that pretension which leads us to exploits unbefitting its dignity and beyond its strength."

Living with John Quincy meant enduring other hazards, as well. Louisa finally conceded that Philadelphia's remarkable Dr. Physick had been correct when he advised her that sleeping with a husband who insisted on keeping the windows open was what caused most of her illnesses. Considering that newlyweds would confront many such differences in preference, Louisa concluded that "a set of questions should be put previous to matrimonial engagement." Such a step would "prevent much mischief."

Since it was far too late to alter her situation, Louisa consoled herself by enthusiastically nursing her husband when his follies brought him low. John Quincy caught a dangerous cold in November 1847 while the couple endured the drafts blowing through open windows in the old house in Quincy. Louisa sat up with him all one Saturday night, helping him overcome a sore throat. Alas, her mate refused to listen to her lecture on prudence, and the next morning set off by foot to attend both church services.

Occasionally Louisa's exhortations succeeded. She was pleased when, with her pushing, John Quincy agreed to address the Massachusetts Historical Society. Founded in Boston in 1791, it was an establishment, Louisa said, where "the very name of Adams has for many years proved an uncongenial sound." Unfortunately, when the day came in May 1843 for her husband's speech, Louisa could not accompany him, since the Society welcomed only gentlemen. The orator went off alone, lost in thought and, it turned out, badly in need of Louisa's guidance.

In his report to his amused wife, John Quincy described how he entered what he took to be the place where the Historical Society met. Not at first taken aback when it proved to be the residence of Abby's sister Ann and her husband, the Reverend Nathaniel Frothingham, John Quincy was shown to a seat in the pastor's study "with a number of persons who I supposed were the Massachusetts Historical Society, though," he admitted, "I could not conceive how they came there." When the assembly did not turn to him for his address and began a business meeting instead, it dawned on the ex-president that he was in the presence of the Massachusetts Congregational Charitable Society. After this discovery, John Quincy was immediately helped to find the audience of historians, which by then was out searching for him.

With increasing patience, the aging Louisa continued coming to terms with her husband and her life. How she did so was beautifully described by Charles in a letter to Abby. His mother, he wrote, "unites tenderness to affection in a manner I have never seen equalled, not even in yourself." There were other admirers, although one was pathetic, John Quincy's old swimming partner and valet, Anthony Guista who in his senility went about Washington loudly insisting that Louisa was the incarnation of the Virgin Mary.

In July 1847, Louisa completed fifty years of marriage. The Golden

Wedding Anniversary was toasted in Quincy, away from the clamor of Washington. Charles and Abby invited a group of old friends to hail the occasion, and John Quincy delighted Louisa by giving her a bracelet. In spite of her gratitude, her thoughts were more bleak than exalted. John Quincy had become very frail. Within a few months, on 23 February 1848, he was dead.

The final moments in the life of Louisa's husband became legendary, partly because he expired in the federal Capitol. He suffered a stroke while beginning a speech in the House of Representatives on 22 February. That afternoon at 2:00 p.m., Louisa was summoned to his side, unaware of what had happened: "God only knows the severity of my trial in the midst of a gaping multitude of men." She had arrived at the Capitol "altogether unsuspicious of the awful shock which awaited me, having heard that my poor husband had had a faint turn from which he had recovered." John Quincy lingered only a few hours, dying before Charles reached Washington. When he arrived, Louisa's son found her tired "but less agitated than I expected." She now acknowledged that the burden of caring for her husband since he had an earlier stroke two years before had nearly exhausted her.

The national tribute paid to John Quincy in death was balm for Louisa. "She retained bitterness to no one," Charles observed, as he looked back over his now widowed mother's long career of suffering and strife. "Her situation seems not a little melancholy, and yet there is an interest about it as the light of day grows softer whilst it declines." The letters Louisa wrote as a widow to Abby and Charles bear no mark of despondency or helplessness. She spent the following summer in Quincy, enjoying as much as ever the fishing, the games with her grandchildren, and the visits with village neighbors. Her thoughts were often on John Quincy, as jottings in her journals show. She composed several poems lauding his career. The unjust treatment of the two Adams presidents, Louisa maintained, would give any dispassionate observer "a deeper insight into the impulses which sway mankind." For Louisa, there was no more to say. This assertion was her last testament concerning public affairs.

During her remaining days, Louisa sought mostly the company of the few surviving members of the Adams and Johnson families. She was clear on one point, now that John Quincy was dead. While he lived, she reminded her relatives, she had endured a regimen of disorder and confusion caused by his disregard for the convenience of others. Now, Louisa announced, life around her must be quiet and regular. "Rely on it, my dear Son," she admonished Charles, "old persons best understand what suits them; and that to harass them with plans or society which they do not incline to adopt only adds to the evils from which they cannot shrink." Both of Louisa's daughters-in-law, Abby and Mary, understood this, and hovered about just as the older woman wished. After visiting Louisa, Abby always regretted leaving, for by now her mother-in-law was "so altered and broken and so touching in her weakness."

On 12 April 1849, Louisa suffered a stroke which ended her cherished custom of summer trips to Quincy. She was stricken while characteristically helping someone, her sister Frye, who had taken ill. For a time the stroke paralyzed Louisa's left side, but she astonished her family by improving rapidly. Her humor and attentiveness in conversation soon returned, and she insisted on trying to feed herself. When she was able to bathe herself, her pleasure at this achievement was boundless, as it was when she could again read, play games, and enjoy long rides in the country.

Now Louisa's letters emphasized her readiness for death, and her wish to welcome it. She reviewed the past, recalling with satisfaction her astonishing feat in 1815 when she traveled from St. Petersburg to Paris. She prepared her will, the main purpose of which was to distribute the $10,000-legacy her brother Tom had left her. Most of the money was given to Mary Hellen Adams and to granddaughter Mary Louisa. There was also a generous amount awarded to Abby's daughter Sister Lou, who, as Louisa noted, bore her name. Her male descendants, Louisa claimed, had been sufficiently cared for by John Quincy. Personal effects were lovingly assigned, much as Abigail had done. Louisa carefully listed shawls, watches, items of silver, jewelry, and other effects. The bulk of Louisa's personal possessions in Washington was bequeathed to Mary and Mary Louisa.

Louisa also wished a proper conclusion to less worldly affairs. In May 1851, a year before her death, Louisa invited Charles to sit beside her for a long talk. Her son never forgot the conversation, one in which she chatted of life's end "in a way so unaffected and natural that I was deeply interested in it." Charles recorded that Louisa had spoken "calmly, clearly, and fluently, yet not out of the level of ordinary conversation." He was much moved by her simple Christian faith, her acknowledgment that she had "no merit for good works," and that she had committed many sins. She stressed how she could now only trust in divine mercy. It was an outlook, Charles said, "which I knew the philosophy of my father did not attain."

In widowhood, Louisa tried especially to be gracious to those of her many callers whom she disliked. Deafness bothered her, and she pretended she had lost "the habit of playing great Lady." Nowadays, she told Charles, "I feel quite foolish when suffering under any marked distinction." She sought to give no offense, however, and chided Mary for insisting on wearing mourning clothes long after John Quincy's death. "One would suppose we lived under feudal laws," Louisa chuckled. She remembered how John Quincy had loathed all black apparel, refusing to wear a black satin vest even when she assured him proper dress required it.

As she grew frail and her memory faltered, Louisa remained bright and full of fun. "I enjoy her very much," Abby noted during what would be a last visit. When Charles made his own pilgrimages to Washington, his mother was still so lively in outlook that he was taken back to scenes long ago in the same house on F Street where she now awaited death. He remembered especially the great ball Louisa gave for General Jackson in January 1824. Such occasions, said Charles, were "the days of gaiety which will never return." He hoped that in old age he might be as tranquil as his mother. Such was Louisa's peaceful state that she refused to share Mary's indignation when the new president, Zachary Taylor and his wife, had not called first upon the widow of John Quincy Adams.

If ever a person enjoyed peace at the last, Louisa Catherine Adams did, having come to terms with herself and life. She died as the clock struck noon on 15 May 1852, with Mary and the few surviving Johnson sisters near. Charles and Abby were in Quincy, whence her son departed at once for Washington, saying "she hath left to me a sweet remembrance and an example of humble imitation." President Taylor's successor, Millard Fillmore, and his cabinet, members of Congress, and a host of friends attended Louisa's last rites. It was a vast concourse, Charles noted. He also observed that both houses of Congress had adjourned in tribute to his late mother, a gesture that would not have gone unnoticed by Louisa. Her regret over the status of American women might have been mollified by knowing she was the first female whose death would bring the nation's legislators respectfully to observe a day of silence.

It was a beautiful May afternoon in Washington when Louisa's coffin was placed in a vault lent by a friend. There it would wait until Charles prepared a final site in Quincy. The Episcopal Church's order for the burial of the dead was read, to Charles' consolation. It was a ritual Louisa had often attended, and its lines were familiar to her. Frequently she had talked of "the resurrection and the life," and of how "in my flesh shall I see God." The minister read the Thirty-ninth Psalm, which contained lines Louisa had often urged John Quincy to heed: "For man walketh in a vain shadow, and disquieteth himself in vain. . . . Every man therefore is but vanity."

Standing at the grave and contemplating the peacefulness at the last of his mother's life, Charles judged the closing words of the burial service as unsurpassingly appropriate. Indeed, he might have thought he heard Louisa herself whispering "Amen" as, over her bier, the minister pronounced, "Blessed are the dead who die in the Lord; even so saith the Spirit, for they rest from their labours."

EPILOGUE

The Crypt

The weather was cold enough in December 1852 for Louisa's corpse to be taken from its temporary repose and brought to Quincy. Her son Charles went to Washington to supervise her final trip. Charles handled these details with his usual efficiency, except that he missed a train connection on the return home. Thus Louisa's remains arrived in Quincy before her son did. Charles had managed to think of everything, even instructing his seventeen-year-old son and namesake, the second Charles Francis Adams, to be at hand should the elder Adams be delayed.

Louisa was to be placed in a crypt located at Quincy's First Parish Church, to whose congregation Adamses had belonged since the 1630s. When a new meeting house had been built in 1828, a vault was dug beneath its portico. The chamber measured fourteen square feet and was reached by stairs from the church vestibule. On 1 April 1828, the coffins of Abigail and John Adams were interred there, placed within granite sarcophagi. When Louisa died, the crypt was doubled in size in order to receive the second President Adams and his lady.

On 16 December, a cold and cloudy day, the younger Charles Adams, along with an undertaker, some laborers, and the velvet-covered coffin of John Quincy Adams were waiting as Louisa's casket was brought to the Quincy church. Until that moment, Louisa's husband had lain in the family tomb across the road in the old cemetery. When the party entered the crypt, it proved easy enough to place Louisa's coffin in its granite encasement. However, stone masons had to be summoned to enlarge the sarcophagus meant for the former president's impressive coffin.

As the work proceeded, young Charles filled the time by ordering John Quincy's coffin opened to see how the corpse had fared. When the lid was lifted, it disclosed a body covered by a glass which quickly clouded with moisture. There was just a moment for onlookers to see what Charles described as "the sunken face of a very old man, on which a short stubbly beard had grown after death." By this time quite a crowd had gathered at the church to watch such entertaining goings-on. It took until late afternoon to put John Quincy safely beside Louisa and place the heavy covering over him. At that point, the elder Charles was present to see the door to the crypt closed and locked. There was no ceremony.

The four occupants were left undisturbed until 1891, when members of the American Antiquarian Society, led by Senator George F. Hoar, asked to view the crypt's interior as part of their visit to scenes associated with the Adams family. Once again Charles Francis Adams II was host for an occasion at the tomb. He took considerable satisfaction in the crypt's condition and in observing his distinguished guests as they "stood around the four stone sarcophagy." He then escorted the spectators to a grassy knoll near the ocean, where his mother Abby rested in the grave she shared with her husband. When Senator Hoar and his party departed, Charles II wondered if the crypt would ever again be opened. It was unlikely, he thought. Charles predicted that both church and grave would soon be forgotten amid the rush of American progress.

Charles was wrong. In 1900, the Daughters of the American Revolution placed an inscription beside the crypt door: "Abigail Adams/As Daughter Wife and Mother/A Model of Domestic Worth/Her Letters are an American Classic/1744–1818." Not until thirty years later did the DAR remember that another first lady was interred beside Abigail and add the following inscription: "Louisa Catherine Adams/Frail of Body, Simple in Tastes, and Retiring in Nature/She Filled the Onerous Positions To Which It Pleased God/To Assign Her With Grace, Dignity, and Fortitude/1775–1852."

Today, nearly a century after Charles Adams II shut the crypt door, it has been reopened, and thousands of persons pay homage annually to Abigail and Louisa and their husbands. There can be few sights more moving for those who cherish the story of America, and particularly of its women, than to see the Adams crypt where two first ladies and two presidents repose. In nearby cemeteries rest many of the other women so dear to Abigail and Louisa: Mary Cranch, Nabby Adams Smith, Kitty Salmon Smith and her daughter Louisa, Mary Hellen Adams and her daughter Fanny, Abby Brooks Adams, and Nancy Harrod Adams and her daughter Lizzie. The resting place of the youngest daughter from Weymouth's parsonage, Elizabeth Shaw Peabody, is the old burying ground in Atkinson, New Hampshire, a cemetery sufficiently hidden that it has escaped vandals and careless visitors. There Elizabeth lies with her daughter Betsy, surrounded by unsullied New England charm.

There is no sign at the Adams crypt of the irony contained there. One of the couples entombed, Abigail and John, had shared a model marital partnership. Yet their son who reposes beside them personified the spirit which overwhelmed the type of marriage Abigail advocated. Driven by ambition and self-centeredness, John Quincy would have permitted his wedded union to obliterate his wife. Only Louisa's strength preserved her dignity and identity. Thus the two Adams females in the crypt knew the best and the worst of times for American women. If Abigail and Louisa's letters should ever be published together, they would speak movingly of how females came to be subordinated in the United States during the first century of national life.

Abigail and Louisa urged that women and men be recognized as equal but different. Only from this complementary design, embroidered by love and mutual respect, could come that accommodation between the sexes which was essential to the good society envisioned by these first ladies. As clear-eyed students of history and human nature, Abigail and Louisa would probably understand how nearly impossible it will be for our age, abounding as it does in prideful gender, selfishness, lust, and violence, to revive the spirit which rests in Quincy's crypt.

Acknowledgments and Sources

In his autobiography, John Adams paid tribute to a woman he never knew, Hannah Bass, his grandmother, who had married Joseph Adams and become the mother of Deacon John Adams, father of President John Adams. Hannah had died in 1705 at the age of thirty-eight, a victim of consumption. She was the granddaughter of Priscilla Mullins and John Alden, and according to John Adams, the world was much poorer for her loss. John placed Grandmother Hannah alongside his mother Susanna Boylston as a powerful influence in his life. A prodigious reader, Hannah Bass was evidently far more learned than most men and women of her time. This was cause enough for John's admiration.

What John acknowledged as his greatest debt to his grandmother was a document written in her hand and left for her descendants, though to John's dismay it had been lost sometime after he had seen it. He recalled that it contained advice and was "wonderfully fine," especially in its plea for learning. Had it not been for Hannah Bass' exhortation, John was certain his father, the deacon, would not have had an "unchangeable determination to give his first son a liberal education." As that eldest son, John Adams saluted the influence of his grandmother, and so should we. Without Hannah Bass' advocacy for education, John Adams would not have won the hand of Abigail Smith. For it was John's mind which drew Abigail to him, just as it was John Quincy's mind which appealed to Louisa.

My own gratitude thus goes first to the memory of Hannah Bass, now dead nearly three hundred years. In preparing this biography, I have also accumulated numerous personal obligations to the living. To begin, without the support of the Massachusetts Historical Society in Boston, nothing worthwhile could be written about any Adams. It is a pleasure to salute that Society as it nears its three-hundredth birthday in 1991. For three centuries it has served as the finest center for historical study in America. For the friendship and help of Louis Leonard Tucker, its director, I am profoundly thankful, as I am for the endless kindness of his associates at the Society: Winifred V. Collins, John D. Cushing, Ross E. Urquhart, Aimee F. Bligh, Patrick B. Flynn, Peter Drummey, and Conrad Wright.

My work on the Adamses began many years ago, so my obligation starts with two figures at the Massachusetts Historical Society who are now retired but still very active. It would be impossible for my wife Joan and me to show Stephen T. Riley, emeritus director, and Alice Riley how much we appreciate what they have done for us. I owe a similar debt to Malcolm Freiberg, emeritus editor of publications at the Society, who has often shown amazing foresight in divining my needs.

My interest in the Adams family became all-consuming after a conversation years ago with the late Lyman Butterfield, the first editor in chief of the Adams Papers. He and his associates brought into being modern scholarship about the Adamses. This book owes much to his memory, and to the invaluable contribution of Robert J. Taylor, emeritus editor in chief, and Richard A. Ryerson, the present editor in chief. The Adams Papers enterprise has recently suffered the loss through retirement of Marc Friedlaender, adjunct editor. For my purposes, I learned more from him than from any source, and I look toward many more years of talk with him and Clara May. Finally, little of this book would have been finished without the support of Celeste Walker, associate editor of the Adams Papers. I thank her heartily.

The spiritual as well as the physical home for friends of the Adams family is, of course, the Adams National Historic Site in Quincy. Under the care of the National Park Service, the Adams mansion, usually called the Old House, along with the cottages where Abigail, Nancy, Louisa, and Phebe lived at one time or another, and the Adams Church and its crypt can be seen today as the Adamses left them. My professional and personal debt to Wilhelmina S. Harris, emeritus superintendent of the Site, is incalculable. For many years she has allowed Joan and me to make her residence in Quincy our home in the Boston area. Mrs. Harris' associate, Marianne Peak, has my thanks for numerous good deeds.

I am also deeply obligated to others in Quincy. The Quincy Historical Society has supported my work in many ways. I am grateful especially to Doris Oberg who, until recently, served as its interim director. To H. Hobart Holly, the historian of that Society, and the source of marvelous help and information for anyone concerned with the story of Quincy, Weymouth, and Braintree, I am especially thankful. He came to my aid, with unfailing good humor, on matters large and trivial.

The kindness of Walter and Dorothy Wrigley turned the visit Joan and

I made to Haverhill and Atkinson into a memorable occasion. Since Walt grew up in Haverhill, I had the advantage of seeing the area through his affectionate gaze, looking upon scenes dear to Elizabeth Shaw Peabody. Undaunted by a cold autumn rain, Dorothy took the photos of Elizabeth's grave and of the Atkinson Academy that appear in this book.

Happily, a lost trove of Adams papers turned up in Virginia, and has been safely reunited with the mass of family materials at the Massachusetts Historical Society. All this is due to the generosity and alertness of Donna Cutts of The Plains, Virginia. When Louisa Adams lived in Washington, she enjoyed the company of Dolley Madison and the Cutts family, among whom Dolley had relatives. Through developments so complicated that only a historically inclined detective would believe it, manuscripts and other materials from Louisa, Mary Hellen Adams, and her daughters came eventually to Mrs. Cutts. She allowed me to study them, and then graciously presented them to the Massachusetts Historical Society. She has my thanks for this decision and for her personal kindness to Joan and me.

A long quest finally turned up the missing portrait of Nancy Harrod Adams. This success was due entirely to help from Leah Lipton of Framingham State College and Roberta Shinn Emerson, Director of the Huntington Galleries. They led me to Mr. and Mrs. L. M. Polan of Huntington, West Virginia, who own the Chester Harding portrait of Mrs. Thomas Boylston Adams. I am grateful to the Polans for their permission to use this portrait as an illustration. I also thank Mary Jane Williams and the University Art Collections of Arizona State University for allowing me to incorporate Gilbert Stuart's portrait of Mrs. Stephen Peabody as an illustration.

When the Dr. Mavis Kelsey Collection of the Bryn Mawr College library acquired letters written by Louisa Adams, Leo M. Dolenski, the manuscript librarian, hastened to see that I had copies of these documents. I thank him and the college for permission to use this material. James H. Hutson, chief of the Manuscript Division of the Library of Congress, helped me with the admirable skill that has aided so many scholars. I am grateful to him and to the Library of Congress for permission to use the Cranch Family Papers and the Shaw Family Papers. Without these collections, it would be impossible to know Mary Cranch and Elizabeth Shaw. I owe a similar debt to the American Antiquarian Society and its director, my good friend Marcus McCorrison. I thank the Society for permission to use its wonderful group of letters by Abigail Adams, Mary Cranch, and Nabby Smith, and for the privilege of reading the diary of Stephen Peabody.

Finally, some personal acknowledgments. They begin with thanks to Carol Wicker for her assistance in the early stages of this manuscript, and to the trustees of the Virginia Historical Society who encouraged my work when I was that organization's director. To William Zinsser, John A. Garraty, and John Morse goes my appreciation for encouraging a stubborn fellow to put aside pen and paper and try writing with a word processor. Now I am only sorry I waited so long.

I am delighted to have the support once again of Oxford University Press, where Sheldon Meyer has been my editor for twenty-five years. Wisdom, patience, and encouragement from him and his colleagues Leona Capeless, Marjorie Mueller, and Sam Tanenhaus have been mainstays for me.

We are taught that the last shall be first, and so it is with my final acknowledgement. The foreword to this book only hints at the contribution my wife Joan Peterson Nagel has made to this biography. She has listened to my ideas, read drafts, made suggestions, and unsnarled genealogical knots. All this and more was done with the good humor and talent she brought to our partnership from the start. Elizabeth Peabody can rest a bit easier, for her view of marriage has not entirely been eclipsed.

It is a simple matter to describe the sources for this book. I have drawn all of my material and ideas from the manuscripts left by the women who have been my subjects. These sources have been supplemented by the letters and journals of several men. Together they offer a deeply personal view of the life and character of the Adamses and those associated with them. Were they less abundant, this book would necessarily have been more superficial.

Fortunately, these materials have been easily available. I say fortunately since I agree with an observation made by John Quincy Adams after he had read some of Nabby's correspondence in 1841: "Letters written in the domestic intercourse of families are necessarily much diversified as to the subjects upon which they are written, as to circumstances to which they relate, to the incidents which they record, and to the state of mind, of health and of temper with which they are composed. Strangers or even members of the family of the writer, who after a lapse of years, read several of them in immediate succession, can scarcely enter into the spirit with which they are animated, but by reading few of them at once and by alternately laying by and taking [them] up again."

John Quincy's advice can still be usefully followed, even given the voluminous character of the Adams papers. I have had at hand and daily depended on the microfilm edition of the Adams Papers. I have heavily relied on Part IV, which includes letters received and other loose papers. Reels 343 to 542 encompass most of the documents pertaining to the Adams women. Part III, which contains miscellany, has Reels 264 to 280, where one can locate Louisa Adams' journals, verses, dramatic compositions, prose writings, and translations. The narrative of her travel from St. Petersburg to Paris is in Reel 268.

Part III also has useful writings by Louisa's brother Thomas Baker Johnson, and by her husband John Quincy Adams, her son Charles Francis Adams, and her father-in-law John Adams. These are scattered through Reels 180 to 262 and 296 to 339. Part of Stephen Peabody's diary is on Reel 341, with the bulk to be found at the American Antiquarian Society. Part III of the Adams Papers also exhibits a few documents left by Nancy Harrod Adams and her daughter Lizzie. Reels 197-198 include items concerning Abigail Adams. Scattered through the diaries and letterbooks of John, John Quincy, and Charles Francis Adams are important insights into the careers of the Adams women. These marvelous sources are contained in Parts I and II of the Adams Papers microfilm edition, Reels 1-179.

For permission to use and quote from the Adams Papers, I am grateful to the Massachusetts Historical Society. Readers who wish to sample the Adams family manuscripts in printed form may consult some of them in a splendid letterpress edition being published by the Belknap Press of the Harvard University Press. To date, thirty volumes have appeared, with an additional one hundred and twenty anticipated. These volumes—they include family correspondence, diaries, and other papers—offer the reader the inestimable benefit of guides and explanations by the editors, unlike the film edition, which leaves scholars to puzzle for themselves.

The collections at the Library of Congress and the American Antiquarian Society are essential to knowing the Adams women. I have earlier thanked the Library of Congress for permission to use the Cranch Family Papers and the Shaw Family Papers. The letters of Abigail, Mary, Elizabeth, and others included in these collections must be united with those in the Adams Papers for a complete story. The same is true of the Abigail Adams Collection at the American Antiquarian Society, whose permission to use these documents I cherish. Many of these letters are printed in Stewart Mitchell (ed.), *New Letters of Abigail Adams, 1788–1801* (Boston, 1947). I am grateful to the Massachusetts Historical Society for being able to study the Paine Family Papers, and the Brooks Family Papers, the Edward Everett Papers, and the Frothingham Papers; the last three collections are important in approaching Abby Brooks.

Except for treatments of Abigail and Louisa, I know of no biographical sketches of the women in this book that I can recommend. Abigail has two good recent biographers: Lynne Withey, *Dearest Friend* (New York, 1981) and Charles W. Akers, *Abigail Adams* (Boston, 1980). An excellent introduction to Louisa is L. H. Butterfield, "Tending a Dragon-Killer: Notes for the Biographer of Mrs. John Quincy Adams," *Proceedings of the*

American Philosophical Society, 118 (April, 1974), 165-78. An interpretation of Louisa which differs from mine is forthcoming in Joan Challinor, "The Mis-Education of Louisa Catherine Johnson," *Proceedings of the Massachusetts Historical Society*, 98 (Boston, 1987). More conventional is the approach in Jack Shepherd, *Cannibals of the Heart: A Personal Biography of Louisa Catherine and John Quincy Adams* (New York, 1980). I look forward to the day when someone will write fully about the three sisters from Weymouth, about Louisa, and about Abby and her daughter Sister Lou. There is much more worth saying concerning these women, for what I have published only begins to tell their story.

Readers who may wish to learn about the history of women in America should start with Carl N. Degler, *At Odds, Women and the Family in America from the Revolution to the Present* (New York, 1980). This excellent book affords a sound background and interpretation for persons who might then proceed into the welcome, rapidly growing, and often contentious literature concerning women in our nation's past.

Index

Subentries in this index refer often to nine women. It may be helpful, therefore, to employ the following forms for their names. The characters below are listed in groups by generation and in the order of their appearance in the story.

MC	MARY SMITH CRANCH
AA	ABIGAIL SMITH ADAMS
ES/P	ELIZABETH SMITH SHAW PEABODY
BN	BETSY CRANCH NORTON
NS	NABBY ADAMS SMITH
LA	LOUISA JOHNSON ADAMS
NA	NANCY HARROD ADAMS
MA	MARY HELLEN ADAMS
ABA	ABBY BROOKS ADAMS